The Complete
SKIING HANDBOOK

A practical illustrated guide to:

Alpine skiing technique and practice • Cross-country skiing • Skiing for children • Free-style • Mountain ski-touring • Deep-powder skiing • Choosing, care and repair of equipment • Pre-ski exercises • Safety • Assessing snow, terrain and weather conditions.

Featuring a guide to over 425 US and Canadian ski areas
Foreword by 'Jungle' Jim Hunter
Former Canadian Olympic skier and national champion

The Complete
SKIING HANDBOOK

Edited by Mark Heller and Doug Godlington

with Jürgen Kemmler and Manfred Vorderwülbecke

MAYFLOWER BOOKS
NEW YORK

Published in the United States by
Mayflower Books, Inc.,
New York, 10022

United Kingdom Edition published by
Martin Dunitz Limited, London

Originally published as: Das Grosse
Skihandbuch

ISBN 0 8317 1670 3

Text filmset by Asco Trade Typesetting
Ltd in Monophoto Garamond
Manufactured in Hong Kong
FIRST AMERICAN EDITION

Contents

The expert on the slopes

Skiing for children

Free-style skiing

Touring and ski mountaineering

Safety for off-trail skiing

Cross-country skiing

Cross-country skiing as a competitive sport

Ski marathons: competitive events for everyone

Skiing vacations

Skiing and the law

Acknowledgements

Hank Tauber, former Coach, U.S. Olympic Ski Team for advice and comments on the manuscript. John F. Henz, President, GRD Weather Center, Denver, Colorado for writing text about weather in the major ski areas of North America. The American Meteorological Society for permission to adapt information on the föhn and chinook wind from their Glossary of Meteorology edited by Ralph E. Huschke and for providing help. The U.S. National Oceanic and Atmospheric Administration for supplying the wind chill tables.

Bill Bachman of International Sports Management Pty Ltd., South Yarra, Victoria, supplied much useful information about skiing in Australia and prepared the guide to Australian ski areas. Margaret Gove for providing useful suggestions about skiing in Australia. Bob Radley of New Zealand Snow Centre, Christchurch for advice on skiing in New Zealand. Valerie Chandler prepared the index.

The photographs on the front and back of the jacket (cross-country skiers), on the title page and on pages 60, 61 and 211 were all taken by Peter Runyon of Runyon Associates, Inc. Vail, Colorado. The photographs on pages 134 and 135 were supplied by the New Zealand Snow Centre.

Preface

There are now many skiing books available, but almost all are either for beginners or, at the other extreme, highly technical manuals. Very few have tried to put across all the most recent trends within this rapidly developing sport.

The Complete Skiing Handbook breaks new ground, presenting a thorough survey of the practical 'nuts and bolts' of all the different types of skiing, at the same time showing how these can be applied to improve style and technique. At every stage, there are step-by-step instructions, drawings and photographs showing just how each movement should be done. We have been helped in this with probably the best collection of colour photographs ever used in a 'how-to' skiing book.

While not neglecting the needs of the beginner, it has been planned with the recreational skier in mind. He or she has probably already reached a moderate level of competence through ski school and personal experience. The vast majority of skiers fall in this broad category so we have constantly tried to answer the kinds of questions they most frequently ask.

Most skiers today are downhill skiers, but a growing number are also discovering the joys of cross-country skiing. For this you do not need to pay the ever-increasing cost of getting up the mountain to start skiing, and often cross-country areas are more accessible with less expensive accomodation. Also, cross-country skiing can be enjoyed by all the family together, regardless of age or athletic ability. Many readers may be surprised by the variety of techniques and the extent that this sport has developed in its own right.

Although ski touring is still a less widely known form of skiing it offers the experienced skier an exhilarating and solitary peace, that nowadays is rarely found on the marked downhill trails of most ski areas. Many of the related subjects are of vital importance to the safety of any skier such as having a basic working knowledge of snow and weather conditions in mountain areas. While not everyone may feel cut out for the breathtaking acrobatics of free-style, it has certainly drawn a great deal more spectator interest to skiing. Even if you do not decide to try free-style for yourself we are sure you will find this section exciting.

Whether you are a beginner or trying to get your jet turns right, we hope this book will provide you with a practical understanding of all these facets of skiing and many more besides. Be sure to enjoy your skiing to the full!

Introduction

Skiing–yesterday and today

If you are learning tennis it makes very little difference whether you learn in Sweden, North America, Switzerland or Australia. The technique is the same everywhere. An Austrian ski instructor in St Anton, however, will often teach in quite a different way from his Italian counterpart in Sestrière, whose own methods will differ from those of a French instructor in Val d'Isère. Equally, there will be differences in teaching methods between a ski instructor in Aspen, Colorado and Stowe, Vermont. Obviously, it would be difficult to tell a Frenchman from a Swiss just from physique or their way of walking – yet every skiing nation has its unmistakable way of skiing. There are a number of reasons for this surprising fact.

If you watch any of the World Cup skiing events on television, you can see for yourself that while all slalom racers may use roughly the same technique, this technique can easily be distinguished from that of giant slalom racers, and especially downhill racers. The majority of world-class skiers have perfected their technique only in one discipline. A few will often win the medals in two events, but trying to find skiers equally strong in all three is like looking for the proverbial needle in the haystack.

A recreational skier, however, needs to be able to do everything: make short, fast turns on bumpy terrain, make long turns on rounded, gentle or moderately steep slopes or change direction while running fast downhill.

So there is no one 'correct' skiing technique. There are various possible ways of skiing, and different factors mean that different features are emphasized. According to geographical situation and snow conditions, different countries tend to stress different technical aspects. The French, therefore, who have many extensive skiing areas above the tree line, particularly favour a kind of giant slalom technique and they emphasize rotation in their turns more than people of other skiing countries. In Italy ski instructors are as fond of children as the rest of their countrymen, and hope to make every *bambino* into a star. Slalom racing is practised every day, on every slope, even by beginners. Short, athletic turns are the favoured method of Italians like Azzurri or Thöni, while countries that have more restricted trails have to tackle more in the way of mogulled trails, like North America where bump-absorbing figures prominently in ski instruction.

Nowdays championship racers only ski on specially prepared trails, while recreational skiers have to be all-rounders, taking everything in their stride, from deep snow to a smooth, hard trail, from powder snow to the slushy conditions of spring. If you have to push heavy snow aside with every movement you make, you need a technique to help you to turn powerfully. If your skis cannot hold on a smooth trail, you need a technique which helps you hold them on their edges.

There is no point in arguing over the 'correct' method of skiing. When Scandinavian skiing came to Central Europe at the end of the last century, no one thought at first of developing the downhill Alpine skiing technique known so well today. The first Alpine skiers found their skis a useful climbing aid – downhill skiing was as uninteresting to them as the descent from a peak is to mountaineers. There was fierce controversy for years over whether this 'Norwegian' style of skiing was more correct than the so-called 'Lilienfeld' method, named after the home of Matthias Zdarsky, inventor of the downhill Alpine technique. Supporters of the 'Norwegian' method, who gave a good deal of space to the various ways of climbing in their instruction manuals thought the Lilienfeld stemming technique practically dangerous. The first ski binding suitable for downhill running, developed by Zdarsky, was condemned by its opponents as an instrument damaging to the feet. The two camps clashed head-on over whether a skier ought to carry two ski poles, or the single Lilienfeld Alpine pole.

Until the thirties, Alpine skiing was a deep-snow sport. Only a powerful style employing sweeping, open movements made it possible for the skier to keep pushing heaps of snow aside. (Cross-country skiers are

still instructed in this method, and may be said to be skiing in an old-fashioned way.) Gradually, however, the increasing number of skiers led to the formation of rutted and hard-packed trails. In these circumstances, it was soon noticed by a few people, using their heads as well as their legs, that the stemming technique was superfluous as soon as a good speed was reached. Yet again there was endless controversy over 'unnatural' stemming techniques, and the most modern of modern skiers claimed parallel turns as the only correct method. Twenty years later the skiing world was cast into uproar yet again when the Austrians, led by Stefan Kruckenhauser, demonstrated their new 'wedel' technique at the 1955 Inter-Ski Congress in Val d'Isère. Traditionalists viewed the fact that you could turn your skis while turning your body in the opposite direction with great suspicion. The heyday of the wedel, when it was admitted that it, and it alone, was the crown of skiing technique, was the only time when a uniform technique was taught almost all over the world. This was for almost religious rather than technical reasons: there was no escaping the gospel according to that absolute authority among skiers, Stefan Kruckenhauser. In imitation of a familiar saying of the golden thirties, he coined the slogan: 'One turn goes round the world.'

A few outsiders stood out, unsuccessfully, against this standardization of Alpine skiing. At exactly this time, for instance, Josef Dahinden of Switzerland had recognized in principle the technique of weight transfer used today, but his 'mambo' technique contained so many inconsistencies that the real nature of his intentions was not understood until years later. It was a Frenchman, Georges Joubert, who broke the hold of the wedel on the ski slopes. Backed

up by the successes of the French racing team, he succeeded in bringing the whole range of Alpine skiing techniques back into use.

The history of the development of skiing techniques also shows how much influence the changes in equipment have had, as well as changes in the state of the trails. As already mentioned, the ski runs gradually became more hard-packed, and this led to a new problem: skiers found their skis slipping away all the time. Lettner's invention of the steel edge was necessary before the high-speed technique associated with the name of Toni Seelos could be developed. From the fifties onwards, wooden skies of the old style began to change: at first they were simply made with a faster, smooth plastic running sole. Compared with materials previously used to make skis, this came to mean that the average speed even of recreational skiers was almost doubled. To put it another way: the skis could be turned more easily because the snow under them slid away more easily. Undoubtedly this development played its part in the rise of the wedel technique, whose graceful elegance and ease made the older technique of exaggerated rotation look positively clumsy.

When Jean Vuarnet, winner of the downhill event at the 1960 Winter Olympics in Squaw Valley, used metal skis for the first time, and Roger Staub, winner of the giant slalom, wore clipped boots, they paved the way for a revolution in skiing technique based on skiing equipment. Modern plastic boots and lightly-built plastic skis mean that, nowadays, every recreational skier can use a variety of techniques in a way that even world-class skiers could not twenty years ago. A plastic ski will track well, whereas an old wooden ski would long have given up. A plastic boot will hold any skis steady at moments when even an Olympic skier in leather boots would have had his ankle collapse under him.

Unlike many other major sports, such as athletics, swimming, football and gymnastics, skiing is not connected with institutions for sports, research – at least not to the same degree. Instruction manuals on the above sports are mainly written by people who have made a study of the subject, while ski books and instruction manuals are nearly always written by private individuals who frame their own opinions on ski instruction. Skiing, therefore, has an odder, more contradictory set of instruction manuals available than almost any other kind of sport. All national skiing instruction schemes have been hallmarked by the personal style of whoever drew them up. The life's work of Stefan Kruckenhauser shows how much influence an author's own experience of skiing conditions can have on the instructional methods he recommends; but for the magnificent slopes of powder snow around St Christoph in Austria it is unlikely that the craze for the wedel would have broken out in the rest of Europe and spread all over the world, as far afield as North America, Asia and Australasia.

Many skiers have become aware of the emergence of two apparently new branches of the sport: free-style acrobatic skiing, and hang-gliding on skis. Free-style skiing is actually as old as modern skiing itself, and the first hang-gliders on skis were seen in 1909.

Obviously there are fashions in skiing. Ten years ago you would only have started out on a cross-country skiing expedition through the back door in the twilight with your skis over your shoulder, for fear of being laughed at. Nowadays it is fashionable.

For at least three generations obstacle or *Gelände* jumping used to be part of any skier's basic repertoire. Nowadays, however, it is rarely practised and is awaiting rediscovery.

We shall have to wait and see whether the trend leads away from the trails towards a greater emphasis on off-trail skiing. Skiing is a changing sport: something that was fashionable yesterday may be forgotten today, and the height of fashion again tomorrow. New variations on the sport are being discovered: while cross-country skiing is promoted almost medicinally as part of the current enthusiasm for keeping fit in Europe, Canada is producing books on cross-country skiing full of information about the reading of trails, understanding the weather, the local flora and fauna. People's interest in skiing depends on the circumstances of the time, and one generation of skiers will have a different idea of the 'real' way to ski from its predecessors.

For almost a hundred years the basic shape of the ski itself has not changed at all. New versions, however, are beginning to appear on the market: in particular, shorter skis. The effects of this are already being felt; the bumps or moguls down the trails are closer, and skiers on the standard long skis have more difficulty making their way through the labyrinth. The new skis make new teaching methods possible, and last, but not least, they make it easier and safer for some beginners to learn skiing: older people, for instance, who have taken up the sport fairly late in life.

One other point should be made: skiing is not like other sports where the same sequence of movements occurs in exactly the same situation, as for instance in long jump, swimming, weight-lifting, competitive skating. The terrain is different at every turn, the snow conditions change, as does the weather which creates widely differing situations with sun, snow, mist, wind, as exist in hardly any other kind of sport.

One might describe the ski run as an opponent and challenge to the skier. Like a chameleon it is always changing – and trying all kinds of ways to throw the skier off his course. Anyone wishing to master such a changing terrain must be able to react in as many different ways. The secret of Alpine skiing is both complicated and simple: you have to be cleverer than the terrain and your enjoyment will increase accordingly.

But you can be *too* clever, especially when it comes to skiing instruction. People do not always try to make it easy for learners to grasp the intricate variety of techniques involved in Alpine skiing. Sometimes they make things much harder by using specialist terms which the beginner can hardly comprehend. For instance, all three German-speaking skiing countries, Germany, Austria and Switzerland, use different terms when talking about the technique of absorbing bumps on trail. They all use the magic word 'anticipation', but all mean something different by it. Making every allowance for the fact that local conditions influence ski instruction differently in different countries, it is hard to see why the slightest variations of movements should all have names of their own as if they were entirely separate. There is a bewildering proliferation of names: the serpentine, the super-parallel turn, the F-F turn, the OK turn, the flying-weight transfer turn, the top turn, the jet turn, the sling turn, the compression turn, the kangaroo turn, the tilt turn, the serpentine sprint, the short turn, the wedel, the godille, and so on. They do not contribute much to our understanding of skiing technique.

This Babel-like terminology is one result of the commercialization of ski instruction. Instead of looking for something in common, some people in the skiing world are positively looking for differences, so that they can claim that their own skiing technique is the only one to be universally taught. The one who suffers is the ordinary skier, who can become thoroughly confused.

It is hoped, however, that in future the skier will not have to cope with so much terminology. He needs to be taught the structure of various movements, to learn about up-unweighting and down-unweighting in his turns, how to twist his body the other way and so on. Then he can develop his own personal style. Skiing is not a series of rigidly prescribed exercises, it is the way you act in certain circumstances in relation to the terrain, adjusting your style to it. This is the only way to use your technique properly, whether in Europe, North America or Australasia.

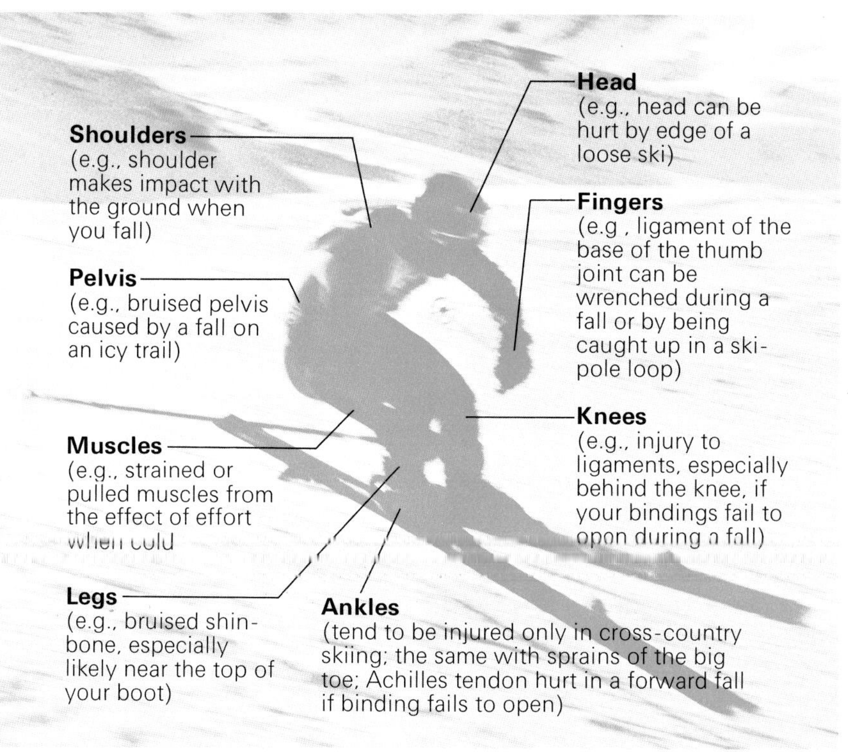
Head
(e.g., head can be hurt by edge of a loose ski)
Shoulders
(e.g., shoulder makes impact with the ground when you fall)
Fingers
(e.g , ligament of the base of the thumb joint can be wrenched during a fall or by being caught up in a ski-pole loop)
Pelvis
(e.g., bruised pelvis caused by a fall on an icy trail)
Knees
(e.g., injury to ligaments, especially behind the knee, if your bindings fail to open during a fall)
Muscles
(e.g., strained or pulled muscles from the effect of effort when cold
Legs
(e.g., bruised shin-bone, especially likely near the top of your boot)
Ankles
(tend to be injured only in cross-country skiing; the same with sprains of the big toe; Achilles tendon hurt in a forward fall if binding fails to open)

Areas at risk

Medical advice for skiers

In our modern society, where life tends to be sedentary but skiing is still growing in popularity, doctors advising on sporting activities often encounter the question of skiing in relation to health.

If the sport is looked at from the point of view of the five main motor demands it makes on the body – strength, speed, flexibility, co-ordination and endurance – it is obvious that the emphasis will be different in Alpine and in cross-country skiing.

Alpine-touring, as a combination of both kinds of skiing, makes demands on the human body similar to those of both Alpine and cross-country skiing.

If we start with the fact that, in training for endurance, the optimum load, especially for heart, lungs and circulation, is for activity to last at least ten minutes, at a heart rate of about 130 per minute, we can see that the average skier is hardly likely to possess the necessary concentration for that kind of endurance in downhill skiing. Alpine skiing also makes considerable demands on strength, speed, flexibility and powers of co-ordination, and the use of all these adds a great deal to a skier's pleasure once he has mastered adequate techniques.

Cross-country skiing makes different demands on the recreational skier's basic physical qualities. Here the main thing is a dynamic, prolonged stimulation which enables the internal organs to adapt themselves to long-term activity, and which makes sport so valuable in preventing or repairing the damage done to bodies in modern life: cross-country skiing is excellent for this.

The risk of accidents or physical incidents in the two branches of the sport differ in much the same way. Accidents are uncommon in cross-country skiing, but more frequent and occasionally serious in Alpine skiing. There are many reasons for the violent effect of a fall on the human organism; the lever arm of the ski, particularly, exerts considerable force on the bones of the lower leg.

Intensive research has been, and still is being, carried out into all the contributory causes of accidents, such as equipment, terrain, psychological attitudes and environmental factors such as the influence of the weather. Many skiing safety campaigns have embodied their results and conclusions. The purpose of such investigation is to reduce still further the inherent risks of skiing and, in view of the great number of skiers, reduce the cost, in terms of lost working days and insurance payments.

Statistics accumulated in a recent study have shed some light on the nature of skiing accidents. In this branch of medicine doctors do not just aim to heal damage sustained in accidents as well and as fast as they can: preventive medicine is seen as more important, and a good starting point for the prevention of accidents is a study of their causes.

Obviously, falls account for the majority of skiing accidents. The best way to avoid falling is to use the correct technique for the prevailing conditions. A good exercise plan will help prepare you physically for the demands of Alpine skiing. A seven-year survey of accident victims has shown that only 5% of them were people who had actively prepared for their skiing, as against 20% who had exercised only sporadically, and 75% who had done no kind of preparation at all. This shows the need for preparatory exercises as an extremely effective way of preventing skiing accidents. Skiing is sometimes seen as a social experience with the chance of making contacts; many people make the basic mistake of seeing it as a way of becoming fit. It would be nearer the truth to say that *being* fit is the best way to ski without risk.

Of course, Alpine skiing does make rather one-sided demands on the human body. Cross-country skiing is an obvious and ideal way to adjust the balance. Ideally skiers should set off for a weekend or a holiday on the slopes with a pair of skis for cross-country (as well as their Alpine skiing equipment), for use in the last half-hour's skiing of the afternoon, or in bad weather. This would round off the physical effects of their downhill skiing in the right way – provided that the necessary foundation of physical fitness had been laid, by, doing pre-ski training.

Ten exercise suggestions

1. Health

Strenuous physical activity should only be undertaken if you are in good health. People more than forty years old who do not go in for any regular form of sport, and anyone who feels uncertain about his or her general health, should consult a doctor first. If you have influenza you ought to be in bed, not doing exercises.

2. Exercising with children

Children should not be forced to do exercises; use your judgement, and be sure they find it fun. They are less physically capable than adults, and should not train so intensively. Children can sustain relatively more severe injuries when skiing than adults, so, in theory, they should be especially well prepared, physically, to go skiing.

3. Warming-up

Before starting serious exercise, muscles, sinews, ligaments and joints should be fairly supple to avoid any risk of injury. Warming up is not done by wearing warm clothing, but by using muscles actively as, for instance, by jogging until you break out in a light sweat.

4. Training to increase endurance

Exercise strenuously at some activity such as running, hill climbing, cycling, swimming, for at least ten minutes without a break. Get your heartbeat rate going at 130 per minute or more. To tell your correct rate, subtract your age from a pulse rate of 200 (for younger people) or 180 (older people).

Example: A forty-five-year-old man trains at a pulse rate of about 150 per minute. Training of this kind is the only way to make sure that lungs, heart and circulation are capable of peak performance.

5. Be kind to your knee joints

Skiing exercises put particular strain on the knee joints, which are often a weak point. Avoid movements which are obviously overstraining to the knees. This, of course, is a general rule for all kinds of exercise.

6. Look after your muscles

Stiff muscles after you have been doing very strenuous exercise are not a bad thing, they simply show you exactly how unfit your muscular system is. The stiffness can be relieved considerably by a hot bath or a massage to loosen the muscles.

7. Train often

It will do you more good to train for ten minutes every day, than for seventy minutes once a week.

Regular exercise will build up muscle strength and stamina.

8. Train on an empty stomach

A full stomach puts more of a strain on your breathing, circulation and suppleness. Do not eat a large meal for two or three hours before exercising – although a cup of tea or coffee with some biscuits will do no harm.

9. Sport makes you fit

A healthy person will feel a general sense of well-being after physical exercise. A persistent feeling of exhaustion could be a danger sign, and its cause ought to be investigated.

10. Exercise sensibly

Exercising too ambitiously can lead to overstrain with consequent risk of injury. Sporting activites should not, for the majority of people, be more than an enjoyable hobby.

If you want to become very fit lead up to it gradually

Equipment

It is a fact of life that a new sport may seem both difficult and expensive for anyone first taking it up. Skiing is no exception and if an entire family is involved the uncontrolled cost can become positively frightening. Most people have a rough idea of what is required for skiing: a pair of skis, some complicated apparatus called safety bindings to hold them on, a pair of poles, some boots and some gloves. The rest, it would seem, can be improvised, but fashion, the neighbours and fellow guests are more likely to induce a desire for conformity.

Skiing is a technical sport carried out in harsh surroundings and, paradoxically, an extremely fashion-conscious occupation. The harsh climatic conditions require technically-sound design; fashion requires variety, novelty and exclusivity. Combined, they can become excessively expensive first time round if you are taken in by an assistant through ignorance.

Many of the more expensive items can be rented until such time that experience and love of the sport requires better and more permanent equipment. Skis, boots and poles are readily available at all winter sports' centres, by the day, week or fortnight. In many countries it is also possible to rent complete ski suits. (Few adults, however, will consider this.) Children present a different problem. Many ski clubs have an exchange-and-mart system where outgrown items can be readily exchanged for hardly-worn, larger sizes. Large families can save by the time-honoured custom of 'handing down', however unpopular this may be with the last in line.

It is difficult to lay down any definite sum which the novice skier will require to equip himself from head to toe (or the former good skier who, for one reason or another, has had to give up the sport for some years). A complete set of underwear, socks, sweat-shirts, pullovers, ski suit and cap will cost, at today's prices, not less than \$320(£160) if sound, but not extravagant models are chosen. A fashion ski suit – one-piece or two-piece – costs from \$440(£220) upwards. It must, however, be stressed that a model produced by Head, Bogner, V de V, or Fusalp will still be sound and still look good years after a cheap substitute has disintegrated.

The technical ski equipment, skis, bindings, boots and poles have to comply with certain minimum technical standards and while there are some extremely cheap sets available from time to time, these are items on which money should not be saved. On the other hand it should not be wasted either. A novice or moderate skier should think about paying upwards of \$320(£160) for the complete set. Specialist skis will cost in the region of \$220(£110), bindings up to \$110(£55) and for boots it would seem that the sky is the limit with electrically heated ultra-designs reaching sums of \$200(£100) and more. Even a good skier, however, can find satisfactory footwear for as little as \$80(£40) – and, strangely enough, such boots will often be easier to ski in than the super-specials.

Children's equipment is disproportionately expensive with little improved performance to show for it. Boots in particular can cost as much as any advanced adult boot and will have an effective life of possibly only a season before the child has grown out of them. Boots for children are a classic case for sharing or purchasing second-hand.

Clothing

In the early days of skiing as a sport, fashion was a minor consideration, especially for men. When women first took up skiing they wore jackets over long skirts, and under their skirts a knicker-bocker style of trousers. In the 1920s they discarded the skirt worn over the trousers. Next came Norwegian ski suits made of thick woollen material, and the forties saw the arrival of the first stretch pants, still cut very wide by later standards. They quickly became uniform ski wear for both men and women. Over the years the rise in popularity of skiing, international racing experience, and the development of the fashion aspect, especially since the coming of man-made fibres, has brought about the situation where ski clothes are a branch of fashion in themselves. Nowadays ski wear can be obtained to suit all tastes in fashion and, more important, it has become highly functional.

Functional ski wear should:

- allow ease of movement
- be water-repellent
- not be a vapour barrier
- insulate from the cold
- have an anti-skid texture
- be easy to care for

It is not intended to go into specific fashion details in this book, since they change so much from season to season. Our main concern is with the materials used.

Ski wear today is mostly made of special synthetic fabrics custom-built for the purpose. This means that ski suits of all designs usually come in fabrics consisting of three layers: a water-repellent surface which does not slide when you fall, which covers a fleece or down thermal interlining, and a lining which allows the skin to breathe. Good quality materials of this sort have these three layers perfectly tailored to each other, especially with regard to the actual manufacture of ski clothing, so that it fits the figure and is elastic.

A rule of thumb:
Bad: elasticity of the surface layer under 20%

Adequate: between 20% and 25%

Very good: 30% and over

Ski wear for the trails and deep snow

A distinction can be made between:

1. The ski suit – an overall or two-piece suit, made of nylon non-slide material.

Either one-piece or two-piece overall-style ski suits are available in nylon non-slide material.

2. A racing suit – made of material with extra elasticity, also available as a one-piece or two-piece.
3. Quilted clothing – made of quilted-filled nylon, for example, ski jackets and waistcoats.
4. Standard gear – ski pants and ski jacket.

The ski suit in the form of an overall has finally conquered the skiing market. It can be bought as a one-piece, or with the top half joined by a zipper around the waist so that it can be taken off and used as a separate ski jacket. Two-piece ski suits usually consist of a dungaree style of suit with a matching ski jacket reaching to waist or hips. In general they fit the body closely, with straight trouser legs. Insets of elastic material at the back, sides and shoulders help the suits stretch more easily. A second cuff inside the trouser leg secures it invisibly, or visibly by means of a strap. So long as they do not fit *too* closely, thermal ski suits of this kind offer the best protection against cold.

Racing suits are cut to fit like a second skin. The use of special mono-elastic or bi-elastic material means that they are adaptable to every movement of the body. Trousers are high-waisted or have the backs and fronts cut high. They can be combined with racing jackets of the same material to make a complete suit, or again can have a top half zipped on to form an overall style. Such suits often have padding at the knees and sides of the trousers and at the elbows and sleeves of the tops, as protection against bumps and falls. The leg is invisibly closed by means of an elastic inner foot or by clip or velcro-type fastenings outside over the boot. This is not a form of ski wear for everyone, because although functional, it is too cold for most people.

Quilted clothing, in the form of ski jackets and quilted waistcoats, is part of a normal ski wardrobe, such garments being worn for extra warmth, especially with racing suits. They act as a form of natural insulation. Real down, not synthetic flock, is used to line the nylon surface, and there is usually the minimum of stitching. Quilted clothing is light and warm, although bulkier than the other items of clothing already mentioned.

Standard gear. The familiar type of stretch ski pants still holds its own along with these three later fashions. Ski pants of this kind are cut very

close to the figure, and fit at the waist, but may also have a high waist or a dungaree-type bib. The legs (reinforced with leather inside at the cuffs, if possible) are held in with an inner foot, the cuffs falling over the boots. Strapped trousers are out of fashion now.

There are no particular rules for **summer skiing** so far as fashion is concerned. Since a ski suit is usually too warm for summer (and not everyone can afford two skiing wardrobes) many people ski in jeans or corduroys, t-shirts, shirts or blouses with sleeveless pullovers. Nylon over-trousers keep the trouser legs from becoming wet. Everyone, however, should have a warm ski jacket (one which will let the skin breathe and is water-repellent), or at least a thinner jacket with a hood.

Ski wear for cross-country skiing

Clothing for cross-country skiing is simpler and cheaper than clothing for Alpine skiing. The difference generally lies in the types of material used and the breeches style of trousers, which are usual for this form of skiing. The material used is thinner than for Alpine skiing, and consists of a special elastic fibre, or a proofed cotton and polyester mix, or a combination of both.

Double-layered materials – water-repellent nylon helanca outside, soft brushed cotton inside – have proved useful in cross-country racing, as have insets to admit ventilation at the back and under the arms.

General hints:

- Clothing for cross-country skiing should be comfortable and allow the skin to breathe.
- Seams must be well finished so as to avoid any danger of them rubbing against a sore place.
- For long cross-country skiing expeditions suits with a windproof lining at the front are useful. These can be improvised by a newspaper worn over the chest.
- A good track suit is perfectly adequate for first attempts.

Ski wear for children

There are so many kinds of ski wear on sale for children that you need to go shopping carefully, and know something about what you are looking for.

Basically, you will find a whole range of adult ski wear scaled down to child size – including racing suits. More details will be given in the section on Skiing for Children (see p. 137).

General hints

- Do not buy clothes that are too close-fitting for children but, on the other hand, do not buy on the principle that the children will 'grow into them'. You must reckon on buying a new skiing outfit for a child every other year.
- In choosing children's ski wear, err on the side of too much warmth rather than vice versa.
- Avoid bulky fur collars, which are of no functional use and are merely a fashion detail. They will be hot and uncomfortable to wear.
- Look for garments with large, roomy pockets which are easy for children to reach into.
- Zippers should have large tags, so that a child can open them quickly even with cold hands. In general, look for clothes which fasten easily.
- Crash helmets for children are essential.

Two-part padded racing suit.

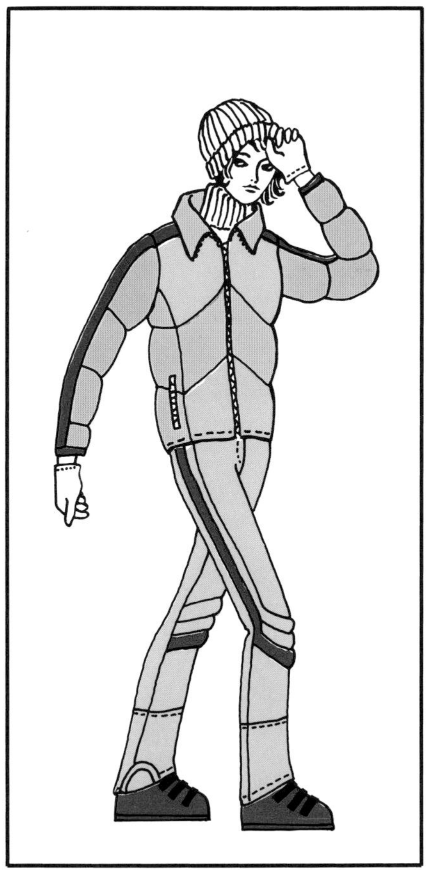

Racing trousers with quilted, down-filled nylon ski jacket.

Dungarees and hooded ski-jacket for children.

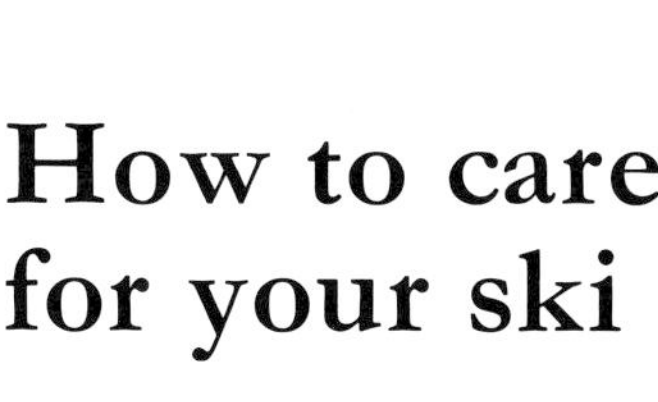

How to care for your ski wear

In general, ski suits, overalls, ski jackets and so on, can be washed at home in a washing machine (use a programme for delicate fabrics). The same goes for sweaters and underwear. Do not wash at too hot a temperature, and use a mild detergent. Don't let your skiing gear become too dirty before you wash it, or marks may be left along the seams. The same thing can happen if you rinse the clothes inadequately. Do not use a fabric softener on coloured ski suits, because the colours will run. Reproofing is important after washing ski clothes, and can be done at home with special aerosol sprays; follow the instructions on the can. It is advisable to re-proof at the start of the season and afterwards at regular intervals, as the protective film wears off after a time. Do not tumble-dry ski clothes; hang them up to drip-dry but not too close to a source of heat.

Quilted clothing can be washed at home too. (A word of caution: the filling will take longer to dry than the covering material, and there may be watermarks left.) Dry cleaning, however, is better.

It is also better to dry clean racing trousers or racing suits.

Spots of food, grease or other substances on ski clothes can be removed with a spot cleaner.

Do not store ski clothes in plastic bags during the summer; cover them with a cotton laundry bag if you like, but in any case make sure they are washed or cleaned before being put away, and if possible keep them hanging in a wardrobe.

Buying ski wear

Bear the following suggestions in mind when buying sports' clothing either for Alpine or cross-country skiing:

- Underwear should be loose; air should be able to circulate through

Accessories for ski wear

Sweaters (wool or wool and synthetic mixtures)	Collarless, closely knitted sweaters are best. Wear them under light roll-neck sweaters, shirts, blouses, scarves. Two sweaters of this kind – one thicker for winter, one thinner for spring – are not just a luxury. Make sure sweaters are not too tight or too short.
Light roll-neck sweater (cotton or mixture of synthetics and natural fibres)	Try not to have too thick a collar; one that has a zipped opening is best.
Hat (wool, nylon or fur) and headband	Fur is advisable only in extreme cold. Smooth, closely knitted, well-fitting wollen caps are best in winter, a nylon cap with a visor for spring. Athletic cross-country skiers will find finely knitted or woven caps or woollen headbands useful. Bright colours for caps (which stand out against the snow) are a good idea if you are touring, skiing off-trail, or for children.
Gloves or mittens (leather, felted wool, fur, nylon, with fleecy lining)	Gloves are better than mittens in general, although mittens offer more protection from the cold. The best kind are leather gloves with a thermal silk lining, padding over the knuckles, a thumb guard and zipper fastener. You may want to wear silk gloves under them. Good quality leather for racing; lined and gathered into the wrist for long expeditions.
Underwear (wool, wool and synthetic mixtures, cotton)	One-piece or two-piece 'long johns'. Cross-country skiers will find a loosely woven fabric is a good idea, since they ought to have underwear which lets the skin breathe well. A top or vest which matches your outerwear can double up as a sweater. In conditions of extreme cold, silk or thermal underwear (made of angora wool) is best.
Socks (wool, cotton towelling)	Thick wool with a cotton towelling (loop-knit) foot are best. Length should reach the top of your boots. For cross-country skiers: knee-length socks (make sure they stay up well). Do not wear darned socks, they may give you blisters.
Waterproof jacket and/or **trousers** (this nylon)	Useful as additional protection from the weather, especially in spring, and for cross-country skiers who are touring.
Scarves (cotton)	Not just a fashion accessory, but very useful for all skiers, especially in a wet snow shower, and for cross-country skiers when skiing in deep snow off the trail and skiing in spring.
Bag (nylon, leather, fur)	You should have room for the absolute essentials in the pockets of your ski suit. Choose a waist purse the right size, with a good strap to hold it in place.
Après-ski boots (leather, plastic)	The best kind for wear when coming off the slope are waterproof plastic, which will be no problem even in slush, with well ridged soles and large, easily closed zipper fasteners and a warm lining. Choose non-slip soles.

Two-piece suit for cross-country skiing, consisting of dungarees and loose jacket.

the weave of the fibres.

- Avoid belts or braces if possible when choosing outerwear, and make sure the kidney area is well protected.
- You do not want your clothes to gape open, but you do want to be able to open them when you want. Clothes with various ways of fastening and opening them are a good idea.
- Ski suits for cross-country skiing should have zippers at the sleeves and in the knee area, as well as at the collar and pockets.
- Ventilation under the arms is important. Top and trousers should be joined by a vertical zipper so that the trousers hang from the top.

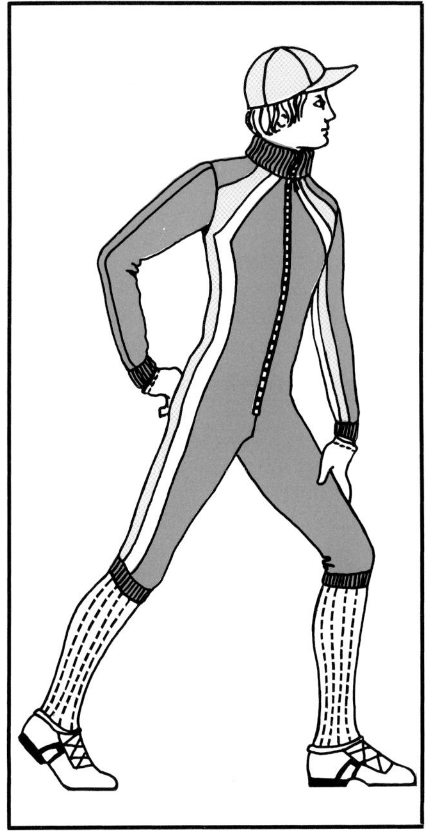

One-piece suit with colour-contrasting stripes.

Dungaree-style ski pants in stretch fabric, with ski jacket.

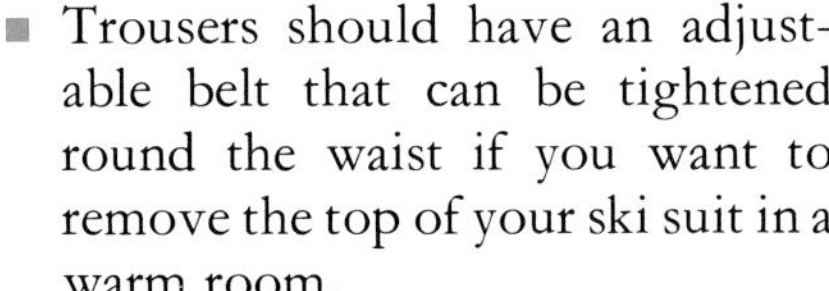

- Trousers should have an adjustable belt that can be tightened round the waist if you want to remove the top of your ski suit in a warm room.

Brief glossary of terms

anti-gliss/anti-slip: material which will not slip on the snow

bi-elastic: material which is stretchable in both directions

flock: synthetic padding of quilted materials, acting as insulation

mono-elastic: material which is stretchable in one direction, usually lengthwise

overall: one-piece ski suit

overdock: visible trouser-leg fastening over the boot, usually clipped

stretch areas: parts of the clothing made to allow additional freedom of movement, for example, at the shoulder, back, and side seams

synthetics: general descriptive term for man-made fibres

Cosmetic protection from the sun

- Rub a suitable cream into all parts of the skin directly exposed to air, sun, cold and wet before skiing as well as overnight.
- Do not use water-based products; choose oil and grease-based creams.
- Apply a protective cream half an hour before going out of doors.
- When buying a cream, look for the amount of light it filters out, which should be given on the label. The more sensitive your skin, the stronger the sun and the longer you expose yourself to it, the more light that should be filtered out.
- Protecting the lips is most important. There are special products for the lips, ranging from those suitable for normal exposure to the sun (on the trails) or for extreme conditions (on glaciers).
- If you want a quick tan, artificial tanning creams can be used; medical opinion considers them safe for the skin.
- Cover-up pencils are available for those prone to freckles.
- After-sun lotions, jellies or, best of all a special ointment from the chemists or drug store, will help avoid any threat of sunburn.
- Do not dab the skin with perfume or cologne tissues in the sun (you could end up with sunburnt spots).
- Protect your hair from the effects of the weather and also your own sweat. Wash greasy hair more often than usual, with a nourishing shampoo. Brush well.

Sunglasses

The first and most important function of a good pair of sunglasses is to protect the eyes from glare, reducing the amount of light that enters the eye. Our sense of sight is normally adjusted to the amount of light we receive in average daylight out of doors when the sky is overcast. In these conditions our vision performs at its best. If there is more light than usual, as, for instance, in springtime in the Alps, glare occurs; a slight rise in intensity above the normal level of light causes reduced sharpness of vi-

The racing look for children. The crash helmet is essential for safety.

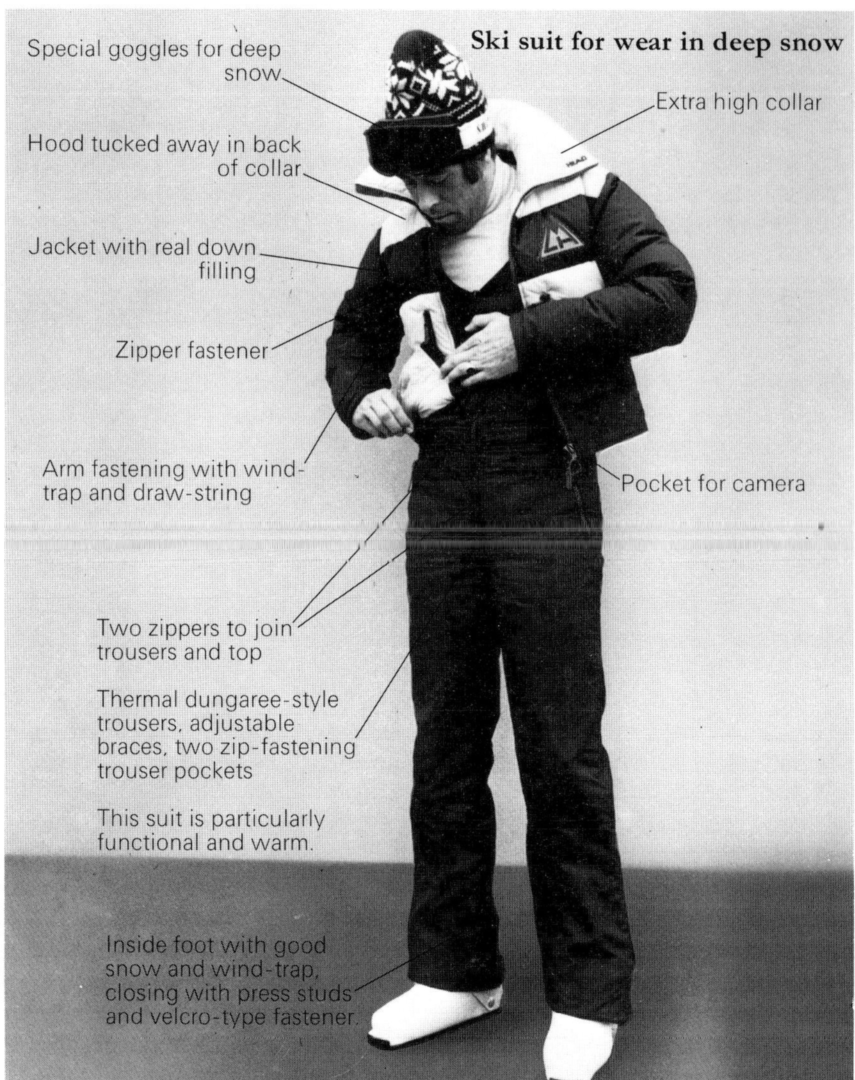

sion and sensitivity of the reflexes. A considerable rise in intensity causes cramp of the eyelids, pain from the glare, and eyelid inflammation. A good pair of sunglasses should filter out at least 50 to 75% of the visible rays of light entering the eye.

Besides the visible rays, invisible ultra-violet rays enter the eye. A distinction must be made between shortwave and longwave ultra-violet rays.

Shortwave rays, with wavelengths up to 315nm at the most (1nm = nanometer = 0,000.001mm.), are easily absorbed by proteins and will destroy them when the dose rises above a certain amount. This type of radiation causes sunburn and inflammation of the conjunctiva (snow-blindness): only the top layers of the conjunctiva are destroyed, and the damage is not permanent, but the pain and limitation of vision are extremely uncomfortable.

Shortwave ultra-violet light is absorbed by most kinds of sunglasses in 'normal' light conditions, but not in the mountains. You must have a pair of glasses with high-quality optical lenses to keep out the ultra-violet rays and to make sure your eyes do not suffer any lasting damage.

Longwave ultra-violet rays, wavelengths between 315 and 400nm (the limit of vision) do no permanent damage to the eyes in normal amounts, i.e., in average daytime conditions. If the eyes are exposed to them for a long time during the day, however, night vision may be affected the following evening. Moreover, people with particularly sensitive eyes may find that their ability to register contrasts is diminished.

Longwave ultra-violet light penetrates ordinary lenses. High-quality optical lenses are necessary to protect your eyes from it.

If you do not want to have your skiing holiday spoilt from the start by painful, running eyes, it is advisable to pay a little extra for really good glasses.

Goggles

Goggles are as important as good sunglasses and are usually worn when it is snowing or the sun is very strong. If your vision is impaired, you will not be able to judge the shape of the terrain – which usually leads to nasty falls.

Some facts about goggles:

- Some makes of goggles are treated in chemical baths to stop them from misting up. First the lenses are given a double-sided coating; this has to be on both sides, for technical reasons, and so must be removed from the outside of the lenses. The coating absorbs water and prevents the formation of droplets on the inside, thus keeping the goggles clear. Misting up can be prevented by polishing the inside surfaces with hair shampoo or washing-up liquid.
- Ventilation is important. Since the capacity of the lenses to absorb water is limited, the air vents should be partly open, while skiing. This will mean the goggles are ventilated as you ski, the anti-fog coating does not have to absorb so much water, and the water already absorbed can evaporate again.
- Be careful when wiping goggles. If snow or water gets into the inside of them – in a fall, for instance – do not wipe the insides. The damp coating scratches easily.

The best way is to shake the snow out of the goggles, then pat the inside of the lenses carefully with a soft cloth. You should never bend the goggles, which can also damage the coating. Although nowadays most drivers are familiar with heated rear windows in cars, we do not yet have heated skiing goggles for emergency situations. Such an invention might solve the problem of misted-up goggles becoming a safety risk.

Skier, ski, boot, binding: a unit

The series of movements we describe as skiing are made possible by the harmonious functioning of all parts of the skier's equipment. This may sound self-evident, but there are two important points to be made:

1. It is the skier himself who moves when skiing, not a vehicle steered by him. Such vehicles could be constructed largely without reference to human physical qualities; less would be asked of them than is asked of skiing equipment.
2. The separate pieces of equipment function together to make various movements possible. This holds true for all aspects of skiing, for example, the performance of a turn or any active safety function, such as the protection of the lower shin from having too great a strain placed on it.

Edging provides an example that illustrates these points:

The processes necessary to edge a ski are decided by the geometrical, flexion and surface qualities of the ski itself, and equally by the height, rigidity and angle of the boot, in some circumstances even by the nature of the binding. The angle at which the lower leg will be leaning over at the time of a safety binding's opening does not depend solely on the adjustment of the heel binding. The height and rigidity of the boot top has a lot to do with it, and so does the shape of the sole and the position of the sliding strip.

When gathering your ski equipment together, always remember the strong influence the different parts of it have on each other.

The following summary of what you require from your most important pieces of ski equipment is the result of study of the subject over the last ten years.

First and foremost, the functional unit of ski, boot and binding has to do two things:

- enable you to steer and control the movement of your skis in the best possible way.
- if you fall, lessen your chances of suffering what is called a 'typical' skiing injury, and also the chances of suffering other injuries connected with falling. (Always use safety bindings: devices to halt loose skis.) And, in general, to keep the moment of stress between skiing and falling to a minimum (this is

The less risk the better in skiing – even though half the fun of skiing is the thrill of taking risks, which this 1930s expert felt as keenly as any mogul king does today.

where the protective function of the ski boot comes in).

You should remember that ski equipment designed to meet the requirements of good skiing will lessen the chances of falling anyway, and with them the risk of injury. In the long run this kind of ski equipment will increase your safety.

So the separate items – boot, ski and binding – should be looked at in the light of the two functions they have to perform. We are leaving aside features such as stability, durability, quality of workmanship; they are very important to the skier, but do not directly influence what happens to you when skiing and when falling.

Skis

The function of skis is to enable the skier to control his sliding movement over the snow in the best possible way. Skis should therefore have good running surfaces and be easy for the skier to control. It can be quite complicated to work out just what combination of qualities will give the best performance by way of the ski's sliding potential, stability, and the actual materials used and its construction. Many forerunners of today's ski have led to the models now available, which do what is asked of them very well. It is easy enough nowadays to describe the physical properties of skis, in detail: length, breadth, flexibility and torsion (or twisting force) all play their part. It is still difficult, however, to decide just what the performance of a certain type of ski will be, judging from such information.

The influence of ski width and side-cut is the clearest:

- Narrow skis are easier to edge, and more suitable for hard surfaces because they exert less pressure than a wider ski of the same length. They demand (and make possible) precise control of the completion phase of a turn, something which only technically expert skiers are capable of.
- Broader skis are more suitable for deep snow, and also for skiers who keep their skis flat on the snow most of the time; therefore, for people who are not very proficient.
- A wide-waisted ski is good for wide turns, a narrower-waisted one for edging and control when changing direction sharply.

It is harder to interpret the effect of a ski's flexibility. The widely held belief that an inflexible or 'stiff' ski is basically more suitable for icy trails, a flexible or 'soft' ski for deep snow, is incorrect. Many racing models with a particularly good grip on the ice are quite soft and many models for deep snow quite stiff. It is more accurate to say that experience has shown that, if side-cut and camber are right, stiff skis usually grip well on ice, but there are many soft models which have a high resistance to torsion and so grip the ice well.

Over a number of years ski manufacturers conducted experiments on skis. Manufacturers first measured the forces operating on the ski, the boot and the foot during a given set of skiing movements. These forces were incorporated into the testing and design of the ski. Lastly, individual skiers assessed the ski and their verdict influenced the final design.

The following qualities sum up a ski's performance:

- Ability to slide
- Ability to turn
- Grip of the edges
- Directional stability

Ability to slide

It is quite easy to objectively determine a ski's ability to slide. Measurements of speed have shown that the skier finds quite small variations of 10% extremely noticeable. It always pays to wax skis and look after the running surface well.

If the ability to slide is no problem in determining performance, gliding over snow and ice in itself is a complicated physical phenomenon, and has not yet been studied thoroughly enough. What happens in the sliding process? Outer (solid) friction and inner (fluid) friction both occur. The outer friction leads to a change in the snow crystals, which become increasingly globular; this begins at the points, and extends to the whole crystal. More and more of the surface area of the crystal is affected by the inner friction. So in skiing the entire-friction process first decreases as speed increases and then increases again as speed continues to increase; this is due to a further increase of internal friction. Extensive measurements made on ice and snow have made it possible to construct useful mathematical models for this process. It also turned out, in measuring adhesive friction on ice (which is dependent on pressure), that melting under pressure is part of the sliding process.

Ability to turn

Until very recently the physics of ski control were totally unknown and skis were made without scientific knowledge. In recent years special bindings have been designed which, with the incorporation of pressure and tension transducers and electronic telemetry, have made it possible to measure the forces used for all the various ski manoeuvres. On the basis of such measurements and a great mass of additional scientific information, the modern ski can now be designed to meet very specific requirements. This information has also been of use in determining the exact moment when muscle forces are brought into play before, during and after a turn and the kind of forces required for different kinds of turns. For example, the greater force required for a series of rapid, linked turns and the comparatively small forces used on slower, wider-radius turns, can now be accurately determined.

This form of measurement demonstrates the difference between types and makes of skis. For example, a comparison of the forces which come into play at the toe of a boot when making a series of fast, short turns can differ by a factor of three in two different, superficially similar skis. This, in simple terms, means that a certain ski requires three times as much effort to turn as does another similar ski. The difference for the moderate ski user is the difference between easy skiing and almost impossible skiing. A comparison between similar skis of identical length shows a decrease in force required of about three–four times for a shortening of ski length from 6½ft to 6ft(2m to 1.85m).

In practical terms, you can test this difference in turning ability by trying out different skis and executing a few turns.

Grip of the edges

You can feel the grip of the edges in two ways when you ski. First, it enables you to follow a particular track on an edged ski, for example, when coming out of a turn. For this it is useful if the grip of the edges extends well behind and in front of the skier, that is, if he is using long skis.

The most important quality of the edges' gripping ability for most skiers is to help avoid side-slip. The braking power of the edges has also been telemetrically measured. Skis are fastened to a trestle with a 165lb (75kg) weight on it, in the snowplough position, and drawn over a smooth artificial ice surface at constant speed. The average tensile force corresponds to the braking power of the ski, which can be used in a braking snowplough, but also of course in braking turns. This is the power that can be used to stop side-slip.

Using new skis, values between 14 and 24 daN have been measured. Braking power declines rapidly with use. After ten days' use, only 60% of the original value was recorded. The grip of the edges, however, can be restored to its original efficiency by filing them, something that can be recommended to all skiers. Correlations between laboratory measurement values and measurement values of ski-edge gripping power have shown that a hardness of about 43 HRC (Rockwell hardness) is particularly good. In other words the edges need to be made of a material, such as a steel/chrome/molybdenum alloy, which matches this hardness.

Directional stability

This means the ability of a ski to make as little as possible vertical and horizontal divergence from its course (fluttering and swimming). Both can easily be observed if you watch skiers. The movements can be recorded telemetrically with transmitters which measure the movements of the skis separately and in comparison with each other.

Choosing the right skis

To start with, it is not sensible or practical to choose a model simply by the description of materials used and method of construction. For it is in the manufacturer's interest to choose and work with the best combinations of materials and construction methods to attain optimum performance. All that interests the buyer is the result. A description of materials and construction, however, *can* tell us something about solidity, quality or durability – but, a little technical knowledge is needed.

Start from the assumption that the lowest price range will not be good enough if you are going to give your skis above-average use.

In general it is true to say that, apart from price and length, too little information about the qualities of a ski is given. Symbols like GT or SL mean little, and the expressions Giant Slalom (once very popular), Slalom and Downhill are kept for specialist racing skis for those three events.

It is a good idea for skiers to read specialist skiing magazines at the beginning of winter, looking for reports on the range of skis and on comparative testing.

A skier should make his choice with an eye to the *performance* of his skis, paying particular attention to their turning ability and the grip of their edges. To a certain extent, these qualities are mutually exclusive. A ski which turns easily will not be so easy to control when edged, a ski which is easy to control and has great directional stability (important at high speeds) is necessarily not so easy to turn. So we have to take these two opposing qualities as a starting point when classifying different models of ski. A European study group has drawn up a system called the LSA system and this, which has turned out to be of considerable practical use, has been adopted by many European manufacturers. It divides skis into three types according to their qualities in performance, as estimated by measurements and practical tests:

L skis: Models which are easy or very easy to turn, even at slow speeds. Suitable for beginners, novices and intermediate skiers, also for advanced skiers who prefer ease of movement to very high speeds and icy trails.

S skis: Models with a strong or noticeably good grip to their edges, which move well and have directional stability even at high speeds. Suitable for more athletic skiers who have developed a good technique and feel thoroughly at home on the snow.

A skis: Models which combine good ability to turn and a noticeably good grip to the edges. Suitable for skiers who want to move easily at a wide range of different speeds both on soft snow and hard trails.

Although this classification system is not universal, it has been followed in all skiing countries insofar as all manufacturers now class their skis into 'standard' 'mid-length' and 'compact' and, within these categories, divide them into classes suitable for beginners and moderate skiers, advanced and moderate skiers, and advanced and expert skiers. Various brand names are given to all these skis.

In addition, skis can also be classed into length categories, i.e., standard, mid and compact and, within these categories, by the average width of the ski. In very general terms, the shorter the ski and the more it is suitable for the novice or the overweight, the wider it will be; a short narrow ski will be unsuitable for deep powder snow and a wide short ski will be less suitable for an icy trail.

A method of selecting the correct ski has been developed. This method classes skiers by sex (i.e., height and weight), ability and speed. Although this table is not an ideal solution it does provide a guideline in a very difficult choice. The table should not be taken as absolute. Tables have been constructed in a number of skiing countries which all give a similar (if possibly, to the user, confusing) answer. The only real solution is to choose a ski from a table similar to this and then to sample the ski on real snow and under normal skiing conditions.

Another method which has been worked out and tested in Germany is a great help when choosing the right model and the right length of ski. This method is simple and is as follows:

Adults

(M = men; W = women)

Use the following table to count up your own points:

- Technical ability:
  - Habitual stem-initiation when changing direction = one point
  - Parallel skiing on well prepared trails = two points
  - Parallel skiing in all snow conditions = three points
- Speed:
  - Leisurely = one point
  - Fast at times = two points
  - Very fast = three points

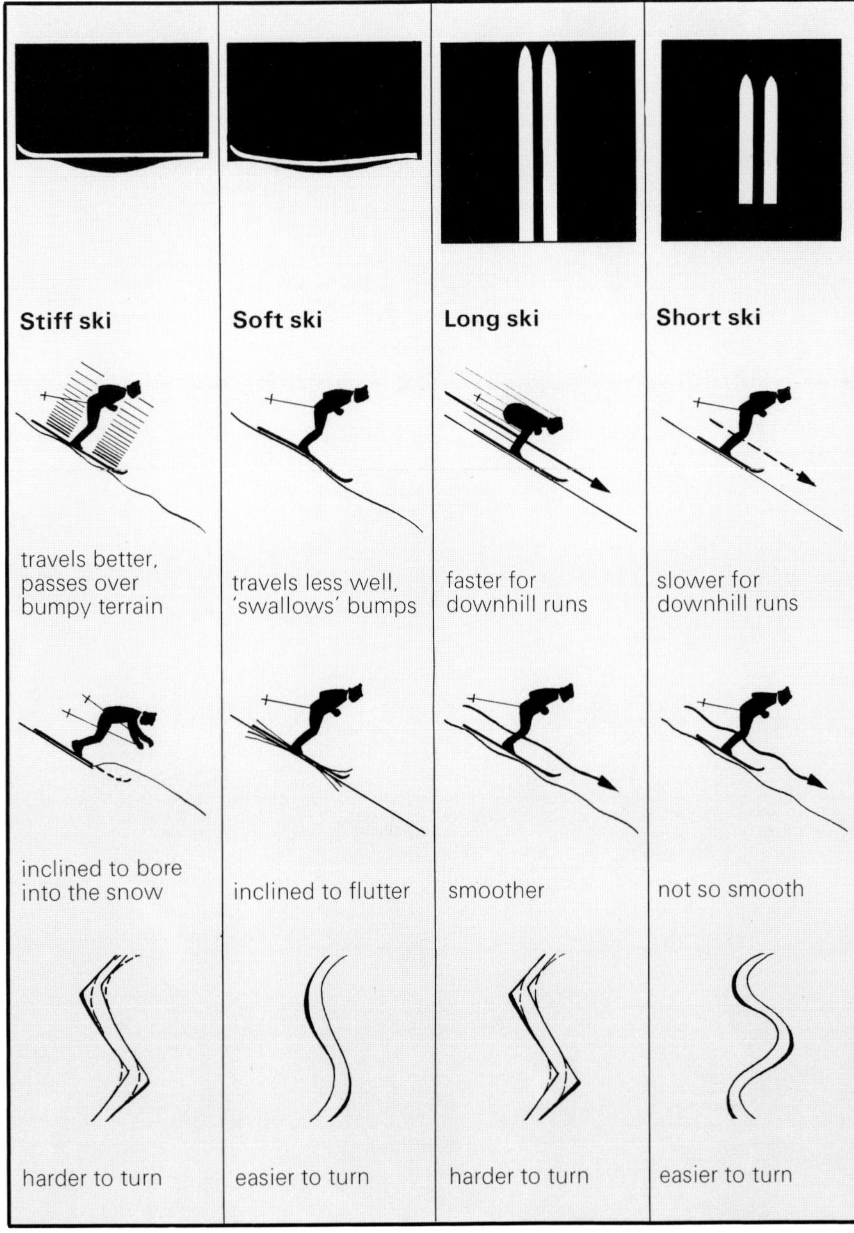

Breadth of ski 180 cm long Points	S 65mm M	W	A 68mm M	W	A 70mm M	W	L 72mm M	W
2	—	—	—	—	160	160	**170**	**160**
3	—	170	170	—	**170**	**160**	180	170
4	190	180	**180**	**170**	180	170	—	—
5	**200**	**190**	190	180	—	—	—	—
6	200 and over		—	—	—	—	—	—

Your point-estimate in the first section will remain the same, but it can vary in the second section.

The table below left shows you the most suitable type of skis (L, A or S) for your point-count, and the length of skis that should be chosen (in centimetres):

Particularly cautious or small skiers – men under 5ft 3in(160cm), women under 5ft(150cm) – can move themselves one box up or to the right from the figures printed in bold type showing ski length; particularly athletic or tall skiers – over 6ft 2in(190cm) for men, over 5ft 9in(180cm) for women – can move one box down or one box to the left.

Skiers who are very heavy (men over 198lb(90kg), women over 165lb(75kg), should choose a more rigid model of ski, so if you have more than four points a longer ski is also advisable.

To avoid confusing terms like 'normal', 'soft', 'compact', the second line down gives the rough measurement of breadth of a ski 5ft 9in(180cm) measured at the narrowest point, in the region of the binding. As will be seen, various lengths of ski occur only in some boxes for each type of ski, for obvious reasons.

Children (up to ten years) and young people (up to sixteen years)

Children's skis are available up to 4ft 3in(130cm) long, skis for young people are available up to 5ft 9in(180cm) long.

Beginners will do best to follow advice from their own ski schools; otherwise, we advise L skis 5ft(150cm) long. The table does not have skis for special purposes in mind (e.g., racing, free-style skiing or high Alpine touring). A good salesman should be able to recommend any customer a ski from the above criteria. Someone who skis only occasionally will not, as a rule, notice much difference between the types.

	Children	Young People
Beginners	at least body height	about body height
Intermediate	body height + 2in (5cm)	body height + 2–4in (5–10cm)
Expert	body height + 4in (10cm)	body height + 6–8in (15–20cm).

Simple tricks to help you choose skis

Place the skis together and see whether the edges are proud of the base. Such skis catch their edges easily and are harder to turn.

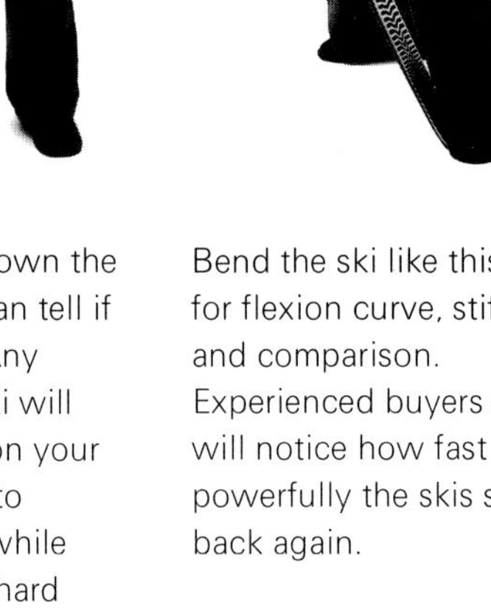

Looking straight down the skis like this you can tell if they are warped. Any distortion of the ski will have a bad effect on your skiing. The ability to maintain stability while twisting the body hard round is particularly important for slalom skis.

Bend the ski like this to test for flexion curve, stiffness and comparison. Experienced buyers of skis will notice how fast and powerfully the skis spring back again.

If you want to test the spatulas (or front end of the skis) for flexibility, bend them at the front like this. Remember that skis for downhill running have softer spatulas and skis for the slalom harder spatulas than a normal all-purpose, 'combi' ski.

Pressing both skis together, see if the running surfaces meet along the whole ski length, as far as the spatula curve.

Factors taken into account	You will need	short –	long
light skiers	shorter skis	*	
heavy skiers	longer skis		*
over forty	shorter skis	*	
under 40	longer skis		*
best for turns	shorter skis	*	
best for speed	longer skis		*
fairly fit	shorter skis	*	
very fit	longer skis		*
deep snow, many large bumps	shorter skis	*	
long smooth trails	longer skis		*
wet snow, granulated snow	shorter skis	*	
dry snow, ice	longer skis		*
stiff skis	shorter skis	*	
soft skis	longer skis		*
skis to grip well	shorter skis	*	
skis to turn well	longer skis		*

Ski boots

No other piece of equipment has so much influence on a skier's movements as his boots. Often, edging, initiating, steering and turning depend more on the quality of your boots than the performance potential of your skis. In general it is perfectly possible to stand on skis successfully fairly early on, but again it depends on your boots. Ski boots are a piece of sporting apparatus; a great deal is asked of them. Many of our requirements are met by various kinds of boots, but in general we seldom find that they are all met in one model.

The most important requirements are:

- Performance
- Safety
- Orthopaedic shape
- Ease in walking and standing

Naturally, the fulfilment of these requirements overlaps to a certain extent, but the distinction makes it easier to understand the function of the boots. The following summary should help you understand how they work.

Performance

The skiing manoeuvres most dependent on your ski boots are edging, weighting of the front of the skis, transferring rotation to the skis, and lifting yourself out of an unintentional back weighting.

Setting the edges precisely is made possible by blocking off the sideways movement of the ankle joint. But the position of the upper part of the boot in relation to the sole is also involved. This will be gone into later, when discussing how to weight the edges of the skis evenly.

Control of movements when weighting the front area is made possible by a progressive forward elasticity of the upper part of the boot. The involvement of the lower leg means that it will be in constant contact with the tongue of the boot. The pivot of the boot movement must be right for the leg movement, that means lower than the geometrical centre of the ankle joint. A really good fit at the heel is essential for this movement.

You will be able to apply your own turning moment to the skis better if you have a really good fit to your heel, ankle joint and entire foot; a roughened lining to the boot is helpful.

An unintentional back-weight position can be avoided by pushing gently upwards and slightly backwards, a movement for which you need sufficient room for the calf muscles.

A boot which is high at the back and front, rigid at the sides, but allowing limited movement at the front will fulfil these requirements well. It should also fit the lower leg in front in such a way that no pain is felt, even when the pressure on the leg is strong and constantly changing.

Safety

The boot should have good shaping round the ankle joint and enclose it with a rigid casing if the joint is to be protected. Many boots come up to standard in this respect nowadays. The result has been a noticeable decrease in the number of ankle injuries suffered in skiing.

The lower leg can only be protected by the heel binding from bending too far for safety if the rigidity and height of the boot give additional protection. A high boot of 8–12in(20–30cm) high inside, becoming steadily less rigid towards the top, decreases the maximum force exerted on the leg at a given moment when it is leaning over, and raises the point at which this force is exerted to where the shin-bone has greater powers of resistance.

Stress when the leg bends (conditional on the corresponding setting of the heel binding) will only be kept less than the breaking point of the lower leg, even under unfavourable conditions (e.g., a strong forward leaning movement of the leg) if the boot fulfils this protective function well because it is properly shaped.

Shaft movement of the boot must be limited to a value less than the terminal position of the ankle joint. This is the only way to avoid ankle injuries which could occur if that barrier was crossed.

This barrier is the point at which the shaft moves 50° forward and is the same at which the break would occur. Unfortunately almost all modern boots show a tendency to give towards the front. This means the shafts of boots are of two types. One is fairly soft and easy to move in from the vertical, and makes it easy to perform the necessary movements when skiing. But if you bend too far forwards the resistance the boots offer is

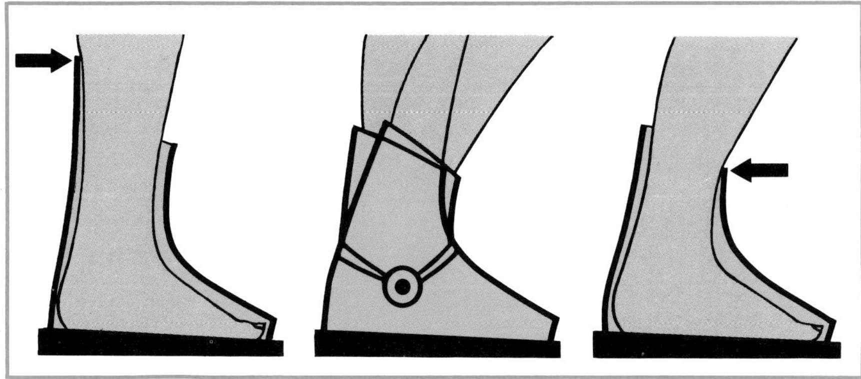

The point of rotation when the shaft moves should fit leg movement. The shaft rigidity should decrease steadily towards the top of the boot.

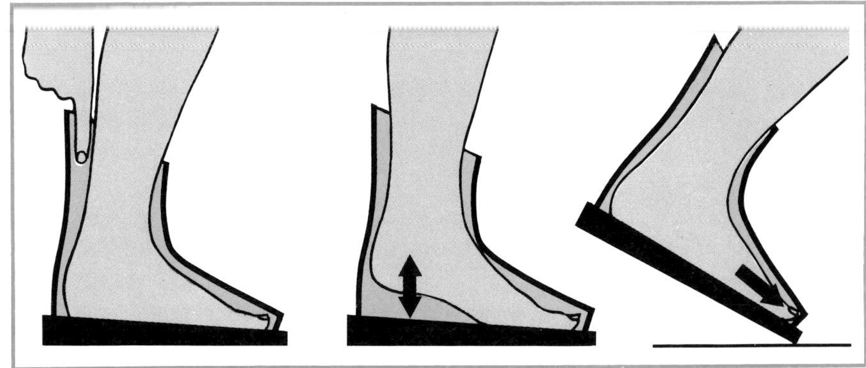

Trying on boots: test (1) the back of the boot (you need at most a finger's breadth of space here); (2) the fit of the heel (no movement up and down); (3) the fit of the toes (plenty of room for the toes to move).

Skiers with knock knees or bandy legs often have problems keeping both skis flat (1) and are inclined to edge one ski more than the other (2). Flattening the skis back after edging is equally difficult (3). A sports' shop can fit a wedge under the binding to tilt the angle the other way and correct your stance (4).

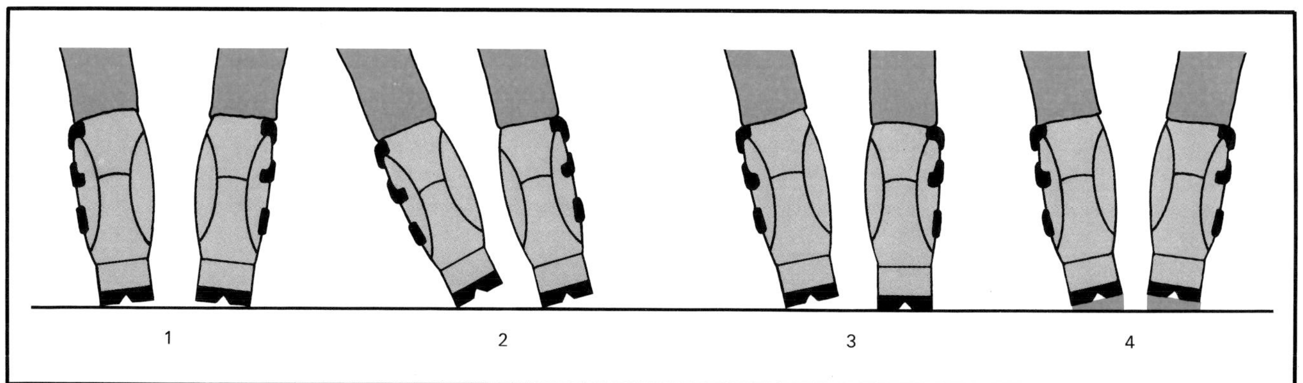

not great enough to avoid the dangerous final position, and, moreover, you cannot exert the necessary pressure on the front of the skis.

The other type of boot is rigid enough to stop you getting further than the final position, but it also holds you back when you are leaning only slightly forwards, so that you do not have the necessary freedom of movement.

Only a progressively elastic shaft gives freedom of movement at small angles, but becomes rigid when the leg angle increases too much.

To ensure that the safety bindings, consisting of toe and heel parts, can function perfectly, the dimensions of the boot soles should conform to international standards. The soles themselves should be rigid enough not to bend or twist. Length should remain fairly constant even with changes in temperature or horizontal pressure at the sides. For this reason, choice of ski boots should be limited to well-established makes.

It is now general practice to design the sole and sole profile of a ski boot so that it will not interfere with the safe operation of the customary low-friction strip of PTFE attached to the ski under the toe of the boot. This is easily visible, as the profile of the sole in an area between $\frac{1}{10}$–$\frac{3}{10}$in(3–8cm) behind the tip of the boot is of a different design.

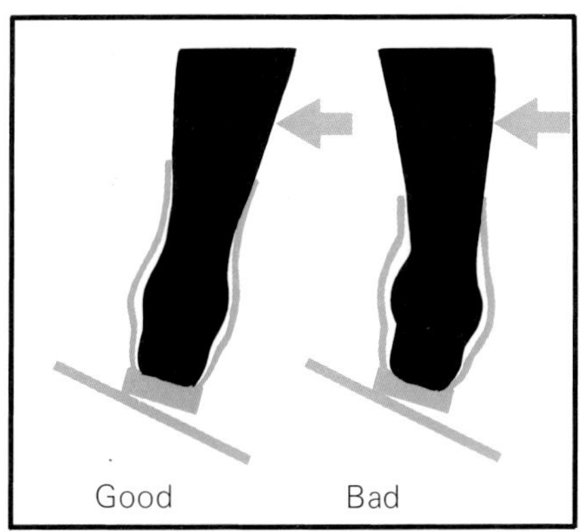

Older models of boots can interfere with the safe operation of ski stoppers. All modern boots are designed to an international standard which ensures the safe use of this device. Most ski sole design is of a non-slip variety and various designs incorporate modifications which are intended to make walking easier.

Due to the curve of the shin-bone, and various muscle formations, high boots bring with them the danger of an uneven weighting of the ski edges. There are some models of boot which alter normal weighting relationships so much that only the outer edges of the skis are weighted. The shape of the inside of the boot and the positioning of the sole have to be such that they produce a more or less even weighting of the edges for the majority of skiers. Uneven edging, however, can be measured and corrected by wedges, so long as it is not something that can only be cured by orthopaedic treatment.

Orthopaedic shape

The shaping of the inside of the boot – with space for toes, the ball of the foot and the ankle, the fit of the heel and the rest of the sole of the foot – must be orthopaedically correct. The greatest pressure is placed against the tongue of the boot when skiing. The tendons of the instep also move a lot when the lower leg is flexed. So this movement must not be impeded by the tongue. Look for a tongue which fits the foot and shin-bone well.

You should find boots on sale for three types of foot: normal, broad across the ball of the foot, and high in the instep. The fit of the boots for different types of feet can also be improved by padding or other devices to fill up excess width inside the boots.

For a very well-fitting boot thermoplastic foam has proved good. Wax can also be thermally applied to give a good fitting. An adjustable inner boot is another method. Air boots, where the inner boot can be pumped up to the right size, mean individual fittings are possible.

Ease in walking and standing

It should be easy to take your boots off and put them on, and the clips should open and close easily. Fastenings should be made so that there is no danger of injury. Ski boots are never suitable for walking in for any distance, but you should still be able to walk a short way in them. You can choose non-slip soles with a good grip and a suitably shaped shaft.

You must be able to stand upright comfortably in your ski boots. In particular, the ordinary skier should avoid boots with a built-in forward lean.

Hints to help you choose your boots

As previously mentioned the techniques of modern skiing demand a tall boot, rigid at the sides, with support when you are leaning back and an elastic shaft allowing movement.

It would be pointless to look for boots in the style of the old, leather boots, possibly because of some painful experiences with modern plastic boots. Any experienced skier getting out his fifteen-year-old touring boots would be surprised to find that he cannot even ski in them today, simply because he has unconsciously become used to the aid provided by modern ski boots. He would also be giving up the obvious ankle protection of modern boots if he went back to the old ones, as well as the protection a tall boot offers the lower leg. Finally, the height of the boot at the back has lessened the frequency of falls and, with it, the risk of injury.

The following hints should help every skier make a sensible choice:

- Although high boots offer everyone more protection for the lower leg, a weaker skier should not choose boots which are excessively high, since they are usually extremely rigid and often have a forward-leaning tendency.
- Skiers who do not ski forcefully should choose boots which are less rigid and more flexible at the front. Women in particular should be careful not to choose boots which are too heavy.
- You should also look for soft boots for children and young people. For child beginners in particular the back of the boot should be no more rigid than is necessary to protect them from falling. Too much support there during normal skiing will lead to an over-rigid style. Since it is easier to dry a removeable inner boot the boots should be lined with a rough-surfaced, absorbent material.
- When trying boots on you should wear a pair of loop-knit or woollen socks such as you will be wearing when actually skiing. It should be easy to put the boots on without any strain, and the same goes for fastening the clips. Make sure there is enough adjustment in the fastenings.
- When the boot is fastened the foot should be held well at the heel, the ankle well supported, the foot supported from below and firmly held down. There should be no feeling of any pinching for the toes need enough room to move.
- If you want to see how the boot will feel during skiing, you should be able to fasten it to the floor with a ski-binding; this is the only way to test it in a backward or forward lean. Leaning forward, you can tell if the boot is flexible enough and especially whether there are areas of pressure in the region of the tongue when you are flexing knees and thighs or exercising pressure on the front of the skis. In the same way you can tell whether the back of the boot presses painfully on the calf musles, and whether it is easy to stand upright again. It is also possible to test the ease with which you can transfer weight, and how well the ankles are supported, if the boots are held down on the floor or fixed to the skis.

If you are choosing a ski boot suitable for touring, the same hints will help you find something suitable both for safety, and for downhill skiing when the terrain demands it. Not many of the boots generally sold for touring are satisfactory in these two points. A touring boot will be stouter in appearance, leading to more friction on the low-friction strip on the safety binding. It is therefore necessary to be sure the upper part of the sole is smooth in the area of the sliding strip. When wearing a plate binding it does not matter if your boots have flexible or rigidly moulded soles.

Safcty bindings

Every fall places a strain on the skier and is the cause of potential injury. The ski can be thought of as a long

lever which gets in the way of a natural fall. This leads to the exertion of large forces and corresponding strain on the skier's legs. If the stress is greater than the strength of the leg, a bone or a joint will break. These injuries are called 'typical' skiing injuries. The function of the safety binding is to protect the skier from them. The principle is to give free play to the union of boot and ski within exact limits of stress, and to do so reliably.

The forces which occur near the bindings in normal skiing – that is to say in circumstances other than a fall – have been extensively measured over the past few years. It has been found that, in normal skiing, a binding has to hold the boot at a far greater force than was previously believed to be the case, so that to calculate correct settings three separate values have to be determined: the control forces (those holding the boot in normal skiing), the holding force (the force required to hold for the peaks of shock that occur in normal skiing) and the disturbance force (those momentary shocks that occur in normal skiing). It is these short-duration shocks (less than 0.1 seconds duration), when skiing over very uneven or icy ground, which can lead to premature release of a binding. As they last for such a short period they cannot cause injury and the binding must be designed to be able to absorb such shocks without opening. (A premature opening can cause serious injury due to an unexpected and unprepared fall.) So correct *adjustment* of the binding is absolutely essential if it is to function correctly.

The facts mentioned above set an upper limit to the adjustment of a binding, determined by susceptibility to injury, and this must not be exceeded. On the other hand, the adjustment must not go below a certain limit, determined by the maximum value of the forces required for skiing.

Once the upper limit is approached, the probability of a 'typical' skiing injury increases. Once you approach the lower limit, the probability of an 'atypical' injury increases, for example, wrenching a shoulder because a ski binding opened prematurely. The minimum probability of both types of injury lies somewhere between the upper and lower limits. The greater the skier's average speed the more likely injury is to occur at higher forces. The question is how to ascertain by experiments the solidity of the human lower leg and related parts of the body, as against the forces and turning moments which occur in skiing.

Well-designed modern bindings can be considered safe if they absorb a defined and measured force (both transient) and, in cases of high-speed skiing, a series of shocks which could culminate in a force sufficient to release the binding.

A really satisfactory binding must be able to do two contradictory

◂ LEFT: adjusting safety bindings.

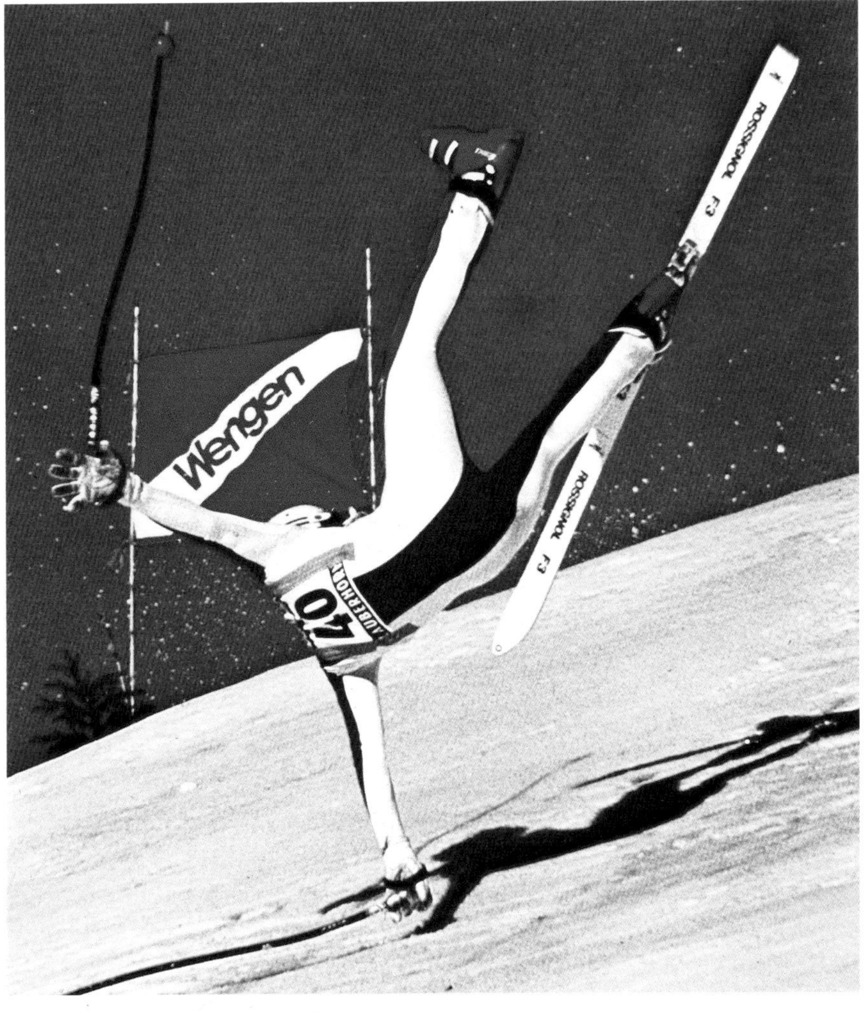

Quick release in rotary, forward and backward falls, as well as lateral falls, is particularly important in racing.

things – release in a slow fall where the build-up of forces could lead to injury and also release instantly if, in a high-speed fall, the momentary force builds up sufficiently to cause injury. All these factors have been combined into international standards for design and no binding which cannot meet these standards is permitted a 'design approved' stamp.

Fracture forces

As a modern ski boot will protect the ankle joint to some extent, the lower shin-bone and its proneness to injury are important in deciding the correct adjustment of the bindings. Of course a skier can increase his leg's resistance to injury by muscle contraction, which will often stop the movement reaching the critical point where injury occurs, but this does not always happen.

If the skier is tired, or takes an unexpected tumble, his muscle reflexes will be partly or entirely out of action. So think of your unprotected leg in the worst (not the best) possible circumstances, when adjusting ski bindings.

Analysis of a fall progression shows, roughly, two types of stress forces:

- Overloading the lower leg's ability to bend (a forward fall)
- Turning about one's own axis (a rotary fall)

Measurements of the fracture load values of bending or rotational forces can be ascertained from the linear measurements of the shin-bone. These are most easily measured by the diameter of the head of the tibia in a living leg because there is not much tissue cushioning at this point.

If you calculate the bending and turning forces in relation to the force which is being exerted by the binding to hold the boot in place, you arrive at a definite figure (which can be measured) above which a fracture would take place. This force, measured at the tip of the boot, is about three–four times the fracture force and it is on this basis that the various tables for setting bindings are calculated.

Choosing, mounting and adjusting safety bindings

On average, five in 10,000 skiers suffer a fracture of the shin-bone every skiing day. Properly chosen, mounted and adjusted bindings decrease the risk to five in 160,000 skiers. In other words only about one in sixteen skiers are skiing with bindings which meet international safety standards.

Choice

The International Study Group for Skiing Safety (IAS) published a list of requirements and testing criteria for bindings in 1969, and gave its seal of approval to many combinations of binding after testing them.

By law all bindings sold in the majority of European countries must reach this standard. The new IAS standards laid down for adults, children and young people (both published in 1974) call for a higher standard and stricter testing criteria for bindings. Once a binding combination has passed its test successfully the IAS will give its seal of approval. Similar criteria have been adopted in North America.

Mounting

One should only combine separate units which match. The work is best done professionally, following the manufacturer's instructions. Most ski equipment shops will fit bindings for a modest additional charge. The reference point for the bindings should be marked on the ski by the manufacturer, either on the left side and/or on the top surface of the ski near the edge. The mark on the ski is matched to a mark on the ski boot, the mark being made on both sides of the boot as close to the ski as possible and coming into the middle of the area occupied by the foot. (If there is no mark on the ski the place can be found by marking a point 6in(15cm) behind the centre point of the ski = half the total projection length measured from the tail. If there is no mark on the boot one can use the centre of the length of the sole as a guide.) Holes must be bored with the correct tools. A manufacturer's specifications will usually be for holes of 4mm, often 3.6mm for models with plastic-tip surface. The correct sole pad or other anti-friction device must be fitted at the right place on the ski; for adults this will be 1–2in(3–5cm) behind the tip of the boot. The binding itself is fitted to the boot according to the assembly instructions after it has been mounted on the skis. One must allow for a play of about 1mm between the sole of the boot and the anti-friction device and be sure that the forward thrust of the boot against the front of the binding is in accordance with the maker's instructions.

Adjustment

The instructions for use of a ski binding will give useful information about adjustment. Every skier should read the instructions carefully and keep them in a safe place.

The IAS adjustment table is given here and is drawn up on the basis of the measurements of fracture forces and normal skiing forces which are described above. The adjustment

IAS adjustment table for bindings

Lower leg diameter, taken at head of shin-bone in cm	Rotary fall release; moment of release in daN m	Horizontal force at tip of boot in daN	Forward fall release; moment of release in daN m	Vertical force at back of heel in daN	**Adjust-ment figure**
Children and young people					
6	0.8	4.5	3	20	$\frac{1}{2}$–1
6.5	1.2	5.5	4	25	1–$1\frac{1}{2}$
7	1.6	7.0	6	30	$1\frac{1}{2}$–2
7.5	2.2	8.5	8	35	2–$2\frac{1}{2}$
8	2.8	10.5	10	40	$2\frac{1}{2}$–3
8.5	3.5	13	13	50	3–4
9	4.5	16	17	65	4–5
9.5	5.5	19	22	80	5–6
Adults up to about fifty years					
7.5	3.0	12	11	45	3
8	3.5	14	13	50	3–4
8.5	4.5	16	16	60	4–5
9	5.5	18	20	70	5–6
9.5	6.5	20	24	80	6–7
10	7.5	22	28	90	7–8
10.5	8.5	25	33	105	8–9
11	9.5	28	38	120	9–10

*Torsion forces are measured in Newtons (N) per metre (m). One Newton/metre is equal to 1 Joule which is equal to 0.74 foot pounds. The forces in skiing are fairly large and consequently are measured in units of 10 Newtons expressed as DecaNewtons (daN)

values are below individual fracture values, but higher than the values necessary in normal skiing. The explanations for use that accompany the table take account of special requirements, for example, for faster or for older skiers. They also contain information for measuring the diameter of the head of the shin-bone (or tibia). This value (and, among other things, age and method of skiing) will give you the correct adjustment of your binding. A provisional adjustment can be made from the instructions that come with your binding. (The new IAS table contains figures for adjustment which will in future be the same for equivalent release values in all conditions.)

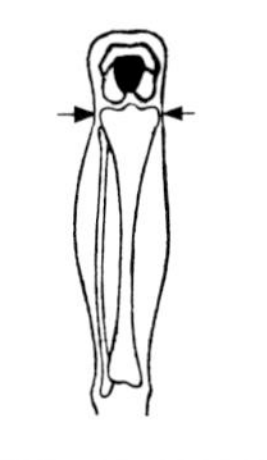

Measurements should be made while you are sitting with knees bent. Calipers should not be pressed tight.

Note: Many methods of assigning a correct release setting have been, and are, used. This particular method is, so far, the only one to be remotely accurate and re-usable. Practice has shown it to be valid for all recreational skiers.

Finally, the toe-binding should be checked for correct release pressure with a suitable test device and, if necessary, readjusted. This is a specialist job and can be done either by the manufacturer or, possibly, in a sports' shop.

Instructions for use of the table

1 centimetre = 0.3937 inches

1. Measure the diameter of the head of the tibia (shin-bone) with a pair of calipers. You can feel the top of the bone on the outside of the leg under the knee joint; take the measurement just above it.

2. Find the values recommended for adjustment of your skis from the table, using the diameter measurement as a guide.
   Example: adult up to fifty years old, shin-bone diameter: $3\frac{1}{3}$in (8.5cm); horizontal force: 16 daN; rotary fall release: 4.5 daN m; vertical force at heel: 60 daN; moment of release falling forwards: 16 daN m; adjustment figure: 4–5. These values can be adjusted accurately to ± 5%.

3. Adults over fifty years should subtract $\frac{1}{5}$–$\frac{2}{5}$in(0.5–1cm) from the shin-bone diameter measurement to find their values.
   Example: adult over fifty years old, shin-bone diameter measured: $3\frac{7}{10}$in(9.5cm); horizontal force: 16–18 daN; rotary fall release: 4.5–5.5 daN m; vertical force: 60–70 daN; moment of release falling forwards: 16–20 daN m; adjustment figure: 4–6.

4. Adults who are very fit and very athletic skiers can adjust resulting values if the diameter measurement is increased by $\frac{1}{5}$in(0.5cm) to, at most, $\frac{2}{5}$in(1cm).

5. In safety conditions where the lever arm used in release diverges

by more than $1\frac{1}{2}$in(4cm) from the length of the sole of the boot (e.g., turntable and plate bindings) the figures given for the release moment in the table do not apply. The release forces can be calculated according to the following equation:

Release force = $\frac{\text{release moment daN m}}{\text{effective lever arm m}}$ daN

6. Adults over sixty years and those with extremely small shin-bone diameter measurements are recommended to use short skis.

7. An approved testing device only should be used to check your adjustments; this is a job for the manufacturer or sports' shop. Since friction between boot and binding plays a part in many binding systems, as a general principle adjustment should be made with dampened or greased contact surfaces. A sole pad or other anti-friction device should be fitted to the ski.

8. Avoid adjustment much tighter than that recommended in the table. It can be dangerous. Nevertheless, if you find it necessary, this usually points to a fault in the binding or its assembly.

9. Check the adjustment of your bindings from time to time. You should always re-adjust them when changing skis, boots or the bindings themselves, and also if you subsequently fit a ski brake.

10. Care and maintenance of the binding to prevent corrosion and accumulation of dirt is essential.

Maintenance

Bindings and their adjustment will only perform correctly if they are carefully treated and maintained. When travelling the bindings should be protected by a ski bag or special wrapping to preserve them from road salt and dirt. Always clean and grease bindings carefully when they become dirty, especially when skiing in summer. Be careful that no screws become loose and that the adjustment has not shifted. Test the toe binding occasionally with the boot in position to see if it goes back into the resting position of its own accord after you have displaced it slightly. If it does it is fairly certain that the release values have not altered dangerously.

Since any part of the functional unit of ski/boot/binding can change, however, you ought to check your binding adjustment thoroughly from time to time, especially at the beginning of winter, with a proper testing device.

Retaining devices to halt loose skis

Fitting of a binding is not complete until a retaining strap or some other similar device has also been fitted.

Every skier needs to wear such a device so that when the binding releases a ski it does not shoot off and endanger other skiers. Poeple who ski slowly will find that a retaining strap is still perfectly satisfactory. Experience has clearly shown, however, that a ski hanging from a retaining strap represents a considerable danger to the skier himself, and the higher his speed the more dangerous it is. This danger can be avoided with a ski brake ('ski-stopper'). It must be one which brakes the ski hard enough to leave it within the area where the skier falls. This also diminishes danger to anyone else. The IAS has also laid down standards for ski brakes, and if you choose one of those you can be sure that it is suitable.

The general requirements of the IAS code of standards are as follows:

- The ski brake must not impede the movement of the ski and the perfect functioning of the safety bindings.
- The ski brake must be constructed in such a way that it will withstand loads without damage.
- The ski brake must work automatically, independently of the skier.
- The ski brake must work perfectly whatever the conditions at the time of skiing (temperature, ice, etc.).
- The ski brake must be made in such a way that it presents no great danger of injury if correctly used.
- The ski brake must brake the ski effectively in all possible positions in relation to the slope, and in all snow conditions and types of trail. It must also come to rest close to the area where the skier has fallen.

Even well-made brakes, however, can present fitting problems. They often make very different demands on ski boots and bindings, and so do not really fit into the functional unit of ski/boot/binding. Even parts which do suit the unit can be wrongly fitted. There are many options for the best place for a brake—for example, more to the back or front of the ski.

The conventional shape of boot sole today often makes it impossible to fit a brake in front of the heel binding, but further forward, just behind the toe, where it will not be so effective. If you do have one fitted in front, be sure that the brake does not impede the sideways release action but has a device to avoid this. In any case, a brake should be fitted professionally. Brakes are often a nuisance in ski maintenance, especially when filing the edges, so it should be easy to remove them. Brakes should be used in racing, or at least in training. The use of a retaining strap in deep snow is recommended because of the possibility of completely losing a 'free' ski.

Ski poles

In Europe, ski poles, like other sporting equipment, have to conform to certain standards laid down by law, and can only be put on the market if they do. They must be made in such a way that no injury to the skier or anyone else can result from their correct use.

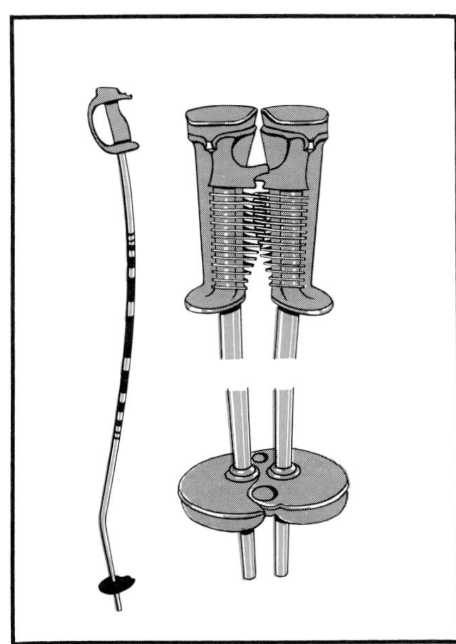

Safety ski stick with in-built fracture points and loopless, anatomically-designed handgrip.

The majority of ski poles on sale today, however, have small faults from the point of view of safety. Various manufacturers have realized this, and fortunately the first steps are already being taken to rectify the matter.

The usual form of injury from the point of a pole – without decreasing its functional use – can be avoided by making the point star-shaped or giving it a crater-shaped groove at the end. The danger when one's body collides with the hand-grip can be lessened by shaping the upper part of the grip to present a large surface area and making it of flexible material, or the pole can be made to bend or collapse telescopically. Finally, injuries suffered when one gets 'hung up' on the end of a pole can be avoided by better shaping of the basket, by making it possible to open the loop or slip the loop off the handle. The grip should be made with the anatomy of the human hand in mind; this means there should be a difference between grips for left and right hands.

Many nasty accidents with ski poles have led the authorities to look into the question of how far safety techniques in general can be applied to improve ski poles. We may expect soon that ski poles which do not come up to safety standards will not be allowed on the market.

Skiing terms

The European Board of Skiing Standards (members: West Germany, Austria, France, Yugoslavia) have made a provisional list defining skiing terms, which we give here. This is the first attempt to do this anywhere in the world. The aim is to have a common language for skiing.

Ski
Gliding runner, very narrow in relation to its length, curving up at the front end to make its passage over obstacles easier. Used for sport and recreation, generally in pairs. Glides over snow and ice (causing liquefaction through friction and pressure), on hard surfaces treated to make them slippery, or on water. Skis used in winter sport come into the category of ski in this definition.

Alpine ski
Principally used fror downhill skiing in hilly areas, under gravitational force. Control of direction and speed is achieved by the combined forward and traversing movements of the skis. Various systems of skiing technique are used to employ the basic physical laws to the best effect. The bottom corners of the running surfaces are usually edged with hard, resistant materials to enable the ski to be controlled when moving sideways.

Cross-country ski
Principally used to move over flat or slightly hilly terrain, especially when propelled by the muscular power of the skier. Changes of direction are mainly performed by stepping. The running surface does not, therefore, need reinforced edges in the same way as the Alpine ski.

Touring ski
A ski suitable both for Alpine skiing techniques and for cross-country skiing.

Giant slalom ski, slalom ski, downhill ski
In Alpine skiing competitions these skis are used in the downhill, giant

slalom and slalom events; they differ to a certain extent according to the requirements of the different events.

Instruction ski
A ski especially designed to suit a given method of ski instruction.

Spatula
Front end of the ski, curved upwards to facilitate passage over obstacles.

Running surface
The sliding underside of the ski that comes in contact with the snow. It is generally made of plastic material with special sliding properties which can be enhanced by the application of wax.

Running groove
Groove running lengthwise along the running surface of the ski, to improve directional stability when the ski is travelling flat over the snow or other material. Alpine and cross-country skis generally have a single groove, skis for ski-jumping generally have more than one.

Ski binding
Device holding the ski boot to the ski which is capable of release and transfers the necessary controlling forces to the ski.

Safety ski binding
Ski binding with a special safety mechanism which transfers controlling force to the ski in normal skiing, and releases the ski from the boot if the force employed rises above an upper limit. It therefore lessens the risk of injury.

Sandwich construction of skis
Method of constructing skis in which the core of the ski is reinforced by layers of material which are more stable and rigid than that of the core on both upper and lower surfaces. The reinforcing materials are employed over the entire breadth of the ski. The core of the ski may be partly hollow.

Box construction of skis
Method of constructing skis in which the outer coating either forms a box shape around the entire ski as seen in cross-section, or is partly extended into the inside of the ski as seen in cross-section. The core of the ski may be partly hollow.

Wooden ski
Ski with wooden core but no strengthening components other than the steel edges, which are stronger than the wood used for the construction.

Metal ski
Ski of sandwich or box construction, where the bearing surfaces are usually made of lightweight metal. The core may be made of any material.

Plastic ski
Ski of sandwich or box construction, with the bearing surfaces made of plastic such as fibreglass, with the exception of the steel edges of the upper edges. The core may be of any material.

Upper surface layer
Ski construction component forming the top layer, serving as protection for the lower layers of the ski as well as fulfilling the functions of an upper surface.

Core
Ski construction component lying between top and bottom bearing surfaces.

Steel edge
Ski construction component forming the lateral limitation of the running surface, usually made of sharpened steel, enabling the sides to grip sufficiently for lateral motive power.

End protector
Ski construction component placed at the end or heel, principally designed to protect the ski from damage.

Sides
Ski construction component placed on the side surface, principally designed to protect the ski from damage.

Upper edge
Ski construction component placed between the upper surface and the sides, principally designed to protect the ski from damage.

Tip protector
Ski construction component protecting the sides, upper surface and running surface of the ski from damage in the spatula area where required.

Running surface base layer
Ski construction component forming the running surface of the ski.

Ease of turning
Defined by the maximum force needed to perform a turn and control it by means of one of the recognized techniques. The ski, the trail and the skiing technique influence the turning force.

Manoeuvrability
The suitability of the ski for the performance of fast linked changes of direction. The ski, the trail and the skiing technique influence manoeuvrability.

Sensitivity
Repeatable (measurable) reaction of the ski to control manoeuvres such as carefully calculated edging and displacement of the centre of gravity.

Edge grip
Suitability of the ski to react to traverse and direction changes in terms

of the edge grip or control. The ski, the trail and the skiing technique influence the edge grip.

Lateral directional stability
Ability of the ski to maintain direction as decided by a control manoeuvre when no further control manoeuvres are performed. Manifestations of instability:

- Excessive turning: ski reacting too readily to a turning manoeuvre
- Tracking: failure to react to a control manoeuvre
- Swimming: periodical wavering to either side

The ski and the trail influence lateral directional stability.

Vertical directional stability
The smoothest and most regular adaptation of a ski to the geometry of the trail over which it is passing. Manifestations of instability:

- Fluttering: vertical oscillation
- Jolting: insufficient absorption of irregularities in the terrain

The ski, the trail and the speed influence vertical directional stability.

These terms apply only to European ski manufacturer's specifications. The United States and Japan have other, though similar, conventionally accepted terms.

Although the specifications and standards of the IAS expressed in DIN numbers are universally accepted in Europe, the American and Japanese manufacturers use other, comparable standards and the American consumer organizations maintain as tight a check of ski equipment as do their European counterparts.

Do-it-yourself ski maintenance

Skiing is a delightful experience when you feel your skis gliding, turning and reacting under you. They can do these things in different ways. They may glide quickly or slowly, turn easily or with difficulty, react quickly, slowly or not at all.

One might suppose that a good ski has all the positive qualities just mentioned and a bad ski all the negative ones, but this is not so.

Strange to say, you will find that even good skis are gliding over the snow more slowly on some days than they did just after you bought them. And suddenly you may wonder why you are having difficulty in turning when you never did before. So maybe the price *was* too high and the salesman was having you on. While there is no art in buying an especially expensive ski, however, there is an art in keeping your skis capable of their best performance even if you did not pay so much for them in the first place. Many people are proud of doing so. All you need is a little practice and the right tools.

An essential for all do-it-yourself work is a firm table or bench – one which will survive a few spots of wax and scratches (1). It should stand in a good light and close to a power point. Next, you need something to hold the ski steady while you work on it (2). There are various possibilities; you can choose according to what you can afford and the alternative uses to which you can put the equipment.

If you decide on a vice, which has the advantage that you can use it for other purposes, make sure the ends of your skis are supported, otherwise you may find a ski bending away from the work. It is even better to

1

2

Holding the ski steady

Necessary	Desirable	Ideal
firm bench or table	clamp or vice	work bench, ski clamp
drawer for storing tools	tool box	board to hang up tools
good light	strong electric light	

have two vices so that you can fit the ski into them at two points. A special clamp designed to hold a ski is the best device of all for it enables you to work fast.

You must also be well organized, for instance, by having the tools you will need in a drawer under the table, so that you can lay hands on them at any time.

It is a good idea to buy a box with special compartments for your tools; one advantage of this is that you can take it with you on your skiing holiday. It is also useful to make a board or locker where you can hang or put your files, screwdrivers, and so on.

Note: If you do not have the time to maintain your skis a good ski shop will do most of the maintenance for you.

Tools

Besides your firm table or bench, which will come in useful for other do-it-yourself jobs, there are certain tools which are more or less essential for ski maintenance (3).

A cabinet-maker's scraper will remove old plastic coating and wax, and a triangular scraper can be used to clean the groove and edges of the ski.

3

You will also need a file to sharpen the edges. These are available in various shapes, from one already set at a right angle to an ordinary smoothing file, which may be cheaper but should be of equally good quality. A file which will smooth the base as well as sharpening the edges is generally used.

You will also need a sheet-metal file for filing the edges if necessary.

A plane with a sharp blade can level out any unevenness on the sole, and comes in useful.

A steel straight-edge is not absolutely necessary but is very useful for anyone wishing to work accurately.

You will need a gas burner for repairing the sole.

The most important tool required is a waxing device; unfortunately it is also the most expensive.

You can simply use an old domestic iron, but nowadays there are devices in which you can melt, mix and apply the wax.

Work will be made much easier if you also have an apparatus for repairing the sole, which does the melting and application of the coating for you.

Materials

Besides your tools, various kinds of ski wax are required. You will need a wax cleaner or de-waxer such as a nitro-cleaner or other suitable industrial de-greaser. Proprietary brands of ski wax removers can be bought in aerosol cans. The de-waxer should remove the very last remnants of old wax from skis after use. Both ski wax and de-waxer are available from ski shops.

Sandpaper of various grades is always useful for do-it-yourself work. It is easier to handle sandpaper if it is held in a sandpapering block.

Fine steel wool, easily obtainable in hardware shops, is useful for cleaning the ski surfaces.

Preparing for the first day's skiing

You have probably noticed already that after touching a number of skis your hands are fairly dirty. This is not surprising when you think that skis manufactured in summer and not sold till autumn or winter have had quite a long time to gather dust.

However, even if your sports' shop has taken the trouble to clean the skis before they go into the shop window, they need treatment before use if you are to get real pleasure out of them from the start.

Modern coatings are prone to oxydization. This layer of oxide gathers on the base like a roughish

Tools for working on skis at home

Essential	Desirable	Ideal
scraper	right-angled file	waxing apparatus with wax basin
file	plane	fine abrasive stone
sandpaper	special waxing iron	mounted file
iron		wax cleaner
wax	nitro-solution for cleaning	sandpaper block

carpet, and will naturally slow you down. Correct treatment eliminates this effect, and is also protective, like the seal on parquet flooring.

After clamping your ski in the vice or clamp, remove the worst of the dust with a cloth.

Then rub the running surfaces thoroughly with fine steel wool.

Make sure your ski is level along its entire length with the help of a good scraper (4). If you hold the narrow edge of the scraper against the ski and push it slowly forward, edges and base should be level (5). (The spatula end does not matter.) The closer the ski is to the ideal the better. If you find that the edges are lower than the base at many points, or all the way along, remove a little of the sole coating with the scraper.

Filing

If the sole is lower than the edges something is wrong, since your ski will run as if it were on rails – this may already have bothered you – and part of the edges must be removed. For this you will need a sheet-metal file. Lay the file flat on the ski at an oblique angle to its length and push forward with both hands, exerting a good deal of pressure (6). Keep checking to see if the edges are at the right level. Make sure you treat the whole length of the ski. Filing at one spot only gives the edge a wavy line and affects the performance of the ski.

But before you undertake this bit of repairing, ask yourself if you are a sufficiently good handyman. If not, it would be better to leave the job to a professional.

Filing will also correct any change in the sharpness of the edges at the tips and ends of the ski. The tips and ends make no difference to the control of the ski when weighted. This area can easily be found by placing the skis together, running surfaces touching, and pressing them flat. Make a mark at the tips and ends of the skis where the running surfaces cease to touch.

From the extreme tip and end of the ski up to this point, the edges can be filed to an almost rounded outline. They do not want to be sharp (7).

The advantage of this treatment is that the edge, particularly inclined to stick ('hook') in hard, packed snow at the spatula end, will be less prone to do so.

Smoothing the edges

The slight roughness left at the edges in manufacture must be removed before the skis are used. Use fine sandpaper (wet-and-dry 100) stretched over a sandpapering block and rub it smoothly over the entire length of the edges, working from the underside of the ski.

Cleaning

Remove any dirt and metal shavings from the underside of the ski with a cloth. Rub the ski thoroughly after

4

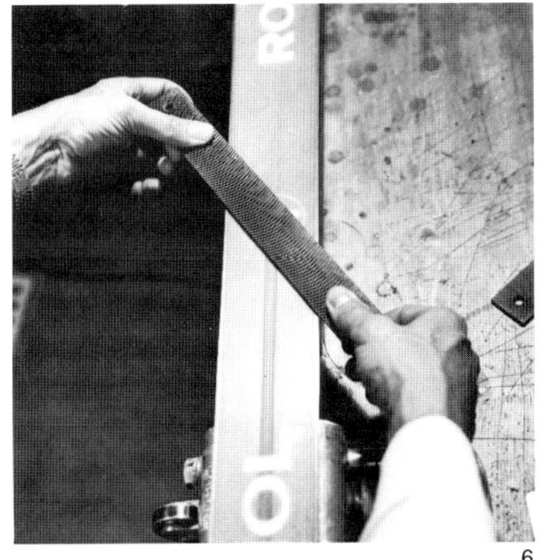

6

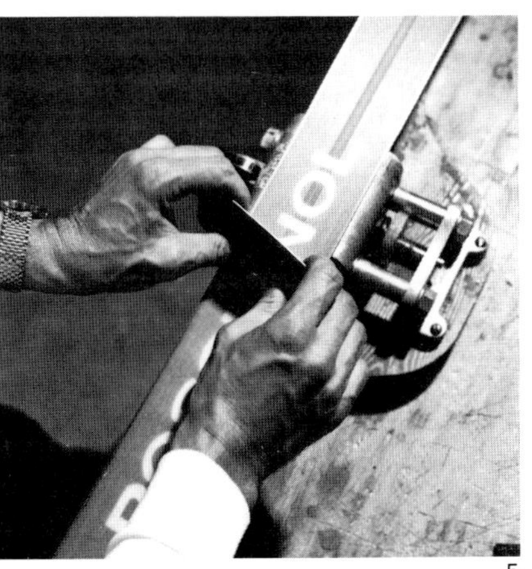

5

7

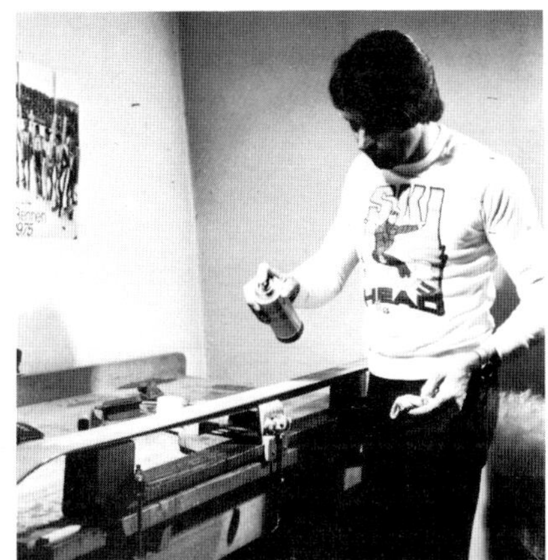

8

using a de-waxer or rub with a cloth dipped in nitro-solution (8). Now the ski is ready for waxing.

Waxing

The best thing to use is a waxing tool sold in ski shops, or an old iron.

When waxing a ski for the first time it is more important to preserve the coating of the base than to prepare the ski to run fast. So you will need to use a soft wax, which will close the fine pores in the coating. Such waxes are usually those which embrace a wide range of temperatures. The colour coding used by most manufacturers is red.

The wax is melted and at the same time applied to the base of the ski (9). If it is not automatically smoothed out at the same time, as happens, for instance, with certain waxes, you must finish by ironing the wax smooth over the ski (10). The iron should be at a temperature of 175°F (80°C). Then run the scraper over the base of the ski so that only a very thin coating of wax remains. This process should be repeated at least once (11). As a general rule, waxing like this is adequate for most snow conditions. If conditions are unusual, however, follow the advice given by wax manufacturers. You will find more information about waxing in the section on Choosing a Wax (p. 44).

Care after skiing

It is best to clean your skis directly after use. Unless you have been skiing on virgin powder snow, the skis will usually be dirty. Traces of dirt, snow and water should be removed as soon as possible, and your best plan is to take a large, soft cloth with you in your rucksack or your car, and use it to wipe the ski, especially the base and edges (take special care with the latter).

Skis should be examined more thoroughly at regular intervals of three to four days and if necessary overhauled.

If the skis have been treated before use as suggested above, there will be no need to sandpaper any rust off the edges. But if you do have to do this, use fine sandpaper. Then rub the base down well, using a wax cleaner.

Filing the edges

It is not always necessary to file the edges. Your edges are likely to need attention, however, if the snow conditions have been very hard and icy, or the snow was not thick enough to cover all stones. Both conditions often occur at the same time, and the performance of your skis will quickly deteriorate.

Preparing for the first day's skiing

Essential	Desirable	Ideal
cleaning waxing	waxing twice removing any slight roughness from edges	smoothing base removing sharpness from edges at spatulas and ends waxing several times

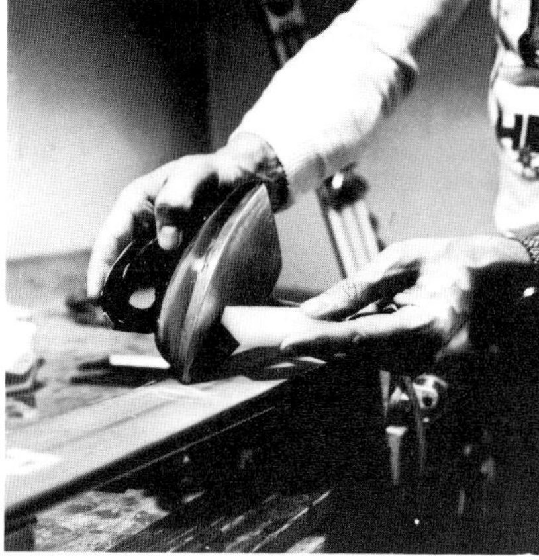

9

11

10

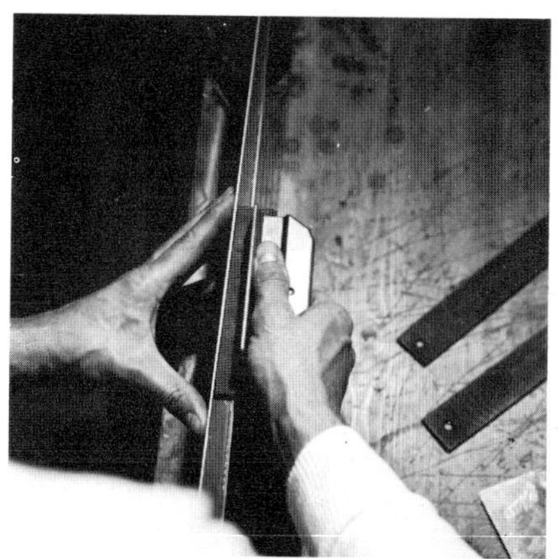

12

Clamp the ski, edge up, in whatever clamping device you are using. Then run the file evenly over the edge to remove the so-called 'beard', a slight irregular fringing which forms on the edge at the underside of the ski (12). Even without travelling over stones, your ski will gradually develop this 'beard' at its edges.

If there are no notches on your skis, that is all you need to do now. If you have notched edges or blunted edges, however, you will have to work on them. A really good file and some expertise in the use of it are necessary. Experienced skiing handymen prefer a large file which has a larger surface area and can have more pressure exerted on it than a smaller one. File the entire edge with a regular motion, working from the spatula down to the end of the ski.

It is very important to be sure you are filing at a right angle to the sole face of the ski. Finally finish off with fine sandpaper or a sanding stone to make the edges perfectly smooth.

If there are any scratches or grooves in the underside of the edge, the skis will have to be professionally repaired, since these cannot usually be repaired at home without risk of damage to the edges.

Repairing the sole

The soft plastic coating on the underside of skis is the most sensitive part, and therefore needs repairing the most often.

Smooth any roughnesses on the sole of the ski with a scraper or a knife, using the knife on any holes with rough edges. Then remove every trace of dirt.

Using a gas burner warm the coating carefully at the spots which need repair.

After this there are three possible ways to repair the sole, depending on the apparatus you are using. The producers of skiing accessories have recently developed devices which can be used for this purpose at home:

- Use an attachment for a soldering iron, shaped like a boot. Place a strip of polyethylene in the boot, from above, and use the whole thing over the damaged area. The attachment can only be used to fill in small gouges (13). P-Tex sticks can also be lit and melted drips used to fill sole scratches (14), before ironing in (15).
- Plastic chips for repairing the base are a good method. After you have prepared the ski as described, place the chips over the damaged areas and iron the plastic into the gouges or cracks with a hot iron. Take care that no small air bubbles form.

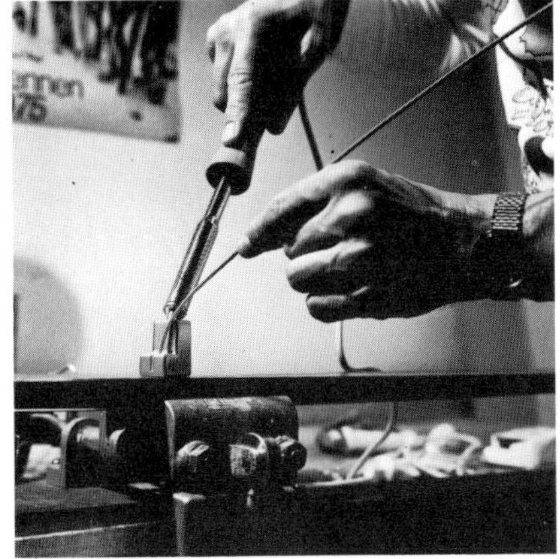

13

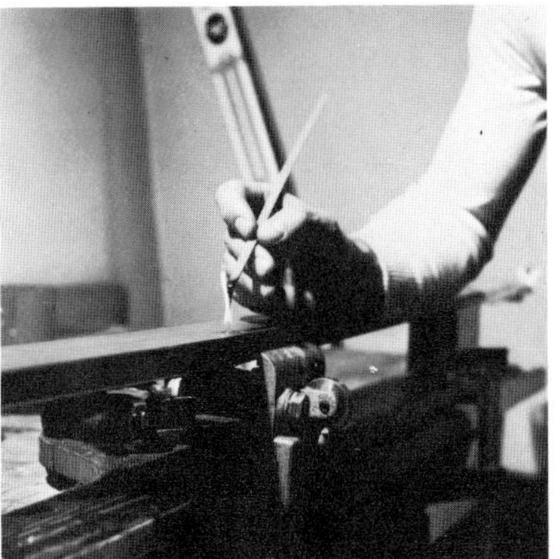

14

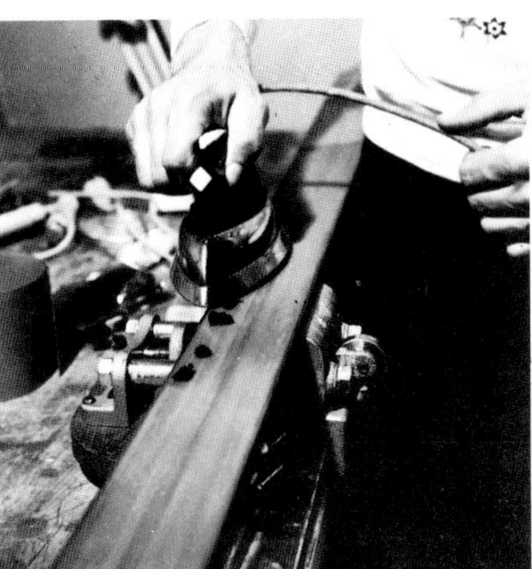

15

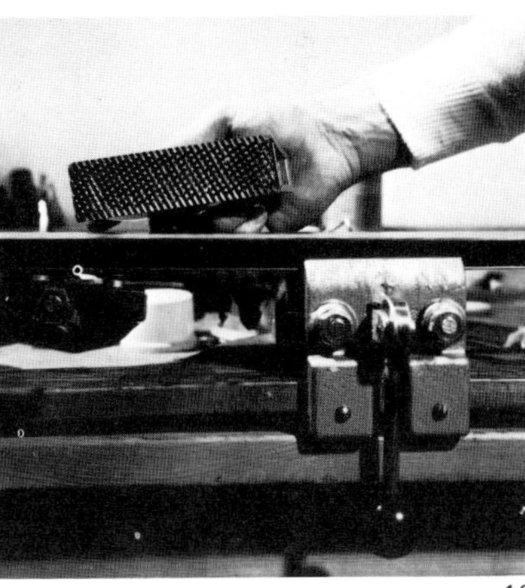

16

- Finally, you could use an attachment fixed to a gas burner into which you place half a plastic repair strip or the plastic chips mentioned above and heat on a fireproof surface, for example, a piece of tin. When the plastic has melted pass the device over the ski, pressing down gently. Keep the flame low as you work. If any smoke appears, turn the heat down at once. Clean the plastic out of the groove of the base with a putty knife or triangular scraper while it is still soft. The apparatus itself can be cleaned with steel wool.

The same procedure must be followed after using any of these three methods of repairing damage to the sole of the ski, since you want to have

Care after skiing

Essential	Desirable	Ideal
cleaning	removing the 'beard' from the edges	filing the edges
occasional waxing	waxing after every use	repairing the base coating

17

it absolutely smooth. Using a file-plane (16), carefully smooth the coating. Exert only slight pressure, or the plane may bite into the coating (17).

Rub the repaired places with fine sandpaper. All signs of damage should have disappeared.

Choosing a wax

A waxed ski runs faster and also turns better. Its sole coating is also better protected from obstacles such as stones and chemicals such as salt. So it is worth taking the trouble to wax ski.

Recently the running surfaces of Alpine skis have been considerably improved. The polyethylene coating which is now generally used is more flexible and porous than previously used materials. It means, however, that a rather different maintenance and waxing technique is necessary.

What happens when skis glide over the snow?

The gliding movement of skis over the snow produces friction and warmth, which consequently causes some of the snow to melt. This creates a thin film of water between the running surface of the ski and the snow over which the ski is gliding. A snow crystal is always six-pointed, but can take many different shapes and form different patterns. New snow consists of sharp-edged crystals which roughen the wax coating and so produce a roughened running surface. This means that the skis will slide better if a hard wax is used. When snow crystals touch solid ground they change shape – the delicate star or prism shapes become rounded and granulated. This change happens fast if the snow is damp or wet. If the temperature is low, it takes longer. In general one can distinguish between the following types of snow crystals after contact with the ground:

- Shortly after snow has fallen – fine, powder snow
- A few days later – 'corn' or granulated snow (the original shape of the snow crystals is barely visible)
- Old snow – coarsely granulated snow (the crystals have lost their original shape and their edges are rounded)

So the question is, what wax to use at different temperatures, and for what kind of skiing?

The following factors must be taken into account:

- If the air temperature is below freezing, the choice of wax depends on:
  - the temperature of the snow
  - the structure of the snow crystals (fine or coarse granulation)
- If the air temperature is above freezing, the choice of wax depends on:
  - the structure of the snow crystals
  - the dampness of the snow

Other factors include the dampness of the air, the exact air temperature, the speed of the skier, the extent of less steep areas on the slope, sun and shade.

How the racers do it

The temperature of the snow is taken at the dividing line between snow and air which is roughly $\frac{1}{5}$–$\frac{1}{5}$in (0.5–1cm) down in the snow. It should be taken at four of five different spots on the course. These measurements must include any flat areas of the course.

The dampness of the air is also important. In damp weather, with new snow up to 32°F(0°C) or lower, the wax must be harder, since the snow crystals are sharp and will penetrate the wax.

Another important factor is the speed which a racer will reach. The reason for 'warmer' waxing at higher speeds lies in the greater friction between the snow and the running surfaces of the skis.

Increased friction means that more water is produced, and so in these circumstances water-repellent waxes are used. If all other conditions are the same, a wax is used for the giant slalom which is 2–4°F(1–2°C) 'warmer' than the wax used for the slalom. In the same way, a wax 5–9°F(3–5°C) 'warmer' is used for downhill racing than for the slalom. It is therefore important to test the sliding qualities of the snow at the speeds one will reach while racing.

If the course has long, fairly level stretches, racers must take them into account when waxing, since the wax will have less effect on a skier's speed on the steep downhill sections than on these more level ones.

In general racers try to aim for the best combination of effects, taking into account *all* factors (including sun or shade, level stretches, and so on), when waxing their skis. Ski waxes are divided into basic waxes and paraffin waxes. The main difficulty in mixing the correct waxes lies in deciding what the proportions of the different kinds should be. Most recreational skiers would not, normally, go to the lengths of mixing their own waxes. This is specialist's work. Base or foundation waxes can be bought in most good ski shops and running waxes covering a wide range of temperatures and snow conditions are available. They are colour-coded from purple (warmest) through red, blue and green (coldest). These waxes should not be confused with cross-country waxes.

The wax should have the following qualities:

1. It should slide well and be water-repellent.
2. It should last well.
3. It should cling to the running surfaces well.

Before beginning the actual waxing, the edges should be smoothed and the running surfaces prepared. The running surfaces should be regularly impregnated with a base wax which will help even out differences in temperature.

Melt the mixture of waxes recommended by the wax manufacturers in a suitable container or waxing apparatus. If you have bought a packet of wax which has no instructions with it, ask for advice in the ski shop.

If you do not have a device for melting and ironing on the wax, melt it in a small pan and paint it on the running surface with a brush (18).

Alternatively, use a waxing machine (iron plus container, electrically heated) to wax the ski (19). Or melt the wax with a waxing iron (20). And apply to the sole of the ski (21).

Clean out the groove and trim the edges of the ski with a triangular scraper (22).

Make sure the coating is scraped very thin. Ideally no wax should come off the coating if slight pressure is exerted with the thumb nail.

Wax should never be polished with the hands, because of the natural tendency of the skin to secrete grease. Use a nylon cloth, such as an old stocking, to polish the coating.

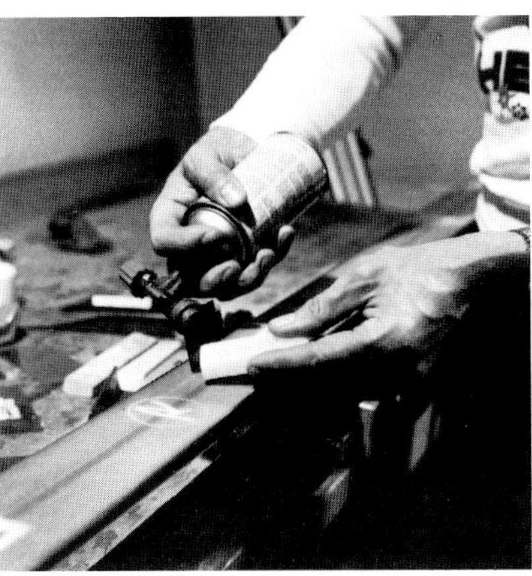

20

18

21

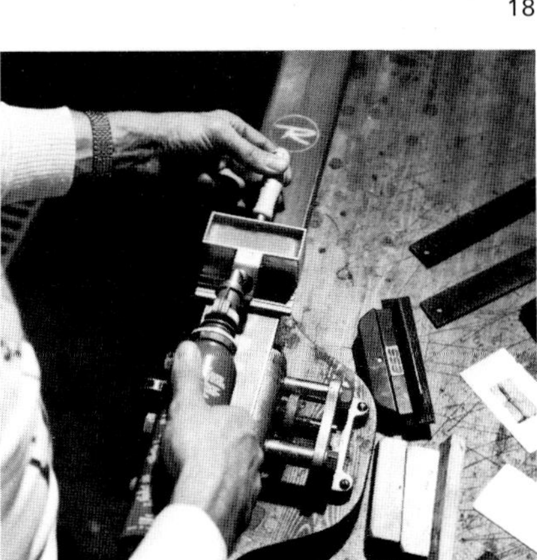

19

22

Before skis are put away or placed together, put narrow plastic bags over their tips and ends; these bags should cover the surfaces that touch when the skis are placed together, that means up to about 16in(40cm) from the ends. This will stop the wax film, so carefully applied, from becoming damaged as the skis rub together when carried.

In fine-grained or new snow, skis prepared for racing should be brought into contact with the snow before the start. In granulated snow, the wax loss is so high that the skis should not come into contact with the snow before a race.

One final bit of advice which will do the upper surface and the bindings of your skis good, as well as the coating of the sole: carry your skis in a ski bag, especially if you are going to transport them by car (23). The money you spend on a bag will be well worth it. You will see why as soon as you take your dry, clean skis out of a ski bag that has been on a car roof as you drove over dirty, wet, salted roads.

It should be mentioned that, for the lazy, and those who have just forgotten to wax their skis, it is possible to improve the sliding quality of your skis with wax from a tube just before you start skiing. This is not the same, however, as proper waxing.

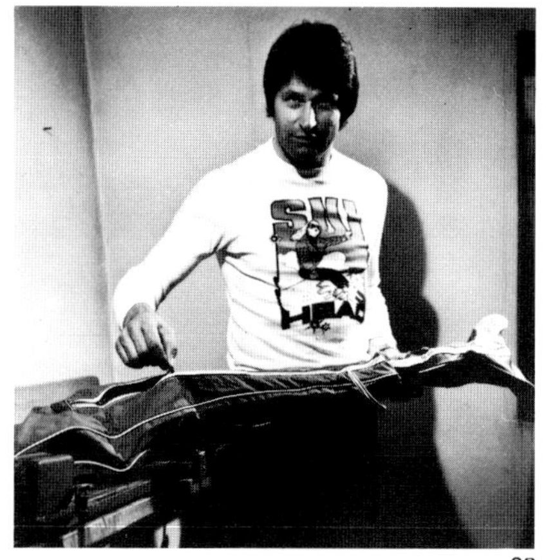

23

Damage and how to repair it

Item	Fault	Cause	Repair
Ski	concave spatula	moulded at too high heat, material warps	file, sandpaper
	glue coming apart	heavy demands on ski, faults in manufacturing, fitting screws too long, varnish damage unrepaired	dry, clean, glue weight down – or send back to manufacturer
	damage to varnish	scratches, collisions	dry, clean, varnish
	loss of protective parts at ends	violent collisions	send for repair
Base	higher than edge	manufacturing fault	sandpaper
	scratches, gouges	passing over stones	clean, repair with polyethylene, smooth, sandpaper
	comes off	long-term effect of damp, heavy demands on skis, manufacturing fault	dry, clean, glue, weight down – or send back
Edges	higher than running surface	manufacturing fault	file, sandpaper
	blunt, rounded	heavy use, passing over stones	file, sandpaper
	notched	passing over stones	file, sandpaper
	too sharp	brand new	sandpaper to 10 in (25 cm) in from each end
	broken	passing over stones	send for repair
Binding	wrongly placed	incorrectly measured or fitted	measure again and readjust
	fitting badly	new boots	measure again, toe binding will often need readjustment
	lost screws	holes bored too large; if fitted to a foam core screws not glued in place	seal holes with glue, fit screws in with Araldite-type adhesive

Storing your equipment in the summer

If you are in any doubt as to whether you will be examining and putting your skis in order at the start of the new skiing season, the alternative is to do so before putting them away for the summer.

First repair the sole of the running surfaces and the edges according to the instructions given above.

Then apply plenty of wax, and leave it on the skis. Make sure the whole of the edges are covered by wax; this is the best way to protect them and the base from oxydization and rust.

It is also a good idea to clean any traces of dirt and salt off the upper surfaces of the skis. You will be surprised to find the skis look nearly as good as new.

It is essential to spray your bindings with a special protective aerosol spray which you can buy from a ski shop. Even if you treat them correctly in every other way, this is the only means of making sure they will function properly next season.

A modern pair of skis can be stored almost anywhere, but try to keep them somewhere where they will not be exposed to great fluctuations of temperature.

There is no need to keep your skis stretched and blocked. Simply place them separately up against a wall, standing them as straight as possible.

Regular servicing

Item	Reason	Service	Frequency
Binding	contact with salt water, corrosion, dirt	take apart, clean, grease	annually
	alteration in release values (wrong adjustment)	check with binding test machine	annually
Edges	blunt, notched	file, sandpaper	at the very least annually; every few days on hard, stony trails
Sole	scratches, gouges	repair with polyethylene strip or chips	after damage occurs
	oxydization	sandpaper, seal with wax	after the season, before the season
Body of ski	damage to varnish	dry, clean, re-varnish	after damage occurs at least annually

Even the best ski maintenance is of no use if you are going to transport your skis 'naked' like this afterwards. In carrying skis on a car roof the bindings at least, and better the whole of the skis, should be protected by a suitable cover.

Skiing exercises

A doctor once commented that anyone going skiing without preparing for it in any way first is a danger not only to himself but also to other people.

You will only really enjoy skiing if you start the winter season in good physical shape. So it is important for everyone to prepare for skiing. Physical fitness is vital if accidents are to be avoided.

Basic training

Anyone who has participated actively in the development of skiing during the last few years will know that people ski faster nowadays than they used to, and they usually ski over bumpier terrain. The skier is assumed to be in better condition, and able to react much faster than he would ever need to do in ordinary daily life. So skiing requires more than a bit of casual preparation; regular training is essential.

The amount of pleasure you get from skiing depends very largely upon your own physical fitness as well as the right equipment. There are few sports where so many factors are involved at the same time: braking to gliding to acceleration, smooth trail to bumpy trail to deep snow, schussing to weight-shifting turns to parallel turns – a whole catalogue of possible types of turn. Many skiers feel too much is being asked of them unnecessarily. One thing is certain, however: if you are in poor physical shape you will never master a perfect technique. Conversely, the better your technique, the more effective is the use you can make of being in good condition. This is as true for the beginner as it is for the racer.

Skiing exercises are the best and most reliable way to get yourself into good condition. With the help of exercises imitating particular skiing movements you can train to do the movements on the ski slopes, and the same is true of the particular muscles you need to use. All this helps you to feel that you are reducing the risk of injury to a minimum.

Everyone needs an individual training plan, with a load adjusted to his own needs and capabilities. It is also important to remember that no one is in peak condition all the time.

There are all sorts of factors which influence a skier's capabilities: a survey of the stresses on the various organs of the body gives an idea of the complete picture. You do not just

Factors determining a skier's capability

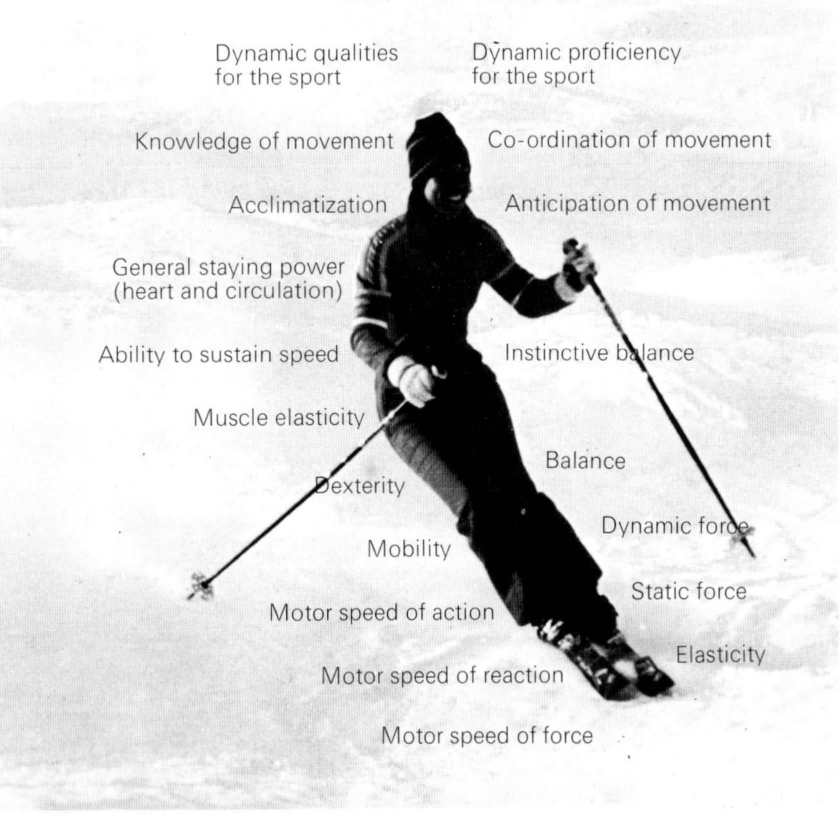

have to train to become fit, you have to maintain fitness – especially outside the skiing season. The aim of preparation is to develop an all-round physical fitness needed during skiing. Everyone should be aware that a skier's individual fitness is the result of training. This is the only way to become aware of one's load capacity in actual skiing. The better your condition, the less the danger of any injury to your health.

Preparation specifically for skiing is quite possible at home, so you do not have to join a group or club. There are all sorts of ways of preparing to ski, however.

Of course there are various training methods, emphasizing different adjustments of the body to the sport, which are nowadays most consistently employed in training athletes for very high performance.

Exercises before going skiing

The most important aims of skiing exercises are:

- to increase general and specific staying power
- to loosen, stretch and strengthen all parts of the body which will be used in skiing
- to imitate typical movement sequences in skiing

Skiing exercises, like the learning of skiing itself, are basically the learning of movements. Many movement sequences used in skiing, like bending/stretching, twisting/twisting back, changing from a forward-leaning to a backward position, weighting with one leg/both legs, can be taught as a kind of 'dry run' in training. In addition there are the basic positions for, say, schussing/traversing/stemming/open and closed ski positions, which can be combined with the movements mentioned above by way of skiing practice.

As well as exercising the basic physical characteristics of force, speed, staying power, mobility and dexterity, skiing exercises aim to train you for specific muscular actions which will be used in real skiing, for example, exerting stress and relaxing it, twisting and untwisting, changing from braking to accelerating muscular activity. The aim is to train passive and dynamic muscle actions alternately. The elasticity of the muscles in particular benefits from this. Skiing exercises make it possible for us to find out the limits of our physical capabilities and the stress we can place on them in skiing. They do not just show us how to adjust our bodies to the sport and correct our movements, they decrease physical and psychological fear and inhibitions or do away with them right from the start.

Skiing exercises can both reassure and motivate. A programme of such exercises, properly understood and carried out, has more to offer than will actually be asked of our bodies when we are skiing, in the way of general movement. On the one hand it counteracts the tendency of expert skiers to concentrate in a one-sided

Determining the degree of fatigue in training

		Optimum load	
Entire training load	Slight training load	Normal training load	Upper limit of load in training or competition
	Slight fatigue	**High fatigue**	**Very high fatigue**
Skin colour	slightly flushed	very flushed	excessive flushing, very red in the face, possibly vomiting
Sweating	slight sweating	heavier sweating (especially the top half of the body)	very heavy sweating (especially the lower part of the body)
Breathing	faster but regular	very fast, sometimes through the mouth	very fast, short, irregular breathing through the mouth
Movements	normal	uncertain movements, 'weak at the knees'	feeble, uncertain movements, staggering
Physical condition	no discomfort	tired, heart beating fast, pain in legs, sensation of weakness	very tired, headache, nausea, stabbing pains in the chest, heavy limbs

way on a few kinds of movement, and on the other hand it gives skiers of all ages and alt all stages of ability plenty of motivation to keep on skiing, as it enables them to imitate skiing techniques off the trail. It is a kind of preparatory school for the ski school itself.

Pulse control

It is especially useful to count your *pulse frequency* for a fitness training programme.

Counting the pulse beats is a simple method of checking the activity of the heart (pulse control).

The measurement of pulse frequency is in pulse beats per minute.

A good rule of thumb for your training load is: 170 to 180 pulse beats a minute minus your age = pulse load-factor.

Wrist Put your two middle fingers on top of the wrist and you should be able to feel your pulse quite easily if you exert slight pressure.

Throat Place a hand around the front of your throat, with the finger ends exerting slight pressure on one side of the larynx and the thumb on the other. If you have been exercising hard, the pressure should be lighter.

How to feel your pulse.

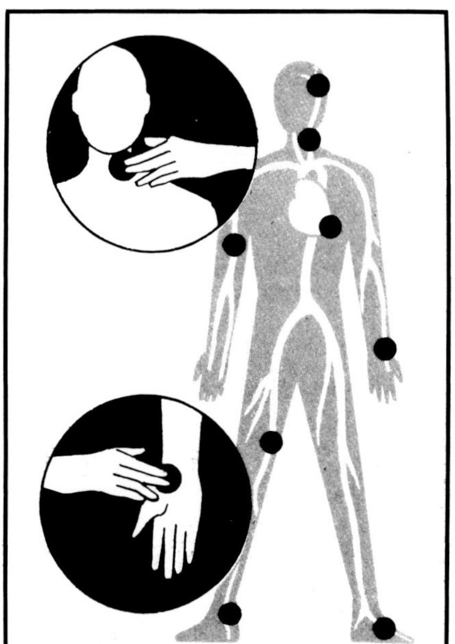

Exercise programmes

Nowadays pre-skiing training programmes are planned according to the condition and the ability of the individual; the needs of the would-be skier are always borne in mind.

General fitness training

Training for general fitness should lay the foundations for a good state of physical health. An all-round athletic programme is the aim. The idea is to train the would-be skier in basic movements and to give a wide-ranging all-round athletic experience. There are all sorts of exercises that will do the job, with or without apparatus. The following exercises have been selected because they need no apparatus and can easily be done at home.

Many skiers prefer to do their preski exercises as part of a group, meeting regularly. If you find this more enjoyable you will certainly do the exercises more conscientously. Contact your local gymnasium to see whether they arrange special pre-ski exercise courses. The further ahead you start doing exercises, the better.

Circuit training

Circuit training has proved itself to be the ideal way of exercising for gen-

General fitness without apparatus
1 shoulders, arm muscles
2 leg muscles
3 stomach muscles
4 back muscles
5 legs, internal organs
6 general body tension
7 stomach muscles
8 jumping power, relaxation
Stage 1: lie on stomach, hands behind back; push-up
Stage 2: jump up from crouching position, with a half-turn
Stage 3: jack-knife
Stage 4: lie on stomach, raise and lower arms and legs simultaneously
Stage 5: running on the spot (skipping)
Stage 6: lying on back, back press-ups; pulling up the legs and then stretching them
Stage 7: sitting up, twist arms and legs in opposite direction, raising legs off the floor
Stage 8: jump up with all limbs extended

Specialized fitness training

Pre-skiing preparation out of the skiing season should not be confined to exercising in a gymnasium. Training out of doors can accustom a skier to various different demands on his abilities (for example, the changing inclination of a slope) and different situations (suiting movements to the terrain and conditions). Ski poles make ideal exercising partners.

Exercise programme:

free running out of doors
- over obstacles
- uphill and downhill
- changing direction frequently.

Circle the legs over the ski poles, alternately left and right.

Wedel in a sitting position, twisting the upper part of the body round in the opposite direction to the legs.

Cross-country skiing movements taking long strides. Alternate leg crouches.

Bend the trunk backwards and forwards, legs wide apart.

Bend the trunk sideways, legs wide apart.

Twist the trunk to left and right.

Cossack dancing, knees well bent; support the arms with the ski poles.

▲ Snow-plough jump.

Jumping backwards and forwards over the ski poles in a crouching position. ▶

Jumping with legs spread sideways and backwards, supporting your arms with the ski poles. ▼

Wedel jumping over the ski poles, alternately left and right. ▶

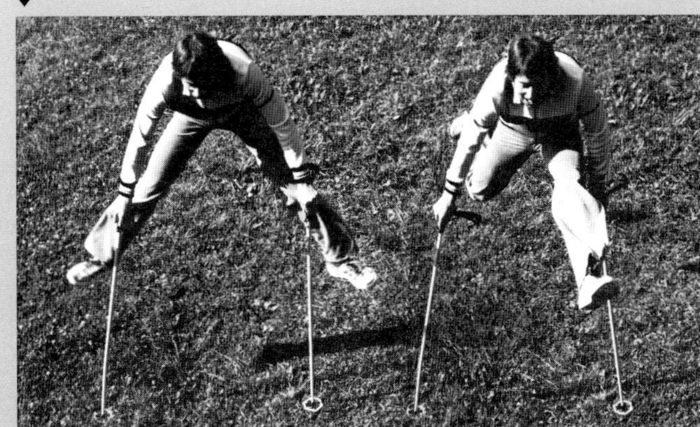

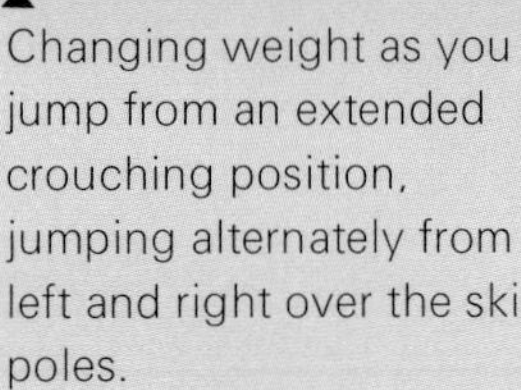

▲ Changing weight as you jump from an extended crouching position, jumping alternately from left and right over the ski poles.

Bending the knees alternately left and right towards the ski poles (good practice for edging). ▶

Ski-mambo: rhythmic twist with counter-rotation. ▶

Balancing on tree trunks in crouching position. ▼

Pre-ski exercises – for the gymnasium or at home

Imitation training is the type of ski exercising where movements actually performed in skiing are practised on one's own, in a group or with partners – 'dry skiing' performed to music if possible. There are many different exercises for all kinds of technical movements and stages of ability. Typical sequences of movement should be rehearsed over and over again in the gymnasium. The same goes for special skiing positions and skiing stances.

Absorbing bumps: alternate between an upright schussing position and a low crouching position. Keep the weight on the entire sole of the foot. Touch the ground to the side with your hands as you crouch down.

Pushing off with both poles: starting from an upright position, swing the arms backwards and forwards. When swinging forward stand upright, when swinging back bend the knees and lean the upper part of the body forward. Breathe in as you stand upright, breathe out as you bend. The emphasis is on the backward swing.

Diagonal stride: alternate leaps in an extended crouching position. Emphasis is on the change of stride (for cross-country skiing).

Alternate between an upright schussing position and a low crouch.

Practise the same movement starting with leg level. Take off from each leg alternately, i.e., stretch one leg out behind and bring it back to the resting position as the arms swing back.

Schussing position: stand balanced on the soles of your feet moving the legs slightly backwards and forwards. Bend and stretch – down and up.

Schussing and snowplough: start from the schussing position, with the legs opened out to the breadth of the hips, crouch and twist the legs, turning your heels out. Repeat the movement rhythmically several times in succession, to give you a fluid down-up-down movement.

Leg twisting: start from an upright position, bend the legs and turn the heels outward. Repeat the movement several times on one side, then alternately left and right, bending and stretching the legs rhythmically.

Ski-mambo: jump rhythmically on the spot, trying to turn the upper part of the body as far as possible in the opposite direction to the legs.

Schussing and traversing: alternate the schussing and traversing positions. Knees should bend forwards and sideways (as for edging) to left and to right. Start by rising into the schussing position, then keep the knees bent and practise a fast alternating 'edging' movement.

Snowplough turn: stretch and bend in the snowplough position with one leg bending particularly far forwards and inwards, come up to the snowplough position again and bend with the other leg in the forward and inward position.

Charleston: alternate jumps from one leg to the other. The legs are kept centred under the body; the outer leg swings outwards and up. Repeat the jump rhythmically, increasing the speed of the take-off.

Fast weight-change: jump strongly and rapidly sideways from one leg to the other. Repeat the movement in rhythmic sequence.

The wedel: starting in the traverse position, push the knees well forwards and sideways (edging position), then twist to the other side (edging position). Practise the alternate edging movement with a down-up-down movement first, then do them in a fast sequence without any vertical movement, keeping the knees bent all the time. Imitate the holding of the ski poles with your arms.

Basic swing turn: a rhythmical sequence of the following movements: traverse position, angle out into snowplough position, bring one leg in and up, return it to a resting position, bend, twist the legs, traverse position.

eral physical fitness. The phrase means that a training programme is put together which places a progressive load on various groups of muscles and, naturally, on the heart and circulation too. The exercises are practised consecutively. This type of training also tests you and allows you to check your capacity. Circuit training always starts with what is called a 'maximum test'. This establishes how often you can do a particular exercise in a given time (say thirty seconds), or if you can do it at all. The maximum performance you have reached then corresponds to 100%. According to what you want to get out of the programme, you can now establish your individual load for yourself. Here are two examples by way of illustration:

1. If you want to increase your strength, effort of about 80% of the maximum performance is necessary; for example, maximum performance: ten push-ups; training performance: eight push-ups.
2. If you want to increase your staying power, aim for an effort of about 25% of maximum performance, although you must continue the movement longer without stopping; for example, maximum performance: ten push-ups; training performance: two to three push-ups repeated many times.

Once you have settled on your circuit programme and got it well established it should be kept up for some time (at least four weeks) until you feel that you can really control your performance. You can aim for additional control by setting a precise time for each movement.

Further improvement in performance can be achieved by:

- Making the pauses between exercises shorter
- Omitting the pauses altogether
- Increasing the training time
- Adding further stages to it

To make sure you still have the right amount of training repeat the maximum test after about four weeks and adjust the programme accordingly.

Preparation for cross-country skiing

Cross-country skiing and touring suddenly have come back into fashion. As the number of would-be cross-country skiers is likely to increase, it is only reasonable to mention preparation for this form of the sport here. (See also the chapter on Cross-country Skiing below.) Cross-country skiing places particular strain on the heart and the circulation. So it is a good idea to prepare ahead by going for long walks, hill walking, hiking and cycling. Cross-country skiing also calls for considerable strength in the muscles of the trunk and arms, so exercises for these muscles should be included in any regular training programme.

Training for staying power

Sequences of outdoor training exercises which can be done in any kind of terrain are a useful form of training for cross-country skiing and offer plenty of variety.

Energetic hill climbing with ski poles will help to strengthen the shoulder muscles. If the training is to be really effective, whatever form the exercise takes the load should be high enough for one to aim for a heart beat of about 140 a minute.

Exercises to increase strength

1. Crouching down, keep one leg bent and stretch the other. Repeat with the other leg stretched. Alternate the movement.
2. Crouching down, jump alternately backwards and forwards.
3. Lying on your side, bend sideways, swinging your free arm up over your head.
4. Sitting up, pull both legs up and stretch to left and right alternately.

Part 1: Warming up:	1. light jogging	Time: 15mins
	2. exercising combined with running (running round trees, running with arms circling, etc.)	Time: 5–10mins
	3. running 110 yd (100m) ten times at increasing speeds	Time: 10mins
Part 2: Rhythmical running:	Five-ten runs over slightly downhill terrain, at a marked rhythm. Loosening-up exercises inbetween runs	Time: 15mins
Part 3: Sprinting:	Five springs of over 325–875 yd (300–800m) with resting periods inbetween	Time: 15mins
Part 4: Unwinding:	light jogging until breathing is back to normal	

Out-of-season summer activities

There are plenty of summer sports suitable for skiers. Some seem almost tailor-made for people, who would otherwise only enjoy winter sports, such as grass skiing and water skiing. Why not try some sport entirely new to you in the summer – such as cycling, tennis, canoeing, skateboarding and wind surfing? There is a wide range to choose from; here is a brief survey:

Sport	Effect
Walking, mountain climbing	Good for the circulation
Cycling	Improves endurance and strengthens the leg muscles
Swimming	Improves flexibility and staying power
Tennis	Good for reflexes, muscles and circulation
Canoeing	Good corrective for the skier's over-worked legs, good for mobility
Water-skiing	Improves balance, strengthens the leg muscles
Wind-surfing	Ideal for skiers: improves balance, strengthens the muscles of the trunk, arms and legs
Skateboarding	Good for balance and general mobility

You may prefer to train on your own rather than attend classes at fixed hours in possibly overcrowded gymnasiums. It might be a good idea to go in for moderate but regular outdoor exercising on the basis of outdoor training methods, as suggested in the plan given here.

Alpine skiing

There are between twenty-five and thirty million skiers in the world. North America has between five–eight million, Japan eight–ten million and Great Britain 300,000. There are between 150,000 and 200,000 skiers in Australia and New Zealand and up to 50,000 skiers from South Africa who ski in Europe.

A great deal of confusion and misleading talk exists about the 'common skier'. There is strong emphasis in all publicity material on 'experts', trails of exceptional difficulty, and high speeds; advertisers attempt to equate the common skier with international racers and, more recently, to the free-style showman-skier. The real-life facts are quite different.

The average, recreational skier is a poor to moderate performer who skis less than twenty days a year, is over twenty-five and under forty-five. Only about 15% of all skiers ever ski the difficult, Black, trails and of these only about 5% do so regularly and with pleasure. Eighty-five per cent of all recreational skiers prefer to ski an easy Red or moderate trail and, given the chance (with no one watching), like to tear down a beginner's trail.

A piece of research carried out in the United States revealed that the majority of skiers never exceed 25mph(40km/h) and they considered 35mph(56km/h) as 'very fast'. The moderate skier skied a moderate trail at an average speed of 15mph (24km/h) while the expert skier would occasionally reach a maximum of 45mph(72km/h) for short periods of straight running. The modern trail is neither designed for high speeds nor would the number of skiers using it permit high speeds. The speed of an expert skier on a steep difficult trail will rarely exceed 25mph but he will lose height very much faster than the moderate skier and it is this which makes him appear to be skiing fast.

In a recent ski survey fifty out of a hundred skiers gave their main reason for skiing as 'better recreational use of free time'. 'Enjoyment, health and fitness' came in second place, followed by 'keeping up with the Jones's'. 'Sporting ambition' was only fourth. 'Having a partner who skis' was mentioned by quite a number of people as a reason for learning and practising the sport; it took last place, but still . . .

More and more people want to learn to ski. Learning to ski may not be very easy, but it is not as difficult as it used to be.

Until quite recently people used to argue about which skiing technique was the *best*; now they tend to discuss which is the *safest*: the answer is any technique which (excluding mistakes) does not put the skier into unnatural physical positions, and allows him to ski efficiently over the terrain.

Skiing is not something you can teach yourself. A ski course given by a qualified instructor is the best way to learn how to ski correctly and safely right from the start. Comprehensive information and explanation, as well as professional guidance in practice, can only be gained from a ski school.

What can ski instruction offer?

The most important thing for a beginner to grasp is probably the fact that progress and ability in skiing *can* be learnt, and the process of learning can be controlled and tested. Every beginner should, as a matter of principle, take a course of instruction suited to his particular requirements. Skiing calls for combinations of movement of the legs, arms and trunk which are not part of our ordinary everyday life, and a beginner should probably start with cross-country skiing. For this reason descriptions of initial technique and methods for the beginner are given in the chapter on Cross-country Skiing (page 166).

So far as learning the basic techniques of skiing are concerned, ski instruction today has to fulfil a number of very different needs. External conditions (terrain, snow, weather) and the individual situation of each pupil as regards age, fitness, skiing ambition, calls for a school type of instruction. This is the idea behind both the instructions for learning technique used in this book and the illustrations of the right way to carry out movements, as shown in the diagrams.

The primary aim of the skier should be to experience many types of movement before gaining much technical mastery. A beginner should aim for a certain level as quickly as possible. This level is determined by familiarity with skiing equipment, ability to glide, a degree of stability and the mastery of the right speed for making the first turns.

Elementary skills such as keeping one's balance and the ability to glide are just as valuable as learning the basic techniques of skiing, and should be practised over and over again. Besides basic technique, the beginner has to learn the rules of the trails and how to use the lifts. These are important parts of skiing experience, and will be the bridge from nursery slopes to skiing on higher slopes.

Ski schools, however, try to be pupil-orientated even in their courses for advanced skiers. There are various different schools offering different techniques, tailored to the needs of the occasional skier who skis only on holiday, the skier who prefers touring and deep-snow skiing, the skier who is a stylist, the athletic skier, right up to the top-class skier for whom skiing is an art. There is an individual skiing instruction programme which has something to offer everyone.

The invisible problems

Any adult, learning to ski, is faced with a series of requirements which are against every instinct. Not only is it a sport which is carried out in an unfamiliar environment (for most of us), but it demands an acceptance of instability. Accustomed by everyday life to resist slips and slides, the novice skier is asked to undertake active sliding using ungainly and unfamiliar implements attached to uncomfortable and clumsy boots. A steep snowy slope is an obstacle to be avoided in normal city life and if circumstance demands that such a surface be negotiated, the instinctive action is to lessen the distance of a fall by leaning as close as possible to the slope. Yet the ski instructor will demand the exact opposite.

The conventional ski teacher and the usual teach-yourself manuals are conspicuous in their disregard for this basic problem and the first task of any novice is to overcome this instinctive dislike and often active opposition to the commands to 'lean out', to look down a slope and to start a downhill slide with active intention.

There are two stages in this first major obstacle to becoming a competent skier. To begin with the novice must learn to think of himself not as a person who has tied two long planks to two huge boots but as a different individual – a person-with-skis, capable of some very strange and unusual feats, such as being able to lean forward at a ridiculous angle and change this to an equally ridiculous angle backwards without losing either balance or position. He is a person who has acquired giant's feet of vast strength capable of stopping the equivalent of five tons with the flick of a foot and a twelve-inch skid.

A driver of an automobile does not feel like a person hurtling along the road; the driver is, in fact, stationary in a completely stable box which happens to be moving along the road at any desired speed. Within this box the driver can relax and perform all driving actions comfortably and totally independent of the speed of the

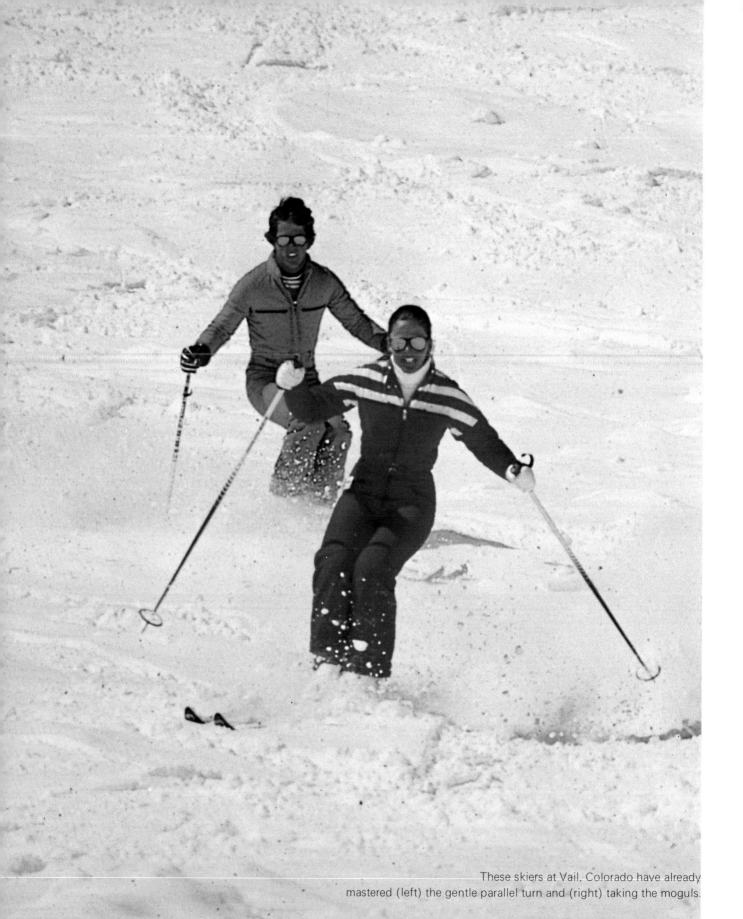

These skiers at Vail, Colorado have already mastered (left) the gentle parallel turn and (right) taking the moguls.

vehicle. A skier is in a very similar situation although closer to the ground and much more aware of speed. Nevertheless, a novice must be persuaded to regard himself as a passenger of a vehicle, himself stationary but moving as a unit – the 'person-with-skis' – and within this imaginary unit is free to perform any required movement in a relaxed fashion. If tense and apprehensive, every movement becomes forced and awkward which in turn leads to mistakes resulting in a fall which, in turn, will make the pupil more tense and apprehensive. Slope-shyness and an inescapable awareness of skis sliding uncontrollably on slippery snow are two attitudes the instructor must help the novice to overcome. The safe artificial slope with its controlled gradients and gentle run-out are the ideal medium for crossing this particular skiing obstacle.

As a skier progresses with the many acquired skills which skiing demands an element of frustration can make itself irritatingly felt. The instructor, professional or amateur will, increasingly, require certain basic body postures as a prerequisite for the correct technical performance of the whole series of basic movements. Over the years, instructions have been shorthanded into such commands as 'bend your knees', 'lean out', 'twist your knees' (or legs or hips). In many cases these are misleading to the novice skier for they have connotations in daily life which are different from those intended by the ski professional. The pupil thinks he is complying with the command but is repeatedly told that he has, in fact, failed to perform the required movement. For the most part this is not a failure of communication but an inability of the average person to correlate his mental image of a body movement with the actual movement performed. This is revealed most embarrassingly by the use of video recorders. In theory this teaching aid should be extremely valuable as it enables the 'victim' to see himself in action and thus be able to correct errors which are manifestly present and visible. In practice, it has been found to work in reverse except in the case of the expert or the competitive skier. Not only does the pupil, novice or intermediate, feel acutely embarrassed at seeing himself behaving in an inexpert and often comic manner, but the visual evidence is in sharp conflict with the physical memory. The result is frustration and retrogression.

Supposed ridicule is one of the major factors resulting in premature drop-out from an adult instruction situation. It can be avoided to a great extent by clever instruction, by avoiding such misleading commands as 'bend your knees' and substituting what might be called fundamental commands to perform apparently unconnected movements which must, by nature of human anatomy, lead to the correct posture. Such a command could be, for example, 'stand on your left (or right) big toe'. The resulting action would automatically produce a flexing of ankle and knee bringing the centre of gravity forward without leading to the unavoidably common 'potty position' which 'bend your knees' usually produces.

Right through a skier's education, the skier himself must be aware that the movements he imagines he is making are not the same as an objective observer would see. Initially every movement must be exaggerated until the acquired skills have become instinctive and 'right' and the formerly supposed exaggeration has become the norm. This is a subjective development which only the skier himself can achieve. It should be added that it applies equally to the supposedly perfect stylist as it does to the novice struggling with his first basic swings.

Expert is a completely relative term. What it means in practical fact is that the skier performs a given set of movements completely instinctively, almost automatically and no part of his conscious thought is occupied by the individual movements which go to make up, for example, a basic parallel. His active thinking is concerned with the placing of the next turn, the surface and terrain conditions, the presence of other skiers and the direction they are taking, while skis, feet, legs and body are going through any variety of complicated co-ordinated movements resulting in a controlled direction or speed change. The command from head to limbs to make a sharp right-handed turn is as instantaneous and automatic as a change in direction while walking down the street. This level of expertise may be limited to the reliable performance of all the techniques up to, and including, a basic parallel. He may fail in the attempt to carry out a linked series of short swings on steep and mogulled ground. An expert on all the common varieties of parallels will come unstuck trying a variety of step-ups and be reduced to having his turns happen rather than planning them, three or four turns in advance. As a form of self-examination a skier can consider himself as having graduated satisfactorily if, at the end of a trail run, he has little memory of any individual turn but only of those which possibly failed; on the other hand he will have a very full recall of sections and passages, of other skiers, snow conditions and even landscape and views.

There is a school of ski thinking that believes that this instinctive, automatic state of technique can be acquired by an exercise of positive thinking, by a yoga-like performance of contemplation before starting a ski run. No one would be so foolish as to decry such preparation and condemn it as foolish. If all these precepts were to be followed, however, the top of the ski lift would be littered by skiers doing exercises, performing deep-breathing self-hypnosis, contemplating the infinite with closed eyes and probably falling flat on their faces at the first turn they performed. Skiing is a pleasurable recreation, the act of skiing should be spontaneous and enjoyable. The recreational skier can safely leave the psychological brain-washing to world champion downhill racers who need to find a crutch with which to help them overcome the inevitable apprehensions before the start of a minute's life-and-death total ski-gamble.

Turns

Many types of turn are described in detail in the ski instruction schemes of the various skiing nations, and these are used according to prevailing situations (terrain, snow, speed). The various different turns are divided into two large groups:

- Turns in which the skier shifts his weight, pushing off from one leg
- Parallel turns, where the skier uses both legs at the same time

Obviously it would be too much to expect many recreational skiers to master the entire range of all the different turns.

As it is not always easy for people unfamiliar with skiing techniques to distinguish between the different turns according to their functional use, we have tried to divide the best-known turns into *universal techniques* and *special techniques*.

One more point: this book is not intended to be a comprehensive manual of instruction in Alpine skiing. The skills which are most important for the recreational skier, however, are described in fairly methodical sequence.

The diagrams showing the performance of a turn represent the actual movements taught, and the accompanying photographs show it being carried out on the trail.

Snow and terrain

An important aspect of Alpine skiing is dealt with in the section on Practical Skiing (p. 108), which is based on years of experience.

In this book the attractive subject of racing has been deliberately omitted. If competitive skiing has any place at all in purely recreational sport then it is in the realm of *Volksskilauf* – the popular marathons as described later in this book (p. 196). To give the ordinary skier detailed information to help him ski safely on and off the trail is more useful than concentrating on the achievements of racers like Thöni, Stenmark, Klammer and Phil Maher.

The diagram on the right, showing skis, explains the types of turn where the weight shifts completely from one leg to the other; the diagram showing feet is used to help explain parallel turns.

The symbols on the right should help you to see at a glance the application of the turn to the prevailing conditions of snow and terrain:

In these days of mass tourism, skiing on the world's ski trails calls for a different attitude and different skiing behaviour, as compared with earlier skiing when fast, athletic skiers racing down the trails were a common sight. Nowadays more attention is paid to such things as safety, consideration for others and defensive and well-controlled skiing.

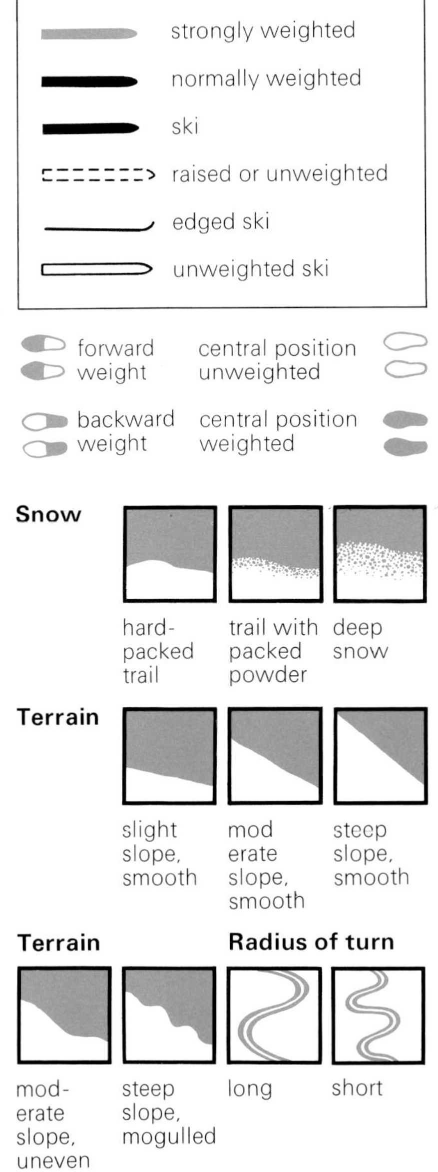

Your first day's skiing

Your first day's skiing will not necessarily be your most enjoyable one. Many, now expert, skiers never forget it all their lives! Here is how you begin:

1. Carrying your skis

Carry your skis over your shoulder with the tips pointing forward and down. And remember: before you turn round, *look* round.

If you are in a group, carry your skis in a vertical position.

2. Putting on your skis

Check your ski bindings regularly, and especially before your first day's skiing. The ski bindings must be professionally adjusted in the sports' shop for your individual fitting, with the aid of a testing device.

Always scrape snow and ice off the sole of your ski boot before putting the ski on. Use either your ski pole or the edge of your ski. Close the ski boots firmly and make sure you have a retaining strap or a ski brake.

Putting your skis on when you are actually on the slope is more difficult. This is the way to do it:

- First place your ski poles in the snow, pointing uphill.
- Then lay the downhill ski safely on the snow, across the fall line, leaving your uphill ski stuck in the snow for the time being.
- Always put the downhill ski on first, then the uphill ski.

3. Holding the poles correctly

Put your hand through the loop from below; close your hand around the handgrip of the ski pole.

This is just the beginning – after all, no one learns everything all at once – there is still a long way to go before you can ski properly. But it will all be worth it ...

4. Getting used to your skis

Before you actually start moving you should become used to the feel of standing on the your skis.

Try the following exercises:

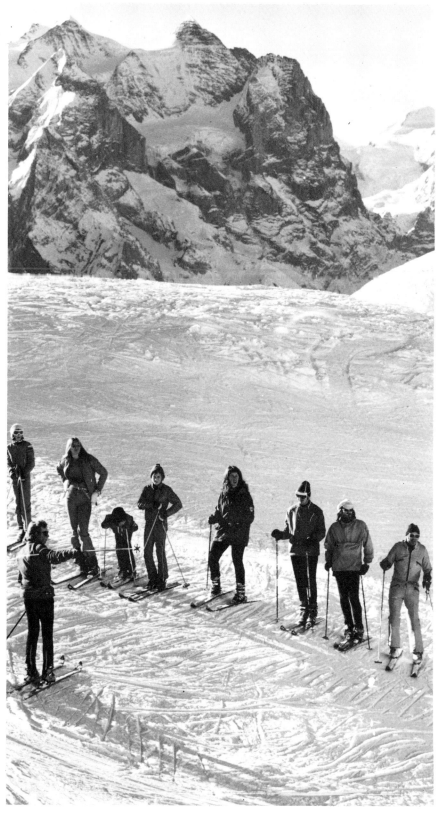

- Stand relaxed, legs slightly apart (to the width of your hips) and parallel. Both skis should be equally weighted. Avoid keeping the skis too close and your knees rigid. Do not bend the upper part of your body too far forward.
- Look straight ahead, not at the tips of your skis. To help you keep your balance hold your arms out to the side a little with the points of your ski poles behind you.
- 'Feel' the snow through the soles of your boots. If you lean alternately forward and back, bending your legs, you will feel the support the boots give you. (You will be changing the weight carried by different parts of the soles of your feet.) Now move your bent knees sideways, to left and to right.

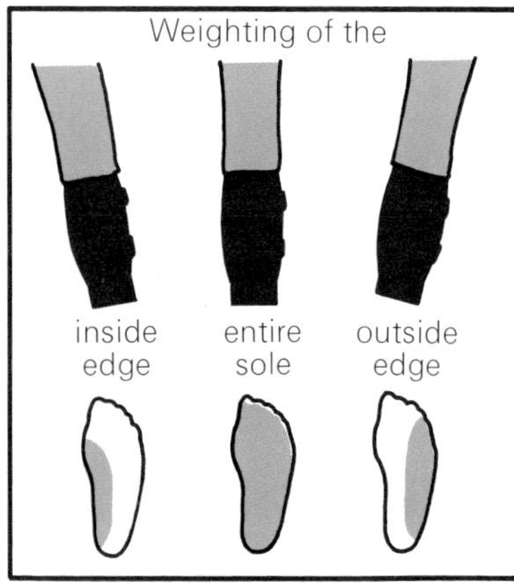

- Lift each ski in turn, move the tip of the ski forward and back, turn it to the right and the left in the air, stamp it on the ground.

These elementary exercises are the starting point from which you will gradually develop that 'feel' for the skis which is so vital in learning to use them. In fact you can practise becoming used to your skis at home – even in the living room.

Types of slope

Travelling over different types of slope is one of the elementary skills of a safe skier. It is very important for a beginner to learn to know and recognize the different features he may encounter.

The most striking types of ski slope are listed below; they are artificially constructed for ski instructors' examinations. A beginner will only learn to know the individual features in the course of his practical skiing, but it does no harm to think about them right from the start.

1. Starting plateau

2. Labyrinth/bobsleigh run

Twisting trench-like feature, as in a well-skied slalom course.

Suitable technique: rotation, inward position, follow the best line the curves allow.

Construction (on artificial course): at least three staggered curves (gates), with high walls either side. Distance from starting plateau: two to three ski lengths.

3. Undulation

Suitable technique: approach with legs slightly apart, ready to bend. *Passive* down-unweighting – preparation to turn – anticipation – turn by twisting legs on the apex. Active upwards twist according to the terrain.

Construction: semi-circular or bell-shaped cross-section. Breadth: about 3yd(3m).

4. Ledge

Suitable technique: approach in more upright position – ready to sink down at the apex – optimum contact of skis with surface – back into compensatory position for next feature (ski jump).

Construction: if possible integrated into the terrain – triangular profile – ascent side longer and less steep – staggered from preceding undulation so that direction must be changed on the last part of the undulation.

5. Ski jump

Suitable technique: jump – controlled passage through the air – soft landing – body ready to shock-absorb before landing.

Construction: height: about $1\frac{1}{2}$yd(1.5m); breadth: one ski length – 'ditch' beyond it about 1yd(1m) long, width of the ski jump – prepared landing ground – enough distance from the next feature (ridge).

6. Ridge

Suitable technique: whatever technique is called for. Advantageous: usually a weight-shifting technique, with compensatory movement.

Construction: length: about 10–23 yd(10–21m) – two direction gates on the ridge – preceded by two direction gates between ski jump and ridge, which determine the angle of entry and regulate speed.

7. Washboard

Suitable technique: approach upright, swallow first wave crouching – rise upright, take the next wave, and so on; do not change direction on the waves – schuss over them – try for optimum contact with the ground.

Construction: three undulations, bell-shaped in profile. Distance between the undulation about one and a half ski lengths – breadth: at least 4yd(4m) – the end of the course should not be the apex of the last wave (completion phase!).

Enough room should be left for the completion phase.

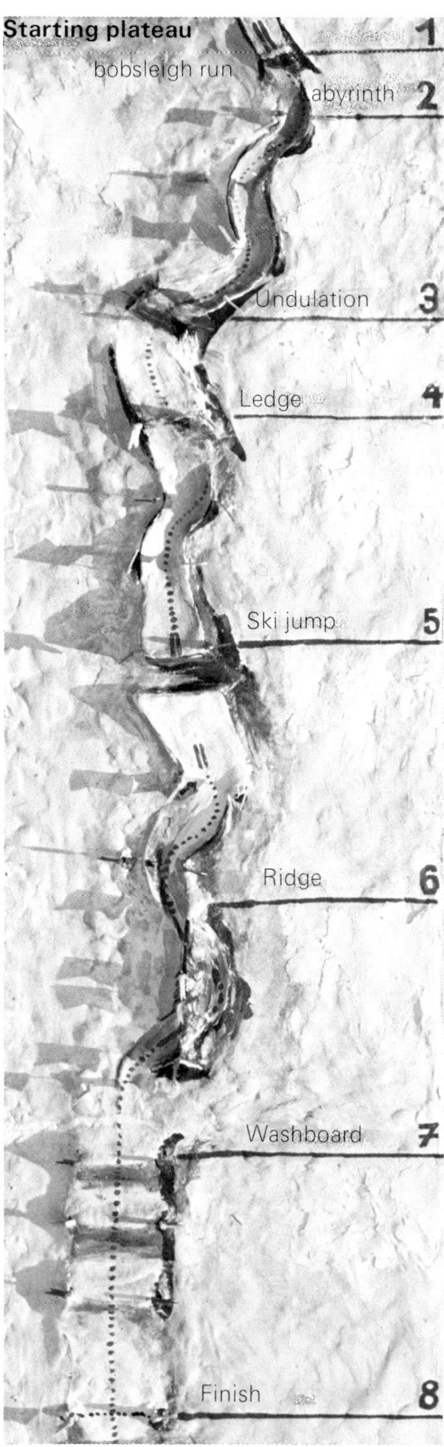

The photograph shows an artificial course with all the different features, as recommended for building by ski schools.

Basic techniques

Walking

Technique

Once your skis are on, the quickest way to become used to them – and they feel clumsy at first – is by ordinary walking. You will also be experiencing for the first time the way the skis slide under you, the way to change weight from one foot to another, and the way to use your poles. Using the correct technique you will be able to move forward on skis smoothly and relatively fast on the level. When *walking* on skis start by trying to push the skis alternately forward, keeping them slightly apart (legs centred under your hips), without raising them off the snow. The rhythmical movement is the same as in ordinary walking, i.e., the weight of the body changes from one ski to the other. With one ski forward the opposite arm and pole are swung forward, and so on, in time with the leg movement.

Ideally a beginner should learn his first steps at an instruction course on cross-country skiing (see p. 170).

Practice

Terrain and snow Start on the level, proceed to walking on uneven terrain and deeper snow.

- It is best to take your first steps on skis on a good, straight, prepared trail (walk both with and without your poles).
- Short walks, for example, from the parking area to the ski slopes, are the best way to 'run yourself in'.
- Diagonal stride: once you are used to walking gradually try to push off harder and achieve a longer slide. Develop a smooth rhythmic movement, with a marked bending and stretching of the legs and well co-ordinated leg and arm movements.
- Practise walking using the diagonal stride with and without poles, making smooth arm movements, both on the level and over undulating terrain.

Double-pole push

Technique

If you are walking on skis over slightly sloping terrain, or on the level over faster snow, you can also use a double push of the poles to help you move faster. To do this swing both poles forward at the same time and thrust them into the snow in front of your feet. Next pull your body up to the poles, bending it at the same time. Once the poles are level with your hips push your arms powerfully back. Finally pull yourself upright again.

Practice

Terrain and snow

- First on the level, then on uneven terrain and deeper snow.
- Try pushing with both poles first on slightly sloping terrain, when sliding with skis parallel.
- Try pushing with both poles hard as you walk on skis up a slight slope.

Skiing exercises

- Leaning slightly forward, legs together, swing the arms smoothly (preparation for walking and running on skis).
- Walk forward, deliberately dragging the legs along the ground.
- Training for pushing off: leaning slightly forward make successive strong stretching movements of the hip, knee and ankle joints of one leg, swinging the opposite arm forward and up. Repeat several times on the same side, then alternate right and left. Practise this standing still and moving forward.
- 'Diagonal stride': jump alternately from foot to foot with a lungeing movement.

Hints

- Rhythmic bending and stretching of the legs.
- Gliding on alternate skis.
- Long glide on the front ski, lower leg forming an angle slightly less than 90° with the front of the ski.
- Relacation of the back leg after taking off and smooth action in bringing the back ski forward.
- If you have trouble getting the rhythm right, it is better to start without poles and move with smooth movements of the arms.

Common mistakes

Keeping the knee joint of the front leg rigid, causing the tip of the ski to rise, with the risk of crossing your skis.

Insufficient displacement of weight from one ski to the other. Raising the front ski right off the snow.

'Mule walking' (leg and arm on the same side).

Skiing exercises

- Practise the double-pole push movement first when standing and then combined with walking movements.
- Alternate lungeing stride and crouching position.
- Do a shoulder stand, spread legs wide as in cross-country skiing.
- Jump and spread legs wide in the air, alternately.
- Do cross-country skiing jumping movements in a prone position.

Hints

- Smooth forward movement will be impeded to a certain extent by your equipment.
- The correct technique for this movement is only possible with cross-country skiing equipment.

Common mistakes

Inadequate thrust of the poles, so that the arms are not fully stretched.

The star turn

Technique

The first way to turn round on the flat is by standing upright and doing a star turn. Move either the tip or the end of a ski out at an angle and then move the other ski up beside it. Repeat the movement step by step until you have completed the turn. Use your ski poles for support.

Practice

- In a standing position, raise one ski and turn it alternately right and left in the air.
- Step sideways from a standing position.
- Perform a star turn in a circle around the tips of your skis.
- Perform a star turn in deep snow.
- Take walking steps at the same time as performing a star turn.

Climbing a slope

Technique

The herringbone is the best way to climb a gentle slope. To make this movement, open out your skis to a wide angle – the steeper the slope, the greater the angle should be. As you climb, press the inner edge of each ski in turn firmly into the snow, raising the end of one ski over the end of the other. The alternate weighting of the skis and use of alternate poles help you move uphill. The best way to climb a steeper slope is side-stepping or half-side-stepping, which requires less effort. Side-stepping is a movement similar to climbing stairs when both feet are placed on the same step before going on to the next. The only difference is that it is performed sideways.

Practice

- The easiest form of climbing on skis is simple *stamping*, but this does not need to be specially taught.
- Use herringbone on slight slopes.
- Use half-side-stepping on rather steeper slopes.
- Use side-stepping on steep slopes.
- The best time to practise the dif-

Elementary skills for learning to ski

As a beginner, you will need to learn:

- A sense of balance
- A sense of sliding
- Edge awareness
- Mobility

Keeping one's balance and learning to slide are the most important skills in the early stages.

There are complicated controls governing the ability of the human body to maintain its *balance*, which also influence its motor functions. It is an interesting fact that stimulation of the sense of balance influences human powers of co-ordination. A practical example: the inhibition of movement and reaction shown by beginners (and by good skiers), due to balancing problems. In ordinary daily life, we do not usually ask much of our motor faculties of balance. We can learn to improve them, however. This will give a better sense of orientation in space, and mistakes of movement can then be quickly corrected. Improvement of balance also lessens, or compensates for, the frequency of dangerous moments which occur in skiing.

There are many ways to improve balance. Sports such as trampoline jumping, roller skating, ice skating, water skiing, skateboarding, even dancing to a certain extent, are all good. You can test your own balancing powers at home. Here are a few simple exercises:

Skiing exercises

- Herringbone: move forwards on the inside edges of your boots in the herringbone position.
- Side-stepping: move sideways, bringing one foot up to the other, keeping the feet edged.
- Side-stepping uphill – stairs or steps.

Hints

- Never raise the whole ski when doing a star turn; leave one end in the snow to act as a pivot.
- Take small steps.

Common mistakes

Raising the tail of a ski when doing a star turn around the tails; this causes the skis to cross.
Holding your poles too far away from you.
Angling the tails of the skis too widely when turning round the tips.

ferent ways of climbing is on the way up to your first gentle downhill run.

- First practise the transition from herringbone to side-stepping on the flat, then when climbing.

Skiing exercises

- Herringbone: move forward on the inside edge of your boots in the herringbone movement.
- Side-stepping: move sideways, bringing one foot up to the other and keep them tilted on their edges.
- Sideways stair-climbing.

Hints

- Climb rhythmically, with a marked alternate weighting of the skis.
- Edge the skis well (press knees inwards or uphill).
- Use a zig-zag route when tackling a long climb, so as to distribute your effort.
- Well-waxed skis will make climbing easier; it is also easier to climb on a softer surface.
- The smoother the snow, the sooner you will need to change from herringbone to side-stepping.

Common mistakes

Insufficient weight displacement and putting the skis down flat when climbing in the herringbone.
When side-stepping, skis not set horizontally (across the fall line).
Insufficient edging.

- Turn your head.
- Jump, twist and turn at the same time.
- Hop on one leg forwards, then backwards, then sideways.
- Stand on one leg, crouch down, stretch the free leg out to the side and describe a figure of eight with it.
- Swing one leg backwards and forwards.
- Stand on one leg and bend the knee.
- Somersault forwards and backwards.
- Practise simple forms of balancing on bars.

Sliding, along with the ability to balance, is one of the first basic skills to be mastered by the skier. Later on, when you are running downhill on the trail, you will find that a certain facility for sliding, and a sense of safety as you slide, are essential for a good run.

If a skier makes noticeably fast progress it can usually be put down to a good 'feel' for skiing, i.e., a 'feel' for sliding.

You can test and improve your feel for sliding before the skiing season begins. Ice skating is an excellent way to do it:

- Taking small steps on the ice, push off with the tip of your skate and slide.
- Skate on one leg only for a time, then on the other.
- Skating on both legs, describe a series of curves.
- Skate in a slalom pattern on the ice.

The kick turn

Technique

Turning is no problem if you are wearing short beginner's skis but with conventional long skis it is rather difficult, and can be dangerous. There are two forms of the kick turn: uphill and downhill.

Starting from a standing position, kick one leg up in front of you, pivot the ski 180° and set it down in its new direction, parallel to the other ski. Then lift and turn the other ski and one pole, so that both skis point in the new direction. In a *downhill kick turn* plant your poles uphill for support and kick up the downhill ski in the first part of the movement. In an *uphill kick turn* plant your poles downhill for support and kick up the uphill ski.

Practice

- Before you do the turn, stand on the flat, well supported on your poles, raise and swing your skis up alternately.
- Do uphill and downhill kick turns on the flat.
- Practise uphill and downhill kick turns on different sorts of terrain, combining them with climbing. Always set your skis across the fall line. Support yourself correctly on your poles.
- On a steep slope, only do a downhill kick turn (you might be left hanging if you try an uphill one!).
- In soft or deep snow, it is advisable to stamp down a firm spot on which to turn before doing the kick turn.

Falling down and getting up

Technique

Before you get up it is a good idea to place your skis *horizontally*, i.e., across the fall line, expecially in steep terrain, and push them down into the snow to make sure they do not slide away. Then either help yourself up with one pole, planted uphill in front of your body, or plant both poles uphill behind your body; next pull up your legs and with one vigorous movement try to push yourself upwards to a standing position.

Practice

- Falling should be practised in the snow itself – don't wait till you actually *have* to fall. When you do fall, try to do what we have
- described.
  Practise getting up, from both sides, several times, on slightly sloping and on steep terrain, on the trail and in deep snow.
- Lie on the ground on your back wearing skis and wave your skis above you. Practice, with skis on, rolling from one side to the other on your back.

Skiing exercises

- Kick forward and back in a relaxed manner, using alternate legs.
- Describe figures of eight smoothly, first with one leg and then with the other.
- Try doing these exercises with your eyes closed, to improve your balance.
- Describe figures of eight sitting or lying down with your legs spread.
- Twist one leg so that the toe points in the opposite direction to the other leg. Practice with both legs, holding a chair, first without touching the ground with your foot and then standing on it.

Hints

- Kick turns call for mobility (especially of the hip joint) as well as a good sense of balance. It is essential to practise correctly for the movement, or you will have difficulty on steep slopes, especially in deep snow.
- Always have three points on which to support yourself.
- Perform the movement briskly, without pausing for too long in the middle.
- Do not let the ski which you are turning sink deeply into the snow on its tail. With compact and middle-length skis there is no need to rest the ski tail.

Common mistakes

Supporting oneself wrongly with the poles; they should not be too close to the body.
Insufficient turning of the body, causing loss of balance.
Bringing round the ski pole before you have got the second ski into position.

Skiing exercises

- From a standing position, let yourself fall sideways, forwards and backwards. Break the fall with your arms, roll over, pull your legs off the ground and stand up.
- Practise falling and getting up while walking and running.
- Sitting cross-legged, get up and sit down again, both with and without support from your arms.
- On a safe steep slope practise falling down the hill, sideways, and rolling over so that your skis are below you. Practise falling while skiing slowly across and down a smooth slope.

Hints

- As you can never be sure, ahead of the event, whether your safety binding will release, try to control your falls, and don't just fall any old how. Turn towards the slope and then let yourself go. Your arms can break the force of the fall considerably.
- The more you bend your knees the greater the danger of injury.
- When standing up place your skis downhill, across the fall line, push up sideways with your arms and stand up in one vigorous movement.
- Emergency falls: on a steep slope always try to fall sideways and back towards the ends of the skis, breaking the force of the fall with the skis themselves.

Common mistakes

Falling forwards is the most dangerous way to fall.

When falling sideways, bending the knees and pressing them uphill.

When standing up, failing to keep the skis across the fall line.

Stretching your legs out before standing up and having your poles too far behind the body.

Schussing

Technique

The basic skiing position is taken up when running straight down the fall line of the slope. It should be as relaxed as possible. Both skis, equally weighted, should lie absolutely flat on the snow. (Take your weight on the entire sole of the foot.) In the early stages keep the skis slightly apart if it helps you to feel better balanced. Have your hip, knee and ankle joints slightly flexed, just far enough to help you absorb unevennesses in the terrain by flexing and extending. The angle of your body should normally be at a right angle to the line of the slope. Sometimes you will find you need to lean a little further back (more weight on the heels).

Carry your sticks pointing behind you, held out to the sides of the body so that they are far enough behind to help you keep your balance better as you go faster. If you want to go particularly fast assume the aerodynamic position known as the egg or tuck (see p. 189). Going over different types of terrain calls for special adaptations of your movements.

Ledge: approach upright – flex – extend.

Drop: approach upright – one ski leading, sitting slightly back.

Bumps and hollows: approach upright – flex as you take the bump – extend.

Practice

Terrain and snow Take off from a point where the slope is only gentle, and there is a flat surface to start from. Finish the run where you can stop without difficulty. Make sure you are on good tracking snow which is not too deep and not on an icy trail. Later you can try steeper and more uneven terrain.

- Run gently down a slight slope in a relaxed manner both with and without poles, with your legs slightly apart.
- Run downhill with a springy flexing and stretching movement of the legs, increasing the movement until it is almost a jump.
- Change between leaning forward and sitting-back positions as you ski down the slope.
- Ski down the slope crouching low.
- Ski downhill on one ski, keeping the tip of the other on the snow but the tail raised off it.
- Ski downhill turning to left and right off your track.

Ledge – drop

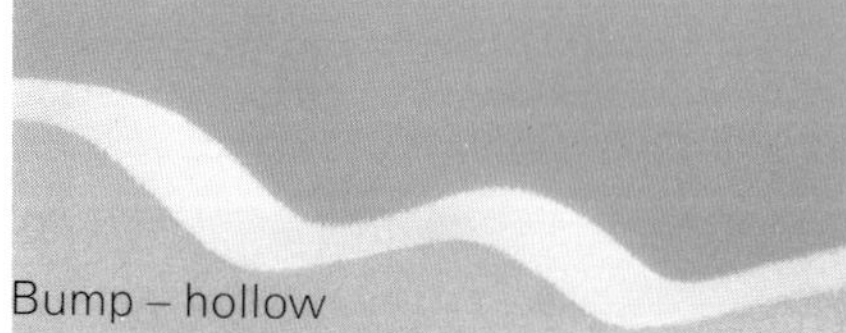

Bump – hollow

- Later you can try downhill running on steeper slopes, and in the egg position.

You must feel fairly secure on your skis, however, before you can get up any speed in downhill running. So it is better not to try going fast until you have learnt your first braking manoeuvres.

Skiing exercises

- Stand in the downhill running position, balancing on the entire sole of the foot. Bounce gently up and down and sway slightly back and forth, with a regular bending movement of your joints.
- Repeat the movement first on one leg only, then on the other.
- Alternate between the upright stance of the downhill running position and a deep crouch.
- Alternate between a knees-bent position and the downhill running position.
- Bounce gently up and down in the egg position.
- Alternate between a knees-bent position and the egg position.
- Alternate between these various positions while running and jumping.
- 'Absorbing bumps': alternate between the upright downhill running position and a deep crouch. Keep your weight on the entire sole of the foot all the time. Bend and stretch up and down, emphasizing the stretching movement.

Hints

- The skis should be perfectly flat and evenly weighted.
- Your stance should be relaxed and ready for movement.
- Keep looking the way you are going, not down at your skis!
- Bumps in the terrain are absorbed by actively bending and stretching your legs. To do this you need a good springy movement of the legs, and must anticipate the necessity for movement as you run downhill.
- 'Keep in contact with the snow' should be the rule when crossing bumpy patches; your skis should remain in contact while you absorb the bumps by using your legs and body.
- Large bumps will only be absorbed if the flexing and extension movement of the legs occurs ahead of the body; this gives you a longer flexing distance. The shock-absorbing movement of the legs, however, is adjusted to the type of terrain you are passing over.
- Lean further forward when gathering speed and when moving from deep snow on to the trail.
- Sit further back when slowing down and when moving from the trail into deep snow.
- To get into the right starting position for downhill running stand across the fall line and do a star turn with heels uphill around the tips of the skis, and support yourself with both poles pushing downhill.

Common mistakes

Keeping the legs too rigid, leaning the upper part of the body too far forward.

Reaching a sitting position by leaning the upper part of the body too far back.

Letting the legs touch, especially at the knees, which causes slight edging.

Sitting down on the ends of your skis.

Holding the arms rigid.

Difficulties with balance.

The snowplough (or wedge)

Technique

The snowplough is skiing with the skis at an angle to each other.

In the 'normal' snowplough position the ends of both skis are spread wide, the tips being about a hand's breadth apart, and both skis are equally weighted. It is advisable not to make the angle *too* wide or it will be more difficult to bend your knees slightly forward and inward. This movement edges the skis inward. Relax the upper part of your body and carry the poles at your side.

From schussing to snowplough: schussing position, with knees slightly bent; as you increase the knee-bend, unweighting the skis, the tails of the skis are thrust out with a twist of both legs, while the knees are pushed in towards each other and forward at the same time.

Snowplough to schussing: start in the snowplough position and bring the skis closer together by rising up slightly. This automatically lessens the amount of edging, and gradually the skis start running together.

Practice

Terrain and snow Practise on a slight, tracking slope, with enough room at the bottom for you to come to a controlled stop.

- First practise the alternation between snowplough and schussing positions standing still. Do it by jumping rhythmically.
- Start off in the schussing position, skis apart, bend your knees to unweight your skis and thrust the ends of the skis apart into the snowplough position. Carry on in the 'snowplough glide' until you come to a halt.
- As before, but while in the snowplough position rise up slightly and return the skis to the schussing position as you run downhill.
- As before, but this time turn the legs both ways several times in

The snowplough turn (or crab)

Technique

Travelling in the snowplough position, a rhythmical down-up-down movement by bending the legs, produces a series of curves. As you flex down, the ski on the outer edge of the curve is turned by the twisting of one leg. The upper part of the body bends forwards and sideways in the same direction at the same time. This increases the weighting and the speed of the turn. Turning your leg right, the curve will go left, and vice versa.

Doing the snowplough turn one aims for pronounced edging, produced by the strong bend of the outer knee.

Practice

Terrain and snow Practise on a gentle well-tracking slope, with room to ski out of your turn at the bottom.

- First get the feel of the rhythmical weighting change of the skis while standing still in the snowplough position.
- Do several turns in succession, close to the fall line, by making a rhythmic down-up-down movement from the legs.

succession while in the snowplough position.
- Alternate between the snowplough glide and the snowplough stop.
- In the snowplough position, practise bending alternate legs.

Skiing exercises
- Practise rhythmical snowplough jumping: change the angle, alternating between a wider and a narrower angle, go sometimes faster and sometimes slower, with and without a springy movement at the end of the jump.
- Bounce gently up and down in the snowplough position; combine this with arm-swinging.
- Practise schussing to snowplough: from the schussing position, with legs centred under your hips, crouch down and turn the legs, twisting the heels outwards. Repeat the movement rhythmically several times, with a continuous down-up-down motion.
- Snowplough to schussing: starting in the snowplough position rise up, closing the legs, dragging the soles of your feet over the floor as you bring them together. Then jump back into the snowplough position.
- Snowplough position: jump and close the legs in the air.
- In press-up position, do snowplough squat-jumping.

Hints
- The snowplough can be described as the first braking technique for a beginner.
- The snowplough position must never be rigidly held.
- Stand in a relaxed manner when in the snowplough position. Do not angle the skis too widely, or it will be harder to push the knees forward and in.
- Schussing to snowplough: open out the legs into an x-shaped position.
- Snowplough to schussing: bring the legs together into a bandy-legged position.
- It is vital to practise turning one leg both ways.
- Use your body weight to help you brake.

Common mistakes
Skis not angled out enough. Skis angled out too much.

Plough angle of the skis and weighting uneven.

Rigid legs, therefore not enough edging.

Tips of skis too far apart.
Crossing tips of the skis.

- Do snowplough turns through vertical gates, emphasizing the turn of the leg.
- Make several short descents, changing your rhythm (use the lifts to return up the slope).

Skiing exercises
- Stand in the snowplough position, heels turned out, toes turned in, legs slightly bent. Practise the rhythmical swaying movement of the upper part of the body. Keep your hips as still as possible.
- As before, but combine the body-swaying with the down-up-down movement, bending the legs.
- Be particularly careful to bend the outer leg further!
- As before, but with hands on hips or at your sides.

Hints
- The turn depends on a rhythmical down-up-down movement, with the knee and ankle joint of the leg on the outside of the curve bending further than the other leg.
- Flex and turn the leg, increasing the weight on the ski and the forward and inward movement of the knee.
- When linking turns, do not stray too far from the fall line.
- Keep the angle of the snowplough position fairly narrow.

Common mistakes
Tips of skis too far apart.

Inner leg too rigid.
Not enough up-and-down movement.

Twisting the upper part of the body too far, outer ski running on ahead.

Skiing in the sitting-back position.

Outer ski slipping away.

Changing weight too soon or too late.

The traverse

Technique

If you want to cross a slope diagonally you will have to do a traverse. The traverse position is founded on the basic skiing position. It is also the fundamental posture for all skiing movements. A comfortable and relaxed traverse position will pay off with years of happy skiing. In order to traverse you must set the uphill edges of your skis well into the snow to stop you sliding sideways. Keep your skis parallel and slightly apart at the start. Push your knees forward and into the slope to set your edges. The upper part of your body compensates for this by leaning out, away from the slope, in the 'comma' position. The upper ski will lead automatically as you turn your shoulders away from the slope. Carry your poles to the sides of your body.

Practice

Terrain and snow Practise on a gently rising slope, with well-trodden snow.

- While standing still, alternate between schussing and traversing positions on a gentle slope.
- Traverse to left and right.
- Practise traversing over a variety of terrains.
- Practise lifting the uphill ski as you traverse, stretching your downhill pole as far away from the body as possible.

Side-slipping

Technique

Side-slipping is a method of skiing downhill with controlled braking power on a steep slope. Swing into the slope with leg rotation, turn the skis uphill to enable you to change direction from the traverse quite sharply. This is the basis of all kinds of turn performed by a rotation movement of the legs. On the crest of a slope or on a bump start from a traverse position by flexing the legs. As you flex, unweighting the ends of your skis, change their direction to point slightly downhill. The movement is controlled by carefully calculated edging of the skis. An important factor in control of the movement is a corresponding twist of your hips against the direction of the turn. The turn may be short, moderate or long according to how much you bend the legs and the change of direction from traverse to fall line.

Practice

Terrain and snow Practise on moderately steep, convex slopes, on snow which allows you a good grip.

- Starting from a traversing position on the crest of a drop, flex low to produce a short uphill turn of the skis. Generally your first attempt to do this will simply produce a sideways sliding motion of the skis. Practise the movement several times on both sides.
- Practise rotating your legs in the down-up-down movement.
- Turn in a fan shape, increasing your angle of approach in the direction of the fall line. You will gradually be executing longer

Skiing exercises

- Alternate schussing and traversing positions. Pay particular attention to the forward and inward movement of the knees which sets the ski edges. Practise a quick change of the edging manoeuvre.
- Practise the forward and sideways movement of the upper part of the body when traversing.
- To loosen up your hip joints, do any kind of bending and twisting body exercise combined with the traversing position.

Hints

- You will need to adjust your traversing position to the inclination of the slope: the steeper and smoother it is, the more you will need to edge your skis. In the normal way the skis are equally weighted; the steeper the slope, the more you will need to weight your downhill ski.
- You will also have to adjust the outward-leaning comma position of your body to the movement of your legs, as influenced by the inclination of the slope.
- The twist of your hips, and therefore the distance the uphill ski is pushed forward, is also determined by the inclination of the slope.

Common mistakes

Weighting the uphill ski.

Pushing the knee of the downhill leg into the back of the uphill knee.

Rigid legs, insufficient edging. Bending the body in toward the slope.

Bending the upper body too far forwards and sideways.

turns. This makes it easier to rotate the legs but harder to control the turn.

- Practise in different kinds of terrain and snow.

Skiing exercises

- Standing still, practise bouncing up and down.
- The leg twist: standing upright, bend the knees while turning the heels outwards. Practise this several times one side, then the other, then alternately right and left, rhythmically bending and stretching the legs.
- Twist your legs to right and left without rising upright.
- Controlling the turn: twist your legs several times in one direction.
- Roll your knees in a circle, first one way and then the other.
- Crouch down and turn your legs alternately right and left.

Hints

- In the normal way a flexing of the knees starts the leg-twisting movement. If you have difficulty at this stage, an up-down movement may start the movement going. The upward movement brings the skis out of the traverse position and flat on the snow, and enables you to follow it with a low downward flexing to start the turn.
- The down movement should result in regular flexing of the ankle, knee and hip joints, and a controlled rotation of the legs.
- If the skis tend to slip away sideways and become out of control set the edges and turn the other way.
- Only twist your legs and not your hips or bottom round to get the leg rotation started.
- You can also side-slip by rolling your knees *away* from the slope, but this is only advisable on steep slopes.

Common mistakes

Weighting the uphill ski and inside edging.

Not enough up-and-down movement to control the manoeuvre.

Turning the outside hip to start side-slipping.

Turning the knees away from the slope to start side-slipping on a slight inclination; danger of losing the edge grip and falling.

Unequal weighting of the skis.

Leaning too far back – risk of slipping backwards.

Leaning too far forward – risk of slipping forwards.

The basic swing

Technique

The basic swing is the first movement that allows you to change direction across the fall line in one continuous motion. Once a beginner has mastered it he can get about on the ski slopes. It is simple to perform: you start from a traverse, in open stance equally weighted, then push with both legs until you are in the snowplough position. Glide in the snowplough position until you face downhill, weighting the outer ski.

Push down, raising the body, then, closing the inside ski to the outside ski, turn the skis out of the fall line and into their new direction. A slight parallel side-slipping effect, knees bent, steers the movement back into a traverse, skis well apart.

The basic swing turn can be done with or without pole-planting; planting your poles helps you push down on the ski inside the curve and transfer your weight to the outside ski, especially when you are linking a number of basic swing turns in quick succession.

Note: The separate parts of the basic swing turn are the traverse, the snowplough curve and a gently controlled parallel side-slipping movement. But the decisive factor is the way you turn the ski out of the fall line and into its new direction. The best way to train for this part of the movement is with the snowplough turn. You will find that doing a series of simple snowplough turns, combined with the traverse, enables you to execute the basic swing turn.

Start by doing long turns, with long traverses and periods of side-slipping. Once you have some experience, make the turns shorter by increasing the force with which you rotate your legs. Keeping the skis well apart makes it easier to control your skis when traversing. The sequence of turns with short traverses enables you to do rhythmical basic swing turns.

Practice

- Practise the snowplough turn: learn how to rotate your legs and change the weighting of your skis by a dynamic succession of snowplough turns (snowplough wedel).
- Do the snowplough turn on both sides, first without and then with pole-planting. Pole-planting supports you as you press down on the ski inside the curve, and makes it easier for you to transfer your weight to the outside ski. The inside arm comes forward and plants the pole, which should be placed between the tip of the ski and your boot.
- Do a 'garland' of snowplough turns: several linked turns slowly executed.
- Basic swing turn: traverse, turn both legs into the snowplough position until you reach the fall line – push down, plant your pole, bring in the inside ski, flex low, turning your legs into a controlled side-slip.
- Improve the steering phase of the turn by practising the uphill part of the side-slipping manoeuvre.
- Try out the basic swing turn in

3

2

1

4

5

6

difficult terrain and snow conditions, varying the frequency of your turns.

Skiing exercises

- Snowplough turn: take up a snowplough position, press down and push up on one leg, bring the leg in to the traverse, bend.
- Repeat several times on each side, then alternate left and right turns.
- Basic swing turn: a rhythmical sequence of this movement – traverse position, angle legs into snowplough position, press down and push up on one leg, bring leg in, bend and turn legs, traverse position.

Common mistakes

Keeping in too low a position when you push off, which . . .
makes it harder to turn the skis at the start of the manoeuvre.
Keeping too upright when you push off, which . . .
means your legs will not turn enough.
Turning the outer hip too much.
Exessive rotation and steering as you turn.

Terrain – snow – frequency of turns

Start on easy slopes, with ski lifts, so that you will have plenty of chances to come down the trail. The radius and rhythm of the turn should be adjusted to the terrain. This diagram shows the ideal type of terrain on which to learn:

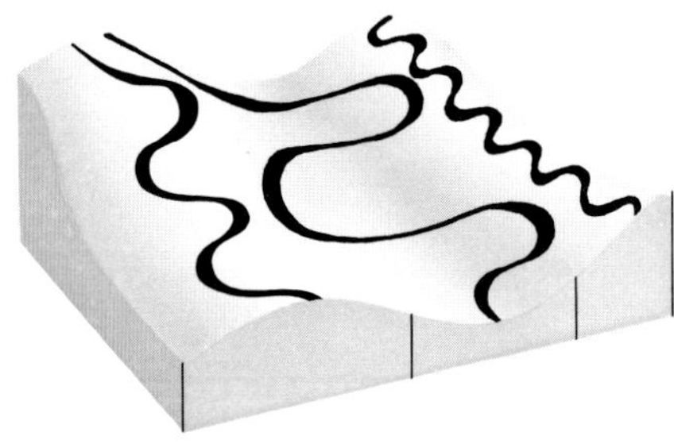

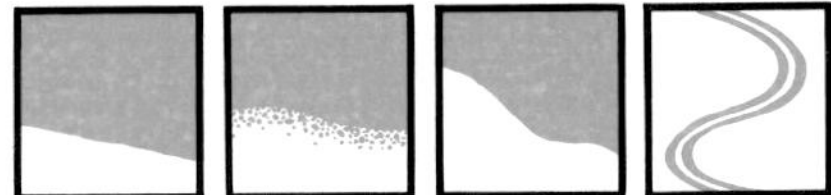

Basic parallel turn

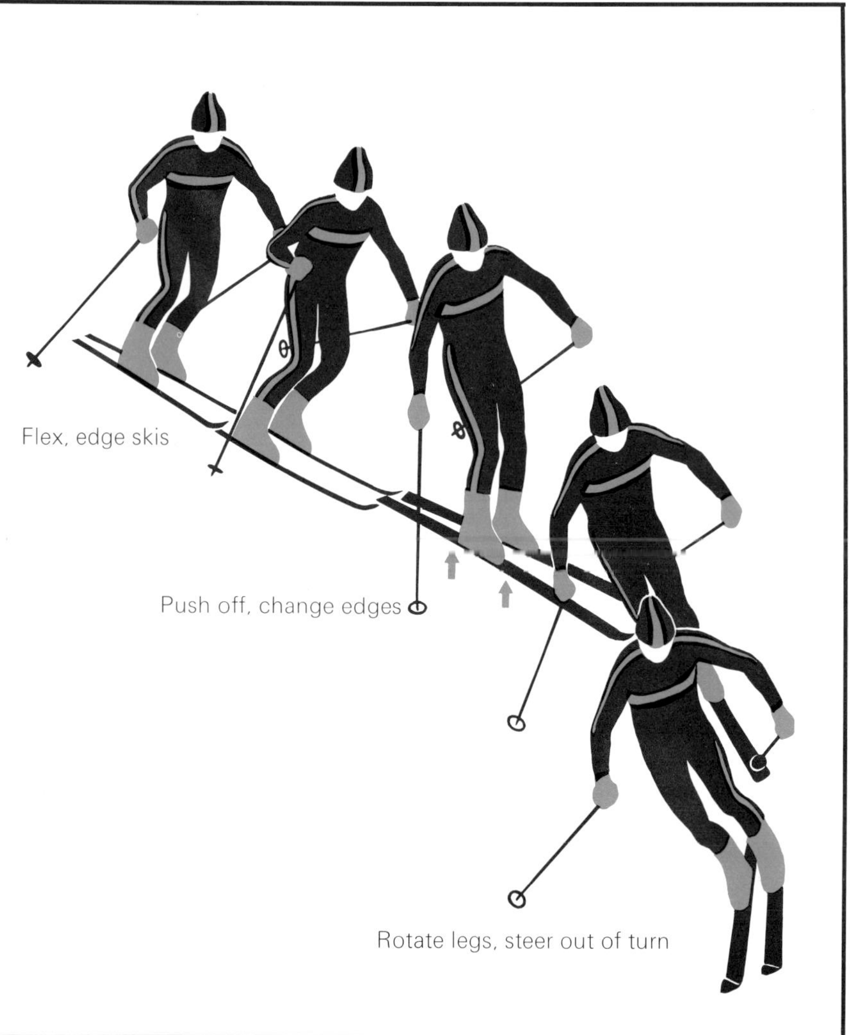

Technique

The basic parallel turn is a mixture of turns involving weight transfer and ordinary parallel turns. It is usually performed from a position in which the skis are parallel and, to a greater or less extent, apart. The turn is started from the traverse; a bend of the knees prepares for the turn itself, and as the knees bend the skier tries to increase the amount of edging (knee leading forward and uphill).

Going into the turn, the skier pushes off and rises up from the downhill ski in the direction of the turn. The setting of the edges changes with the change of weighting. As the skier flexes down again the skis are turned further in the new direction. During the change of edging and the turning of the legs the upper part of the body leans further forward with the movement of the turn. Planting the ski pole helps the pushing off movement. When weighting is more evenly distributed on both legs the powerful pushing-off movement can lead to a hop into the air; if too much weight is concentrated on one leg at the pushing-off moment the usual result is a kind of step taken by the downhill ski towards the uphill ski.

Control of the turn as the skier flexes down is combined with a twist of the hips in the opposite direction and a forward and sideways bend of the upper part of the body. Preparation for the next turn begins during the final, steered phase of the basic swing turn.

Note: there are three essential things to practise: preparation for the swing turn (flexing and edging), a strong pushing-off movement in the direction of the turn, followed by a change of edging, and control of the turn (steering its direction by twisting the legs round). The aim is to calculate the amounts of down-up-down movement, weighting and speed which will lead to a turning radius suitable to the terrain. Increase in the frequency of the turns gives rise to a wedel effect consisting of rhythmical changes of direction close to the fall line.

Practice

- First one should practise the pushing-off movement and the slight movement of recovery after the hop; practise jumping in a stationary position and when moving down the fall line.
- The simplest form of the basic parallel turn is to change direction on a gentle slope by means of rhythmical hops to left and right with the tails of your skis pointing outwards. Start with skis well apart, hopping at only a slight angle.
- Practise the turn as a fan shape. Execute basic parallel swing turns from the fall line, bringing your line of approach gradually closer to the traverse.
- Repeat several linked turns.
- Practise the turn in more difficult conditions of terrain and snow, varying the frequency of turns.

1

2

3

4

Skiing exercises

- Hop rhythmically with both legs to left and right, bending and stretching.
- Hop rhythmically on one leg to left and right, taking off as strongly as you can.
- Push up from the traversing position (legs centred under your hips), then bend down and turn your legs in the other direction. Alternate this movement to left and right.

Terrain – snow – frequency of turns

Practise first on gently sloping terrain, then on moderate, rounded slopes, and on snow surface with a good grip; a certain amount of unevenness will be a help.

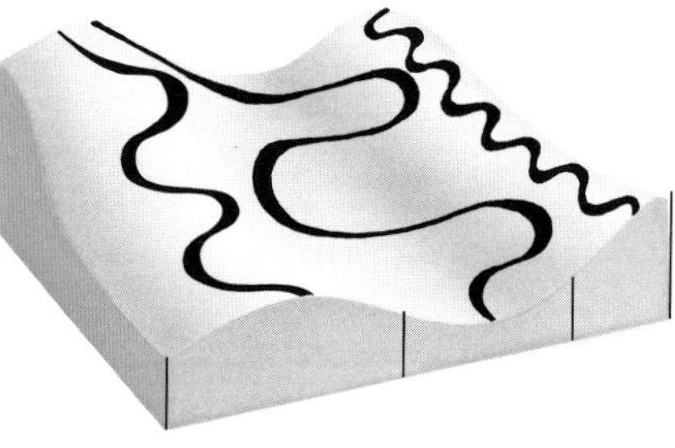

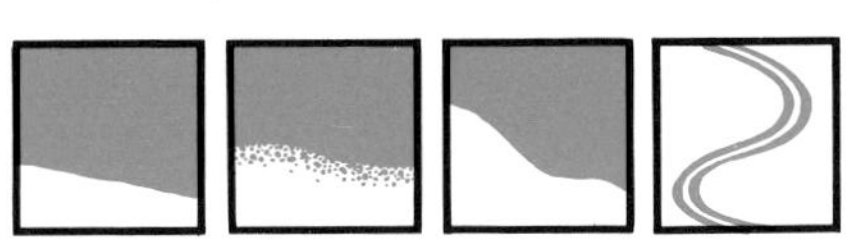

Common mistakes

Failing to flex enough before you push off leads to . . .
too weak a pushing-off movement and insufficient weight transfer.

Failing to rise high enough as you push off . . .
makes it more difficult to turn the skis as you go into the turn.

Failing to flex low enough after you push off . . .
means you cannot turn your legs far enough.

Trail signs

Ski trails are marked so that a skier will be warned of the degree of difficulty to be expected and, in the course of skiing the trail, be warned of possible dangers and obstacles ahead. For many years attempts have been made to introduce an international, standard form of sign-posting.

There are at present two distinct types of trail markings – the one used, more or less universally, in Europe, and the one used in the United States. Australia and Canada appear to use either or both.

The European standard is based on three (occasionally four) standards: Black, very difficult and difficult, Red, moderate to difficult and Blue, easy to moderate. Occasionally, Green is also used to indicate a beginner's trail of considerable ease. These markings appear before reaching the trail, and on the trail, in the form of posts with circular coloured discs which also carry the trail number and location number.

In the United States, a combination of both colour and shape is used and a relative or comparative scale of difficulty is implied. Most Difficult is shown in black on a diamond, More Difficult is shown on a square blue sign and Easiest on a round green disc.

In addition a number of signs can be found on the trail indicating steep bumps, gullies, narrow passages, ski-lift crossings and the like. The signs used are visual and are similar to international road signs. They are self-explanatory. Danger owing to avalanches is shown by a red hexagonal in the United States and by a yellow and black oblong in Europe which bears the words *Achtung Geschlossen – Lawinengefahr* or *Attention, Fermé – Danger d'Avalanche*. Always be sure to check the system of trail signs.

International rules of the ski trail

Fair play in skiing: ten rules

These rules are beginning to be generally adopted as the basis of a Highway Code for the ski trails.

1. Consideration for others
Every skier should ski in such a way that he never places anyone else in danger.

2. Control of speed and movements
Every skier should adjust his speed and movements to his own degree of expertise, as well as to the terrain and weather conditions.

3. Choice of track
A skier approaching another from behind must choose his course so that he does not endanger the skier ahead.

4. Overtaking
The rules about overtaking are not rigid – a skier can overtake from above or below, on the left or the right, but must do so at a distance which allows the skier being overtaken enough room for all his movements.

5. Skiers lower down the slope and traversing
Any skier wishing to join a trail at a lower point on the slope, or traverse an area, must look up and down the slope to make sure he can do so without danger to himself or others.

6. Stopping during a downhill run
Every skier must avoid stopping at points where the trail is narrow, or where he cannot be seen by oncoming skiers. If he falls at such a point, he must move away from it as quickly as possible.

7. Climbing a slope
A skier climbing the slope may only use the outside edge of a trail, and must leave that free as well if visibility is poor. The same applies to skiers coming down a slope on foot.

8. Observing the trail signs

Every skier must observe the trail markers and other trail signs.

9. Accidents
It is every skier's duty to help at the scene of an accident.

10. Identification
Everyone involved in an accident, whether as participant or witness, must give particulars of his identification.

For skiers in groups

People do not just ski in groups when they are having lessons at a ski school; they often do so on their own account. It is advisable to learn a few of the unwritten 'rules of the game' for safe skiing in groups, to make sure your friendly group skiing expedition is not spoilt by an accident.

1. As a matter of principle, every skier within the group should observe the international rules of the trail.
2. Before you set off on a downhill run you should discuss who is to lead the group and who is to bring up the rear. Both skiers should be a little more experienced than the other members of the group. You should also decide the order in which each of the other members of the group will ski. The weaker or slower skiers will determine the pace and the route of the run. Always keep in sight of each other, especially in snowfall or mist. Do not short-cut the radius of the leader's turns.
3. Always come to a halt below the other members of the group. However sure of yourself you feel, never stop in such a way that you could have a fall where the group is standing.
4. When stopping in a narrow place, always remember that the skier following you will need room to turn off the trail too, so avoid obstructing the run-out.
5. When coming up to ski-tow tracks or forks in the trail, always wait for each other in a safe place so as to make sure the group keeps together, even in poor visibility. It is advisable to do the same when getting on and off the lift.

Using the lifts – safely

Nowadays we can hardly imagine skiing without the use of lifts. It is essential, however, to learn the correct use of a lift particularly when the lift is of the ski-tow type, and for beginners the first ride up the slope on a lift may well present more problems than the first downhill run. If there is no opportunity to learn how to get on a lift during your ski lessons, you should learn about the difficulties – and, most important, about the rules – before you actually use one.

Ski-tows

You can practise on the flat, with a partner. When you are first using a lift in earnest, choose a quiet time when the lifts are not crowded – if only to save yourself from looking silly in front of a long queue if you happen to fail in your attempt to get on. Try to go up with an experienced partner, and have a good look at the way to do it before you start. If you have finally decided to buy a lift ticket, warn the lift attendant.

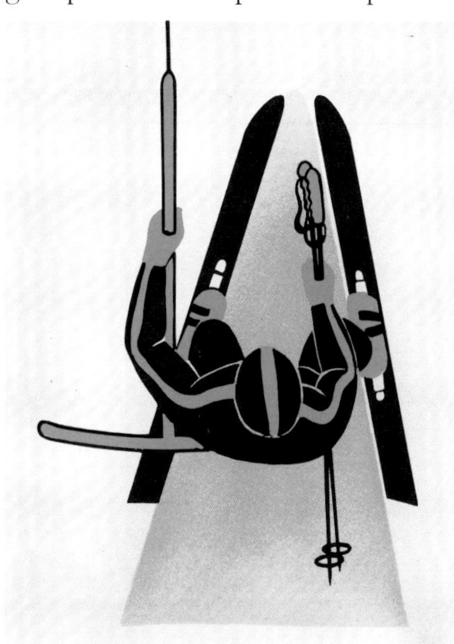

If the ski-tow goes downhill part of the way, it is best to brake in the snowplough position.

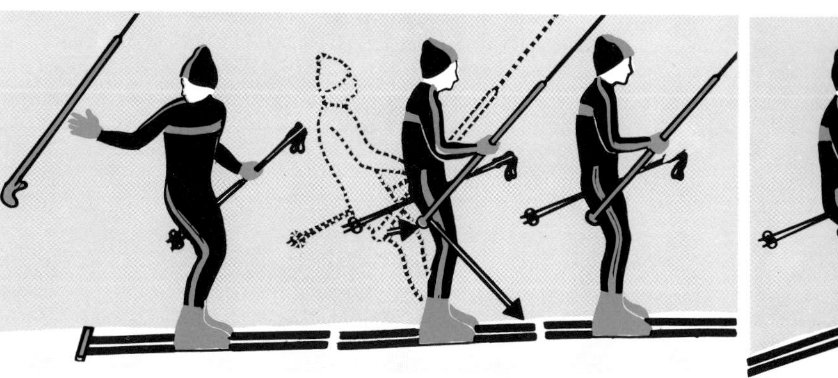

Getting on and starting: do not sit on the T-bar.

Riding: absorb bumps and dips by flexing and stretching your legs.

The rest of the procedure is as follows:

1. Standing in line
Stand in line in an orderly way, in single file if the lift is a button lift, in pairs if it is a T-bar lift; this way you will not harm your own skis or anyone else's, and will avoid congestion.

2. Getting on
Move briskly up to the point where you get on the lift, hold both poles in your outside hand, leaving your other hand free to hold the bar.

3. Starting off
Do not sit down on the arm of the T-bar! Remain standing, leaning lightly back against the arm, and let yourself be pulled uphill. Sliding your skis forward in the direction you are going will make it easier to start.

4. Riding up the slope
Keep both skis evenly weighted and apart. Do not lean outwards, or towards your partner and you will keep your balance better.

5. Keeping to the tracks
Keep your skis going along the tracks worn by other lift passengers, do not let them waver into a 'slalom' movement across the tracks, do not get off the ski-tow too soon or you may endanger yourself and others.

6. What to do if you fall
If you have a fall while going up, get out of the way at once, since there is no way for the person coming up after to avoid you easily.

7. Preparing to get off
Prepare to get off the lift in good time. Make sure the arm of the T-bar

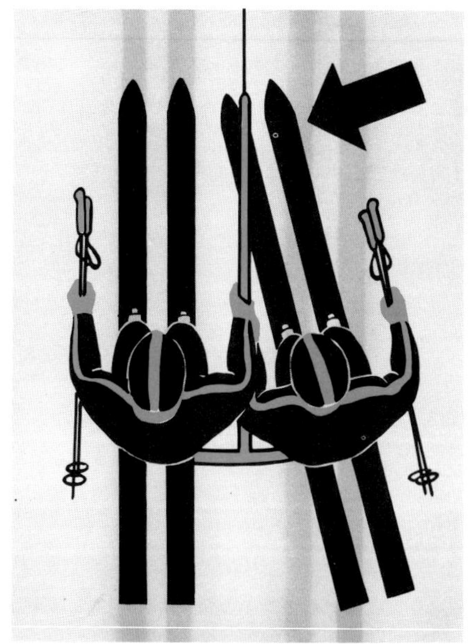

Always stay in the track.

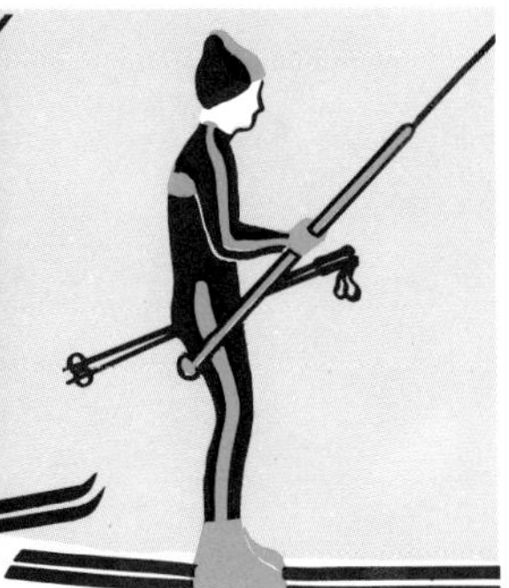

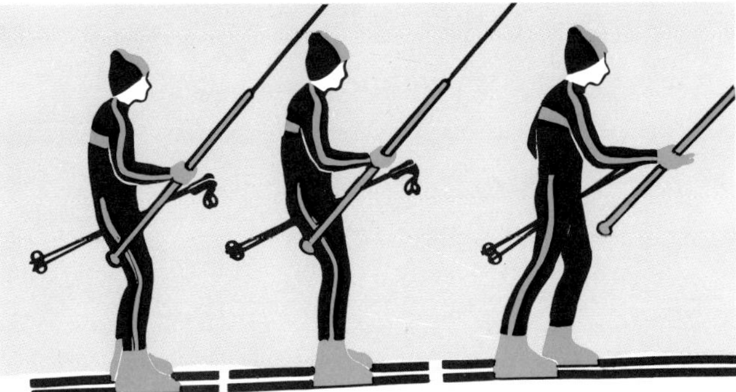

Getting off: do not let go of the bar too soon.

is not caught in your clothing.

8. Getting off

Step briskly off the lift, letting the bar swing gently free in the direction it is going; do not toss it thoughtlessly aside.

9. Moving away from the lift

Move off at once, leaving room for the skiers coming up after you, so that there is no danger of a collision or of your getting hit by an empty T-bar.

This suggested code for the use of ski lifts was drawn up after years of practical experience.

Chairlifts

In the United States Jim Curran invented the chairlift and installed the first one at Sun Valley in 1936. It is a wonderful sensation for a skier to ride up above the snow-covered slopes in a chairlift – provided, of course, the sun is shinning, because otherwise you can have a chilly and uncomfortable ride. You should always wear warm clothes.

1. Stand in line in an orderly way, poles held in your outside hand.
2. Move briskly but carefully up to the getting-on point.
3. Look back as you are getting on.
4. If you are carrying your skis (hold them upright while waiting to get on), try to put them down on the space provided (if any). If you are wearing them, take care you keep the tips up during the ride.
5. Once in your seat, swing the metal 'gate' which acts as a safety bar into place. It is usually combined with a footrest for your skis.
6. Do not swing during the ride.
7. There is usually a sign on the last of the masts carrying the chairlifts to let you know you are approaching the top. Raise the safety bar in good time.
8. Raise the tips of your skis as you approach the ramp.
9. Slide briskly off the lift and move away from the ramp at once.
10. Do some warming-up exercises before you start skiing downhill.

And one more point:

You will generally find information about the trails, trail markings, closure of trails, presence of trail-grooming machines, and any danger of avalanches displayed in the area where you line up for the lifts. Every skier should take this chance to become thoroughly acquainted with local conditions at the time.

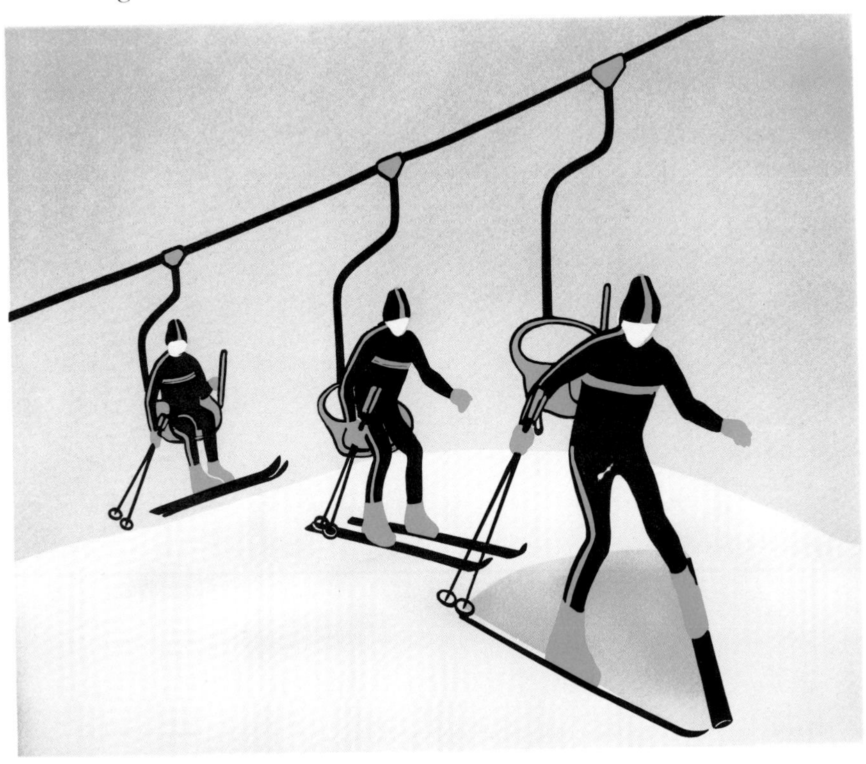

When getting off a chairlift you will usually find you are at the top of a small slope. Beginners should try to brake in the snowplough position.

Warming-up exercises before you start skiing

Many sportsmen and women, whether footballers, swimmers, athletes or others, regard warming-up as a routine part of their training. Putting up a good performance in competitive sport can depend upon it. What about skiers? The large majority ignore the desirability of warming-up before they start in spite of the fact that they may have come a long way up in a chairlift, in spite of temperatures of 18°F(− 10°C) or lower and in spite of snowstorms, stiff limbs and cold hands. Luckily, attitudes have now begun to change.

Overall ski-suits and over-trousers, in short, the general improvement of ski equipment, all help the skier keep out the cold. But only the cold! The result of chilled muscles is a noticeable loss of elasticity as well as poor physical co-ordination. This means a skier cannot control his movements accurately and will usually try to make up for it by exerting more force. The high muscle tone which results can then lead to the tearing of muscles and ligaments.

So warming-up before you start skiing is well worth it, since a few exercises (for the muscles of your legs, ligaments, for your shoulder, arm and trunk muscles) are enough to loosen up muscles and joints, get your circulation and breathing working better, in fact get your entire body into better shape for the skiing you are about to do. So it is not advisable to start when cold, especially not after a long ride up the slope in a chairlift or on a ski-tow. Exercises are a safeguard against the danger of injury incurred from being cold, and if you have already warmed up you will also find that you do your first turns better. Warming-up is especially valuable for skiers on a beginners' course, who will find it increases their ability to learn a complicated sequence of movements.

Start slowly; you don't want to injure yourself while doing the exercises themselves. Practise the various exercises until you feel you are at the top of your form. Never move off downhill with cold feet.

To get you warm:
Jump up in the air, swinging your arms up, alternating your legs between the snowplough position and the schussing position

Loosening up:
Arms swinging as for cross-country skiing.
Swing your arms up to your shoulders.

Mobility of the shoulders:
Rapid arm circling in both directions; circle both arms at once.

Mobility of the trunk:
Bend and stretch, co-ordinating your knee bends and arm swinging forward and back.

For cold hands:
Swing the arms forward and back; cross and stretch the arms vigorously.

Preparing to run downhill:
Rapid jumping, transferring the weight from one leg to the other and raising the end of the ski off the snow.

Mobility of the hips:
Circle hips and trunk forwards and backwards, hands on hips.

Leg-stretching exercise:
Go down into a sitting-back crouching position and stand up again.

Before starting downhill:
Practise pushing up and edging your skis hard.

For cold fingers and the circulation of your thighs:
Slap your left and right thighs alternately.

Universal techniques

Up-unweighting parallel

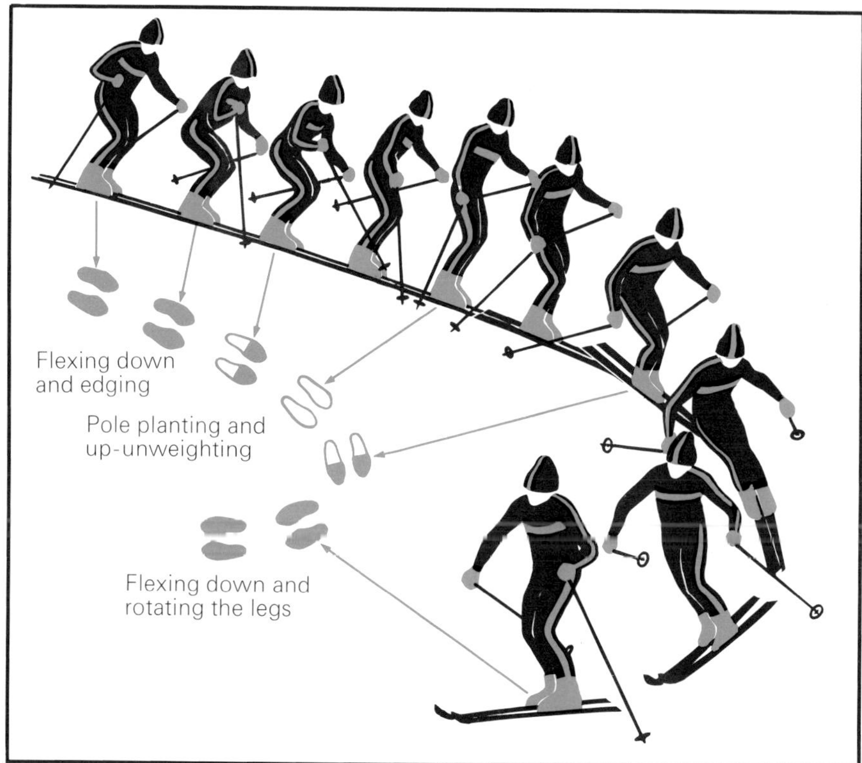

Technique

The up-unweighted parallel is a 'classic' way to change direction while skiing; every skier still aims to perform this turn. The change of direction across the fall line is executed by means of a down-up-down movement combined with a push-off and rolling movement of both legs.

Starting from the traverse, the skis are first edged uphill (down movement). This uphill edging is necessary for the subsequent up movement when the skier pushes up with both legs, twisting them round, to start his turn. The skis are then edged the other way, the skier flexes and turns them into the new direction. During the change of edging and the twist of the legs, the skier's upper body follows the movement. He plants his pole to help him take off and twist his legs. As he goes down again, the steering of the turn is combined with a rotation of the hips and a forward lean of the upper part of the body. There should be just the right amount of fluid down-up-down movement to produce a smooth edge change and an even turning radius.

Note: there are two essential elements of this turn to be practised:

- Edging and initiation push
- Edge change and control of the turn by leg rotation

The poles should be planted rhythmically so as to help you turn, i.e., you should plant your pole ahead of you (do not *swing* it out ahead) as you go down before turning. Control your turn according to the terrain by rotating your hips and compensating with the upper part of your body (forwards and sideways). If you are linking several turns do not traverse between them.

Practice

- First practise pushing off with both legs and recovering gently after this upwards push; practise pushing up while standing still and while moving across the fall line, both with and without pole-planting.
- The simplest form of this turn is angled hopping on the flat, i.e., rhythmical upward hopping movements with both legs, to left and to right, ski tails outwards.
- Start by practising hopping at a slight angle only, skis apart.
- Training for a soft landing: having gone into the turn, increase the angle of the movement by planting your uphill pole, until you are about to start out of the fall line. Refine leg rotation and the ski position.
- Link several turns in quick succession on a gentle slope: your first attempts at the wedel. Intensify this movement till you are doing a broad wedel movement close to the fall line.
- Training for edging your skis: practise both while standing still, and while traversing and planting your poles on a moderately steep slope.
- Practise the turn in its easier form (the basic parallel swing turn).
- You will find that with repetition and increasing speed and linking turns freely, controlled parallels are possible.

Skiing exercises

- Bend and stretch the legs and hop rhythmically at the same time.
- Up unweighting: hop alternately to right and left with both legs, taking off vigorously and landing softly. Repeat rhythmically several times in succession.

1

2

3

4

- Practise for edging: starting from the traversing position, push the knees strongly forwards and inwards. Do the movement alternately to left and to right.
- To perfect your down-up-down movement: turn the legs alternately to left and right in a continuous movement.

Common mistakes

Insufficient edging at the end of a turn leads to ...
too weak a take-off.
Too weak a take-off, with an inadequate upwards thrust, leads to ...
difficulty in edge-changing, a poor turn of the skis.
An inadequate upwards thrust of the body leads to ...
rotation as you start the turn.
Too weak a twisting movement of the legs after pushing up leads to ...
difficulty in turning the skis.
Inadequate downward flexing while twisting hips forwards and sideways, leads to ...
a poor steering phase.

Terrain – snow – frequency of turns

First gently sloping, then moderately steep.

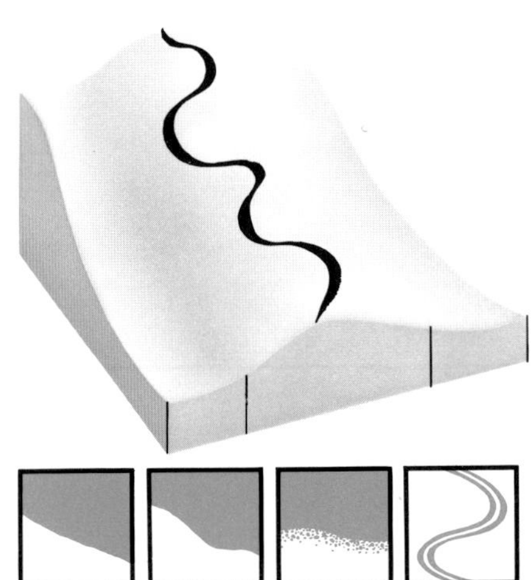

The short swing

Technique

The short swing with its fluid down-up-down movement enables you to link tight turns near the fall line and to ski downhill with great control over your movements even on narrow, steep sections of the trail. In principle the technique of the short swing is the same as that of the parallel turn. There are two important elements in this manoeuvre:

- A rhythmically active sequence of movements close to the fall line performed at a specified frequency.
- Stronger edging and a faster initiation.

Note: fast bending and stretching of the ankle, knee and hip joints. Do not pause at any point in the manoeuvre.

The upward initiation must be started rapidly and allowed to die out.

The downward unweighting, during which you rotate your legs, should start slowly and increase in speed. The knees are pressed hard forward and uphill, thus edging the skis. The upper part of the body and the position of the poles should be steady, although performing the corresponding balancing movements. Plant the poles rhythmically and alternately between your bindings and the tips of your skis. Control your speed by increased rotation of your legs (and thus your edging) and not by side-slipping.

Experts can refine the technique of the parallel and short swing until they can ski without any vertical movement, turning the skis around the axis of the legs. They prepare for the run early by twisting the hips and the upper part of the body in the direction of the turn. The main activity in the turn is in the sideways angling of the thighs and knees (you need a good knees-bent position to do it).

This technique calls for well-trained leg muscles; the main problem is to get your anticipation right, that is,coordinating your skis and leg positioning with the counter-movement of your hips and the upper part of your body. It is simply a turn for trail skiing, pure and simple, and enables you to control your parallel skiing whether you are going fast or slowly. When training, practising control of your down-up-down movement and the edging of your skis is particularly valuable.

Practice

- You can perform an easy version of the short turn by shortening the radius of the parallel turn.
- Pushing off well, execute several short turns close to the fall line.
- Carry out end-form short turns with varying rhythm in various kinds of terrain.
- Traversing short swings: perform several short swings from a traverse. This will improve your edging and the angling of your legs.
- Perform short swings, making sure your edges bite hard.

Skiing exercises

- Wedel hopping: jump rhythmically off both feet, turning in alternate directions.
- The wedel: in a traversing position, press the knees hard forwards and sideways (edging), then twist the other way (edging). Start by practising the change of edging

with a down-up-down movement, then repeat faster without any upwards thrust.

- Variations of hopping: hop on your heels, on the full sole of the foot, and on the balls of the feet.

Common mistakes

Insufficient edging at the end of the turn leads to . . .
too weak a pushing-off movement.
Bending the knees too far before pushing off leads to . . .
a sitting-back position as you start the turn.
Rotating your legs too little after you push off leads to . . .
difficulty in turning the skis.
Insufficient vertical movement (or a tendency to lean forward) leads to . . .
difficulties in keeping your turns rhythmical.
Keeping your skis too flat on the snow leads to . . .
lack of control.
Planting your poles inaccurately leads to . . .
difficulties in keeping your turns rhythmical.

Terrain – snow – frequency of turns

Moderately steep and steep slopes, almost all kinds of snow (packed trails, deep snow).

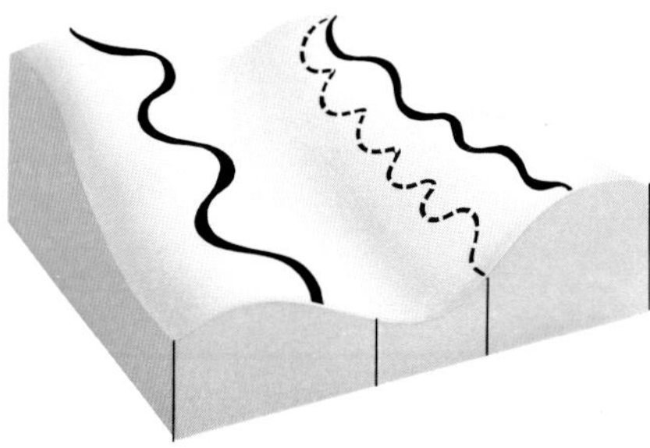

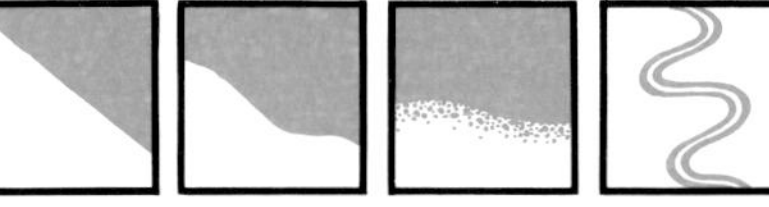

The compression turn

Technique

If you want to ski well in very bumpy terrain you will have to be able to turn while absorbing the bumps. The compression turn is the ideal manoeuvre for a good skier on uneven terrain. The legs take over the function of shock-absorbers, bending and stretching to absorb or 'swallow' the bumps, while the upper part of the body stays still.

The start of your rotation takes place on the crest of a bump, at the moment when the skis are still centrally placed and resistance to turning will be at its least. A laterally planted pole downhill helps to stabilize and support you. In absorbing the bump the legs are pushed up in front of your body by the bump itself, so the actual swallowing is more of a passive movement of the legs. Immediately afterwards you actively stretch the legs as you move down the other side of the bump, so as to keep in contact with the snow.

Unlike the parallel turn, however, the movement involves extension of the legs pointing downwards (weighting of the edges). You are therefore performing a kind of kicking movement to keep in contact with the ground, especially in the dips. In practice, there are two forms of this turn:

- the passive form, in which you let the bumps push your legs up in front of your body.
- the active form, where you actively bend your knees up in front of your body as you flex (compression turn).

Note: approach in a relatively upright stance with both skis weighted (to help you keep your balance).

Anticipation is important in preparing for the turn.

When 'swallowing' the bump by actively bending your legs up in front of your body, giving you more scope for a springy action, do not lean back on your heels.

Keep your upper body steady and erect. Start twisting round by rotating the legs while your knees are still bent, so as to make use of the down-unweighting. Plant a pole laterally downhill to support you. Extend the legs downwards. Turn on the crest of the bump, while only the centre of your skis is touching the snow. Keep the upper part of your body facing downhill as you ski. Adjust your bump-absorbing movement to the terrain.

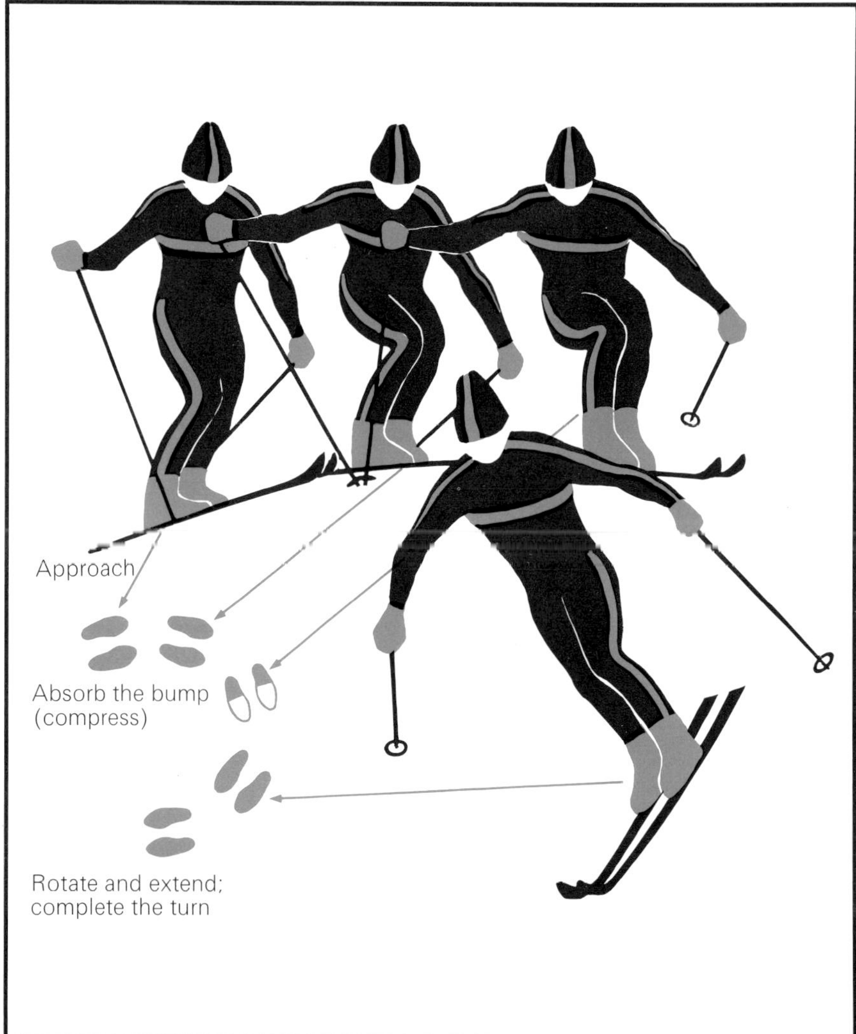

Practice

- Start by practising absorbing bumps by bending and stretching the legs as you run straight downhill. Then try the same thing in a traverse.
- As before, but turn your skis on top of the bump. Sequence of movements: bend and turn, stretch and turn.
- Do several turns in succession on bumpy terrain.
- Ski in bumpy terrain at a higher speed, keeping in contact with the snow by extending your legs energetically downwards. Ski round the bumps instead of turning.

1

2

3

4

5

6

Skiing exercises

- Jump, crouching down and then extending the legs.
- 'Bump-absorbing': alternate between an upright schussing position and a low crouch. Bend and stretch – down and up.
- Touch the floor to the sides of your feet.
- 'Bump-absorbing turn': jump, crouching down and then extending the legs in the air. Crouch down quickly, turn alternately left and right, extending the legs.
- 'Bump-absorbing' in press-up position: bend and stretch the legs alternately (squat-jumps).

Common mistakes

A cramped style of skiing leads to . . . difficulty in maintaining your rhythm and adjusting your movements to the terrain.

Keeping too upright as you ski leads to . . . inadequate absorbing of bumps and weak turning.

Failure to stretch your legs actively enough downwards leads to . . . insufficient turning as you extend the legs and poor absorbing of the dip.

Sitting too far back leads to . . . a pronounced back wards-leaning position

Insufficiently elastic legs lead to . . . difficulty in keeping in contact with the ground.

Terrain – snow – frequency of turns

Moderately steep but bumpy slopes, on snow giving a good grip.

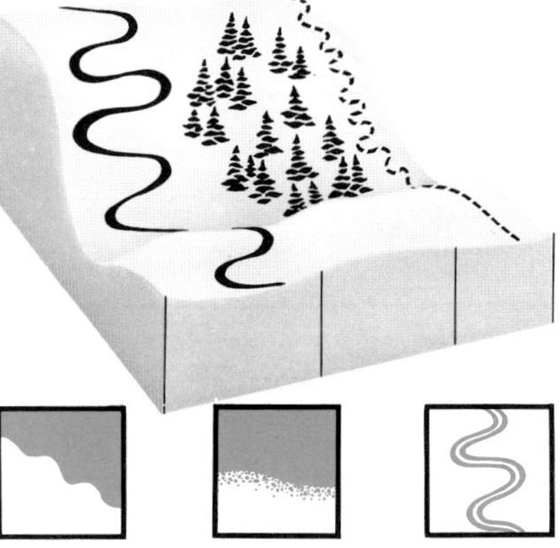

Stem step turn with uphill ski stemmed

2

3

The step turn

Technique

Turning while stepping from one ski to the other is a modern technique developed from racing, and is now becoming increasingly popular in modern skiing because of its adaptability. Its salient characteristic is the step-transfer of weighting from one ski to the other.

There are many variations of the technique, depending upon the skier's position before the turn and the way in which it is carried out. The principle of the manoeuvre, however, is always the same: the skier comes into it out of a traverse or a preceding turn, places increasing weight on the downhill ski, and tries to prepare for a stepping-off movement from the downhill ski by pressing his downhill knee forwards and uphill. Taking off with the help of a vigorous pole-plant, he then steps his weight on the other ski and starts the next change of direction. As he turns, the ski which is now weighted is edged on the other side, and he steps up the ski from which he has taken off. The turn is controlled by the twisting movement of the legs, and a strong edging manoeuvre, as well as the forwards and sideways movement of the upper part of the body.

Features common to all step turns

- One ski is more heavily weighted than the other.
- The skier steps his weight from one ski to the other, as in ordinary walking.
- Edging in turning, and the transfer of edging from one side of the ski to the other, are very marked.
- The turn usually starts with rotation (a forwards twisting movement of the outside hip).
- The turn is usually controlled by torsion (bringing back the outside hip).

The technique of these turns is ex-

1

4

Stem step turn from downhill stemmed ski

tremely adaptable: for instance, one can use a stem turn with weight transfer to brake, use a parallel turn with weight transfer to glide and use a scissors step turn with weight transfer to gather speed. You can shift your weight from outside ski to outside ski and from inside ski to inside ski. You can use the method to absorb bumps on uneven trails, you can use it in the sitting-back position. You can use it to execute long-radius and short-radius turns, with and without pole-planting.

It has just one limitation: it cannot be used to the full in soft or deep snow. Once the basic sequence of movements involved in turns with weight transfer has been mastered you will recognize the advantages of this dynamic technique:

- The freedom of the legs to move increases your ability to react and gives you a greater sense of security.
- Stepping the skis and turning your skis while weighted, enables you to grip a hard trail better with your edges.
- The fluid sequence of movements makes it easier to gain speed.

The principle of step turns has something to offer every skier – so long as he does not put elegance of style before all other considerations. It is easily the most adaptable of skiing techniques, since it can be applied in all sorts of different situations. According to the position of the skis, it is possible to distinguish between:

Stem step turn: either the uphill or the downhill ski is angled before weight is transferred. The effect is to brake the skier's progress to a greater or lesser extent.

Parallel step turn: this kind of turn can be executed with skis close together or well apart. It is a gliding turn for good skiers and is popular with racers.

Parallel step turn, skis close together

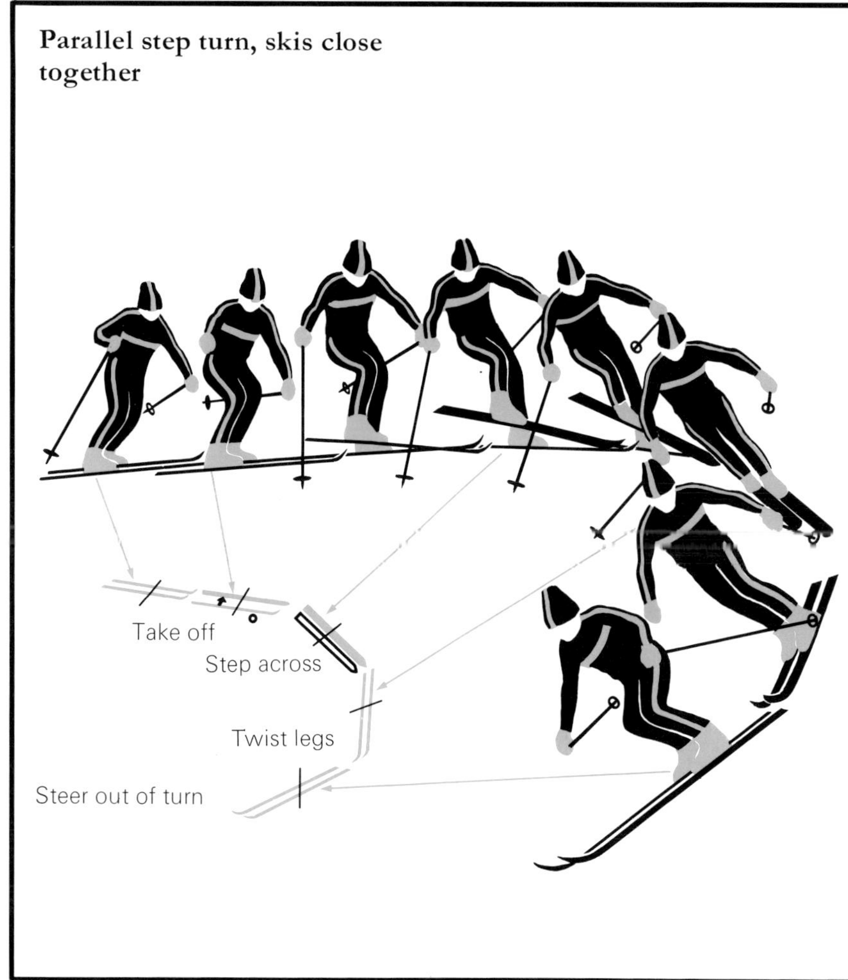

Acceleration stepping action: a dynamic variant. The pushing-off movement causes acceleration; a rhythmical series of short turns involves weight transfer.

Once you have understood the basic movement of the weight-transfer turns (see basic swing, p. 80), try the following turns:

Scissor step turn

This athletic version of a step turn can easily be learnt from trained skiers. The decisive phase of such a turn is the scissor-like opening of the skis before take off, in order to gain height. This manoeuvre distinguishes the turn from other forms of turn involving weight transfer. The fluid and dynamic sequence of movements helps to increase the speed of the turn. You may already have practised the basic form of this step turn when skating to turn and when stepping from ski to ski to describe a curve.

Stem step turn

- Do several short basic swing turns in rhythmical succession, progressively increasing the push-off from the edge set of the downhill ski.
- Do medium-radius step turns, stemming out the downhill ski.
- Do uphill stem step turns, short to long radius.

Parallel step turn

- 'Jumping with step across', bringing up the ski from which you have taken off.
- From a schussing position, place one ski to the side and parallel, step across to it, steer the turn by rotating your legs.
- Do a succession of turns with step action, medium radius, from an increasingly shallow traverse.
- Starting from the traverse, change to the other traverse using a parallel turn involving step action and rotation of the legs.
- Do step turns with skis well apart.
- Do step turns with skis close together, increasing your speed and raising the inside ski.
- Do long turns with step action, paying particular attention to a carving control of the turn.
- Do quicker push-off step turns.
- Do short swings involving stepping action on bumpy terrain.

Terrain – snow – frequency of turns

Start on a gentle slope, proceed to hard, steep trails of all kinds.

1. Downhill stemmed ski, uphill stemmed ski.
2. Parallel step turn, uphill stemmed ski.
3. Uphill stemmed ski, downhill stemmed ski.

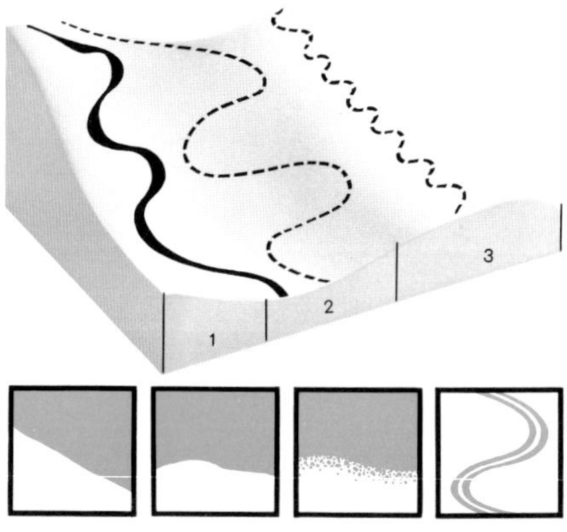

Skiing exercises

- Stem step turn (uphill ski stemmed): starting from a traversing position, angle out to a stemming position, press down and rise up, bring up the other foot and go down again in the new traversing position.
- Parallel step turn (feet apart): in a traversing position, open the legs parallel with a step to the side, press down and rise up, bring up the other foot and go down again in the new traversing position.
- Acceleration stepping action: jump rapidly and vigorously from one leg to the other in a rhythmical sequence.

Common mistakes

Pushing off with too little force leads to ...
inadequate weighting change to stepped ski.
Rotating the legs too little leads to ...
difficulty in turning the skis.
Insufficient down movement (knees forwards and uphill) and forwards and sideways bending lead to ...
poor steering phase.
Badly judged upwards movement leads to ...
difficulty in getting a good sequence of turns.
Lack of precision of pole-planting leads to ...
difficulties with your co-ordination.

Stem step turn

Lack of precision in stemming out/weighted uphill ski/unweighted downhill ski, leads to ...
difficulty in stepping your weight across.

Parallel step turn

Failure to position and keep your skis parallel leads to ...
difficulty in co-ordination when stepping across and steering the turn.

Step turn with quicker push off

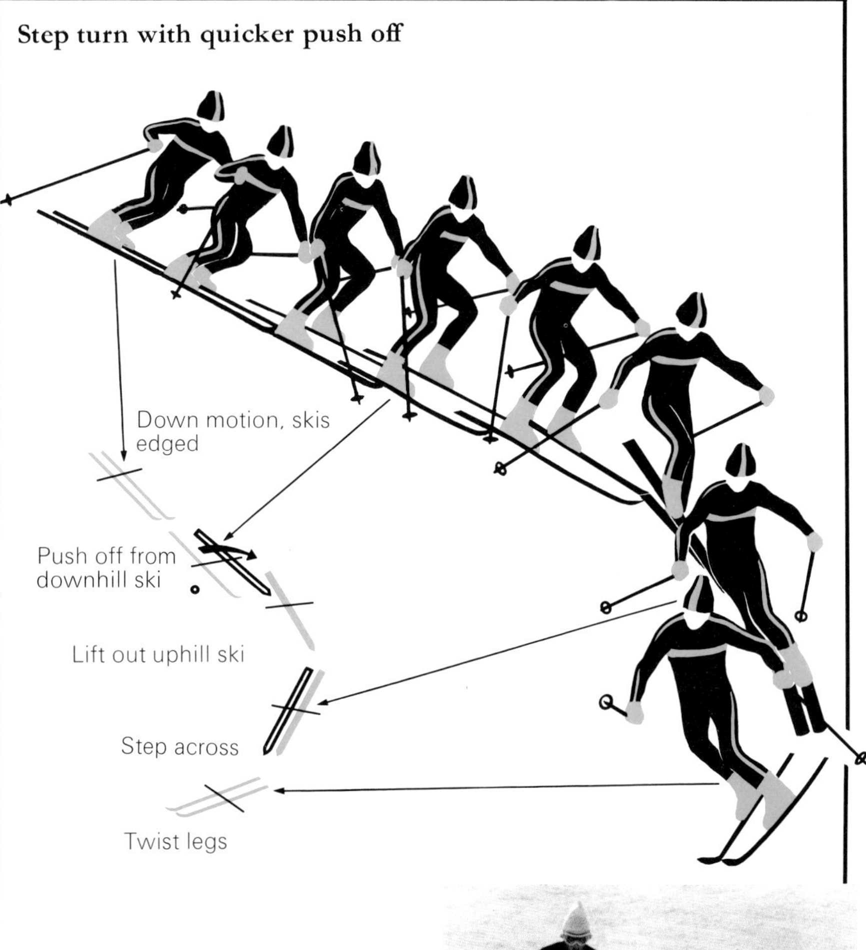

Important: a strong twisting take-off movement with one leg from the edge of the downhill ski (unweighting). Marked stepping action, combined with an obvious change of weighting to the other ski. Twist the legs to steer out of the turn as you crouch down.

Terrain – snow – frequency of turns

Accelerating stepping action.

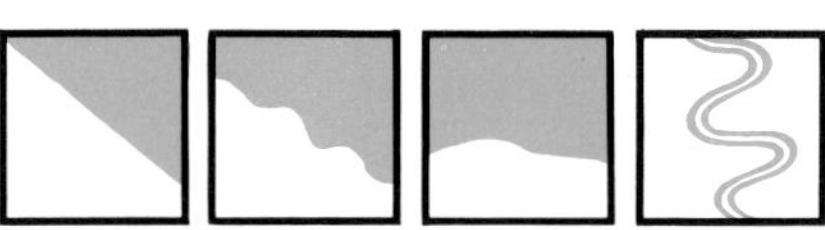

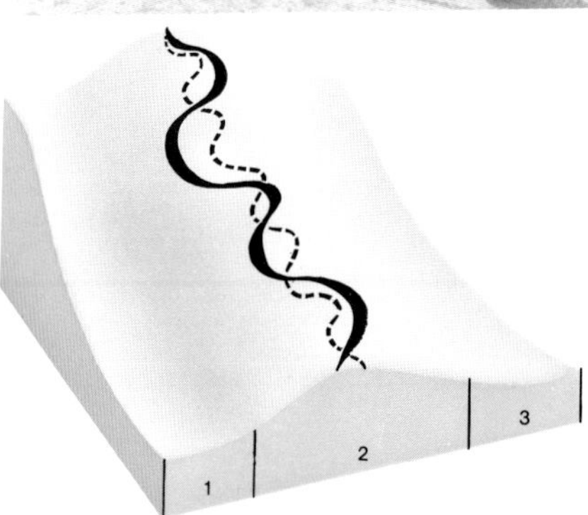

Special techniques

The rotation turn

Technique

At high speed it is useful to be able to change the edges as smoothly and as early as possible, especially to maintain an even weighting of the skis. The rotation turn enables you to do this without a strong unweighting movement and with a moderate amount of upward movement. As its name indicates, the turn is steered by a slight rotating movement, which resembles that of a motor-cycle rider leaning into a curve, i.e., the upper part of the body makes a horizontal forwards movement into the new direction.

Rotation is a turning movement of the hips and upper body anticipating the next change of direction, which gives rise to a turning impulse and transfers to the skis. The arm on the outside of the curve also twists round during the turn to reinforce the movement. The turn is steered, with both skis weighted, by twisting the legs in the normal way, or by a fairly strongly marked leaning-in position, after the rotation movement has been stopped in the fall line by the use of the hips.

This technique is relatively restful to perform on gentle or moderately steep slopes (or when doing a giant slalom through gates set well apart), and for that reason has been called 'the idler's turn'. It guarantees particularly dynamic steering of your skis at high speed.

Note: the rotation turn can be done with or without up-unweighting. The twisting movement of the turn should not go round too far; after you have changed the edges block the rotation of the body.

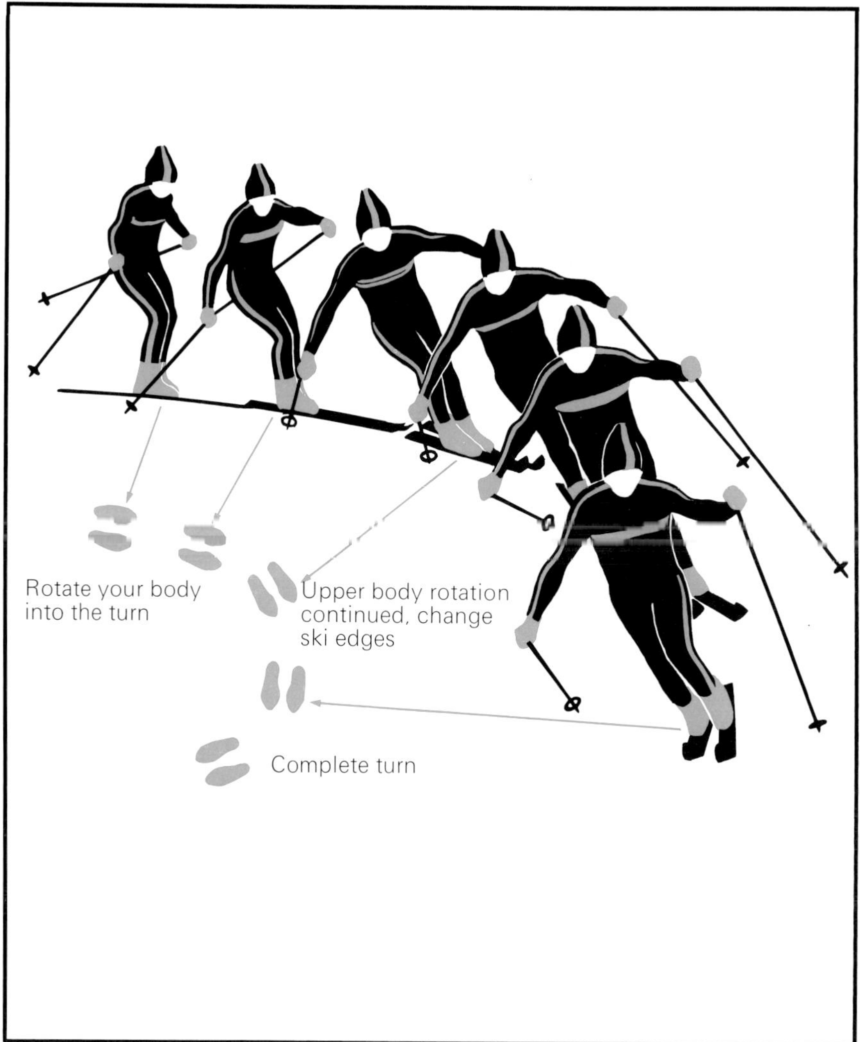

Practice

- The best way to start practising is to do parallel turns with a moderate upward movement.
- Coming out of the schussing position, twist the whole body into a turn (leaning-in position) and steer for some way on your edges.
- Steer the turn uphill, weighting the inside ski.
- Practise several rotation turns in succession, with a graduated increase in speed, on the trail and in deep snow.
- Repeat several turns in succession with a longer radius, on a gentle slope.

Terrain – snow – frequency of turns

Gentle or moderately sloping terrain; good trails can also be tried in deep snow.

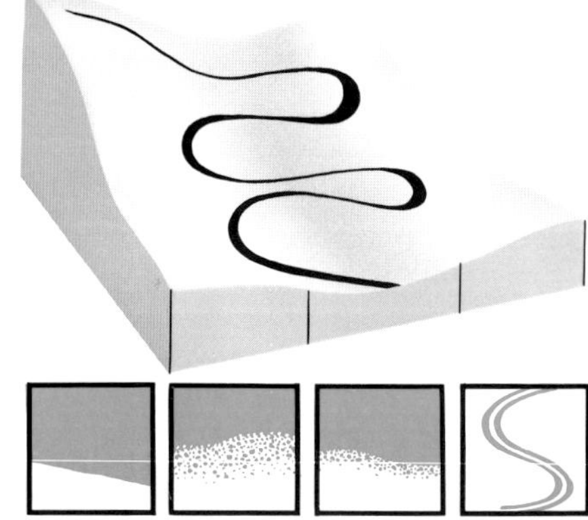

The jet turn

Technique

The jet turn is a favourite among modern forms of turn. The technique comes from racing, where it is often used as a means of acceleration. An expert skier uses jet turns mainly on a bumpy trail, in types of snow where it is difficult to turn, and on steep slopes. The jet movement – a forward push of the skis as you flex down – facilitates the change of edging and the start of the turn.

Begin by going down from an erect position and make the jet movement; this means that you are briefly in a sitting-back position as the turn starts. The upper part of your body is also leaning inwards at the beginning of the turn, a position accentuated by the planting of your pole well out to the side. Each turn is steered by a carefully controlled rotation of the legs.

When you are doing jet turns on a bumpy trail they are performed with a bump-absorbing movement, a useful technique to adopt, as it means you can extend your legs around the bumps.

Note: visually it seems that this is a turn performed in a sitting-back position, but this is not so in terms of the actual movement. The active forward push of the feet in front of the body at the start of the turn automatically leads to a brief moment in which you are sitting back, but this movement must be compensated for as far as possible in the steering phase, i.e., in the course of the turn there is a simultaneous bending-and-stretching movement of the legs vertically and horizontally, with the upper part of the body also moving over sideways to help correct your balance. You should adjust the jetting movement itself to your speed and the terrain.

Practice

- Do a turn uphill with a strong downhill pole-plant, sitting back at the end of the turn, and, using anticipation, twist the tips of your skis downhill.
- Repeat a succession of several such turns in garland form.
- Starting from a traverse position (both skis weighted), do the jet movement and twist your legs. Starting the turn on a bump will help.
- Do a succession of such turns on bumpy terrain.
- Practise jet turns on all types of terrain.

Terrain – snow – frequency of turns

Moderately steep, bumpy terrain; later try the jet turn in deep snow.

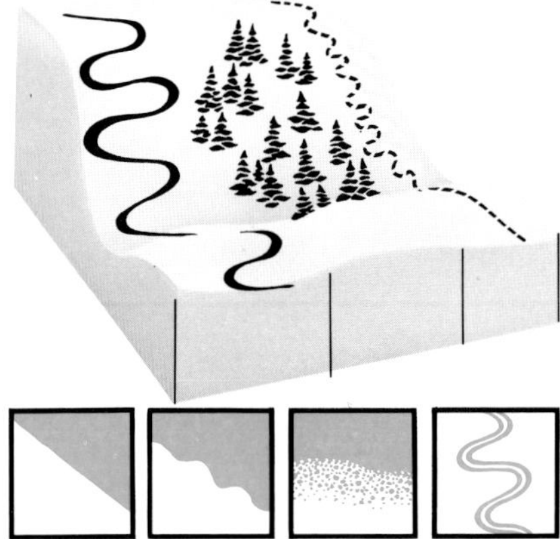

The down-motion turn

The down-motion turn is mainly used on slopes which are icy and have a smooth surface, where it is possible to react quickly and keep in constant contact with the ground.

Technique

Go into the turn by a sink-down motion, in direct contrast to the parallel turn with up-unweighting. The remainder of the turning movement and the steering of your skis occurs as you rise up again.

Approaching in an upright stance, flex the legs quickly, with an active down movement; this is the only way to achieve the unweighting you need to initiate the turn. At the peak moment of unweighting, change your edging and start to rotate. The upward movement, leading to a marked stretching and twisting movement, follows directly on from the downward movement.

The greatest difficulty in this turn is at the beginning, where it depends upon simultaneous down flexing and a change of edging at the peak moment of unweighting. Unlike the parallel turn with up-unweighting, the down-up movement is not a smooth one, but is more sudden and rhythmically different. Similarly, the alternation of unweighting and weighting is technically different, and in the steering phase of the turn there is the danger of edging your skis the wrong way, especially in 'marbled snow'.

Note: after approaching in an upright position, flex downwards fast and start rotating the skis at the moment of greatest unweighting (down-unweighting); begin twisting the legs by changing your edge-set with knees bent. Control the further rotation of your body and the steering of your skis as you rise up. Extend the legs strongly downwards.

Practice

- Start by practising the stretching-and-twisting movement, a 'new' way to steer the skis; turn uphill from a crouching position twisting your legs as you stretch them.
- Do the down-motion turn, planting your poles to left and right, from the fall line and over the fall line.
- Do a succession of turns on a slight gradient, without traversing.
- Do the turns on a steeper slope, accentuating the twist of your legs in the crouching position. Control the stretching-and-twisting movement according to the suitability of the terrain and your speed to the steering of your turn.

Terrain – snow – frequency of turns

Gently sloping trails, or well-prepared practice slopes. Later, try the turn on moderately steep slopes with a smooth surface, which is hard rather than soft.

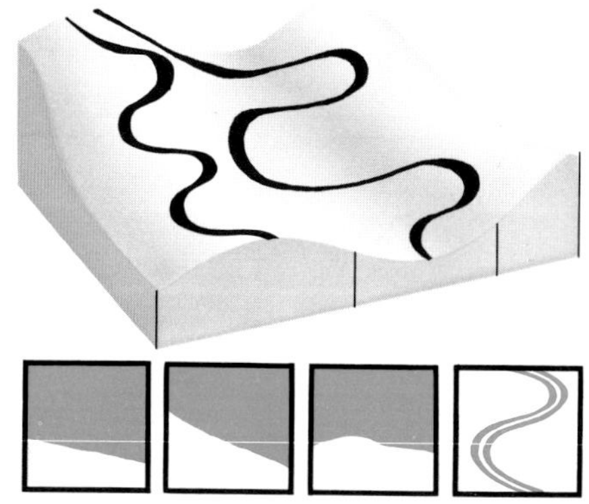

The inner ski turn

The inner ski turn is another artistic variant of turns involving weight transfer.

Until recently inner ski turns were only in the repertoire of expert stylists, but it is now known that almost all good skiers sometimes do certain turns in what would have been considered an 'incorrect' way in the classic sense (i.e., skiing on the inside ski), during competitive skiing, especially the slalom and free-style skiing. First and most important, this turn is good for your technical expertise, the feel for edges and your sense of balance. It has its place in the training programme of all athletically-inclined skiers. There are several forms of turn executed on the inside ski. One of the smoothest is the inside ski turn on one leg, on alternate sides.

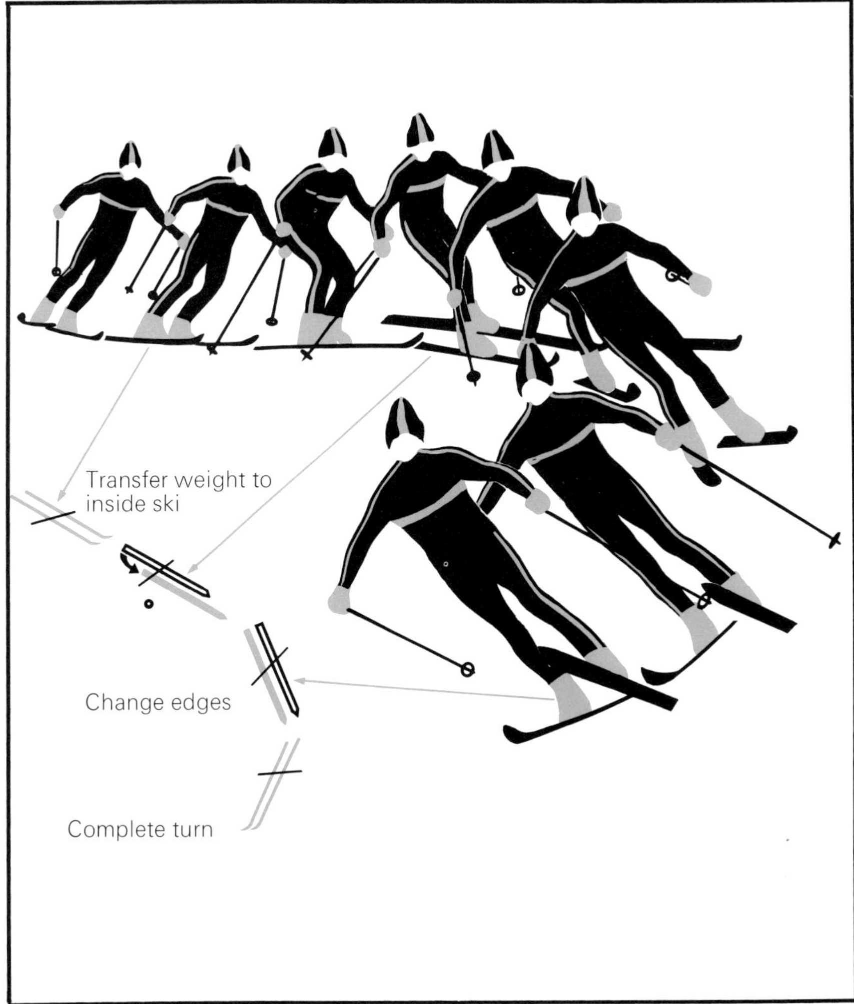

Technique

During the steering phase of the preceding turn, the inside ski has more and more weight placed on it. Before reaching the fall line transfer weight to the new inside ski. The change of weighting and of edging and the start of your twist round are combined with a marked tilt of the upper part of the body in the new direction of the turn (leaning inwards); as you do this you can partly raise the ski on the outside of the curve off the snow. In the steering phase any wobbling can be compensated for by a yielding bend of the leg on which you are standing. The shorter the radius of the turn, the faster the pushing-off movement. Inside ski turns performed in quick succession are called 'charleston turns'.

Note: each turn is performed by the transfer of weight from one inside ski to the next. The landing must be on the outer edge (important for your pushing-off movement). The rhythm is similar to that of the short swing.

Practice

- A skating step is useful as a preliminary form of practice.
- Next start doing a turn on the inside ski out of a downhill run, raising the outside ski.
- Now try hopping carefully from one inside ski to the next as you run more slowly downhill.
- Do a rhythmical succession of alternate turns close to the fall line.
- Do variations of inside ski turns, with differing radius and speed, and without raising the outside ski.

Terrain – snow – frequency of turns

First on a slightly sloping trail, then on any kind of terrain.

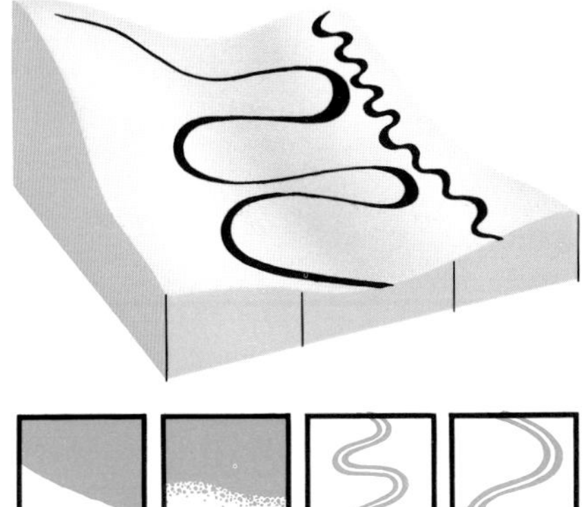

The racing step turn

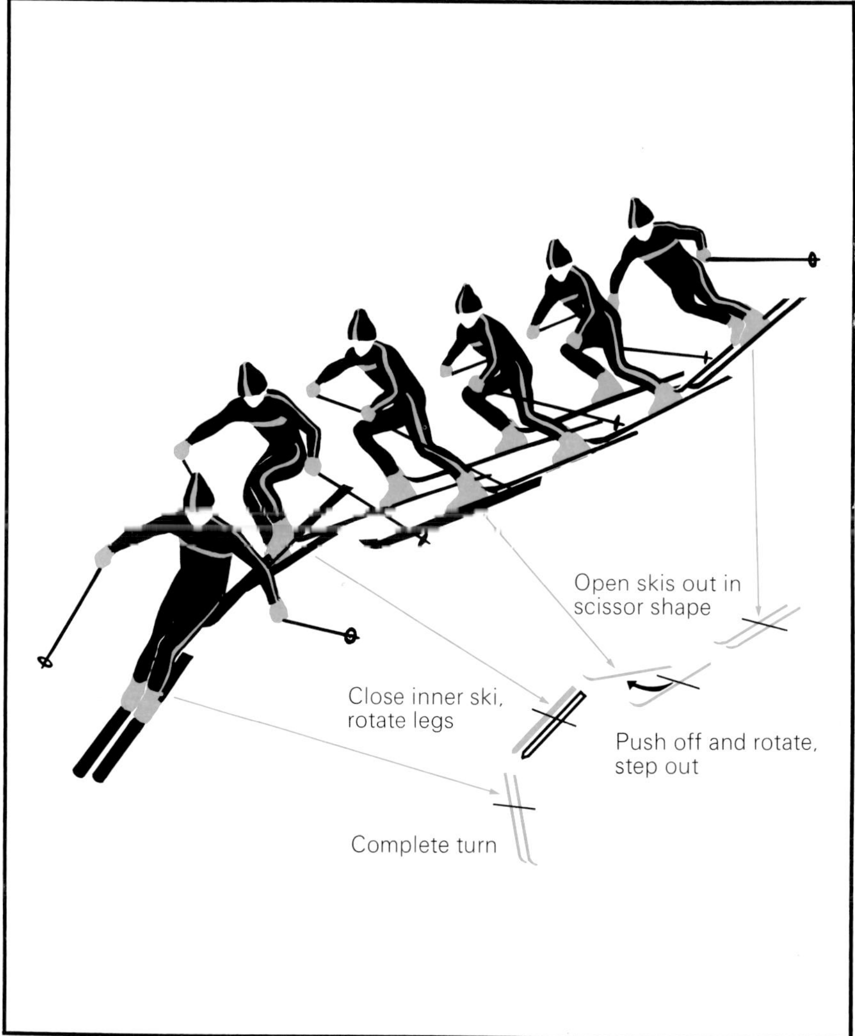

Technique

The step turn is familiar as a kind of turn involving stepping out, especially in racing technique. This form of athletic step turn can easily be learnt from trained skiers. The decisive phase of the movement in this turn is the scissor-like opening of the skis before pushing off. This distinguishes it from other forms of turn involving stepping across.

Even for athletic skiers, it is an extremely useful variant of such turns on fairly level stretches. From a steep approach, the turn is steered uphill and away from the fall line by the scissor-like opening of the skis. As you step out the angled ski, push off and rotate strongly from the outside ski (acceleration of speed), the movement taking you forwards and sideways. Then close the ski from which you have pushed off and place it parallel with the other.

The second part of the turn is an ordinary parallel turn in which you rotate your legs and increase the edge-set in the steering phase.

Note: after steering the turn with increased edge-set, go into the next turn with the uphill scissor movement. Push off and twist strongly forwards and sideways off the edge of your lower ski from a low position, and step out your upper ski (acceleration).

Bring your other ski up parallel and tilt over your edges, rotating your legs. The pushing-off-and-twisting movement must follow smoothly on from the pushing-off movement and take you into the curve of the manoeuvre. Transferring your weight and twisting the skis while weighted allows your edges to get a good grip.

The free movement of your legs increases your ability to react and gives you a better sense of security on steep slopes. To do the turn perfectly you must have well-trained leg muscles, as well as an extremely good feel for your edges.

Practice

There are two things to be practised first:

1. The scissoring movement
2. The pushing-off and twisting movement

- As preliminary practice do skating steps and describe curves out of the fall line on a gentle slope (training for the scissor-like angling of the skis and the thrusting movement).
- Start with a step turn out of an approach in the fall line; practise single turns to left and to right.
- Change your angle of approach progressively into a traverse. This will automatically increase the radius of the turn.
- Do a succession of several stepping turns on a slight slope, controlling your increase of acceleration. Let the skis slide properly in the steering phase.
- Do step turns, actively transferring your weight.

1

2

3

4

- Do step turns through gates (training for giant slalom). A short, fast variant of the stepping turn used in the slalom is the so-called *scissor turn*. It is the technique chiefly used by slalom racers for off-set vertical gates.

Skiing exercises

- Pushing off and stepping across: the best way to train is to do skating-style jumps in a slightly crouched position.
- Scissor step turn: from a traverse position, angle out one leg to the side, toes pointing outwards, push off, step out the angled leg, bring up the other leg into new traverse position, crouch down.
- As a preliminary, practise taking steps with alternate angling of the legs. Start with wide steps, then take long ones.

Terrain – snow – frequency of turns

Almost level terrain is ideal at the start. Later do the turn on a moderately steep slope with a good gripping surface which is hard rather than soft.

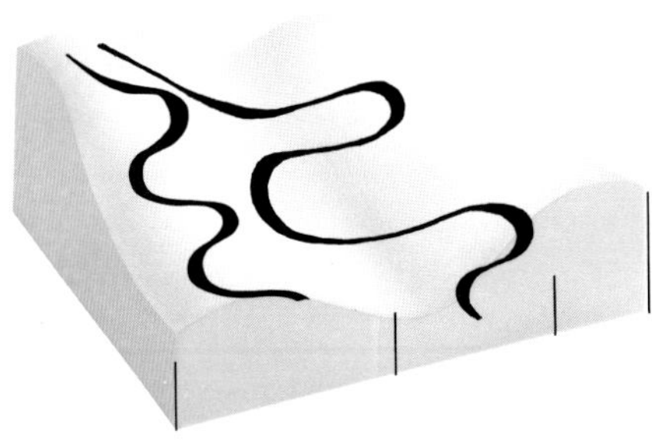

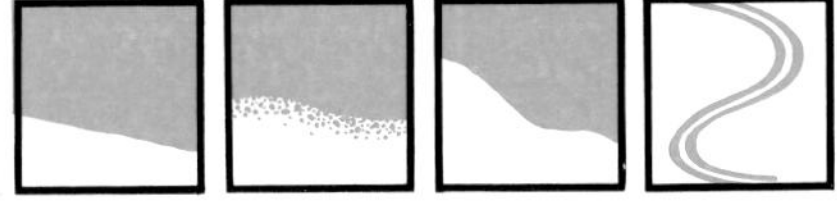

Some frequent mistakes

In the course of skiing, every skier develops a style of his own: his personal technique and movements. In order to perform a given movement in the right way, as previously shown in the various kinds of turns, you will need to have a mental image of the movement, i.e., know in your own mind how the movement can be executed.

Recognizing and correcting your own mistakes is a very different matter. Once the faults are recognized and their reason known they can generally be corrected.

Experts use a technique called 'seeing a movement'. Coaches with sufficient experience and imagination can project the current 'mental image' sequence on to the movement actually performed. Then they can see where the skier is departing from the ideal sequence of movements, assess his mistakes and set them right. One must start by concentrating on the general impression of the movement, and only then on its component parts. There are three things to look out for:

- Development of the movement, i.e., departures from the 'ideal' technique.
- Timing of the movement, i.e., rhythm (acceleration, delay).
- Force of the movement, i.e., at what point greatest force is applied (too early or too late).

Generally, the things that can affect a skier's form (and with it, his sense of security) so that he begins to doubt his ability are usually minor matters and bad habits. If you feel there is something wrong, do not give up at once: take a look at the following pictures of common faults. You may see yourself among them.

These are the faults most commonly observed (rather exaggeratedly described, as being positively 'wrong'), and they can easily be corrected.

Many faults arise from a bad skiing position. The more relaxed your position the better. Ankle, knee and hip joints should be slightly flexed so that unevennesses in the terrain can be absorbed by bending and stretching. A central position is always the safest, for beginners and experts alike. Your skis are evenly weighted, your body centred over them. Keep checking up on your basic position and correcting it.

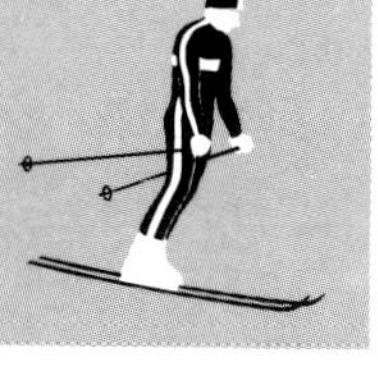

1. Basic position
Too upright: stretched position.
Too low: crouching position.

2. Weighting
Too little weighting of the front of the skis: sitting too far back.
Too little weighting of the back of the skis: leaning too far forward.
Bad: pressing your downhill knee into the back of your uphill knee when traversing. Result: knock-kneed position as you traverse, uneven edging, knee joints bending unequally.

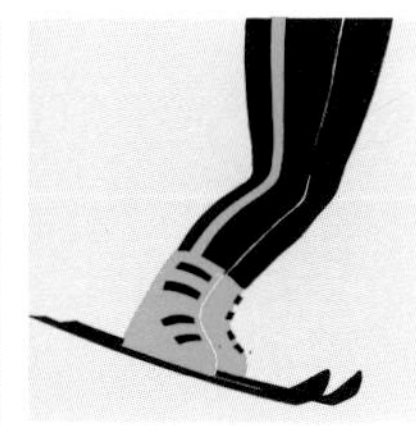

Better: keep knees side by side.

3. Ski control
Knees too far in: knock-kneed position.
Knees too far out: bandy-legged position.

4. Position of the head
Bad: looking down at your skis while skiing. Result: incorrect stance, inability to see ahead, dangerous on trails.
Better: keep looking the way you are going.

5. Position of your arms
Bad: arms stretching downwards. Result: leads to a cramped style, in-

adequate movement of the legs, too much movement of the trunk, difficulty in keeping your balance at higher speeds.
Better: keep the arms slightly forwards and to the side of the hips.

6. Planting your poles
Bad: exaggerated forward swing. Result: delay in the pole-planting, pole planted too close to the ski, hindering the skier instead of giving support, often leading to twisting the outside hip too far, insufficient edging.
Better: plant the poles with the lower part of the arm facing slightly downhill, out to your side between the tip of the ski and the tip of your boot at the moment of edging.

7. Initiating a turn
Bad: stiff legs, too little movement of the knees, upper part of the body bent forwards. Result: difficulty in initiating the turn since there is not enough unweighting. Poor edging, since you can only move the knees sideways to edge the skis in combination with a forward movement.
Better: an active downward movement, bringing the knees forwards and sideways.

8. Controlling a turn
Bad: leaning over into the curve as you turn. Result: turning too far, insufficient edge grip, poor steering. Danger of tilting the inside edge too far, risk of falling.
Better: counter-rotate the hips as you flex down. Bend the upper part of the body forwards and sideways. Keep the upper part of the body facing downhill.

9. Turning
Bad: sitting back and weighting the ends of your skis as you cross the fall line at the beginning of the turn and during the turn itself.
Result: weighting the ends of the skis makes it harder to turn them, the skis may slip away and go out of control, leading to edging the wrong way and crossing the tips of the skis; a common cause of an unintentional stop-turn.

Better: keep to a central position as much as you can – if anything, lean forward slightly; saves strength and is safer. The sitting-back position is only for brief use to save your balance in emergency.

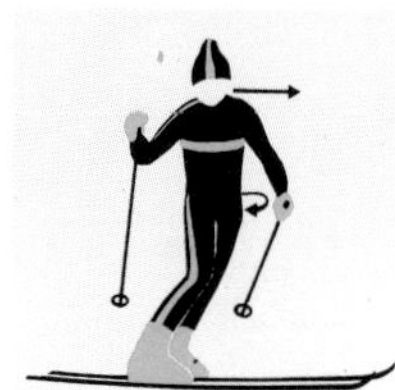

10. Anticipation
Anticipation plays an important part in skiing. It means starting a turn by rotating the uphill hip in the direction of the turn itself. The movement is transferred to the thighs and knees and brings the skis flat, making it easier to change their edging.
Bad: rotating the outside hip forward, head looking back, as preparation for the following turn. Result: incorrect anticipation, making it harder to go into the turn, no fluid transition from turn to turn.
Better: rotating the uphill hip in the direction of the next turn (only as far as the fall line), marked rotation of the legs, with a fluid change edging, head facing the way you are going, looking for the right place to turn, well-controlled turns.

11. Turning
Bad: keeping your skis too close together when you are a beginner. Result: difficulty in keeping your balance, exaggerated, uncontrolled and useless movements of arms and trunk, insecurity.
Better: keep your skis further apart for more security and controlled skiing.

Practical skiing

Skiing technique today means first and foremost a functional style of skiing which will give you security – security means you can act in the right way in your everyday skiing.

Practical skiing means a functional way of using your skis in the right way for any situation that you may come across, with due regard to the basic knowledge of skiing technique. Skiing technique itself may be a fairly complicated subject, and is in a constant process of development, but on the whole skiing problems really remain much the same.

Every skier should aim to be able to ski on any kind of terrain, within his own ability, without falling. So skiers must learn to be adaptable, always keeping an eye open for the constantly changing conditions of terrain and snow they may encounter.

To do that yoù need plenty of experience, not just in respect of skiing technique, but in assessing the make-up of various terrains and judging the snow conditions.

It is only through practical skiing that every skier develops the ability to react safely and rapidly to different situations, and develops it to the extent he needs.

Skiing technique

Both the challenge and the difficulty of skiing arise from having to pay attention to several different things at the same time. Here is an example:

A skier is coming down a moderately steep slope, doing basic swings; the slope is considerably broken by bumps (result of the local terrain) and rutted by tracks (result of new snow). As he goes downhill he has to bear the following things in mind, sometimes all at once, sometimes in an overlapping sequence:

- Guilding the skis parallel in alternating directions, angling them out into the snowplough position, bringing them back parallel. The changing position of the skis is accompanied by a down-up-down movement of the legs.
- The changing position of the skis brings with it a change in the relationship of different parts of the ski to the snow (edging).
- As well as executing movements of this kind with his legs, the skier has to keep his upper body in a certain position, and has to plant his ski pole at a certain moment.
- At the same time he has to observe the terrain and adjust his speed and the radius of his turns to it, take into consideration the type of snow present as well as keep an eye open for other skiers, so as to avoid collisions. On top of all this he also has to keep his balance.

This example shows that the co-ordination of all these movements, actions and observations is a lot to ask of a beginner or an inexperienced skier, so that failures and mistakes are quite likely to occur. The result is:

- Fear and insecurity.
- Defensive reactions of one kind or another – mostly the wrong kind.
- Physically, an inhibited style; mentally, tension.
- The possible danger of injury arising from falls, particularly if other factors such as bad weather (snowfalls, poor visibility in mist), overcrowded trails and so on are present at the same time.

Many skiers find their reactions are particularly negative on a crowded trial. If they then encounter unexpected obstacles in the terrain, a situation arises which generally inhibits or diminishes the skier's ability to act correctly.

But there are certain dangers which threaten even an experienced skier. Many people think that with so many different kinds of turns being taught in ski instruction schemes, they have to learn as many of them as possible.

What you really need is to have an idea in your own mind of how to adapt the turns learnt during ski instruction to the terrain, snow, your speed, the frequency of your turns, the position of your skis and the way you control them – before you can judge which turn is the best to use in what terrain and in what kind of snow.

There are many different ways of dealing with different conditions. Many techniques are equally useful, and differ only slightly from each other. They do not all, by any means, offer a guarantee of good skiing over every kind of terrain.

Once you have learnt the basic

Technique		Beginners	Advanced	Experts	Racers
Basic technique	Snowplough, snowplough turn	2	0		
	Traversing, side-slipping	2	2	1	0
	Basic swing	3	2	1	1
Step turns	**Step-up turns involving weight transfer**				
	With downhill stemming	1	3	3	2
	With uphill stemming	1	2	1	1
	Parallel open and closed	0	3	3	2
	With accelerating push-off movement	0	1	3	3
	Scissoring movement uphill	0	0	2	3
	Scissoring movement downhill	0	0	2	3
Parallel turns	**Turns with up-unweighting**				
	Parallel turn	0	2	3	2
	Short swing	0	2	3	3
	Rotation turn	0	1	1	2
	Turns with down-unweighting				
	Bump-absorbing compression turn	0	1	3	3
	Parallel down-unweighting	0	1	2	3
	Jet turn	0	0	3	3

0 = not applicable 1 = possible 2 = important 3 = intensive

techniques, step-up turns and parallel turns of various kinds, you have a fair amount of technical knowledge, but you are not really a skier until you have got past the nursery slopes and learnt how to apply the movements to different terrain in different conditions – and, most important, how to do so safely. People used to put style first, but these days it has given way to more functional considerations.

Experience shows that some techniques and turns are not equally good for every stage of ability in learning to ski. For example, a racer would not use a stem turn and a beginner would find little application for a stepped, carved turn.

The above table is intended to show the general reader how to apply the movements and turns described in this book. Taking the forms of turn described in the ski instruction programme of the previous chapter as a starting point, it is suggested that you now practise them as shown in this table.

The following qualification should be made: the table is drawn up for regular skiers of normal talent, in good training.

What turns and technique do you need to know?

So far as safe skiing is concerned, the average skier does not need to know all the turns mentioned in this table. It is more worthwhile to concentrate on a small number of techniques. The photographs show five techniques which would, at a pinch, see you through any situation and get you safely down the mountain, whether you have to deal with gentle or steep slopes, ice, packed trail or deep snow, good weather, snowfalls or mist.

Row 1 Basic swing.
Row 2 Traversing, side-slipping.
Row 3 Parallel turn.
Row 4 Bump-absorbing (compression) turn.
Row 5 Twisting and hopping round (jump-turn)

1
2
3
4
5

Characteristics

Bad skier	Good skier
Always skis with the same turn frequency	Adjusts the frequency of turns to the terrain
Unweights too much or too little when flexing or thrusting	Controls up-unweighting, has a preference for down-unweighting
Does not plant poles accurately	Uses poles well to support himself and help turn
Uncontrolled change of edging	Progressive change of edges
Often gets skis at the wrong angle	Controls turns well
Always uses the same leg movement	Varies his leg movement to the circumstances; alternates between leg movement on both legs (parallel turns) and on one leg (step turns)
Unco-ordinated leg and trunk movements	Good co-ordination between legs and trunk
Uses too much strength	Skis more sensitively, concentrating on skis, edges and poles
Makes long traverses	Skis near the fall line
Skis over bumps	Skis round bumps, into the dips
Sets edges clumsily at the beginning of a turn	Sets edges with precision
Often finds himself airborne	Keeps in contact with the snow, even on bumpy terrain
Skids frequently when steering turns	Carves turns
Skis too fast and insecurely	Skis in a controlled, secure style
Cannot brake in time	Can stop quickly at any moment
Skis in an 'angular' way	Skis in a 'rounded' way
Skis without control	Controls movements
Has difficulty keeping balance	Keeps correcting balance
Often stops	Keeps on the move for long periods
Gets annoyed when skiing; is not really master of any technique	Enjoys skiing. Has mastered the most important techniques
Skis with legs in a fixed crouch	Does not get tired so soon, is well loosened up

Characteristics

Bad skier	Good skier
Is out of condition, has stiff muscles and cramp after skiing	Keeps varying the flexing movement of legs (tension – relaxation)
Twists joints too far when turning	Makes controlled and moderate movements of the joints
Usually skis leaning inwards and sitting back	Suits the position of his body to the terrain
Often skis in the snowplough position	Avoids skiing in the snowplough position
Forces his technique on the terrain, fights the terrain	Looks for the right kind of terrain for the turns he wants to make
Avoids difficult terrain on principle	Ventures into difficult terrain from time to time
Does not recognize own faults	Learns from mistakes

Emergency braking

However good his technique, a skier should always keep safety in mind. So one important question to ask yourself is: can I stop quickly if some obstacle suddenly appears?

Here are a few exercises to practise, to help improve your skiing technique:

Beginners
Slow down your speed with the snowplough when schussing downhill and by side-slipping when traversing. Increase the set of your edges as you do so, and you will come to a well-controlled stop.
Practice: alternate rhythmically between a narrow and a wide angle in the snowplough. Alternate between schussing and the snowplough downhill. Starting from a traverse, side-slip to get the skis across the fall line. Side-slip edging and flattening the skis several times. Practise the movement on both sides.

Intermediate skiers
The best way to brake is to stem downhill for a short braking movement, and to do an uphill turn for a longer, controlled braking movement.
Practice: do uphill turns. Do step-up turns, stemming the downhill ski.

Experts
Control your speed on steep slopes by short turns after the fall line, pushing off with one leg or both legs. If you have to brake suddenly, it will often be sufficient to put strong sideways pressure briefly on the strongly edged outside ski before a new turn. This is called broadening your track.
Practice: do short turns in steep terrain with a marked horizontal placing of the skis and increased edging. Do short turns in the direction of the traverse. Practise often on steep, hard trails and in bumpy terrain. Try coming out of a schuss covering as little ground as possible as your turn off. Practise a good, safe 'stopping turn'.

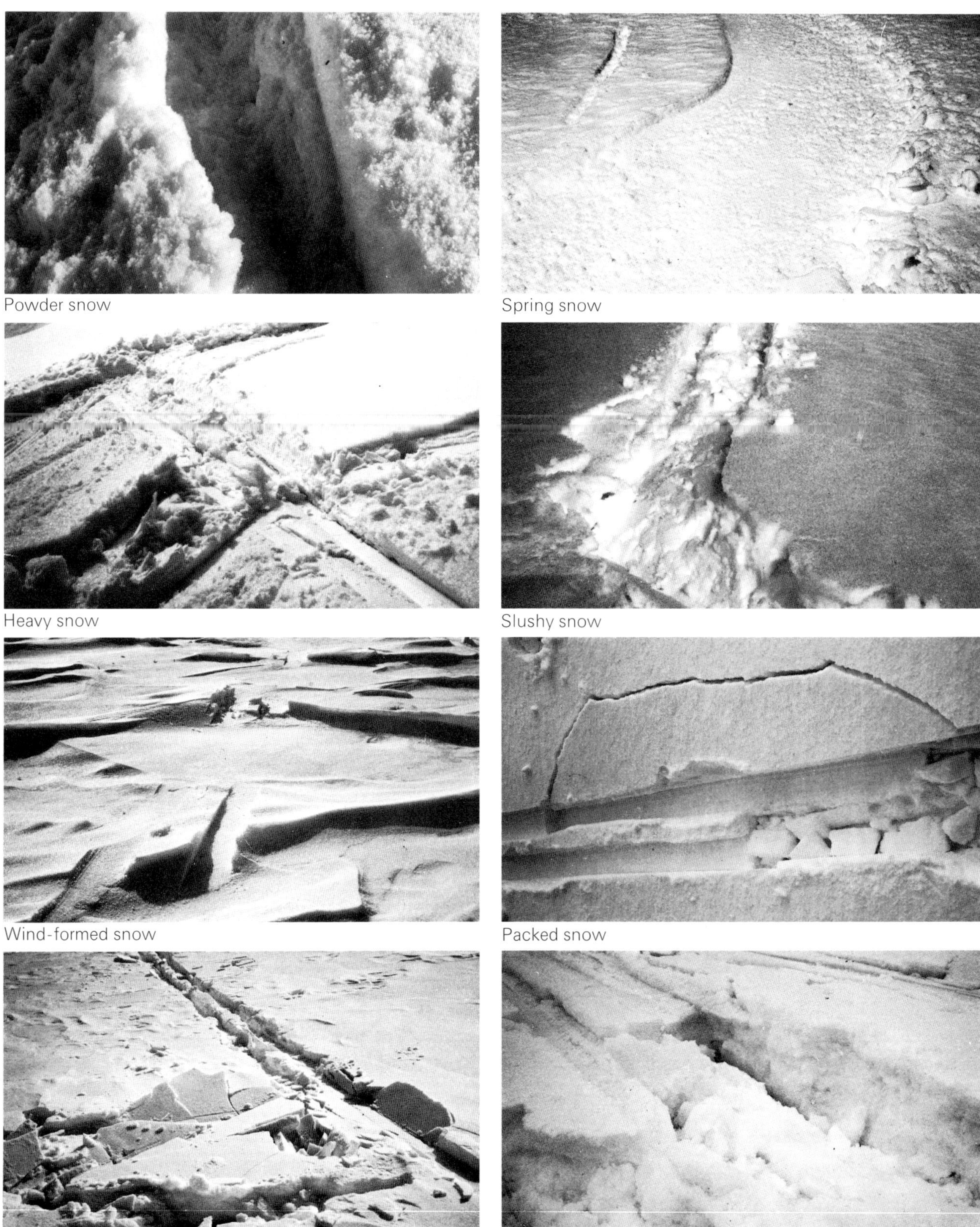

Powder snow

Spring snow

Heavy snow

Slushy snow

Wind-formed snow

Packed snow

Crusted snow

Rotten snow

Snow and terrain

In cities, snow means cold and wet. To skiers, snow is a substance of almost infinite variety, and there are many factors which can influence its character:

- Sun and shade
- Wind and mist
- Temperature
- Height above sea level
- Time of day
- Season of the year
- Depth of snow
- Situation and inclination of the slope.

Ski trails will vary accordingly, and you should learn to analyse the type of snow and adjust your skiing technique to it. In general, you can distinguish between the following types of snow:

New snow: snow which has fallen within the last twenty-four hours.

Old snow: snow which has a different structure, due to its having settled (and other influences), one to two days after it fell as new snow.

Powder snow: loose new snow which has fallen at temperatures below freezing.

Packed snow: new snow pressed together by the wind. Formation of wind slabs.

Heavy snow: snow with a high moisture content. Occurs when snow falls at around freezing point. Sticky!

Corn or spring snow: old snow in the spring, with a coarse, granulated structure.

Crust: snow which has formed a hard surface from repeated freezing and thawing and the influence of wind pressure. A dangerous sliding surface under newly fallen snow!

Rotten or slushy snow: spring snow which is thawed by the sun in the daytime. Heavy going.

There are halfway or transitional forms between these kinds of snow, which may or may not increase the skier's pleasure, according to the way the trail is groomed. And even a good skier must keep re-adjusting to the snow.

Groomed trails are safer

Groomed trails are always safer! Although more and more skiers are coming up the slopes by lift or cable car every year, the biggest drop off in the number of injuries was observed when the trails started to be groomed by machines and cleared of dangerous obstacles. This fact is not so self-evident as it may at first appear. Experts on safety in the various Alpine countries have argued quite strongly over the question: the opponents of groomed trails argued that broad and supposedly safe trails in the big winter sports' resorts were also more conducive to uncontrolled speeding downhill. This so-called 'highway effect' has not, havever, been so noticeable as was previously supposed.

In spite of good mechanical preparation of the trails, however, you may still find conditions unpleasant when skiing. While a freshly rolled cold powder snow trail is soft as a carpet to ski on, rolling at an air temperature of about 32°F(0°C) after a great deal of new snow can get it into a state resembling miniature cobblestones, and you will not be able to ski comfortably on it.

Skiing is equally uncomfortable when deep tracks, ruts and furrows in slushy snow freeze hard overnight. Ice and snow together are a treacherous combination, and can spoil a good day's skiing. The danger is not so much that the skier will break his legs, but that he will hurt himself when he falls, and strain himself in trying to control his skis again.

The most typical 'leg-breaking' snow is usually new snow which has turned so heavy and mushy because of rain or a rise in temperature that if you happen to fall (and your binding does not release), your ski dives into it and cannot be freed.

Skiing is also dangerous when there is only a thinnish layer of snow on rocky ground, and roots or branches can catch a ski. In these conditions you should ski slowly, as you should on scanty snow cover in the spring.

Mechanically groomed trails can have their disadvantages, so be careful, especially when they have just been rolled!

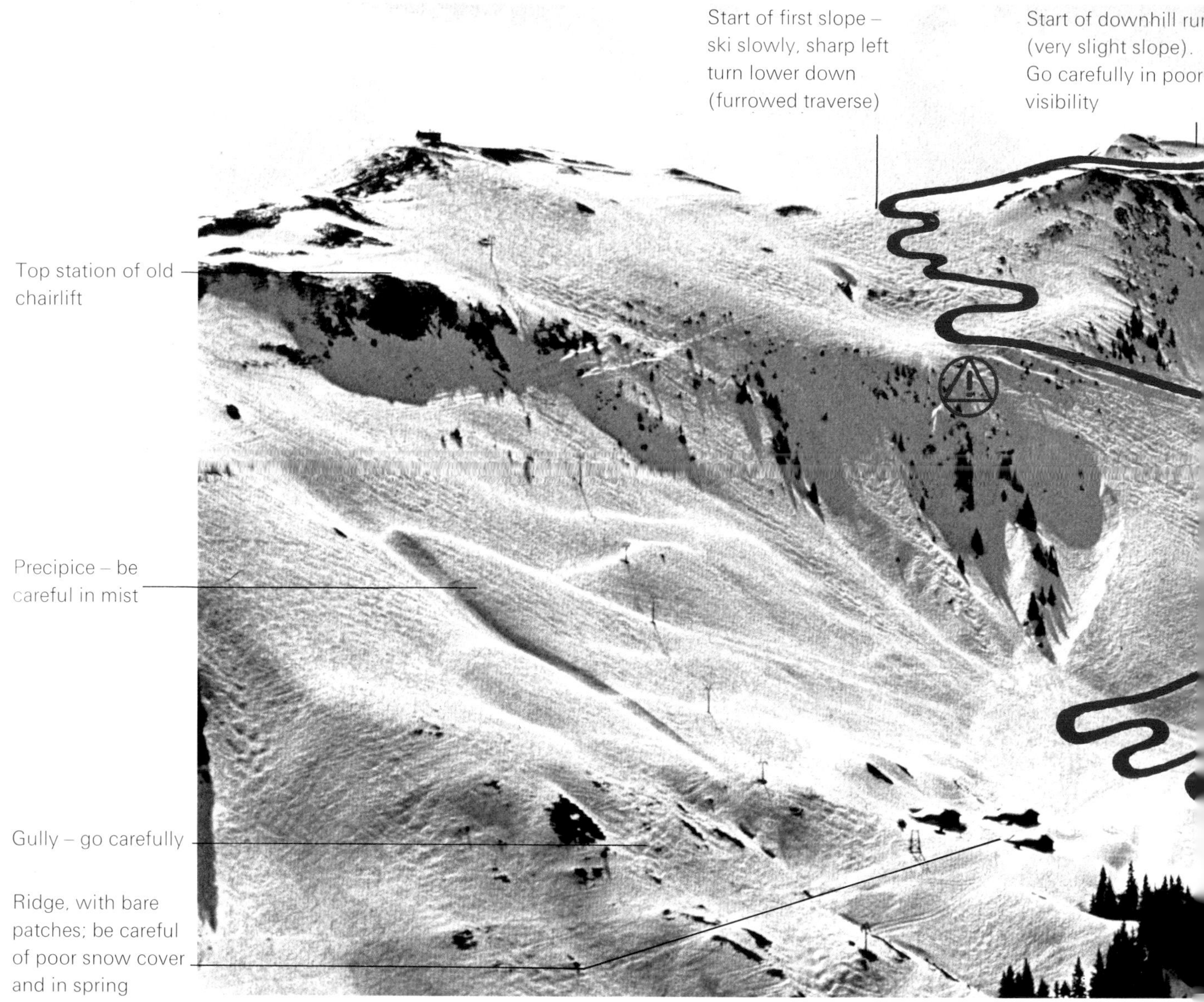

Analysing the terrain

Our aim is not merely to have some interesting skiing, but to become safer and more circumspect skiers.

Try to develop a sixth sense for the lie of the land. The photomontage above shows how this can be done.

Scene: the classic skiing region of the Hahnenkamm at Kitzbühel in the Austrian Tirol, which skiers first see from this angle.

The following five points should be checked:

1. Study trail maps showing the lifts, the trail links, the different routes, the difficulty of the runs, and information about lift passes and prices.
2. What are the predominant snow conditions? Snow conditions can change according to the height above sea level, the way the slope faces, the air temperature, the weather, wind, clouds, mist, sun, time of year, number of skiers using the slopes, the timberline, grooming of the runs, substructure of the runs.
3. Where is the nearest first-aid post (which will have a telephone) and where can you find a place to stop for rest and refreshment?
4. What special obstacles can you notice, for example, precipices or gullies, and what landmarks are visible which will help you to orientate yourself, for example,

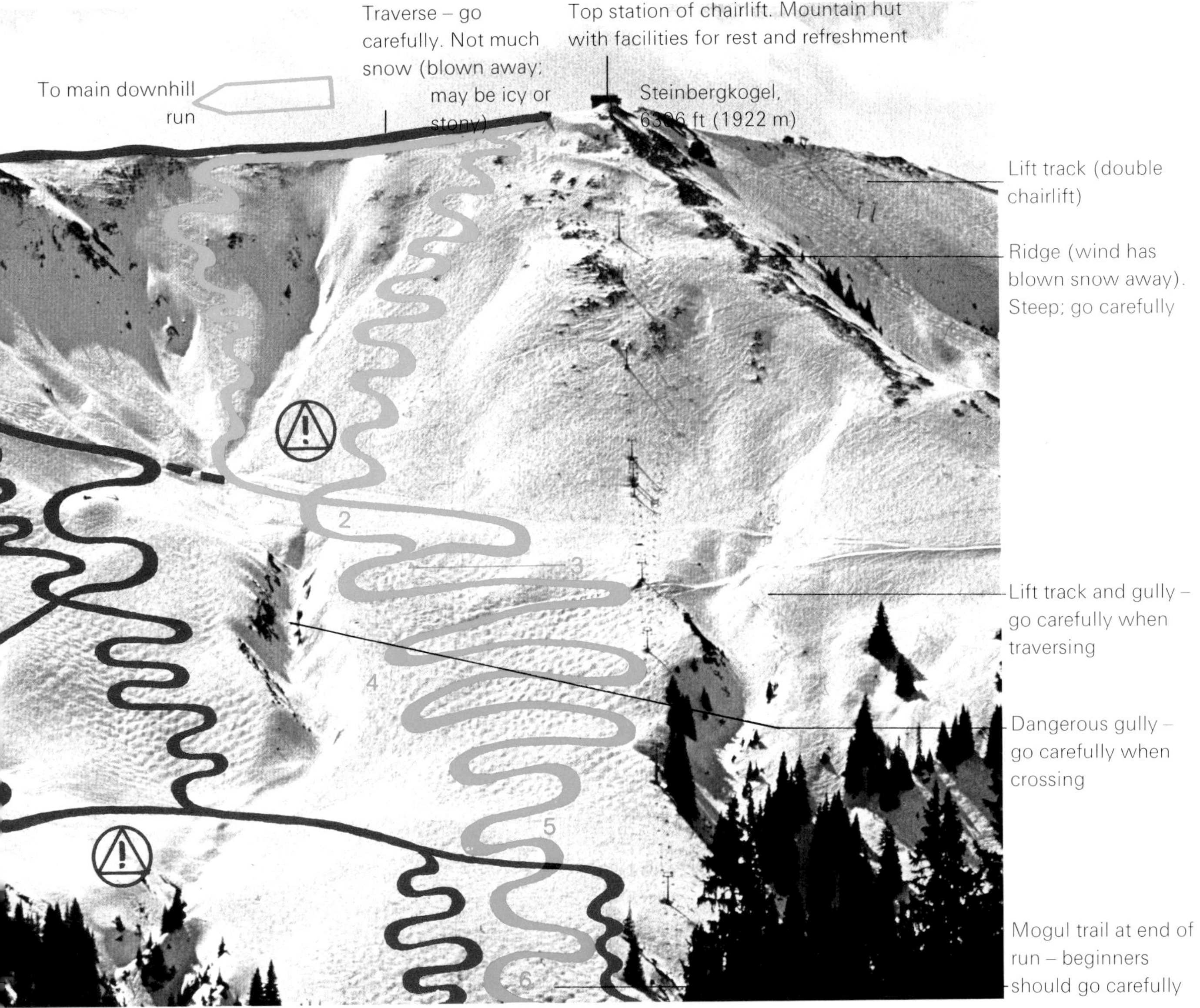

lift tracks, mountain huts or forested areas?

5. What markings, warning signs and notices of prohibition, for example, 'Avalanche Danger' must one look out for?

You might then make a detailed analysis of the terrain, as has been done above.

Analysing the downhill runs

The problem points to notice are:

1. A very steep, dangerous starting slope, risk of encountering wind slab areas (cornices formed by the wind).
2. A possibly dangerous traverse if skiers higher up the mountain set off an avalanche. Do not linger at this point.
3. Careful – downhill run crossing from the left. Watch out for other skiers crossing your path.
4. Be careful of the gully; do not ski too near its edge.
5. Careful – downhill run crossing from the right. Watch out for other skiers crossing your path.
6. Careful – slope becomes steeper. The run becomes narrower; moguls are larger and closer.

Skiing on trails

There are other aspects of practical skiing to be thought of, besides the basic facts about the snow and terrain. A knowledge of the trail rules is essential, as well as using the lifts correctly and understanding the trail signs. In the course of time experience will teach you to recognize dangerous places, distinguish between easy and difficult or dangerous sections, to behave sensibly in bad weather and so on.

Most skiers are so concerned about themselves as they ski that they generally fail to notice the changing aspect of the terrain, the alternation of sections in sunlight and in shade, trail markers and landmarks. It is essential to keep your head up and your eyes looking forward on the trail! Just as a driver develops a kind of 'sixth sense' in the course of time, a good skier should become used to taking in, and interpreting, the terrain at a glance. Many skiers shoot blindly downhill and it is for this reason that accidents occur because the run turned out to be too difficult, or the skier did not register the danger points. Most accident victims are not even able to give a clear description of conditions on the trail, let alone the difficulty and geographical features of the run on which they were skiing.

Here are some hints to help you use the trails in the right way:

- Get to know the international trail rules and the trail signs. Learn the correct way to use lifts, and how to keep clear of vehicles on the trail.
- When buying your ski equipment, remember to keep the safety essentials in mind, and remember to keep checking the functioning of your ski bindings as recommended in the IAS table (p.35).
- Always bear in mind the possible risk your clothing may represent as you are skiing. Your outer clothing should be slip-resistant.
- Warm up your chilled muscles by doing some exercises before you start skiing downhill. A quarter of all skiing accidents happen during the first part of the descent and are caused by 'starting cold'.
- Many skiing incidents are caused by skiing too fast, poor skiing technique, and failure to judge situations and one's own powers of reaction. The risk of accident can be reduced by skiing safely, improving your technique and by behaving carefully on the trail.
- Pay particular attention to signs indicating dangerous or close areas: look out for gullies, holes, bare patches, precipices, rocks, bridges, narrow passages.
- Find out the grade of the runs.
- If necessary (with children and timid skiers) ask the lift staff to slow down the lift as skiers get on or off.
- Unfortunately there are still some lifts (mostly button lifts) which carry the skier away too fast. Usually they are of the self-service type. Avoid lifts like these if you do not feel up to the situation. Be careful with children.
- Before you start, ask the lift attendant if the lift tracks are icy or rutted.
- When waiting for the lift, if the place where you are waiting does not seem safe watch out for skiers coming towards the lift too fast, so as to avoid a collision.
- Even when riding up on a ski-tow collisions with other skiers are possible. Look out for other skiers to left and right of the ski tracks who could endanger you if they fell. In particular, watch out for the would-be wedel stylists who like to perform close to the lifts, especially after falls of new snow.
- If you are skiing in a group or as a family, you should always stop at the end of the run below your partner or the person standing lowest down in the group.
- Many accidents happen at the beginning of the day, or during the last runs of the day when the skier may be overtired or the trail icy and more dangerous after sunset. Skiing accidents are particularly common on the third day of a holiday, when performance tends to reach a 'low'. Consider having a rest day.
- Children are in particular danger on the trail. They may often be physically fitter than adults, but they usually have less staying power or concentration.
- Alpine racing often tempts young people, or spectators who ski, to emulate the racers' aggressive style. Everyone should realize that the style of a top-class racer is combined with a high, though calculated risk factor.
- You should be particularly careful when there are warning notices telling you of the presence of trail-grooming vehicles on the slope. These vehicles are usually painted brightly and have blinking lights.
- Keep as safe a distance as you can between yourself and these vehicles. A skier can get out of the way

of a vehicle more easily than the other way round.

- Brightly coloured ski jackets and ski pants are not only fashionable, but also safer. Skiers wearing bright colours are more easily seen by other skiers.

- If there is not much snow on trails and slopes you must be especially careful. A fall on ice or hard crust can lead to nasty abrasions and bruises, when normally no harm would result on soft snow. Hard, icy trails are often very difficult for less experienced skiers. All skiers should get into the habit of wearing some form of head covering. An ordinary woollen hat can be a sensible form of protection.

- The skiers in most danger are beginners and those who try to show off. It is easy to explain and excuse this fact where beginners are concerned and it usually arises from lack of experience. Often they do not know how much they are capable of, and venture on downhill runs which they should have avoided. But above-average skiers are a different matter. They may be trying to show their expertise and too often overestimate their abilities and reach speeds where they are no longer in control.

- A skier who is determined to have a record number of descents under his belt is in particular danger. Even if a skier is reluctant to admit it, fatigue and loss of concentration are frequent causes of incidents. Do you want to be another accident statistic?

Even a lift track is not immune from avalanches as this wind-slab slide shows. It was started by the ski track above the lift.

◂ Shade on the north side – sun on the south side. The snow will not stay powdery so long on the south-facing slope in the northern hemisphere.

Every skiing region is different, according to its height above sea level, the nature of the terrain and the snow. Winters in the northern hemisphere high-mountain areas such as the Alps and the Rocky Mountains follow a certain definite pattern. ▸

Factors influencing snow conditions

A beginner naturally finds it hard to adapt himself to changing snow conditions, and to cope with trails in some of the conditions already described. His dream of skiing can rapidly become a nightmare. But every skier must go through this experience once in a skiing lifetime.

It is a good idea to learn about the factors influencing snow conditions.

The three main factors are:

- time of year
- height above sea level of the skiing area
- direction the slope faces

All three mutually influence each other, and according to the location of a ski resort they give rise to its prevailing conditions of snow and its skiing character. Sometimes it would be more sensible for skiers to study these aspects rather than listen to snow forecasts.

In all skiing areas the timberline (usually between approximately 6000–6500ft (1800–2000m) above sea level in the Alps and up to 9840ft (3000m) in the Rockies) plays a certain part. Though almost all skiers want to ski on higher and higher slopes, and above all on slopes above 6500ft (2000m) which will be sure of snow, an experienced skier knows that trees can be a useful landmark in mist or poor visibility, as well as giving some protection from strong winds – and he values them accordingly.

Note: For skiers in Australia, New Zealand and other parts of the southern hemisphere read 'north' for 'south' and vice versa.

North-facing slopes

Advantages: little sun, so snow conditions are usually good (cold) in the middle of winter. Snow lies longer in the spring. Good for skiing in deep snow.

Disadvantages: trails are sometimes icy, especially in wooded areas. Going up in a lift can be very cold in early and mid-winter. Almost no spring snow until very late in the season.

South-facing slopes

Advantages: plenty of sun, high temperature in the daytime and cold frosty nights usually result in spring-like snow conditions even in mid-winter. Not so cold on the lifts.

Disadvantages: powder snow does not last long; bare patches appear fast. Easily-broken crust often forms off the trails. Poor snow conditions from midday onwards in spring.

East and west-facing slopes

The sun is on east-facing slopes in the morning and on west-facing slopes in the afternoon. Conditions correspond to a combination of the features of north and south-facing slopes. There are usually inbetween slopes. North-west slopes offer a longer skiing season than south-west slopes.

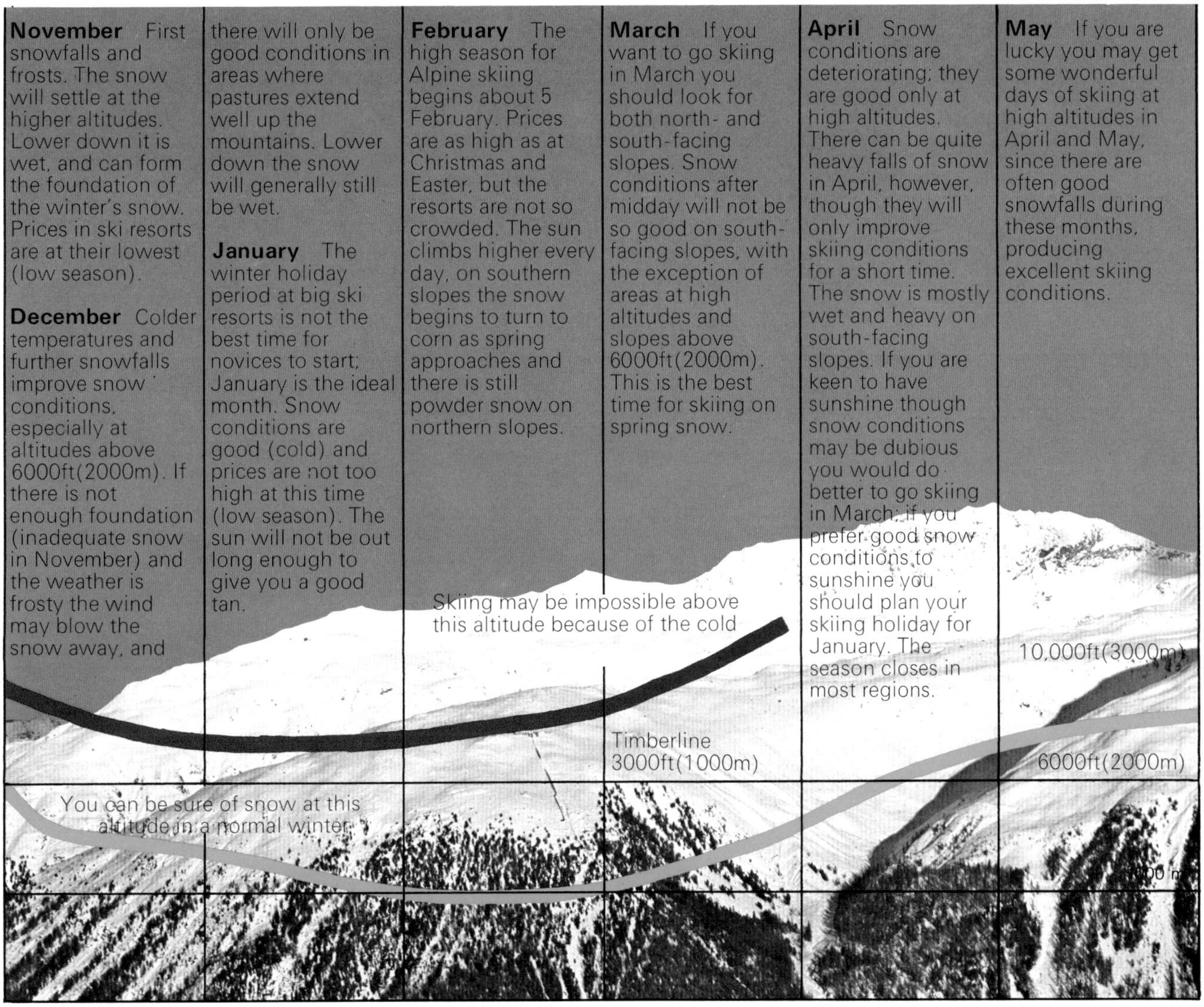

November First snowfalls and frosts. The snow will settle at the higher altitudes. Lower down it is wet, and can form the foundation of the winter's snow. Prices in ski resorts are at their lowest (low season).

December Colder temperatures and further snowfalls improve snow conditions, especially at altitudes above 6000ft(2000m). If there is not enough foundation (inadequate snow in November) and the weather is frosty the wind may blow the snow away, and there will only be good conditions in areas where pastures extend well up the mountains. Lower down the snow will generally still be wet.

January The winter holiday period at big ski resorts is not the best time for novices to start; January is the ideal month. Snow conditions are good (cold) and prices are not too high at this time (low season). The sun will not be out long enough to give you a good tan.

February The high season for Alpine skiing begins about 5 February. Prices are as high as at Christmas and Easter, but the resorts are not so crowded. The sun climbs higher every day, on southern slopes the snow begins to turn to corn as spring approaches and there is still powder snow on northern slopes.

March If you want to go skiing in March you should look for both north- and south-facing slopes. Snow conditions after midday will not be so good on south-facing slopes, with the exception of areas at high altitudes and slopes above 6000ft(2000m). This is the best time for skiing on spring snow.

April Snow conditions are deteriorating; they are good only at high altitudes. There can be quite heavy falls of snow in April, however, though they will only improve skiing conditions for a short time. The snow is mostly wet and heavy on south-facing slopes. If you are keen to have sunshine though snow conditions may be dubious you would do better to go skiing in March; if you prefer good snow conditions to sunshine you should plan your skiing holiday for January. The season closes in most regions.

May If you are lucky you may get some wonderful days of skiing at high altitudes in April and May, since there are often good snowfalls during these months, producing excellent skiing conditions.

Skiing may be impossible above this altitude because of the cold

10,000ft(3000m)

Timberline 3000ft(1000m)

6000ft(2000m)

You can be sure of snow at this altitude in a normal winter

In Australia and New Zealand north-facing slopes receive the sun and south-facing slopes are colder. Snow generally falls above 3300ft (1000m) and stays on the ground above about 5000ft(1500m).

Adjusting your technique to the terrain

During ski instruction you are mainly concerned with flexing, edging, rotation and so on; putting your skiing into actual practice is more demanding. Every terrain is different and you have to learn how to cope with slopes, bumps or moguls and dips, gently sloping and steep runs.

The following eight kinds of terrain, shown in a simple diagrammatic form, represent typical situations which are found relatively often.

These examples demonstrate:

- how to ski best on different types of terrain
- what particular kinds of turn have been found to be the most useful on each terrain
- whether short or long-radius turns are best
- ease or difficulty of the terrain
- what familiar skiing techniques to use on it

Trail conditions are assumed to be normal. The kinds of turn recommended are described in detail in the chapter on Alpine Skiing (p. 58).

Hints: By way of training, go over each terrain once in your mind. Try to find the route which is best suited to your capabilities, and get to know the terrain better in this way.

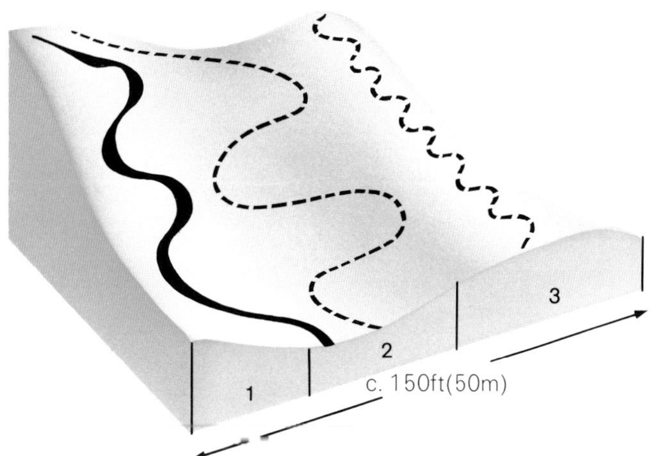

easier

basic swings (1)
parallel turns:
short swings (1)

more difficult

parallel turns:
parallel turn with up-unweighting (2)
down-motion parallel (2)
short swings (3)
rotation turn (2)
turns with weight transfer:
scissor step turn (2)

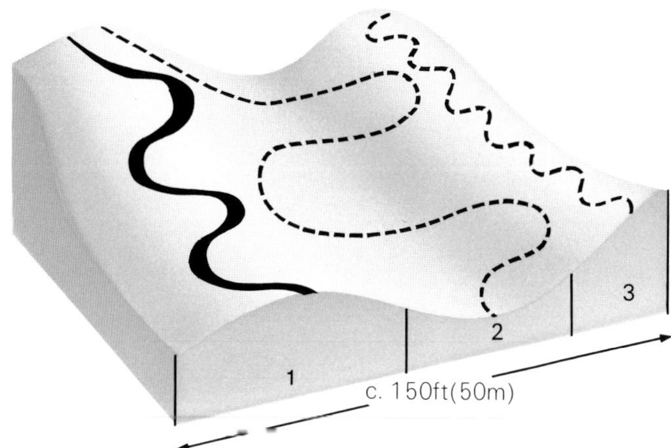

easier

basic swings (1)
step-up turns:
stem step turn (1)
parallel turns:
short swings (1)

more difficult

parallel turns:
parallel turn with up-unweighting (2)
short swings (3)

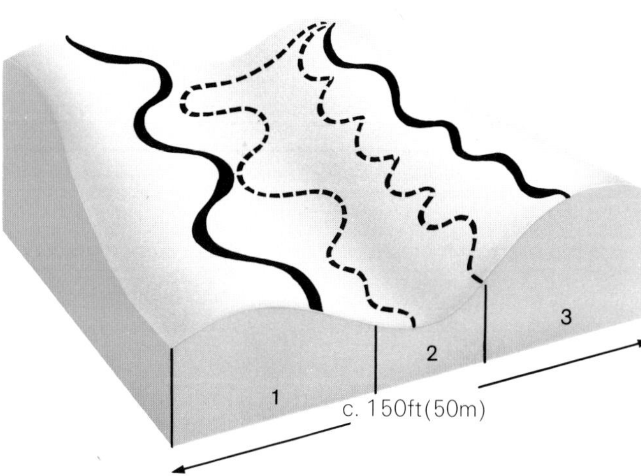

easier

snowplough turn (3)
basic swings (1)
step-up turns:
stem step turn (1)
parallel turns:
short swings (1)
possibly the wedel (3)

more difficult

parallel turns:
short swings (2)
parallel turns with down-unweighting (2)
parallel turns with up-unweighting (2)
traversing short swings (3)

1
2
3
c. 150ft(50m)

easier

basic swings (2)
parallel turns:
parallel turns with up-unweighting (2)
short swings (3)

more difficult

parallel turns:
short swings (1)
parallel turns with down-unweighting (1)

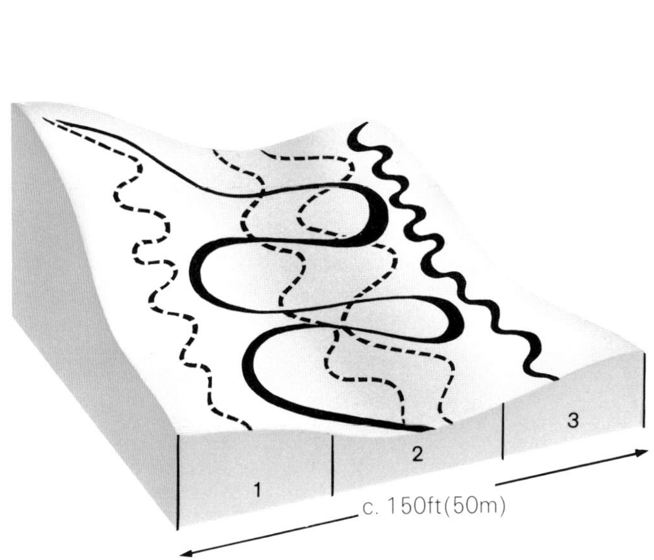

easier

basic swings (2)
parallel turns:
parallel turns with up-unweighting (2)
short swings (3)
rotation turn (2)
combination of parallel turns with up-unweighting (2, 1) and step turns (2, 3)

more difficult

parallel turns:
short swings (1+2)
parallel turns with down-unweighting (2)
compression turn (3)
step-up turns:
accelerating step turn combination (2, 3) and parallel turns with up-unweighting (2, 1)

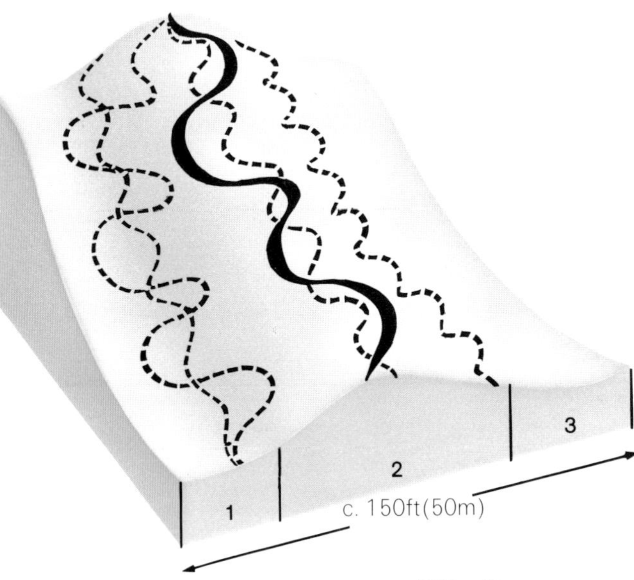

easier

basic swings
parallel turns:
parallel turns with up-unweighting (2)
step-up turns:
stem step turn (2)
parallel step turn (2)
accelerating step turn (2)

more difficult

parallel turns:
short swings (1)
compression turns (2)
traversing short swings (3)
combination of parallel turns with up-unweighting and step turns (1)

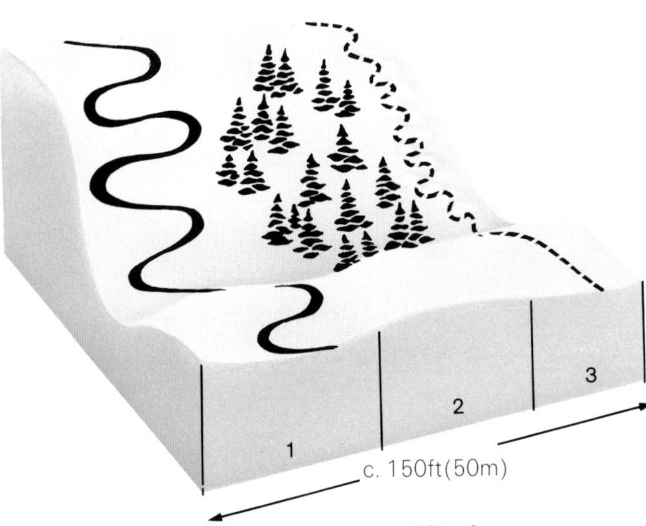

easier

basic swings (1)
parallel turns:
parallel turns with up-unweighting (1)
step-up turns:
stem step turn (1)
parallel step turn (1)

more difficult

parallel turns:
compression turn (3)
step-up turns:
accelerating step turn (3)
It is inadvisable to ski through the trees (2)!

c. 150ft(50m)

easier

snowplough turn/traversing/basic swing turns
parallel turns:
parallel turns with up-unweighting, or wedel

more difficult

parallel turns:
wedel or short swings
down-motion turns

A good eye for the terrain

It is relatively easy to learn how to ski safely from the point of view of technique. An experienced skier is not just technically perfect and reliable, however, he is also able to apply his technique, with all the different turns he has learnt, to the terrain. In the course of his practical skiing every skier should learn how to observe the terrain closely, so as to become a good skier across all kinds of country. Only someone who is using eyes, brain and legs together will get all the enjoyment he can from skiing.

The general shape of the ground can tell you a great deal about the problems of skiing. Analysing the route and the turns, the expert has a fluid, rhythmical style, rational and precise, fast but well controlled. The most important criteria by which to judge a skier's run are:

- speed
- the safety factor
- variety of technique
- use of the terrain

All this can be learnt, but it takes time, experience and practice. A good ski instructor can be an invaluable help.

The illustrations show more or less typical situations on a normal downhill run. The blue routes show:

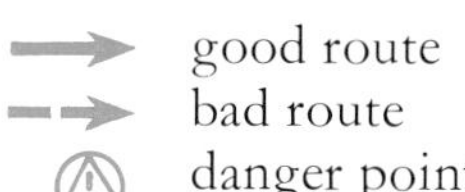

good route
bad route
danger point

Example 1: a narrow ski 'road', with a steep drop on the downhill side and a snowbank on the uphill side, view of path partly concealed, icy, not much snow covering.
Method: ski on the downhill side, where the surface will usually give the best hold. Do not schuss round

1

2

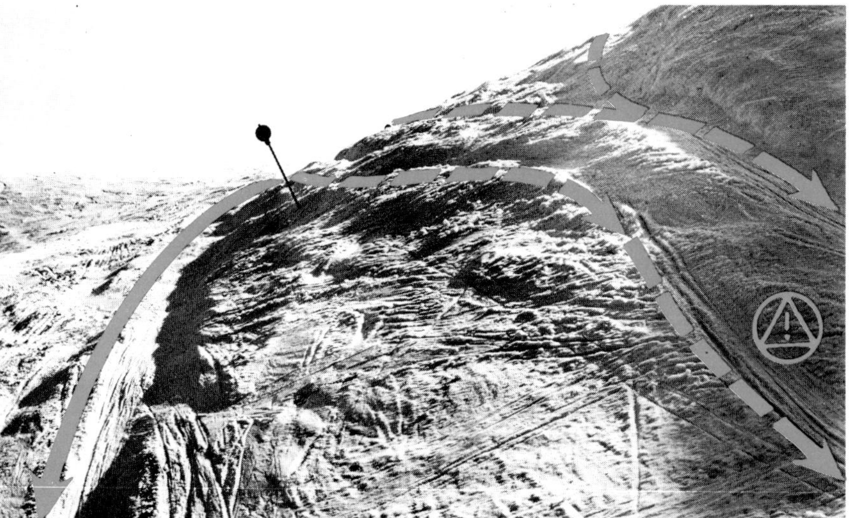

3

bends when you cannot see ahead! It is better to snowplough in the middle of the path or side-slip at the edge.

Example 2: a wide ski 'road', view clear, route marked, tempting you to cut the corner.
Method: follow the markers; in poor visibility it could be unwise to cut corners (you might find a ditch or gully). Never mechanically follow other people's tracks.

Example 3: several traverse tracks on ridge, icy ruts.
Method: when traversing on an icy surface always look for the least steep and the sunniest (and therefore softest) route.

Example 4: skiing down between two ski-tows.
Method: it is a bad habit, and can be dangerous to ski between two lift racks, especially when there is plenty of room on the trail. If you have to, keep close to the fall line. Cross the lift tracks only at indicated points.

Example 5: bumpy ground on a ridge above a slope.
Method: if the ground becomes steep, change to a well-controlled speed in good time. Always look for the sunny routes in mogulled terrain and on icy trails.

Example 6: steep slope with moguls, narrowing at the bottom to a ski bridge.
Method: make your turns as wide as possible until the slope becomes gentler, cross the bridge at a well-controlled speed. If your speed is not controlled the sudden change from steep to flat ground just before the bridge could cause you to fall.

4

5

6

7 

Example 7: mogulled ridge with ruts across it, not much view ahead. *Method:* as you cannot tell what is going to happen on the other side of the ridge, ski as slowly as possible and as low as possible on the gentler slope.

8 

Example 8: mogulled terrain with possible avalanche danger (wind-slab), in new snow conditions. *Method:* always ski as close as you can to the fall line on slopes like this. Keep to the trail, be careful as you cross below the icy ridge.

9 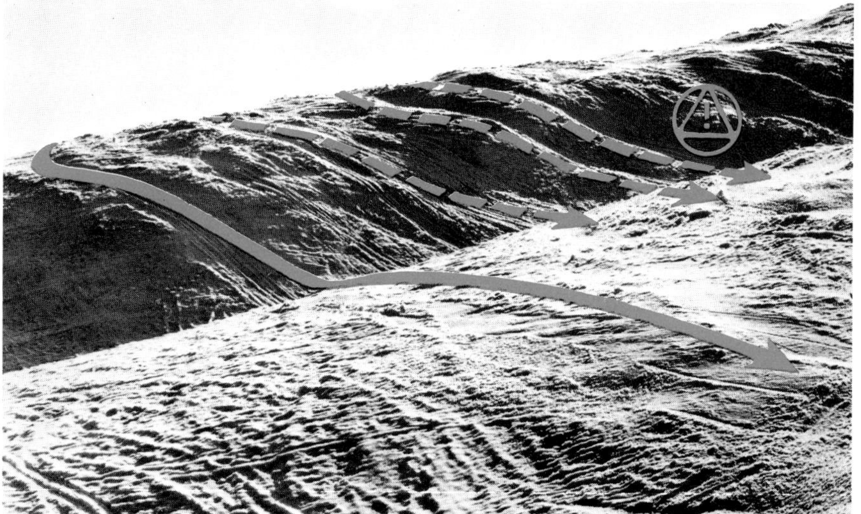

Example 9: gully between two ridges, view ahead concealed. *Method:* in poor visibility you would usually see a gully like this too late, and would probably fall, since you would first find yourself going faster and then your speed would be braked as you started up the opposite slope. Turn aside on the first crest, have a good look at the terrain ahead, and traverse carefully down.

Example 10: trail with bare patches.
Method: sudden steep drops will often show icy or bare patches, which is the result of many people skiing over the same spot. Ski as high as possible, where the snow has not been worn away. Do not follow the transverse ruts.

10

Example 11: end of the run, entrance to the lift.
Method: a wide slope ending in a narrow entrance to the lift area. If you head straight for the entrance you are endangering skiers who may be waiting for the lift. Even a small error can lead to a collision, because the lift line cannot get out of the way. It is safter to turn off outside the queue area and walk across to the lift line.

11

Example 12: a spring run, bare patches.
Method: bare patches appear first on convex slopes, and you cannot see them from above. So always look for the dips or gullies of a slope, where the snow will usually lie longer. Do not follow the traverses.

12

The expert on the slopes

Are you afraid of poorly groomed trails? Or skiing the moguls? Do you have difficulty getting a grip on steep, icy slopes? Can you ski deep powder? If you are an average skier with a certain amount of experience, and cannot answer 'yes' to these questions, the following suggestions might help.

Skiing moguls

Nowadays small bumps are regarded as quite helpful to skiers for turning, but trails with many moguls usually present skiers with problems. As everyone knows, the traditional parallel turn with its marked down up down movement is not particularly useful when you are negotiating moguls. To be comfortable on a mogulled trail the compression turn is essential (see p. 94).

Step turns on a mogul trail.

During this turn your legs act as shock-absorbers, you absorb the bumps by bending and stretching your legs while your upper body does not move much. The turning movement starts on the crest of a mogul at the moment when the skis are on the open and friction is minimal. A pole planted to your side is necessary to stabilize you. As you absorb the bump your legs flex in front of your body, and thus the 'swallowing' of a bump is more of a passive than an active bend of the legs. Directly afterwards you start actively extending your legs in a kind of downward kicking movement, so as to keep in contact with the snow.

To avoid excessive bouncing in very bumpy terrain, experts try to ski round the bumps rather than directly over them. If possible, during the turn, skiers should keep in constant contact with the ground. Naturally the absorbing movement of the legs must be adjusted to the terrain and to your speed. The upper part of your body should always be facing downhill. Experts will do mogul-absorbing compression turns either on both legs (parallel turns) or on one leg (step-up).

Hints

- You must practise skiing on mogul terrain as well as learning the technique.
- The most difficult part is keeping in contact with the ground, the easiest part is turning the skis. Extremes of vertical movement (active unweighting) are wrong, use of passive unweighting is right. The faster you go, the less unweighting you need!
- The fast turn of the skis quite often means the upper part of the body does not follow the skis. Try to keep the upper body downhill of the skis; this will help good anticipation for the next turn.
- Each mogul produces a counter-

1

2

3

4

pressure which is swallowed by the elasticity of joints and muscles. The leg muscles must not be relaxed. A skiing 'feel' for pressure must be acquired.

- Pole planting is an important support. The pole must always be planted well out to the side and downhill. Pole planting brings the upper part of the body into the right position.
- Exaggerated compression of the legs (sitting too far back) must be avoided. Skiing in a sitting-back position is a strain and often results in crossing the ski tips on a bump. Suit the compression movement to the bumps.
- On very mogulled trails jet turns are useful. The bumps are circled rather than crossed, so that one is not carried into the air above them. The jet movement occurs on the side of the bump.
- At high speed the bump-absorbing movements become an active, retracting 'pull-up' of the legs. The retraction leg movement must take place at the right moment to lead into the leg-stretching movement as the bump is crossed.

The pictures and diagram show an ideal ski route through very mogulled terrain The blue and red lines show short and long radius turns. It is not a good idea to ski over the top of high moguls (black line) unless speed is low.

Skiing on ice

Skiing on icy trails presents problems identical with those of skiing on steep slopes. Fear of losing control tempts the skier to lean into the slope and adopt a passive rather than active style. Particular problems are encountered by skiers who use strong unweighting movements to turn their skis, and skiers who are too upright, with too little edge-pressure.

Expert skiers are distinguished not just by their elegance of style or an extreme sitting-back position, but by their ski control and, in particular, by the way they place the running surfaces of their skis in relation to the snow. It is noticeable that they either keep their skis moving optimally, or edge them briefly and correctly. In other words, they avoid unnecessary edging, but when it *is* desirable to set the edges, they do so to the best possible effect.

Hints

- The reason for poor edging can be blunt edges or loose boots. Provided neither of these is the culprit, the correct ski control and body position will be the decisive factors in edging.
- The steeper and smoother the slope, the more strongly you need to set your edges – in traversing as well as in turning. The edges are set by a forwards and sideways pressure of the knees, while the upper part of the body compensates for the movement by bending forwards and out to the side (outward angulation). The decisive factor is the amount of edg-

Skiing on an icy trail, setting the edges hard. A brief change of edging (unweighting phase) and an active stretch of the legs as the skier steers out of the turn (weighting phase).

Jumping over a ridge: LEFT, in an active crouching position; RIGHT, rather more acrobatically: a 'tip drop' (only for experts)

ing, which should be correct for the terrain, snow conditions and speed.

- Many skiers are at fault in judging the amount of edging on hard trails by trying to cling to the slope. The result is they push their skis downhill and start an uncontrolled skid. Only experience can lead to the instinctively correct edge-set.
- Edge-set during a turn is the second problem. This must take place at exactly the correct spot and correct moment of the turn, a point dependent upon the nature of slope and turn. This is absolutely essential for a skier racing through a slalom course.
- There is no point in edging continuously; the likely result will be ski-chatter in which the edges lose contact with the snow and the ski becomes even less secure than it would if lying flat. It is better to have a certain amount of edging power in reserve, to be brought into play at the right moment.
- It is advisable to edge the skis during a weighted rather than an unweighting phase. In any case, the edges must be weighted briefly and actively.
- The best line is close to the fall line in difficult and icy terrain. It is usually easier to control speed with a succession of short turns than with overlong traverses. Edge contact must never be lost.
- There are easier stretches even on the iciest slopes. These should be chosen as there will be a better hold for a turn; a traverse can link them up.

Gelände jump

Gelände (or terrain) jumping is not merely a matter of courage or something done by showy skiers, it is a useful skill which every skier should be able to employ to some extent. Terrain jumping is part of downhill running as much as turns and schusses, and the main purpose is to cross ridges or large undulations in the terrain. Properly carried out, it increases the skier's control, since mastering the skill of jumping adds one more technique for unexpected situations on unfamiliar and difficult terrain.

Powder snow skiing

Skiing in deep powder snow is a skier's dream, although there is nothing dream-like about the skills needed to enjoy skiing in any kind of deep snow. There can be a gap, however, between the wish and the deed: between trying to ski in deep snow and being able to do so. It is a recurrent challenge and a precise balancing game played with skis and slopes.

The snow

Deep snow is not necessarily powder snow. 'Deep snow' is any snow surface which allows the skis to sink sufficiently to cover them. There are three basic varieties, according to their consistency:

- deep snow in which you can ski easily (powder snow, spring snow)
- deep snow in which it is possible to ski normally (heavy snow, slushy snow)
- deep snow in which it is only possible to ski with difficulty (compressed snow, wind-packed snow, breakable crust, rotten snow)

Deep-snow skiers must be able to recognize these different types of snow. All can be met during a single run on various slope exposures and, if recognized, the worst can be avoided. Every deep-snow skier is exposed to an increased danger of finding an avalanche slope and an elementary knowledge of snow craft is as important as the basic deep-snow skiing expertise.

Equipment
Whether or not deep-snow skiing is a pleasure depends, in part, on having the right skis. The rest of the equipment is the same as for trail skiing. Skis should be easy to turn, their spatulas flexible and not too strongly curved; it is best to choose from groups L and A (see the section on Ski Equipment, pp. 16–47). Compact skis about head high and with broader spatulas have proved very satisfactory. In contrast to trail skiing, a ski brake is not recommended for deep-snow skiing because your skis can become buried and lost in the snow after a fall; a retaining strap is better. Straps and properly adjusted ski bindings (they may require a different setting for deep snow) are most important. Correctly waxed skis will also help.

Technique
In principle, deep-snow skiing calls for a sound ski technique on a groomed trail. Anyone can get by with a basic parallel turn in light, loose new snow an inch or so deep, providing skis are close together and equally weighted. In deeper snow and difficult snow, skiing technique has to be varied to suit the situation. There is no typical or specialized deep-snow skiing technique, and no specific turns; efficient, correct application of known skills is the key.

1

2

3

4

To master the technique for skiing in deep powder you need to have a feeling at all times for:
—the movement and position of your body
—the proper weighting of the skis in relation to the speed and radius of your turns.
The two sequences show a combination of jet and compression turns. Notice the active movement of the legs, while at the same time keeping the upper part of the body still.

Hints

- Even the experts have to keep re-adjusting their skiing to the prevailing type of snow. In practice, every variation of skiing is used in deep snow.
- Deep-snow skiing calls for experience and a good 'feel' for skiing.
- Even weighting of both skis and a slight sitting-back position are particularly important. Skis are banked through the snow, rather than edged.
- Less leaning out, more leaning in and rotation, keeping the upper part of your body still, and a probing ski pole planting are advisable.

- A higher speed and fall-line turns make rotation easier. The problem here is the even weighting of both skis, which can only be achieved by a constant speed. The slower the speed, the greater the danger of the skis running on different levels within the snow. The closer to the fall line, the easier it is to weight both skis equally.

- At higher speeds there are the following effects: the greater force with which the snow accumulates in the spatula area forces the tails of the skis into a curve, making it easier to drift sideways. This is why soft skis are important: the harder the skis, the greater the speed required in order to turn easily.

- Skiing in deep snow is by 'feel' and it is necessary to acquire an instinct for the right skiing position and body balance: Ski weighting must be adjusted to speed and radius of turn. The photograph series show a mixture of jet and compression turns – active leg movement and quiet upper body.

- Exaggerated unweighting movements, which increase the time taken for unweighting, are a help to the inexperienced deep-snow skier. It is then easier to start and steer the turns.

- A slightly delayed upwards movement in a parallel turn is better, as deep snow hinders a strong push; downward flexing should be a gentle movement. Too much movement of the trunk, especially too much forward bending, is not helpful.

- A mixture of a jet and compression turn is one good technique for deep-snow skiing. The basic swing, parallel turn with up-unweighting, short swings and rotation turns are also suitable. It is wise to be able to perform some or all of these turns with an impeccable technique on a groomed trail before attempting them in deep snow, which permits no technical error.

1

2

3

4

- The characteristic feature of the compression turn is the active movement in which both legs are flexed in front of your body during unweighting. This upwards pull of the legs unweights the skis, freeing them to rotate the legs for the new turn. The regained ground pressure is felt when the legs are stretched and rotated.

- Falls are all part of deep-snow skiing, and are inevitable sooner or later. They often look impressively dramatic but are usually harmless. Getting up is often more of a problem.

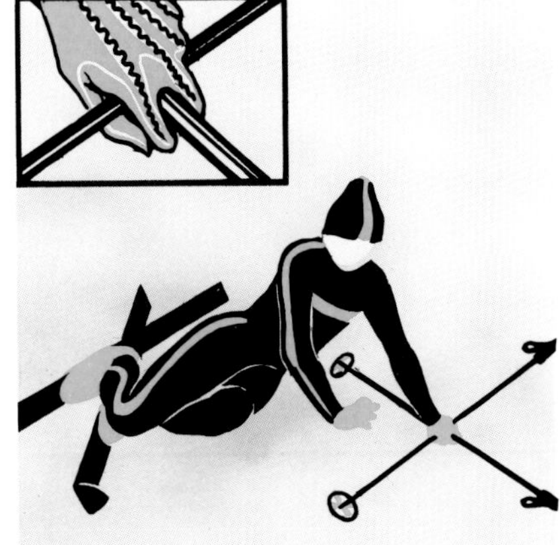
This position of your poles can be very helpful to get you back up in bottomless powder snow.

RIGHT: These young beginners are at ski school at Coronet Peak, Otago, New Zealand.

Skiing for children

When children first start skiing they regard the sport as just one of the many pleasures of winter. Many adults have forgotton this a long time ago.

Advice for parents

When we set out to make skiers of our children we tend to be guided too much by our own feelings and ideas, overlooking the fact that children should have fun as they learn to ski.

Let children become accustomed to the outdoor winter world before they try skiing; but be sure they have warm and practical outdoor clothes and keep early play periods short.

Skiing equipment for children

'It will do for the children' is not the way to start a first day's skiing. Unnecessary failures can be put down to children wearing skis too long for them, handed down from an older brother, ski boots with four pairs of socks to make them fit, or using poles more suitable for pole vaulting. Quite apart from the fact that the wrong sort of equipment may well cause a child to dislike the sport from the start, you cannot hope that they will make any real progress while using it. Naturally cost is an important factor, but in the long run the 'best buy' will be good quality equipment which will last some time and can, reasonably, be handed on. Bindings and skis are vitally important for comfort and safety, and it is better to pay for good quality and pay less frequently, than to economise and have to make frequent purchases.

There is such a great variety of equipment available that choice can become very digcult. A good sports' shop with trained staff should be able to give valuable help and advice.

Skis

'Play skis' are the best for small children between the ages of two and five (see Getting Used to Ski Equipment, p. 140). From the wide variety available, a short, broad plastic ski with a simple strap binding has proved its worth in practice. The uncomplicated binding allows children to start by wearing gum boots or almost any other kind of footwear. Scales on the running surfaces help to avoid the frustration of sliding backwards. But play skis of this kind, which are excellent and uncomplicated to start with, are not suitable for long-term use in Alpine skiing. Once a child has learnt to run downhill and is about to start doing turns, he or she needs normal Alpine skis with a proper running surface and edges, as well as ski boots and good efficient safety bindings.

On average, the length of the skis should be the same as the child's height. The current trend is for shorter skis for children, as is the case for adults (see table, p. 27). With children, who are light and full of movement, edging is not so important as the ease with which the skis will turn. This is the advantage of a shorter ski. Children should not have skis longer than their own height until they can ski really well, executing parallel turns quickly and safely. It is amazing how many parents give in to their children's irrational demands to buy longer skis. When buying skis for a child it is better to buy them too short than too long.

The trend today is for children's wear to follow that of adults as closely as possible. A down waistcoat is very practical.

Ski bindings

There are many good bindings for children which meet approved international standards. A layman (and even an expert) cannot take in the whole array of tests and standards applied to children's bindings. It is obvious, however, that the big ski binding manufacturers are keen to have their products tested and passed by neutral organizations and customers have come to recognize that if children's bindings are to perform as they should they must be of a high standard.

A safety binding is incomplete without a retaining strap. Unfortunately these can be rather complicated for children. It is up to the parents to seek a device which will be easy to handle.

Ski brakes

Ski brakes are steadily gaining popularity with adults. Unfortunately they can, as yet, only be fitted to skis over 4ft 6in(140cm) long. A ski brake can be recommended for children who ski well and fast, since it can avoid injuries caused by the 'backlash' of a ski held by a retaining strap. But if the ski brake is to work perfectly the entire sole of the ski boot must be as smooth as possible. Soles with deep, broad ridges are not suitable for use with a ski brake.

Ski boots

As with adults, a child's skiing technique and the progress he makes in learning to ski will depend to a considerable extent on a properly chosen pair of ski boots. The basic requirements are rigidity at the sides, flexibility at the front and smooth soles to help the safety bindings release. Children's boots should be as simple as possible to fasten. Boots which are a little on the large side, leaving room for growth, are acceptable; the upper limit is reached when there is room for a finger between the child's heel and his boot if he is trying the boots on while wearing a pair of thick woollen socks (or two pairs of thinner ones). At the beginning this extra space can be filled up with another pair of socks.

Clothing

The trend in ski wear for children is to be as close to adult ski wear as possible. There are brightly coloured suits on the market, tight-fitting snowsuits with a good stretch, racing trousers padded at the knees, sweaters with shoulder-guards for slalom – in short, everything calculated to make a child's heart beat faster while his parents groan when they see the cost! Not all the latest skiing fashions are practical for children, and parents should take a child's age and skiing ability into consideration when buying. Children who live in the mountains, with ski slopes just outside the door, will need different clothes from children whose families have to make an expedition and drive for hours before reaching the slopes.

A one-piece, water-resistant, brightly coloured snowsuit is best for very small children (two to five years old). Once a child is past the stage of simply playing and can begin to learn properly (from about five years upwards), a warm two-piece suit, consisting of ski pants and ski jacket, is better because of the warmth it gives. If parents are going to give in to a child's wish to have a 'real' racing outfit, an additional pair of overtrousers for cold days, to be worn over the racing ski pants, are a good idea. Trousers like these have zippered sides which means they can be put on and taken off while the child is still wearing ski boots. Down-filled ski jackets and waistcoats are now available for children over five years old. Unfortunately, too few parents understand the importance of suitable underwear. Thin synthetic-fibre tights and vests mean a lot of heat loss, which cannot always be replaced by the heavy outer clothing. Money spent on thermal underwear for skiing is a good investment. The same goes for mittens or gloves. If you want to give your children goggles which hardly mist up at all, the new double lens kind are a good buy.Ski wear for children should, at least in theory, be functional rather than fashionable.

Learning should be fun!

To begin with, children are ideally suited physically to learn how to ski quickly and easily – learning can be child's play to them! They like to feel that skiing is a game; they should enjoy everything new they do, without it seeming like school, and they should not be pushed too hard.

To say children are ideally suited physically to learn skiing, refers first and foremost to the excellent natural sense of balance a child has from about the age of six or seven. Perhaps the best possible age for a child to start skiing is between six and nine, when his co-ordination of movement is well developed. One cannot talk about a 'right moment' for every child, however. Children often differ widely in their physical development at any given age; there are early starters and late starters in sport and in ordinary daily life. Let a child try – and if he does not seem ready to learn skiing, in spite of having good instruction, put it off till next winter.

All parents ought to keep this in mind when they put their children on skis. Being too eager and ambitious, putting pressure on a child, may have the opposite effect from the one intended. If a child is having no fun he will *not* find it child's play to learn to ski; his style will be cramped and inhibited.

As a rough guide to the progress children can make at different ages, the following is a summary drawn from practical experience:

- Two-six years old – getting used to the snow and the slopes.
- Six-ten years old – the play element should be emphasized.
- Ten-twelve years old – organized instruction.
- Twelve-sixteen years old – serious training (if required).

Getting children used to skis and snow

You cannot take children skiing until they are over four years old, but they can get used to the feel of skis and ski poles and the surroundings of skiing (snow, cold) as soon as they can walk. Practical experience has shown over and over again that very young children between the ages of two and six should only prepare for skiing as play, ideally with one or other parent.

The reason for this is that, up to the age of about six, children tend to teach themselves: they play, learn and experience things on their own. Their motor skills are not yet fully developed which means they will feel un-

How children ski:
using step turns and the rotation technique without pole-planting
leaning forward
legs in knock-kneed position, wide apart turning the trunk a great deal.

certain of themselves even when performing quite simple movements. (This can irritate an ambitious and impatient father's nerves.) Add various toys like sledges, skates, play skis, poles or sliding toys, and the child's sense of insecurity can rapidly increase, leading to fear and dislike of skiing. It is most important for parents to give each child individual attention, to be very patient, and praise every successful move, however simple.

Other reasons why small children should not start taking ski instruction until they are older is that they lack powers of concentration at an early age, and their attention is easily distracted. An instructor teaching a group must have the whole group's attention directed at him, or to practising a given movement. He cannot

hope for the full attention of small children, who often want to do something else even before he has finished explaining what *he* wants them to do. Only patient parents who have no ambitious plans for their children can slowly get them used to snow and cold, ski equipment and skiing, so that they will have fun all the time. Early preparation of this kind will mean that children learn faster later on.

Ski schools, with what they call a skiing kindergarten for this age group, should offer only very simple

ski instruction, suitable for children of nursery-school age. The children should be allowed to follow their own inclinations, in an area set apart from the rest of the slopes.

Most parents know their children will not become good swimmers if they are made to go into deep, cold water early on. Modern methods of teaching swimming accustom a child to the water slowly, as a matter of course; starting in shallow, warm water, the child can play and splash about.

But there is a tendency to expect far too much of small children when they start skiing. They are literally torn from a warm room to make their first attempts at skiing in a harsh environment. Faced with snow and cold, unwieldy equipment and advice which may or may not be good, it is not surprising that children do not succeed immediately.

Early on, and without having pressure brought to bear, a child should gradually get used to the wintry conditions of skiing, and this should precede skiing itself. There are all sorts of ways children can familiarize themselves with the snow and the cold – stamping about in the snow, using snow to build with, having a snowball fight, rolling about in the snow, tobogganing and sliding, are all ways a child can get accustomed to snow.

Getting used to ski equipment

Short, light 'play skis' are proving very valuable in getting a child used to the feel of skis for the first time. They can be used for sliding downhill – and tried out at home for sliding on the sitting-room carpet, or while shovelling snow. They are very short, have no sharp edges and corners, and so there is no danger to the child. His play ski kit is completed by poles. They should be lightweight and have blunt ends. At the 'play ski' stage the child is not aiming to execute turns, just getting used to the feel of the equipment and the sensation of sliding. It should be so much fun that children will look forward to their next skiing adventure without being pressured by their parents.

A few things a child can do when out on skis for the first time:

- Take small steps – like a dwarf
- Take big steps – like a giant
- Take fast steps – like a weasel
- Stamp – like an elephant
- Walk round Daddy like a Red Indian
- Hold on to the end of the toboggan while Daddy pulls it
- 'Ski-tow lift' – Daddy pulling with both ski poles
- Sliding on one ski
- Making pictures out of ski tracks in the snow: flowers, stars, Christmas trees, fishbones, railway tracks, and so on.

And after you have accustomed your children to the snow, send them to a ski instructor to learn skiing properly. They will learn faster, more enjoyable and more securely with a group of other children of their own age.

Skiing for children aged six to ten

A course of ski instruction is the ideal basis for learning at this age. It is encouraging for a child to have playmates of his own age, with the same aims and problems. And children

who have started school will be used to a certain amount of discipline. Unfortunately children at the lower end of this age group will still find it difficult to think as a group. They are not interested in team efforts such as getting into various formations, they are interested in their own performance.

The instructor will find that praise is extremely helpful in teaching children. Adults would describe it as flattery to be praised even for a poorish performance – not children! They feel encouraged; praise will spur them on to do better. When considering the various methods of instruction used at this age, it is possible that the step-turn technique is best for children between the ages of six and ten, because of the resemblance to the normal movement of walking, and the natural reflexes of standing on one leg. Although many children may look as if they are skiing very well on both legs, they transfer their weight very easily, though without any marked vertical movement and without a noticeable raising of the inside ski. They are also much better than adults at making use of centrifugal forces for turning. When running downhill, skiing in curves or turning, the knock-kneed position into which children's legs go means they are naturally inclined to angle their skis. This means that there is usually no need to spend a long time teaching the snowplough.

The instructor can stretch a point and allow a slight stemming position to be considered as an open parallel position until the child reaches a higher grade; it would be inadvisable to try to turn this secure position, too soon, into a more elegant position with skis close together. This is a mistake which is often made. It makes a child feel less secure, and increases the problems of edging.

When children are turning, they should be allowed to use rotation of the trunk when starting a turn, and at the start they should also be allowed rotation when steering the turn. This is a natural way for a child to ski; the niceties of counter-rotating the upper part of the body and rotating the legs can be kept for a later stage.

There are various ways, some shorter than others, whereby an instructor can bring his pupils to the stage of learning step turns, which comes at the learning phase (ages ten to twelve) and the training phase (ages twelve to sixteen); these ways vary according to the talent, age and constitution of the children.

Possible ways for a child to prepare for parallel turns

Variety of talent and variety of technique call for a variety of ways to teach children skiing. Children should have proper instruction: they will learn faster, more safely and have more fun at ski school.

Free-style skiing

Free-style, acrobatic or hot-dog skiing is a playful, athletic skiing style full of artistic jumps. The repertoire of free-style skiing is as varied, colourful and individual as the elements that go to make it up – and as young as the enthusiastic participants of this variation of the sport.

In North America free-style skiing has been part of the ski-instruction programme for some years, and more and more European skiers are becoming fascinated by this style of skiing; it is beginning to be taken seriously. Shorter skis have been a major factor in the development of free-style as a special branch of skiing.

Free-style skiing is the *haute école* of skiing: a mixture of acrobatics, exhibition skiing, stylish jumps and tightrope walking in a carnival atmosphere. There are no limits to the wealth of ideas which invent more and more tricks. To be a free-style skier, however, requires above-average dexterity and mobility, elastic muscles, an excellent sense of balance, good physical fitness and plenty of nerve. If you want to be a free-style skier you must also be an expert skier.

It is not surprising that this new style of skiing attracts athletic skiers and, among them, people who do not want to race, but who simply enjoy skiing for the fun of it.

A famous and successful family of free-style skiers: the Garhammer family; left to right, Franz, Hedi, Fuzzy and Ernst. Fuzzy Garhammer was one of the pioneers of free-style skiing in Europe and has given a lot of stimulus to this new branch of the sport.

Is it dangerous?

Free-style skiing is sometimes misunderstood, and the acrobatic, hot-dog and trick skiers who practise it are on the defensive against the popular opinion that free-style skiing is particularly dangerous. The first free-style or hot-dog competitive events started in the United States in about 1970. They were more concerned with daring hot-dog stunts than with perfection of style, or technique. The results were severe injuries, sometimes crippling the performers, and even death.

A few responsibly-minded people were quick to form an association to set limits to the sport; strict rules were laid down which, for instance, banned the double somersault, insisted on people being properly qualified before they were licensed to perform, laid down the height of ski jumps, and so on. This brought better techniques and more safety to free-style skiing. What had started out as a kind of 'crazy gang' show became a serious and tough sporting discipline. Looked at in this way it is no longer a dangerous sport. Indeed, free-style skiing can be an aid to safety, since acrobatic training of this kind certainly helps skiers to move nimbly and avoid dangers on the trail, and this is why it is included here.

Technique

Many people think that free-style skiing is something quite new, but this is not so, as a glance back to the history of skiing over the last fifty years will show. As early as 1929 a skiing manual by Dr Fritz Reuel, himself an active figure-skater, appeared under the title of *New Possibilities in Skiing*. This book, probably the first of the free-style skiing manuals, contains the basic principles and forms of movement still found today.

Technique is still developing, and while new ways of practising acrobatic skiing are being created every winter it is not feasible to give definitive versions of the kinds of turn used. Look at the news-stands, particularly in North America, and at the increasing number of free-style magazines and you will get some idea of the immense variety of free-style skiing. Further material can be found in various skiing books published during the last few years.

The technique of free-style skiing evolves smoothly from that of skiing with step turns, since most of the free-style turns are performed on one leg. The following are among the well-known turns:

- The Flamingo turn
- The Reuel turn
- The Charleston turn
- The Fuzzy turn
- The Art Furrer turn

After that come turns executed on both legs or one leg around 180° or 360°, performed either with rotation into, or against the direction of, the turn. Travelling backwards in the snowplough position is a good basic exercise to help one understand how to do these turns. The next steps taken in learning free-style skiing are:

- Turning uphill on both legs around 180°
- Turning across the fall line on both legs

One of the easiest of acrobatic turns: the flamingo turn, where several turns are performed on the same ski.

- Stem turn with weight transfer travelling backwards in the scissor position
- Turning on one leg around 180°
- Turning on one leg around 360°, changing the lead ski

Note: the rotation should be performed with the body relatively upright and with no pressure on the spatula area of the skis. Control of the front half of the ski is consequently very important.

Step-overs should not be attempted until the steps above have been learnt: approaching on the downhill ski, in a traverse, the uphill ski is swung up and replaced below the downhill ski, turning uphill.

ABOVE: take-off and flight phases of a backward somersault. The jumps are divided into:

1: Upright jumps (e.g., the splits, the back-scratcher, the daffy).
2: Jumps rotating about the longitudinal axis of the body (e.g., the helicopter).
3: Jumps turning about the transverse axis of the body (e.g., forward and backward somersaults).

LEFT: ballet dancing on skis: a study in movement, showing how jumps, turns and steps are harmoniously combined.

Ballet dancing on skis

Once the basic movements have been practised the next stage is ballet dancing on skis – waltzing on skis, turns in both directions, the peacock's tail, the helicopter, the tornado, the axel and so on.

Ballet dancing on skis combines turns, jumps and steps; the stepping movements form the basis of the style, linking the turns and jumps harmoniously. Many of the movements are directly related to figure skating.

Hints

- The most important aid to learning is using skis of the right length, i.e., body height minus 4 in(10 cm). Many manufacturers produce special skis for free-style skiing.
- Always warm up well by doing exercises before the first movement.
- Practise the basic movements without skis.
- Always practise movements on both sides.
- Turning on an inclined plane calls for a particularly good sense of balance and edge feel. Anticipation and front-of-ski control are important.
- Experience alone will lead to precision.
- Ballet dancing on skis needs music: translating the music into movement offers plenty of opportunities for self-expression.
- Good, 'dry' forms of training are gymnastics, diving, trampolining. Ice skating can be a great help.

The relationship of free-style skiing to figure skating is particularly obvious when a couple perform together.

The free-style skier's repertoire

As well as the moves and turns which go to make up ballet dancing on skis, there are the stances, for example, on the tips or tails of your skis, and walking on the tips. Competitive free-style skiing includes events for pair skiing, since nearly all the elements of ballet dancing on skis can be performed by couples as well as individuals.

Aerial jumps, however, are the most spectacular – and the most dangerous – feature of free-style skiing. Any kind of 'do-it-yourself' method can be extremely dangerous. There are speical courses available both for beginners and experts in the summer (water-skiing and trampolining) as well as in winter.

A great test of athletic ability is combining a mogul run with jumping. The mogul run is down a mogul trail and differs from ordinary skiing over moguls in that the free-style skier does not try to avoid the moguls; on the contrary, he attacks them. For reasons of safety to other skiers, however, an all-out attack on the moguls should be kept for special training areas or competitive events and should not be carried out down the public trails.

Competitive events

The following are the most important competitive events in free-style skiing:

Moguls

Moguls are run on a steep, bumpy trail; the skier should make the best possible use of the terrain to perform a fast, exciting and well-controlled run.

> Length: about 1000ft(300m);
> breadth: about 65ft(20m);
> gradient: about 45%.

Jumping in the course of a run can raise the competitor's marks, but he must not twist forwards or backwards in a jump.

Marks awarded: speed, technique, style, elegance, jumps, dynamic force, control.

The time for the course is set by a pacemaker who skiis round the course beforehand, and marks are awarded according to this ideal time. Sitting down or falling costs the competitor marks.

Ballet

Competitors moving at a normal speed perform dance steps, twists, acrobatic turns and jumps on a gentle, smooth slope, as free from bumps as possible, to music of the competitor's choice.

> Length: about 650ft(200m);
> breadth: about 165ft(50m);
> gradient: about 20%.

Marks awarded: style, rhythm, elegance, choreography, precision, inventiveness, grade of difficulty and fluidity of the sequence. Translating music into movement ('artistic impression') earns marks.

Aerials

This event does not depend on the actual length or speed of the jumps so much as on acrobatic ability. Three ski jumps of a standard size are built on a slope of moderate steepness, and the competitor jumps from all three in turn.

1. ski jump platform for forward somersault jumps
2. ski jump platform for backward somersault jumps
3. ski jump platform for jumps performed upright and jumps rotating about the transverse axis of the body

Marks awarded: position of the body, position of skis and poles, controlled landing. The individual jumps are marked according to their degree of difficulty, similar to high diving.

Only free-style skiers with licences can take part in competitive events. Five qualified and experienced judges decide on the placing of competitors by marks awarded in a similar way to that used by ice-skating judges.

The future:

There is growing interest by commercial sponsors to have free-style skiers and teams as entertainers before and during various competitive ski events. This stimulus has brought the aerial acrobatics very close to a circus turn where daring and innovation are combined with grace to become a natural target for television cameras and a captive audience. At the same time, the ballet discipline is coming closer to a pure art form using carefully choreographed figures and sequences. The emergence of a well-defined partner routine in free-style skiing is reminiscent of the elegance of ice-skating.

Anything is possible in free-style skiing: couples racing in a parallel slalom on one pair of skis – for the fun of it.

Touring and ski mountaineering

Alpine touring seems, in theory, to be a mixture of cross-country skiing, downhill skiing, and even free-style skiing. In practice it is not so simple. Everyone realizes, when avalanche disasters hit the headlines, that touring has its own special dangers. Accidents happen to touring skiers because of carelessness, inadequate knowledge, and poor preparation for the expedition as well as poor equipment. It is understandable enough that not all the thousands of skiers around nowadays will have the same amount of experience and the same instinct for mountains that used to characterize all skiers who went touring. This is why it is so important that everyone who wants to start touring takes some steps to acquire basic mountain knowledge. There are a number of special deep-snow and avalanche courses open to the public. But there is more than that to preparing for a skiing tour and carrying it out successfully. The following suggestions are by way of advice to all who are toying with the idea of trying this classic form of Alpine skiing, but do not have the opportunity or the luck to be able to take part in a suitable course and to familiarize themselves with the demands and dangers of touring. No book can really replace the practical experience of a mountain expert, any more than you can learn to sail by just reading a book on the subject.

There are some basic principles, however, that can be laid down.

Skiing ability

In general, touring calls for a solid knowledge of skiing technique on the trail. The skier must have a complete command of technique but need not be expert. Step turns involving weight transfer (stemming both up and downhill) is a minimum requirement, as is some experience of skiing in poor snow conditions,. in difficult terrain, and with a back pack. A completely reliable stationary 'kick' turn is a must. The experience of snow conditions that a good skier possesses will pay off in downhill running.

Physical fitness

Touring requires a certain mental toughness and special physical training. Physical fitness for trail skiing can be far from fit for touring. Cross-country skiing, hill walking, cycling, long-distance running are all good basic training. But it is equally important to be acclimatized to altitude, since many touring expeditions will go to altitudes where the lack of oxygen becomes noticeable. The partial pressure of oxygen – with the air pressure – decreases with height, and from about 13,000ft (4000m) above sea level, altitude sickness, with symptoms such as headache, dizziness and nausea, as well as mental confusion, is not uncommon. Normally there is no altitude problem below about 6500ft(2000m); at about 10,000ft(3000m) the oxygen content of the air is reduced to about 70 per cent and it is noticeable.

Ideally, acclimatization at a lower altitude is to be recommended; it will certainly pay off during any subsequent touring expeditions. Skiers who live a long way from the mountains can make up for their lack of opportunity to adjust to high altitudes, at least partially, by a good training scheme to get themselves into condition.

Equipment

Touring is only enjoyable if the equipment fulfils the special requirements for this kind of skiing.

Clothing

As a general principle, ski wear should be warm, absorb perspiration, let the skin breathe, and be windproof and water-resistant. It should include suitable underwear such as long johns, a long wool or cotton vest and knee-length socks which are not too thick. Ski pants which are not too close-fitting, with legs falling over the boots or, in spring, breeches-style trousers and leggings are customary for outer wear. You will also need two sweaters – thin rather than thick – a quilted or down-filled ski jacket, over-trousers with long zippers to fasten them and thin outer ski jacket against wind, a wollen hat, lined ski gloves or silk gloves worn under woollen mittens. It is particularly important to use a good suncream with a filter factor of four to six, lip salve, and good sunglasses.

Skis, boots and bindings

Skis for touring are more or less identical to skis for use in deep snow: ease of turning and ability to grip on ice, as well as light in weight, are the most important criteria.

Touring boots must be suitable for walking as well as skiing. They must be comfortable for climbing with or without skis and they must be able to take light crampons, and give good ski control on downhill runs.

Buildings for Alpine touring which are perhaps the most important part of the equipment, should meet four requirements:

- A binding for touring must be a high-quality safety binding for use in downhill skiing.
- A binding for touring must be light, and allow the heel to rise freely for climbing in any kind of terrain.
- A binding for touring must be practical in use.
- A binding for touring must work perfectly even in poor weather conditions and at low temperatures.

One binding among the many available, which has had extensive use, is the ISER binding, which can be recommended without reservation as a good binding for touring; it is easily and quickly adjusted for climbing or downhill running. The adjustment does not depend on moveable parts, so it cannot be affected if frozen. When adjusting the binding to downhill, snow which has got into the locking device is automatically expelled.

It is also easy to get in and out of the binding with a certain amount of snow under the boot soles: the large self-centring sole holder makes it easy to get into one of these bindings even

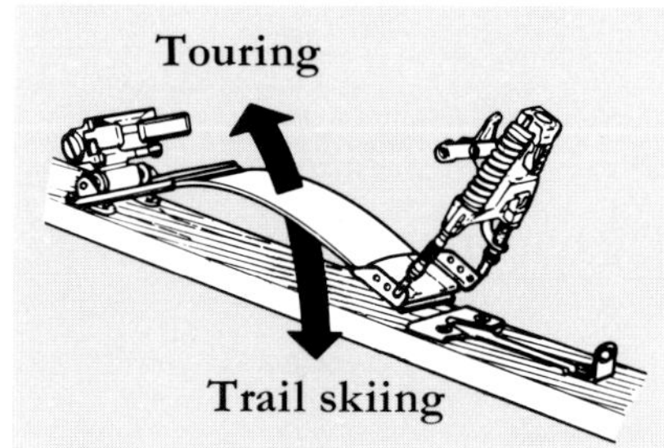

No problems in switching from downhill running to climbing.

in deep snow. Not all bindings that snap into place easily in a warm room will do the same on a steep slope!

Before skiing with any new touring binding for the first time, it should be tried out at home, switching the adjustment several times from touring to downhill skiing, and refitting the binding after it has successfully released in the course of a fall.

Careful binding adjustment is very important in touring.

In addition to your basic equipment the following are required for ski mountaineering and touring:

Climbing skins which either clip or stick on. Properly handled the stick-on kind is the best as it does not collect snow lumps and is light and takes up little space. There are also combined clip-and-stick skins. In either case spare sticking compound should be carried. The adhesive surface should be renewed after ten-fifteen tours. Snow blades for crusted and icy snow are advisable.

Rucksack: a touring rucksack for one-day tours; for longer expeditions you will need a suitable back pack (not a frame pack) with built-in sections for carrying skis.

For navigation: large-scale map, route guide, compass, altimeter, route sketch.

Emergency rations (minimum): one to two packets of concentrated food, dextrose, salt tablets, tea.

Equipment for glaciers: $\frac{1}{3}$in(8mm) rope, harness, two prusik loops, ice axe, crampons.

Safety equipment: a space-blanket or equivalent on all tours. For longer tours: avalanche cord, plastic splint, electronic avalanche bleeper for each member of the party, sterile dressings, 4in(10cm) wide elastic bandage, adhesive plaster, triangular bandage for sling, concentrated dextrose, safety pins, small pair of scissors.

Preparing to go touring

Besides having the ability to ski safely, good physical fitness, and the right equipment, the skier who intends to go touring needs a sound

When climbing uphill, put safety first. Avoid extreme changes of direction and make use of helpful features of the terrain. Look before you ski.

knowledge of the dangers of the mountains, particularly avalanches (see Avalanches, p. 152), mountain weather (Weather Lore for Skiers, p. 158), navigation and mountain craft. All this is part of his general know-how. Most important is an awareness of the potential risks.

If there is any doubt at all as to whether it is safe, caution is better than a rescue. Expert advice before the start should not be disdained.

Every experienced ski tourer knows the importance of getting advice from a good mountain guide and of being able to navigate by using a map, a compass and an altimeter. Studying maps and route guides and listening to the weather forecast and the avalanche reports are basic preparations. Once off the trail the skier must become self-reliant; this implies a certain amount of independence in skiing performance as well as an ability to assess dangers and react to them correctly. The snow conditions will not be ideal, and the tried and trusted swing turn will be the best choice (see p. 80 above). The swing turn, which has a braking effect, is still a good guarantee of safe downhill skiing, especially when laden with a backpack and touring equipment.

RIGHT: Take long strides on gentle slopes and smaller steps on steep slopes. On gentle slopes you can contour – do kick-turns on steep slopes to change direction.

ABOVE: Climbing tracks will quickly disappear if it is snowing or the wind is blowing.

BELOW: Never climb or ski on a cornice or below one. It could break and/or avalanche. Keep to the weather side of the slope.

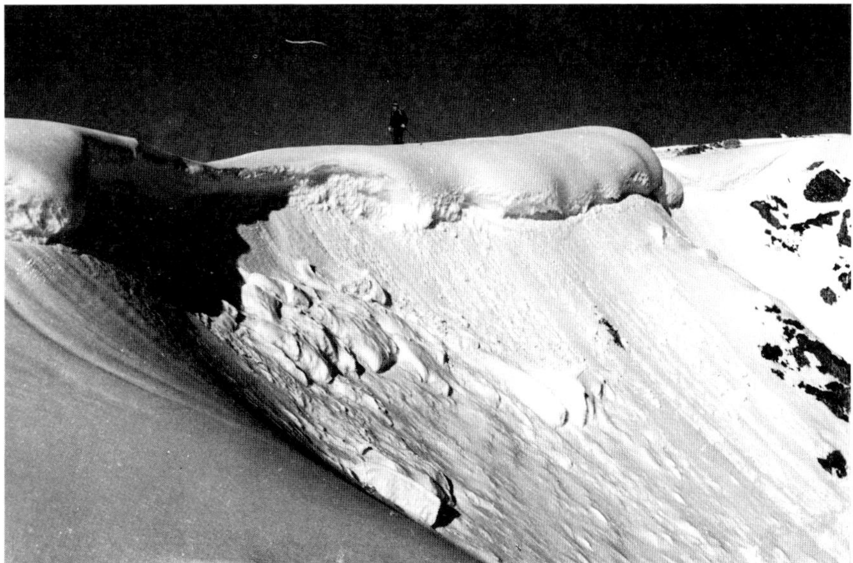

International mountain distress signals

- Six signals per minute, repeated at regular intervals with a one-minute pause in between.
- Answer from the rescue team: three signals per minute.
- Signals may be acoustic or visual. In an emergency everyone is duty bound to help.

Safety for off-trail skiing

Safety for off-trail skiing

There are several dangers when skiing in the mountains. They can be classed as *subjective* and *objective* dangers.

Subject dangers (those arising from the skier himself) include fatigue, strain, chill and exposure, overestimation of one's own capability, physical and psychological strain, for example, vertigo and sickness.

Objective dangers (those arising from the skier's environment) include weather hazards, snow and terrain conditions, and the greatest danger of all – avalanches. As an example, over the last fifteen years more than 800 people have died in avalanches in the Alps. Every time the same questions are asked: could tragedies of this kind have been avoided? Were the skiers careless? Are these fatal accidents acts of God?

Experts who have studied avalanches believe that at least 90% of all such accidents are the fault of the skiers themselves. A groomed trail surrounded by forest and running out in a flat area, or a very gentle slope may be completely safe from avalanches. But even this rule has its exceptions: avalanches have been known on slopes with a gradient of only 14°. The great masses of snow slide down at speeds of up to 186 mph(300 km/h) and with pressure of up to 100 t/m^3 (tonnes per cubic metre). A skier who fails to observe an avalanche warning sign, or ignores it, is running the same risk as a man who starts to cross a railway line at an ungated level crossing with an express train approaching him.

In the normal course of events skiers on the trail are safe from avalanches, providing they obey the directions given by the lift companies, ski schools and trail patrols.

Good signposting. Bad signposting.

Useful points to know

The U.S. Forestry Service Avalanche Centre, Atta, Utah, the Swiss Federal Avalanche Research Centre and many other organizations have published leaflets for the use of skiers with particular emphasis on avalanche dangers.

Avalanches

Avalanches are the cause of about 50 per cent of all fatal accidents in the Alps. Australia has had few avalanche victims and there have only been three deaths from avalanche in New Zealand in the last twenty years.

Nevertheless, danger from avalanches threatens skiers on the trails as well as skiers touring in the mountains. Once buried in an avalanche there is danger of death from suffocation, along with death from cold or from shock and injury. The chances of survival are minimal. Buried under 6ft(1.50m) of snow the prospect of staying alive sinks to 10% after two hours. In practice this means that it is vital for well-organized help to get to work within the two hours after an avalanche has fallen. This will depend upon other skiers on the spot; organized mountain rescue teams do not generally reach the scene of the accident until much later.

Causes of avalanches

Avalanches are caused by the effects which snow, weather and terrain have upon each other. Avalanches are possible when there is:

- More than 1ft(30cm) of new snow.
- Formation of snowdrifts of compressed slab snow by the wind on the lee sides of slopes (especially below the crest of a ridge), sometimes even without any new snowfall.
- Warmth and moisture which affect the snow cover, particularly when the föhn or chinook is blowing, it is raining, or the sun is shining fiercely.
- Formation of unstable snow cover, especially when so-called 'swim snow' is present in lower layers or surface frost has been snowed over.
- Smooth unbroken terrain sheltered from the prevailing wind, usually facing north-east to south-

Dry loose-snow avalanche (single-point breakaway).

Dry full-depth avalanche (slab-type breakaway).

east, where the slope has a gradient of over 15°. The most dangerous slopes have a gradient between 28° and 45°.

Types of avalanche

There are many different kinds of avalanche, distinguished by their appearance and the conditions under which they have been formed. Wind-slab avalanches are the most dangerous for skiers; in over 90% of all accidents to touring skiers they are set off by the skiers themselves.

Touring skiers also run the risk of wet snow avalanches in spring; these are avalanches of loose surface snow, and though they are small in volume they can be very dangerous because of the weight of the snow; 35cu.ft(1m^3) of powder snow weights 110lb(50kg). The same volume of spring snow weighs 880lb(400kg). Wind-slab avalanches are often very large, move very fast, and, most important of all, can be set off from a considerable distance away. Wind slab may not be easy to recognize, depending on its degree of solidity, since it can be covered with new snow, and may still be unstable weeks after its formation.

Starting out on a touring expedition

- It is essential to obtain information about the weather and snow conditions in the area where you intend to ski. This is available through avalanche bulletins, avalanche and weather forecasts in the press, television and radio, from the mountain patrols and clubs, from guides and the landlords of mountain huts.
- Make sure your party consists of people with adequate skiing ability and the right kind of equipment (falls and general incompetence mean a considerable rise in the risks the party runs).
- The leader *must* be able to assess the danger of avalanches over the chosen route.

Choosing the route and safety while on it

- If possible steer clear of any terrain where there may be risk of avalanches.
- If slopes can be avoided where there is avalanche danger do not traverse across them.
- Climb slopes as close to the fall line as possible, if necessary on foot with skis off. If a traverse in a danger zone is unavoidable it should be made as high up the slope as possible, on a downhill line.
- Keep enough distance between the members of the party (going downhill as well) for there to be only one person in the danger area at a time. In any case it is advisable to keep a distance between skiers, so as not to overload the slope.
- When skiing in groups, get someone to give warning at a safe point where there is a good view of the danger area.

Behaviour in avalanche-dangerous terrain

- Add a modern electronic avalanche bleeper to your equipment. (Remember to switch it on to transmit at the start of the day!)
- Be aware of any potential danger. Wear or trail an avalanche cord. (An avalanche cord 33ft(10m) long is the best prospect a buried skier has of being found. Arrows clipped to the cord point to the wearer.)
- Loosen or release all bulky objects (bindings, retaining straps, loops of poles, waist strap of your rucksack, and so on). This is the general principle to adopt if you have no intention of escaping by

Your route downhill should always avoid slopes where there is any hint of avalanche danger. Be cautious on steep north-east slopes (centre of picture). It would be safer to run downhill near the trees, left. Avalanche danger is greatest on the right.

Keep a careful eye open for fences, stones, rocks, tree stumps and trenches as you run downhill. Adjust your technique, speed and choice of route to the terrain.

Navigation

Alpine touring routes are not sign-posted and frequently untracked. No Alpine weather can be relied on to stay fine indefinitely and the bright blue sky with sparkling snow can change to an impenetrable mist in a matter of minutes. For this reason every tour should be carefully mapped and a detailed route plan or sketch prepared.

The navigation instruments you will need are – a reliable compass, an altimeter which must be re-set at every clearly identifiable point, a reliable map, preferably of a scale of 1:25,000 and a watch. The navigational co-ordinates – direction, height and distance (time) can be accurately fixed with these instruments.

The sketch plan should show each direction change, identified by a natural feature if possible (for example – a rock face, river, ravine or huts) which will be visible under poor weather conditions. The compass course should be clearly written. In addition each direction change should also be identified by the height read off from the contour lines on the map. The estimated walking time should also be included; this can be calculated using the rough guide – climbing at 1000ft(300m) per hour, skiing downhill at about 2000ft (600m) per hour in poor visibility.

Wherever possible the system of 'deliberate error' should be used when approaching a final destination or a major route change. This consists of plotting a course which will lead to a point several hundred yards to one side of the destination and identified by a marked natural feature (such as a forest border, road, path, ravine, or long cliff). When this natural feature has been reached, the skier will be able to judge for himself whether he is either on one particular side of his route or the other.

running downhill.

- Wear all clothing, even in warm weather, as a protection against hypothermia if buried in an avalanche.

Self-help in an avalanche

- Schuss downhill if this way of escape is still possible.
- Get rid of bulky objects (skis, poles and so on).
- When the avalanche catches you, try to make swimming movements to keep on the surface and perhaps reach the edge of the avalanche.
- Before the avalanche stops moving get into a crouching position, making a breathing space in front of your face with your hands and around your chest with your arms and elbows.
- Try to free yourself, do not struggle hysterically. Keep some strength in reserve. If trying to free yourself it is important to be orientated, and the easiest way is to let saliva trickle out of your mouth. If it seems impossible to get free, remain still to conserve energy.
- Sounds carry well inwards and outwards, so shout if there is someone nearby. Do not fight the feeling of drowsiness that may overcome you; a sleeping person needs less oxygen, and may still be rescued after several days. Giving yourself up for lost is fatal.
- Hope for rescue and keep listening; keeping alert can lessen the effects of shock.

First rescue attempts

An electronic avalanche bleeper is extremely useful in rescue attempts if the whole group, including the buried person, are equiped with bleepers – as it makes location instantly possible. If not, other measures must be adopted:

- Watch the person caught in the avalanche until the slide stops.
- Notice the point at which it caught him, the point at which he disappeared, and the point at which he and/or the avalanche stopped, and place objects to mark these spots.
- Station someone to give warning, in case of any subsequent slides.
- Search the surface area of the avalanche in silence while listening for any sounds.

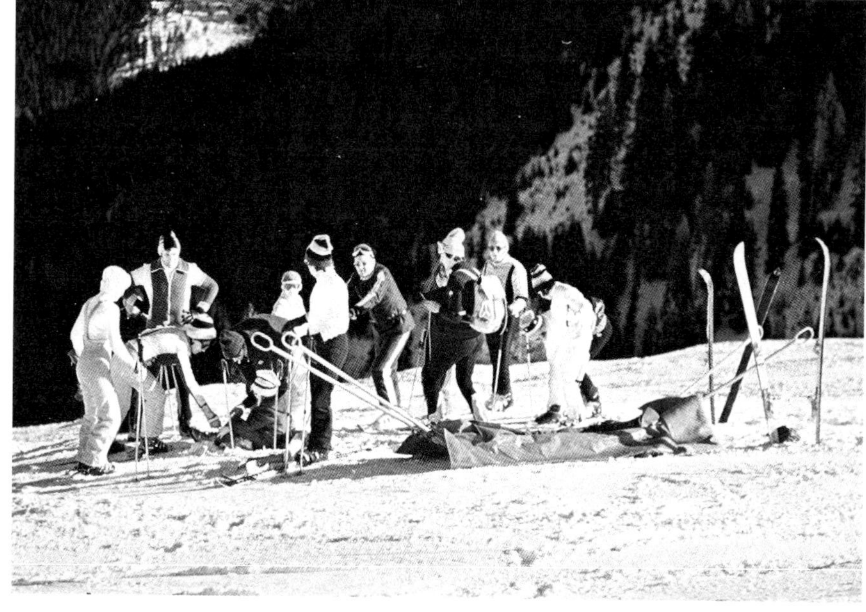

- Send two people for help (when reporting an accident give the following details: where, when, how, whom). Use map references or a diagram. Write the details down at the site of the accident.
- Those still on the scene should first try probing the area most likely to produce results (the part of the avalanche running down from the point at which the skier disappeared to the point at which the avalanche stopped); use suitable probes (these are light, portable avalanche sounds) or, if necessary, ski poles and skis. Probe at intervals of 30in(75cm) each way, to a depth of at least 3ft(1m). Gradually extend the area of your search, marking off the areas already searched.

Avalanche rescue and first aid

- Once you have found where the victim is by probing or by the bleeper, free nose and mouth.
- If unconscious, start resuscitation (mouth-to-mouth or nose breathing) after cleaning snow from air-ways, while other members of the party continue to dig the victim out.
- Lay him on his side in a prepared, sheltered place.
- Keep him warm by body contact and dry clothing. Only use hot drinks if he is conscious and cooperative. On no account give him alcohol.
- Attend to any injuries, such as open wounds or broken limbs. (But see section on First Aid, and also on Accidents below.)
- Do not move the victim until he regains consciousness and the first effects of shock wear off. Never let a shocked person or someone suffering from hypothermia stand up.

First aid

Safe skiing is the motto of this book and the emphasis is on prevention. Accidents, however, *can* happen to anyone at any time, so a prudent skier should know what can be done and what not to do.

For any serious ski mountaineering expedition lasting several days it must be assumed that the group (two or more skiers) is totally self-dependent and any injury or accident must, in the first instance, be dealt with by the group. Though in general neither injury nor accident is a common occurrence in ski mountaineering, it does involve a distinctly greater risk than trail skiing. It is therefore essential that even minor discomforts, such as blisters, small cuts, grazes, digestive upsets, colds, coughs and sneezes be treated adequately and immediately. Even the most minor distress can lead to serious risk of exposure due to making only slow time in adverse weather.

In addition to the normal and conventional first-aid materials such as bandages, cotton wool, band-aids and the like, which should be the individual responsibility of the members of the party, it might be advisable to carry a basic list of suitable medicines. These can best be obtained through your own doctor. Unless one member of the party is a qualified nurse or doctor, strong drugs of the pain-killing variety or antibiotics should be avoided. Their use at altitude can be dangerous. Aspirin, or similar approved compounds, will deal with most minor pains and cough drops or sweets will alleviate coughs and sore throats. Strict diet and personal hygiene will avoid stomach upsets and liberal use of disinfectants will prevent minor grazes and cuts from becoming infected.

Every ski-touring party should carry a repair kit consisting of pliers, screwdriver, wire, nylon cord, spare binding parts and special ski binding tools.

Accidents

Although skiing injuries are a fraction of what was once a common occurrence, most trail skiers will, sooner or later, come across some unfortunate skier who has suffered a fall sufficiently serious to require the presence of the rescue patrol and transport from the ski slope. Like any such incident, it produces either a feeling of helplessness or an officious and probably incompetent and ignorant bystander who will, with great energy, do everything wrong.

There is a golden rule to all first aid – do as little as possible as efficiently as possible; in practice this usually means doing nothing more than providing some elementary comfort and a human presence until the competent people arrive with trained expertise and equipment. It is the art of doing nothing that can briefly be described.

'Can I help?' is the first question. Many falls look dramatic and the victim will often be slightly bemused for an instant. If there is an injury, he will be quick to answer.

Retrieve ski or skis and/or gently remove still attached ski or skis and place them, tail-first, in the snow so that they form a cross above the victim. Work from below the skier and do not move him crudely by pulling or pushing or attempted lifting. The simplest way is to offer two crossed arms from in front and below the skier allowing him to pull himself into a more comfortable position. Under no circumstances should a leg or legs be forcibly moved into a fresh position. It will often ease an injured skier if a seat is scooped out in the snow so that he does not tend to slide downhill. This can be done quite simply without any displacement of the victim.

One, or preferably two, of the bystanders should be asked if they would mind reporting the accident to the nearest lift terminal. The location should be defined by the name of the trail – ideally giving the number of the nearest trail marker (the number indicates the precise position on the trail on a master plan in the rescue service hut). It is best to write this down. It is also a good idea to warn those going for rescue not to be in too much of a hurry and so avoid adding to the casualties.

In general, it takes about half an hour from the moment that an accident has been seen to the arrival of the rescue patrol. There is not very much that can be done during this waiting period except to provide comfort and companionship and, if required or circumstances seem to demand it, additional clothing, something warm or waterproof to sit on. The text books will recommend hot sweet drinks to combat primary shock, but few if any skiers on the trails will be carrying a thermos or heating apparatus. If there is any hot sweet tea available, however, it is sound medicine. Under no circumstance make use of any kind of drugs or alcohol. Minor cuts and abrasions can be ignored unless the bleeding is sufficient to be a nuisance.

Collisions

Unfortunately many of today's skiing accidents are the result of collisions and such collisions can have much the same results as an automobile accident. Obviously a serious open wound with copious bleeding must be attended to and the simplest method of doing this is by pressing a large pressure pad of any non-fluffy material on to the wound. Tourniquets in the mountains in winter conditions are a dangerous approach as the restriction of circulation in a limb can lead rapidly to frost damage. They should only be used in cases of dangerous arterial bleeding (above the injury) or copious venous bleeding (below the injury).

Unconsciousness resulting from a head injury or any other major injury should not immediately be treated as a case of imminent death and mouth-to-mouth rescuscitation started. This is only required where breathing has stopped (for at least thirty seconds) or there is no pulse to be felt (at the neck not the wrist). An unconscious person should be laid flat, if possible legs higher than head, and the head turned sideways and any obstruction to the nose or mouth cleared away.

Fainting after even a minor injury is not uncommon. There are nearly always warning signs and the victim will almost certainly give warning – 'I'm afraid I'm about to faint' – and immediately fold up. He will recover within a short time and can be helped to do so by having his head placed lower than his heart.

The greatest danger in any mountain injury is hypothermia, that is to say a lowering of the core temperature of the body which occurs when heat loss from the skin surface and breathing is in excess of heat replacement from normal body metabolism. The danger is greatest if there is wind as well as low temperature.

The so-called 'windchill' is now well documented and precise tables have been established showing the effective heat losses when even moderate temperatures are accompanied by a wind. Hypothermia is not a thing which is very likely to be encountered during the course of normal trail skiing with modern efficient ski clothing, but it is an ever-present danger in any case of injury, if rescue is not available within a reasonable time. The symptoms are unexpected lassitude, incoherence, impairment of vision, limb weakness and extreme irritability. Immediate treatment is required and should consist of immobilization, body contact warmth and early rescue.

Other injuries

Two very common injuries or complaints are minor frostbite and snow blindness. The former, usually affecting finger-tips, toes, nose-tip or ear lobes (and less commonly cheeks) shows itself as a dead white patch which feels hard and is insensible. Most commonly applied treatments are dangerous old-wives' tales. The affected part should NOT be rubbed with snow or with anything else. It should not be beaten or waved about (this is for an earlier stage before the affected part has become frozen). The best first-aid treatment is to keep the frost-bitten part covered, go immediately to the nearest day lodge, warming hut or rescue hut and then place the affected part into cold water which must be slowly warmed up by repeated changes until feeling is restored and the whiteness disappears. If this does not happen quickly medical aid should be sought as early as possible. It is advisable in any case to see a doctor after even a minor frostbite as the area can easily become infected and will almost certainly blister.

Snow blindness is really quite inexcusable and is the result of failing to wear sunglasses or tinted goggles even in dull weather. It is caused by an excess of ultra-violet light and is, in effect, a sunburn of the cornea. It is extremely painful and disabling and takes two to three days to heal. Medical aid should be sought, though, if this is not available, eye-pads soaked in cold tea or any proprietary eye-bath solution, rest, darkness and mild painkillers are the best adjunct to patience.

Weather lore for skiers

A little practical weather lore is useful for all skiers.

The most important meteorological phenomena occur about 9 miles (15 km) above the earth's surface. Air, which conveys these meteorological phenomena, is a mixture of gases comprising:

- 78% nitrogen
- 21% oxygen
- 1% other gases (e.g., argon, carbon dioxide)

Water vapour, the real 'weather maker', is present in the air in quantities which vary a great deal – between 0.2% and 4%. The greater the amount of water vapour present, the damper the air will be. According to the air temperature, water vapour becomes either an invisible gas, a liquid or a solid.

The amount of ozone is variable too; ozone is essential as it absorbs excess ultra-violet radiation. The atmosphere also contains tiny particles of dust and other chemical and organic matter which come partly from space. These suspended particles act as the nucleii of condensation in the formation of rainfall. If they are present in concentrated form they obstruct the rays of the sun. This effect is most noticeable in valleys, and decreases with higher altitude.

Thermal energy comes from the sun. The rays of the sun warm the surface of the earth and heat the atmosphere from below. The amount of sun a given part of the earth receives varies with geographical latitude, the time of day and the season of the year. Part of the sun's rays are absorbed (reflected or scattered) in the atmosphere.

Wind

The movement of the air is described as wind; this movement is the result of compensation between high and low pressure areas.

There is a close connection between wind and the weather in many areas. A wind blows between the mountains and the valleys; this is caused by a drop in pressure as the result of different temperatures on the valley floor and the mountain heights.

Note: the valley wind blows towards the mountains in the late morning and early afternoon. It is more noticeable in summer than in winter, when cold air lying in the valley slows it down.

The mountain wind blows down towards the valley in the evening.

Mountain and valley winds are localized air currents which are most effective in fine weather conditions; thus they are also described as 'fair weather wind'.

But even the narrowest mountain valley is affected by the distribution of atmospheric pressure on a larger scale. When mountain people speak of a quarter from which rain and storms come, or a 'bad weather wind', they are relying on generations of experience which have shown them that a change in the weather depends on the wind coming from certain directions – indicating low-pressure areas in the case of bad weather. The opposite – high pres-

The Beaufort scale of wind force

Beaufort number	Description	Mph (km/h)	Effects of wind
0	Calm	$\frac{1}{2}$ (1)	No wind, smoke rises vertically
1	Light air	$\frac{1}{2}$–3 (1–5)	Direction shown by smoke but not by wind vanes
2	Light breeze	4–7 (6–11)	Wind felt on face, leaves rustle, wind vanes move
3	Gentle breeze	8–12 (12–19)	Leaves and twigs in motion, wind extends light flag
4	Moderate breeze	13–17(20–28)	Raises dust, loose paper, moves small branches
5	Fresh breeze	18–24(29–38)	Small trees in leaf begin to sway, crests form on waves. In winter, break off any touring expedition in high mountains and intense cold
6	Strong breeze	25–30(39–49)	Large branches moving, whistling in telegraph wires, difficulty with umbrellas
7	Moderate gale	31–38(50–61)	Whole trees in motion, difficult to walk against the wind. Break off any touring expedition in high mountains in summer
8	Fresh gale	39–45(62–74)	Twigs break off trees; progress impeded
9	Strong gale	46–54(75–88)	Slight structural damage to houses, chimney pots and slates blown off
10	Whole gale	55–63(89–102)	Trees uprooted, considerable structural damage to houses
11	Storm	64–72(103–117)	Widespread damage. Seldom occurs inland
12	Hurricane	73 and over (118 and over)	Devastation

sure areas – will bring fine weather. Since mountains and valleys deflect air currents and force them into certain paths, there is a great deal of variation in mountain weather, which can often surprise those who were not brought up in the mountains.

Important: take the advice of a mountain guide, a warden or ranger.

Wind and weather in the northern hemisphere mountains

The western face of the Rocky Mountains, the Bugaboos, Sierras and Wasatch (Utah)

- South-west to north-west winds are usually 'bad weather winds' when low clouds are present. In the Sierras south to west winds are usually 'bad weather winds'.
- North to east to south-east winds are usually 'fair weather winds'. N.B. these tendencies are more marked when atmospheric pressure is falling or rising rapidly.
- South to south-west winds indicate low pressure disturbance to the west.
- North-east to south-east winds may indicate the coming of a föhn or chinook (called Santa Ana or Newhall wind in Sierras) if lenticular clouds are present. May be followed by bad weather in two or three days.

N.B. rapid pressure falls with increasing clouds means bad weather if winds are south-west or west. Pressure rises with high clouds signal fair weather.

The eastern face of the Rocky Mountains, the Bugaboos, Sierras and Wasatch (Utah)

Eastern-face weather is much more difficult to characterize and a variety of weather sequences is possible.

- North-east to south-east winds below mountain-top level are usually 'bad weather winds' when attended by rapidly falling or rising pressures.
- South-east to south winds indicate bad weather to come.
- South-west to north-west winds are usually 'fair weather winds', except for the 1400–4000ft (500–1500m) nearest the mountain peak.

As a general rule, independent of location:

If there is a strong fall in pressure, accompanied by winds blowing up into the mountains, with increasing cloud cover, you can expect the weather to change for the worse.

In high mountain regions there is a particular danger of squally winds blowing at high speeds. The danger is especially high when lenticular clouds are present.

New England and eastern Canada

- North-east to south-east winds are usually 'bad weather winds'.
- South-east to north-west winds are usually 'fair weather winds'. N.B. snowfall in the New England mountains is strongly affected by storms along the Atlantic seaboard. A westerly wind sometimes brings light snowfall and a chinook effect, though not as marked as in the Rockies.

The Alps

The northern face

- North-west to north winds are usually 'bad weather winds'.
- North-east to south-east winds are usually 'fair weather winds'.
- West winds indicate low-pressure disturbance.
- South-west and south winds may indicate the coming of clear periods with föhn-like conditions, to be followed later (one or two days) by bad weather.

The southern face

- East to south-east winds are usually 'bad weather winds'.
- North-west to north winds are usually 'fair weather winds'.
- South and south-west winds indicate bad weather to come.

As a general rule, independent of the locality:

If there is a strong fall in pressure, accompanied by a wind blowing against the cloud formation, you can expect the weather to change for the worse in the near future.

Wind chill table (0°F temperature)

Wind mph	35	30	25	20	15	10	5	0	−5	−10	−15
5	33	27	21	19	12	7	0	−5	−10	−15	−21
10	22	16	10	3	−3	−9	−15	−22	−27	−34	−40
15	16	9	2	−5	−11	−18	−25	−31	−38	−45	−51
20	12	4	−3	−10	−17	−24	−31	−39	−46	−53	−60
25	8	1	−7	−15	−22	−29	−36	−44	−51	−59	−66
30	6	−2	−10	−18	−25	−33	−41	−49	−56	−64	−71
35	4	−4	−12	−20	−27	−35	−43	−52	−58	−67	−74
40	3	−5	−13	−21	−29	−37	−45	−53	−60	−69	−76

Wind and weather in the southern hemisphere mountains

Australia

- West to south-west winds are usually 'bad weather winds'.
- North winds are usually 'fair weather winds'.

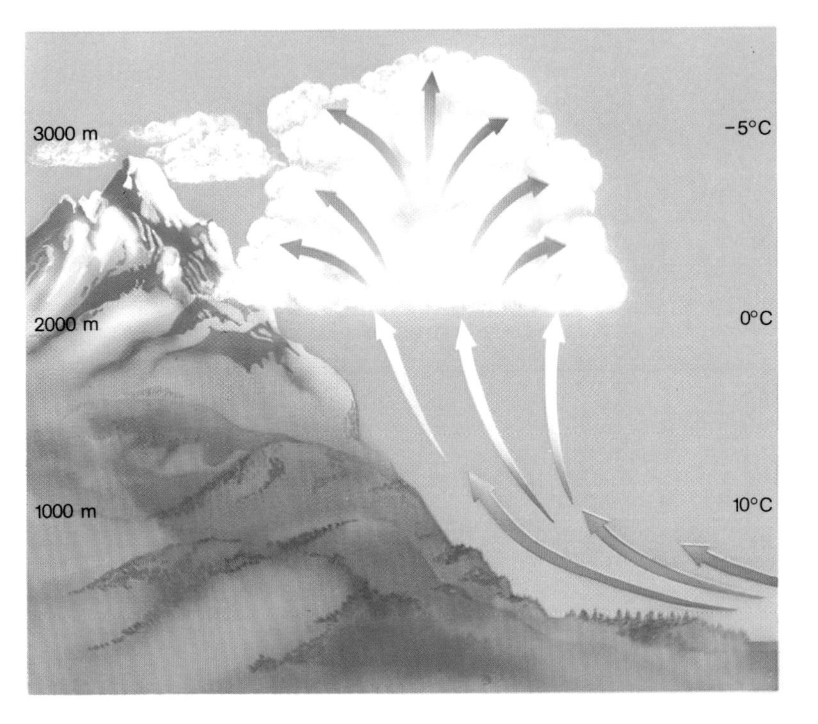

Warm air from down in the valley rises, cooling off as it does so. The relative humidity increases. After reaching saturation point water vapour condenses, clouds form.

New South Wales mountains will often get easterly snowfalls that miss the Victorian Alps.

If south-west winds combine with a low-pressure system they will often bring snow. Penetration of the land mass depends on the strength and intensity of the depression, i.e., the southernmost resorts will get more snow than those further north in New South Wales. The snow is usually in a state of slow melt during the day so knee-deep powder snow is unusual.

New Zealand

- South to south-west winds are usually 'bad weather winds'.
- North-west winds are usually 'fair weather winds'.

Thaws are caused by the 'Nor Wester' which drops heavy precipitation on the western slopes and reaches the lee flank in the east as a warm dry wind.

In the mountain areas there are excellent snow conditions with almost universal power snow.

Atmospheric pressure is due to the fact that the air has mass. Atmospheric pressure is measured in:

Millimetres of mercury (Torr, mmHg) or millibars (mb)

The relation between the two pressure measurements is:

1 mmHg = 1.333 mb
1 mb = 0.750 mmHg

Atmospheric pressure decreases with height. In the lower levels of the atmosphere air pressure decreases by 1mm mercury column (= 1.3mb) per 11m rise in height.

Altimeters can also be used as barometers. Air pressure differs according to time and place, so it is necessary to adjust an altimeter to a known height before use. The following are important points to note in making weather observations:

1. Rising or falling atmospheric pressure.
2. Speed with which the pressure rises or falls.

Atmospheric pressure

Cold air is heavy and presses the barometer down. High pressure effects a rise in temperature and a decrease in the humidity of the air. This is connected with the dispersal of clouds. Warm air is light. The rising of warm air leads to a cooling of the air and the formation of clouds. In

State of barometer	Millibars/hour	Weather
Rising	0.25–0.5	high-pressure situation approaching (fine weather for some time)
Rising	1–2	intermediate high, clear periods of short duration
Falling	0.25–0.5	low-pressure situation approaching (poor weather for some time)
Falling	1–2	stormy weather situation, thunderstorms in summer

this case the barometer shows falling pressure.

Clearly marked local variations from the norm can occur. The temperature and humidity of the air play a large part.

Atmospheric pressure is shown on weather maps by lines, corresponding to air pressure (isobars), of five millibars apart. The distance between the isobars shows the prevalent variation in pressure:

Distance between isobars	Pressure gradient	Weather
small	large	turbulent (stormy)
large	slight	calm (little wind)

Air temperature

Air temperature is a very important meteorological element, together with atmospheric pressure and wind, particularly where weather in the mountains is concerned.

The warming and cooling of air in the valleys and up on the mountains, in connection with mountain winds and valley winds has already been discussed (see above). Air masses (of different temperatures) which flow into the valleys and over the mountains have even more effect on the weather: warm air comes from the south, arctic air from the north. (In the southern hemisphere the direction is reversed: warm air comes from the north, cold air from the south.)

Air temperature decreases with altitude. With no cloud formation, rising air will cool off by about 4°F(1°C) per 328ft(100m) increase in height. Air with relative humidity of 100% will only cool off by 2°F(0.5°C) as it rises.

Compared to mountain temperatures, valley areas at the same altitude are colder in winter and warmer in summer. Valley areas also have a marked progression of temperatures during the day which is not found on mountains. In winter the lowest nightime temperature is reached sooner on the mountains than in the valleys. The highest daytime temperature in summer, however, is reached at about the same time on the mountains and in the valleys.

Humidity

Strictly speaking, there is no point in measuring the air temperature if one does not also know something about the water-vapour content of the air. The long-distance view you get on the mountains will tell you something about the humidity and temperature of the air:

Cold air means better long-distance visibility than warm air.

Cold polar air, however, is also drier than warm air from the subtropics.

Visibility, the colour of the sky, and sunset colours all indicate the state of the weather:

- Stable weather conditions may be expected if the valleys remain misty and visibility higher up is good.
- Clear weather in the valleys, with overcast weather higher up on the mountains, indicates a change in the weather.
- An obvious decrease in visibility high in the mountains indicates an increase of humity in the air within twenty-four hours. Clouds and rain may be expected.
- Sunset colours of orange and red-brown are a sign of continuing good weather.
- Sunset colours of yellow and yellowish-green are a sign that the weather is about to change.
- If the blue of the sky turns to grey, the appearance of clouds and thunderstorms in summer may be expected.

The 'relative humidity' mentioned in weather reports gives the relationship between the water vapour present in the air to the highest possible amount of water vapour at a given temperature, expressed as a percentage. If humid air cools off the relative humidity rises (up to 100%, at which point the air cannot absorb more humidity and clouds and rain occur). If it warms up, the relative humidity falls (not usually below 10% even in very dry conditions). Excess water vapour in the air gives rise to the following different formations: clouds, mist, dew (it can also turn to ice, and snow, sleet and hail may be expected). There are two main types of clouds:

- Cumulus clouds
- Stratus clouds

The look of the clouds tells us something about the weather. Piled-up masses of cumulus cloud indicate changeable weather, such as occurs when masses of cold and warm air meet. Such weather is accompanied by showers of rain, snowfalls and sometimes thunderstorms.

By way of contrast, stratus clouds usually extend horizontally over the sky, forming almost unbroken cloud cover. Stratus clouds give steadier rain, because there is no stormy movement of the air. They are described as 'stable' cloud formations, as opposed to the 'unstable' cumulus clouds. Stable and unstable cloud strata can often alternate very quickly. Showers therefore fall most often in the afternoon, when the morning and midday sun has warmed the lower layers of air. Simultaneous cumulus and stratus cloud formations point to changeable weather and all kinds of surprises.

The föhn or chinook

Föhn is a typical Alpine weather situation – and an excellent example of the way rising and falling air affects the mountains. The föhn is a wind blowing down the mountainside, and is particularly marked on the north side of the Alps, although that is not the only place where it occurs. (In the Rocky Mountains and High Sierras this wind is sometimes called the chinook; see below.)

In Europe the föhn appears at its strongest on the eastern side of an area of low pressure over France. Its characteristics are:

- Protracted fall in atmospheric pressure.
- A strong south wind in the mountains.
- Damp air forced to rise on the southern side of the Alps.
- Heavy cloud formation and rain on the southern side of the Alps.
- Air higher up, which is less humid, streams into the valleys on the northern side of the Alps as it warms up and loses more moisture.
- Squally winds on the northern side of the Alps, dry, warm air, frequently very good visibility, formation of lenticular-shaped föhn clouds.

Though the föhn may blow for several days, if the low is stationary over France the situation is a sign of bad weather.

Note: if the wind changes from south and south-west to west to north-west, and clouds come up, a cold front can be expected.

The föhn can also blow on the southern side of the Alps: heavy rain falls on the northern side of the Alps as the result of a situation where there is high pressure over the eastern Atlantic and low pressure over the Baltic. Stormy winds blow from the north with the result that there is clearer, drier weather on the southern side of the Alps.

The effect of the föhn on the southern side of the Alps is bound up with rising atmospheric pressure, and in this case it indicates a settled period of fine weather.

Föhn winds on the southern side of the Alps usually occur in January and July. The showers on the northern side of the Alps in January are accompanied by heavy snowfall.

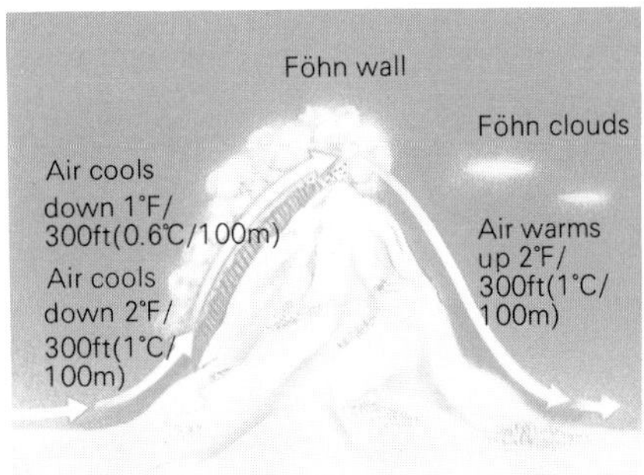

Chinook occurs on the eastern side of the Rocky Mountains The higher elevations may be affected by chinook wall clouds and snow squalls. At lower elevations west to north-west winds with rapidly falling or rising pressure indicates the coming of chinook. When it sets in after a spell of intense cold, the temperature can rise by 20–40°F(– 6–4°C) in fifteen minutes.

After the first rise, the temperature may fluctuate violently, as it comes alternately under the influence of patches of warm and cold air. The sky is usually clear over the plains with the mountains covered by the characteristic chinook arch of heavy cloud.

The factor of special importance to skiers is that the warm air blowing either on the eastern side of the Rocky Mountains, or on the northern side of the Alps, starts the snow melting. The danger of avalanches can become acute.

Föhn is known by a wide variety of local names. In New Zealand a föhn blowing from the Southern Alps onto the Canterbury plains is known as a Nor Wester. A north wind in Australia, blowing from the centre of the continent, usually heralds a melt or rain.

Snowfall

It depends on the temperature whether water vapour is precipitated as rain or snow.

Note: always look out for zero temperature in the mountains and the line at which it appears. Snow will fall at about 330ft(100m) below this line. Snow showers may occur in temperatures of 41–45°F(5–8°C). If a skier finds rain in the valley he may find snow falling up in the mountains, but he might also get sleet and squally winds. Study the weather forecasts thoroughly before setting out on a long touring expedition, and ask local people for advice.

Showers do not fall equally heavily everywhere, even over the same range of mountains.

For skiers

The formation and state of snow cover depends primarily on the prevailing temperatures in the mountains. Higher up there will be more snow, and it will lie longer. A good permanent snow cover may be expected during winter at altitudes above 6000ft(2000m).

The snow cover on the mountains is usually composed of different kinds of snow. Stresses form between the different kinds. Stormy winds also lead to uneven distribution of the different kinds of snow, especially high up in the mountains.

Wind causes the formation of wind

slab and drifting. The excess snow will break away from steep slopes.

Differences in the composition of snow cover, and the effect of the wind upon it, are among the basic causes of avalanches.

High pressure

Large-scale variations in atmospheric pressure are a feature of meteorological phenomena in the mountains as well as elsewhere.

Note: in a high-pressure area the air comes downwards, becomes warmer in the process, and clouds disperse. Fine, warm weather may be expected when pressure is high.

In fact the weather is often different – and in particular there may be a difference between weather down in the valleys and up on the mountains. In autumn and winter especially, air from the high-pressure area cannot usually get right down to the ground. The reason for this is that the strong radiation leads to the formation of cold air pockets near the ground; these are damp, and generally keep the currents of air off. So a mist persists all day in the valleys. Up on the mountains, however, the sun will be shining, it will be warm for the time of year, and long-distance visibility will usually be good.

Stable high-pressure areas occur in winter. The air is cold and dry. When the weather is clear in the mountain valleys we get severe frosts which are even harder over the snow cover. Such high-pressure areas occur in the northern hemisphere particularly in January and February but they may also occur at the end of November and in the first half of December.

There are usually a great many showers during the Alpine summer. Long periods of fine weather are rare in the Alps at this time of year.

Low pressure

In a low-pressure area the air rises, cooling off and becoming moister as it does so; cloud formation and showers of rain or snow occur.

Low pressure, however, does not automatically foretell bad weather. A mixture of cold and warm masses of air in the low-pressure area means we may get surprises.

In a low-pressure area there is a good deal of difference between the effects on the weather of warm and cold fronts. Precipitation in the region of a warm front usually takes the form of rain or steady snowfall. Precipitation in the region of a cold front is more showery and often accompanied by thunderstorms, even in winter. After a cold front there are often clear periods (formation of an intermediate high). Strong radiation losses over the ground mean that in winter the warm air from a 'low' cannot reach the layers of air closest to the ground. Therefore the effect of a low-pressure area on the weather is delayed.

Large-scale meteorological situations such as this can affect the weather for a whole week. They usually occur in July, August, November and January in the northern hemisphere.

The appearance of the clouds tells us something about the weather. The piled cumulus clouds indicate unstable weather, such as occurs when cold and warm masses of air meet. Stratus clouds in the background.

Cross-country skiing

It is not surprising that cross-country or Nordic skiing has become increasingly popular over the last few years and it cannot be pure chance that the greatest rate of growth has happened in those countries which have been devoted to Alpine skiing. In many places the downhill trails have reached the limits of their capacity at weekends and in the high season, whereas cross-country skiing offers an alternative which presents no such problem. No wonder that many passionately keen Alpine skiers are enjoying Nordic skiing, both touring and cross-country.

While the pressures and bustle, technology and regimentation of the commercial world have made their way into many areas of Alpine skiing, the cross-country skier can still find the opportunity to escape from it all. Someone whose career makes great demands on him is not so likely to find the relaxation and recreation he needs on overcrowded trails. Understandably, many holiday-makers prefer to go their own way in their free time and enjoy the charm of the winter landscape in peace and quiet. Cross-country skiing can be practised everywhere where there is snow, at any time, after work, or at weekends, and it appeals particularly to those people who like to enjoy skiing without expense and competitive sporting pressures.

An essential part of the sport's appeal seems to be that it is never regarded as just a way of keeping fit but is always a pleasant form of recreation. And why not admit – even if it seems eccentric in the twentieth century – that travelling on skis through a snowy winter landscape, away from the centres of the tourist industry, can help us achieve a fresh emotional and psychological balance.

There are many more advantages that cross country skiing can offer: the equipment is simpler and cheaper and there are no overcrowded slopes. Money and time wasted on lifts and trains is saved and, compared to downhill skiing, the risk of injury, whether to yourself or others, is minimal.

Most publications, particularly in Europe, emphasize the beneficial effects of cross-country skiing to health. It should be a minor motivation but medical studies of sport state unequivocally that cross-country skiing is an ideal way to improve the performance of heart, circulation, lungs and metabolism, and is good preventive medicine for the effects of a normal sedentary way of life. Lack of good regular exercise, often combined with psychological stress, is a major cause of many illnesses of modern life.

Quite apart from the health aspect, cross-country skiing is an excellent way to lose weight. It has been established that the exercise taken during cross-country skiing burns up a great many calories: 500–700 per hour!

Cross-country skiing is a fine example of the kind of sport that may be enjoyed all your life. It is not necessary to be young and athletic to go cross-country skiing, nor ultra-fit and ambitious. Anyone who can walk can learn the basics of skiing technique quickly and easily. The devotees of the sport range from children to grandfathers, from novices to experts, from skiers who practise the sport for recreational (and even health reasons) to competitive sportsmen and women. You only have to go skiing in Norway on a Sunday to realize this.

Cross-country skiing – rambling

Ski rambling is usually regarded as the first step to the more athletic cross-country skiing (*langlauf* in German). Rambling excursions on skis have a value of their own, and a place alongside the more athletic forms of cross-country skiing.

Walking on skis is exactly what it sounds like, although perhaps it would be more correct to say step-by-step gliding. In quite a short time a complete beginner can move forward on the flat on his two narrow skis. The right terrain (see below) is essential to master the art easily. The first aim is not for a technically perfect gliding step, but only the ability to move slowly forward over the snow.

Cross-country skiing through a snowy winter landscape, away from the hurry and bustle of the centres of tourism, is coming to be a popular alternative to downhill Alpine skiing.

This means there are no great technical hurdles to be overcome before enjoying the sport. It makes few demands on athletic performance and expertise, so even an awkward beginner is in no danger of making himself look silly or failing completely. It is no secret that fear of public failure and disgracing oneself athletically keeps many people from taking up sports. This is certainly true of Alpine skiing, for nearly half the guests in some winter sports' resorts are non-skiers. These are the very people who need not worry about trying out a pair of cross-country skis.

The experience of cross-country skiing is not so much an athletic one as a way to enjoy the countryside: you can ski cross-country in natural surroundings, go for excursions through the winter landscape, even ski in places that are closed off in summer because they are under cultivation. Perhaps the illusion of a personal freedom of movement is part of the pleasure.

Most important of all, cross-country skiing as a recreational sport offers people who live far away from mountains a chance to try this simple form of skiing without any great outlay of time and money. They may also experience the charm of the winter landscape at the same time. Since there is no special level of performance that has to be reached in simple walking on skis, there is no age limit. People of seventy or eighty can still make their way comfortably along the trails, and five-year-old children enjoy following in their parents' tracks.

The latter, of course, will only be true if the excursion is geared to the children's needs. Walking on skis for too long, with no games and no particular aim in mind, is as boring for children as a traditional family walk on a Sunday. So parents should make sure there is some variety: they could play a tracking game, show the children how to follow animal trails, organize a game of hide-and-seek, and then their children will be keen to join them.

Children have little trouble learning the technique of cross-country skiing. They have a more natural sense of movement than adults. And even the keenest cross-country skiing enthusiasts among parents should not make the mistake of withholding Alpine skiing from their children. A ski course for children will be more fun on a slope than on a level trail! It

is not usual to find children who develop a real, permanent love for cross-country skiing before the age of ten. Up to that age, parents must adapt themselves to their children's needs on cross-country skiing outings. Once children are older, simple ski rambling can become a true family sport.

In fact cross-country skiing along the trails is one of the few ways in which a whole family *can* practise the same sport together. And this is quite an important point, since it is an unfortunate fact that many families find they are separated in their free time and at weekends by different sporting interests and capabilities. Even wives and mothers, however, who refuse to join in, say, tennis, Alpine skiing or cycling because they are 'not the sporting type' can easily take part in a family cross-country skiing outing.

One could also say that cross-country skiing is the ideal recreational sport for less athletic women, since it encourages them (generally under-represented in sport) to take part.

Whether skiing with your family or with a group of friends, cross-country skiing can be recommended as a particularly companionable, recreational sport. Things are taken relatively easily, breathing is simple and you can chat to each other. And the route of any good expedition may well lead to a café or inn somewhere near the end of the journey, where you can refresh yourself after your efforts . . .

First steps

Anyone starting out on narrow cross-country skis for the first time is well advised to attend a school for beginners. The time will be well spent in that it will reduce frustration later on; if you try to teach yourself you can easily finish up with problems when you get out on to a trail.

An experienced instructor – or an expert cross-country skier friend – can choose the right kind of terrain, explain and demonstrate movements and correct mistakes, and be able to assess your progress.

On the other hand, the basic movements of walking on skis are not so hard to learn, and a self-taught skier may be able to master them. If you are in this situation read the section on technique and methods of cross-country skiing, and work out the necessary basic knowledge for yourself.

Suitable equipment (see below) is as important as it is for Alpine skiing. If the choice is 'no-wax' skis which, in theory, need no waxing it is still important to prepare and wax them in order to get a good grip on the snow and to ensure that the skis do not slide away at every step.

Terrain

To begin with, it is better that the terrain is as flat as possible, with an even covering of snow. First steps will succeed even better on a well-prepared trail. A beginner will only feel comfortable on such a trail if he can use it without being disturbed. Constant requests from other skiers to give way are embarrassing and can fluster a novice.

A well-organized cross-country school will have a special learner's loop professionally laid out and prepared.

- Trails for learners should run parallel, at a distance of about 10ft(3m) from each other to keep pupils from getting in each other's way; they are generally about 200–250(60–80m) long.
- The distance between left and right ski should be about the breadth of the hips, and the trail itself should be deep enough to ensure that the skis remain in the grooves. This makes it easier to control the skis while gliding, and a beginner can concentrate on keeping his balance.
- In new or deep snow, tracks for the ski poles are prepared on either side of the trail, so that a beginner does not 'collapse' when planting poles and so lose his balance.
- The snow is flattened at either end of the trail, to make it easier to turn (using the star turn).
- The instructor's trail which runs parallel crosses the pupils' trails about 30ft(10m) before the end of the trails.

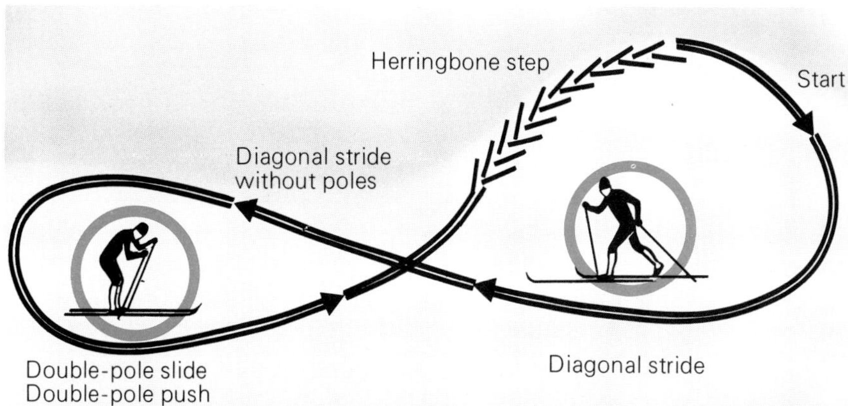

- The straight parallel trails are surrounded by a circular looped trail, where more varied walks can be done.

The instructor should find suitable terrain for learning how to climb and come down slopes; these slopes should be close to the learner's loop. Success in learning depends to a great extent on having just the right gradient for a first attempt at gliding using both poles together, climbing and coming downhill. A slight inclination is sufficient to begin with.

Getting up after a fall

It is inevitable that first steps will result in the first fall, a gentle occurrence with cross-country skis, as the link of ski, boot and leg is loose. A fall is, more or less, an involuntary sitting-down.

There is no compulsory or orthodox way of getting up. Every beginner will find the method most suitable to himself, according to the situation and his own dexterity. In general, there should be no hurry.

- Place skis tidily together and pull them to one side, parallel, and partly under your body.
- Slip hands out of the loops of the poles.
- Place the poles together and use as a support while standing up in a normal fashion, as if there were no skis around.

Getting used to your equipment

If you can walk, you can walk on cross-country skis.

The skis which are loosely held to boots, and the long poles which at first are only used for balance, take a little getting used to, particularly after the heavy fixed weight of Alpine equipment. The initial reaction is one of instability, lightness and length. A few minutes' skiing is sufficient to demonstrate the simplicity of cross-country equipment.

The basic step – the diagonal stride

It is important not to walk about, raising the skis off the snow. The skis should be pushed forward step by step along the trail, sliding or gliding, and kept in contact with the snow. This, of course, is only possible if your knees are flexed and the first steps are relatively short. The cross-country ski binding gives full freedom to the heel.

Arms and poles are supports which move in the same way as they would when walking without skis on: as the right ski is pushed forward, the left arm and pole are ready to plant the pole forward – and so on alternately. The step is called the *diagonal stride* because of this diagonally opposite movement of arms and legs. The most common mistake at this stage is to bring the right ski and the right arm and pole forward at the same time – followed by the same movement on the other side.

This should be corrected by practising the stride and slide without the use of poles.

The star turn

The first introduction to this technique occurs, at the latest, when turning round at the end of the trail. This is done by stepping round with the skis forming the radius of a circle, using either the front or back of the skis as its central point, raising, angling and putting down the skis alternately. Small steps are advisable and the ski should be lifted by the toes.

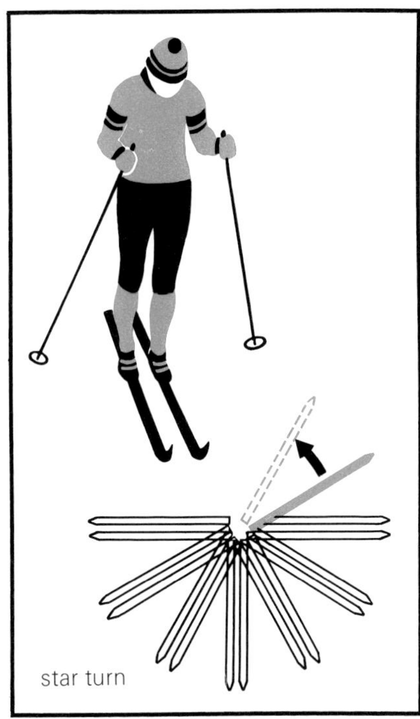
star turn

Diagonal stride without poles

Practise without poles is the best way to advance from walking to gliding as easily as possible, and to acquire a rhythmical co-ordination of arms and legs. Arms, legs and skis should be relaxed; the arms swing in a loose diagonal movement in relation to the leg movement, as in normal walking. As the right arm swings forward, the left ski is pushed forward; then the left arm and right ski come forward. The steps should not be too hurried or too short and the skis should be allowed to glide. The centre of gravity of the body must remain no further back than the knee and foot of the leading leg (see diagram, over page).

Double pole glide

The first experience of sliding should be on a well-prepared, flat or slightly sloping trail. The movement is merely a push forward with the help of both poles as opposed to walking with a stepping motion. Both feet are flat on the skis, ankles flexed, knee and hip joints slightly fixed, and both poles pushed backwards. This movement should not be done too vigorously or made with too long a thrust, for this will result in a loss of balance; it is better to repeat the double pole plant several times at short intervals.

Diagonal stride with pole planting

Pole planting with the diagonal stride is a secondary consideration to begin with; legs and arms moving correctly and smoothly in a good rhythm is more important than a vigorous pole plant. The slightly bent arm is swung forward, holding the pole loosely by its grip (the arm does not swing up above eye level). The pole should be planted close to the trail about level with the body; as speed and rhythm

First steps on narrow cross-country skis should be taken under the supervision of a qualified ski instructor.

1

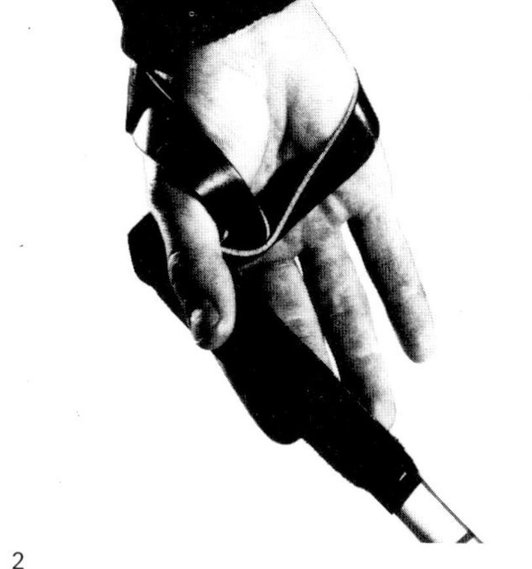

2

increase it can be planted further forward. In this way the pole forms an acute angle with the front of the ski.

The body is first pulled and then pushed past the pole, and finally the arm, swinging back, is loosely extended. During the pulling phase the hand should grasp the handle lightly (1) – during the pushing phase it is relaxed (2) and the loop takes the pressure.

As the walking or running rhythm becomes more assured, the poles should be planted more vigorously and pushed off more strongly. (Once the movement achieves a definite glide on one leg, it will be necessary to make a marked backward-stretching movement of the arm to help to slow the rhythm of the arm and pole movements.)

From walking to gliding

Once the entire movement involved in the diagonal stride has been more or less mastered and the rhythm of arms and legs is assured, more emphasis must be placed on the pushing-off and sliding movements. This is how it is done:

1. The leg is used to push off backwards, while the poles as they are planted alternately are used as a more active support. This will gradually lead to a sliding process.

2. Sliding for longer on the front, weighted ski, while the other leg swings loosely out behind should be practised and will help with balancing problems.

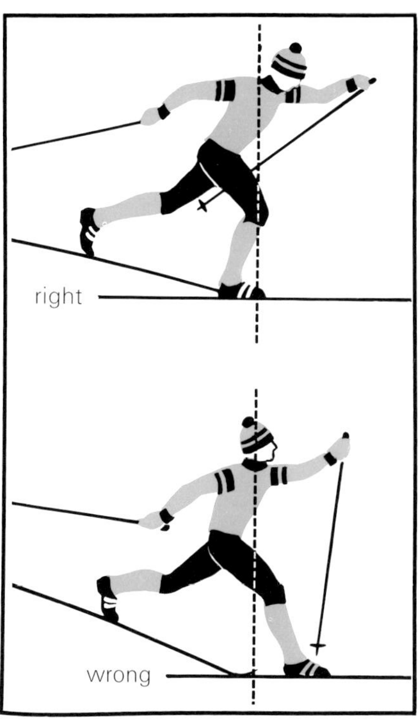

Very important: your centre of gravity must be above the leg which is sliding, i.e., the knee of that leg must be bent far enough to be above the foot. If the lower part of the leg is pushed too far forward at this stage of the movement it is easy to get the centre of gravity too far back. The lower leg will then be forming an angle of more than 90° with the front of the ski, whereas it should be less. This incorrect movement will make it harder to maintain balance, and the back leg will be put down on the snow again too soon and too far back. The result will be an involuntary sliding on both legs.

If the centre of gravity of the body is where it should be, however, around the axis above the foot and knee of the leg which is sliding, it will be easier to slide on one leg and put the other ski down again on the snow close to it.

Double pole push

The first experience of this technique was pushing forward to slide (see above); now push vigorously backwards with both poles at once on a slight downhill slope. Skis must be parallel and level with each other. Standing up, both poles and both arms are swung forwards. The poles are then placed vertically (in front of both feet) and the arms start a pulling and pushing movement. The upper part of the body bends forward, the arms pull the body up to the poles and finally push it briskly past them and forward, while the weight of the body, resting on the poles, helps the push. After a final pressure, by an emphatic backwards swing of the arms, the movement is completed. As this is done, ankle, knee and hip joints are well bent before rising up again, ready to bring arms and poles forward once more.

It is important to breathe out well during the bend and pushing movement and to breathe in well while standing up again. The musculature of the trunk relaxes, and the standing-up phase becomes a brief moment for recovery.

Climbing a slope

A slight slope can be climbed using the diagonal stride without any difficulty. Steps should be shorter, the centre of gravity rather further forward, and skis set down in the trail more vigorously. Naturally pole planting and arm movements must also be intensified.

If the slope is steeper, the *herring-bone step* is used. Keeping to the rhythm of the diagonal stride, the tips of the skis are angled out at every step, setting the inner edges of the skis so that they do not slip back. The steeper the slope, the more wide the angle of the skis and the stronger the necessary support from arms and poles.

Side-stepping can be used to get past short stretches of steep gradient, like banks of snow at the side of a path. This entails climbing sideways with the skis parallel, as if going upstairs sideways. The uphill ski and pole is raised and set down first, and then the downhill ski and pole is brought up beside them.

To climb across a moderately steep slope, the technique of *half side-stepping* is used. The basic movement is the same as side-stepping, but the uphill ski is set down pointing diagonally forwards as well as sideways.

Cross-country skiing downhill

Every cross-country skier is going to find himself in difficulty at some point in his runs when he finds his skis are sliding downhill on sloping terrain, or on a sloping trail where he is gathering speed. He will find out that coming downhill on narrow cross-country skis with a binding that leaves the heel free is difficult, and calls for considerable skill and a good sense of balance. So learning how to come down a slope properly should be part of the programme when learning cross-country skiing.

It is important to choose the right terrain for learning to come downhill: a very slightly inclined slope with plenty of flat space to run out at the bottom is quite enough for a beginner. The pupil must be able to stop himself at the end of the run. The

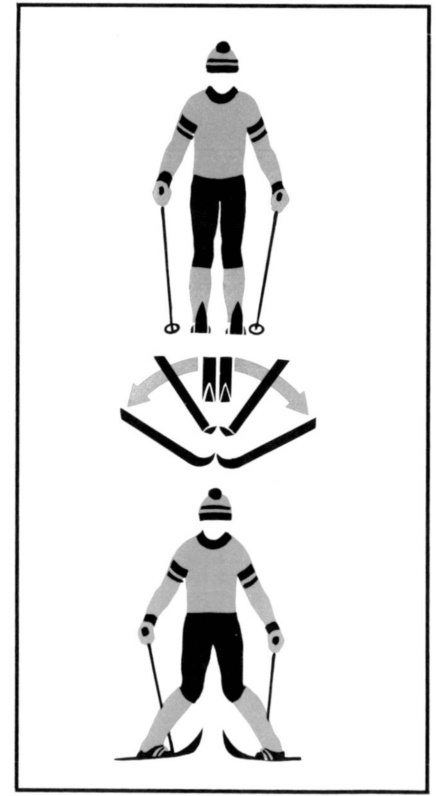

stance should be practised stationary and on the flat.

Weight should be evenly distributed between the heels and the balls of the feet. Ankle, knee and hip joints are bent, arms relaxed, poles with their tips pointing backwards.

As the heels are not fastened to the skis (in contrast to Alpine skiing) any excessive movement brings with it the risk of a forward fall. The position of the skis should be rather apart, to correspond to the track, i.e., roughly centred below the hips.

After stationary practice a gentle slope should be attempted with one or two pushes with both poles. Any feeling of insecurity is more easily dealt with by crouching slightly rather than standing upright.

The following hints are useful when travelling too fast or wanting to stop.

In soft snow, ski off the trail into deep snow; this has a very effective braking action. When skiing into deep snow it is best to push one ski slightly forward, while keeping the weight well back.

If the snow on either side of the trail is hard or has been trodden smooth, speed can be controlled by using the *snowplough* position. As in Alpine skiing, the tips of your skis are turned in and the ends out. The knees are bent forwards and inwards to start the movement, twisting the heels out so that the skis are set on their inside edges.

As a last resort if neither of these two methods will control the speed a controlled fall at the right moment is the best solution. It is unlikely that an injury will result if the fall is sideways or backwards.

Negotiating changes of ground

A ridge

Approaching a ridge in an upright position, the body is flexed while crossing the ridge, the upper body leaning forwards. Once over the ridge the legs are extended.

An undulation

Undulations should be swallowed by bending and stretching of the legs. As the undulation is approached, ankle, knee and hip joints should begin to flex to the undulation. Then legs and body are again extended before starting to flex again as the next undulation is reached.

A dip

Take a dip with legs bent, one ski pushed forward (stepping position), the body sitting slightly back to absorb the pressure of the slope on the opposite side. It is a similar position to that taken when skiing off the trail into deep snow.

Once a beginner has mastered the techniques of the diagonal stride, use of the double pole push, climbing up a slope and skiing down one, he is ready for his first cross-country ski excursion.

Ideally, the first stage should consist of practice on a short circular trail laid out so that its features call for the use of all the techniques learned so far (see diagram on p. 171).

Gradually the length and difficulty of the trail can be increased to provide an idea of the limit of skill and physical endurance.

Before a first expedition on an unknown trail, you should find out its length and difficulty. Public cross-country skiing trails are signposted showing length and difficulty.

Hints for cross-country ramblers

While short rambles do not call for much planning and preparation, longer touring excursions should be properly prepared.

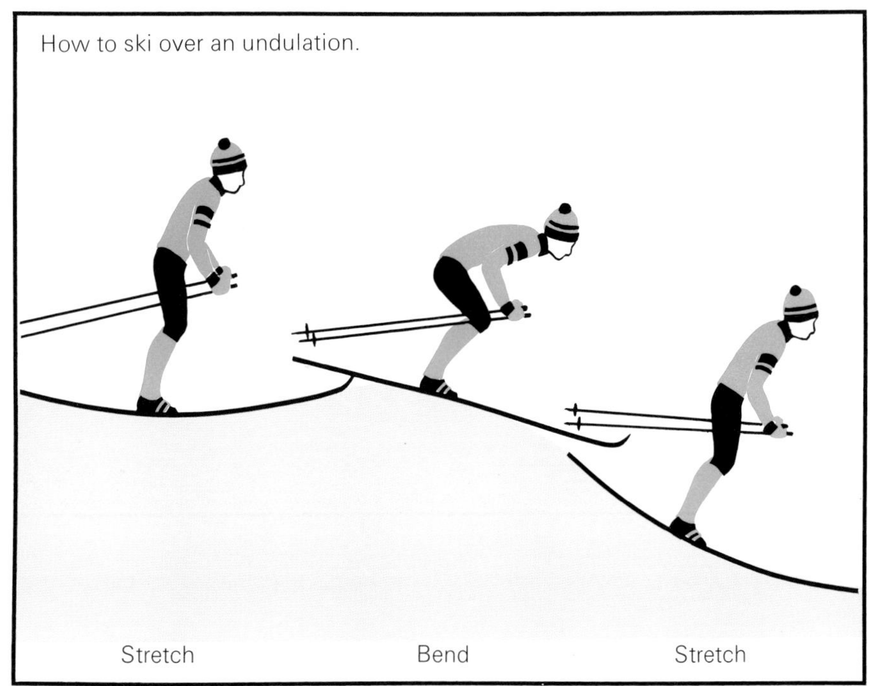

How to ski over an undulation.

- The length and nature of the excursion should be tailored to the needs of the members of the party.
- A timetable is a useful preparation. Then, if bad snow or weather conditions are encountered and the party realizes that they will not get as far as hoped for, an intermediate goal already planned on your schedule can be substituted.
- If the excursion is not going to lead back to the starting point the return must be taken care of.
- Every member of the party must be given information about the location of the trip, its length, the time it will take to complete, the equipment required and any other details before the start.
- Check equipment before starting.
- Arrange for someone to bring up the rear (not the weakest member of the party).
- If the trail is not prepared, the fittest members of the party should take turns in leading.
- The distance between members of the party should not become too great; people should be able to get in touch with each other at any time.
- Adjust speed and performance to the weakest member of the party.
- Poorly waxed skis must be thoroughly re-waxed.
- No risks should be taken when skiing down slopes! It is better to carry skis over difficult spots.

The cross-country skier's code

The growing popularity of cross-country skiing has its darker side; there is evidence of more and more accidents occurring in the course of what is, in itself, a comparatively harmless sport. They are mainly caused by bad conduct on the part of skiers.

Rules (similar to those for Alpine skiing) have consequently been drawn up by the juridical committee of the FIS, which should decrease the accident rate.

1. Consideration for others

Every cross-country skier should act in such a way that he does not injure any other skier or place himself at risk.

2. Signposts and direction markers

Obey the signs: ski on trails only in the direction indicated.

3. Choice of trail

Skiers must ski in the right-hand trail on double or multiple trails. Skiers in groups must ski in single file on the right-hand trail.

4. Overtaking

Skiers may overtake on the left or the right on an empty trail, or outside the prepared trails. The skier in front need not move off the trail, but he should move aside if he thinks he can do so without danger.

5. Skiers coming in different directions

Skiers meeting as they ski in opposite directions should give way to the right. Skiers going uphill should give way to skiers coming downhill.

6. Position of poles

When overtaking, being overtaken or meeting and passing other skiers, poles must be kept close to the body.

7. Suiting speed to the conditions

On downhill sections especially, every cross-country skier must suit his speed and behaviour to his degree

of expertise, the type of terrain, the number of other skiers and the visibility. He must keep at a safe distance from the skier ahead. If necessary he must allow himself to fall in order to avoid a collision.

8. The trails must be kept clear
A stationary skier must stay off the trail. In the case of a fall, the trail must be cleared as soon as possible.

9. Assistance
It is everyone's duty to assist in cases of accidents.

10. Identification
In the case of an accident every skier, whether personally involved or a witness (i.e., whether responsible for the accident or not), must give evidence of his identification.

These ten rules are comparable to the U. S. trail skiers' code.

Cross-country skiing – *langlauf*

Langlauf is the more athletic variety of cross-country skiing – running rather than walking on skis, and only a few years ago it was still regarded as a sport appealing only to a few tough individualists and extreme ascetics. With the growing popularity of cross-country skiing as a recreational sport, thousands of people have discovered that it does not mean, predominantly, work and hardship; it means fun and the pleasure of fast movement.

Though this is a more athletic version of cross-country skiing than simple cross-country rambling on skis, it has the same good points:

- It is a healthy means of recreation to ski through the winter landscape, away from the hustle and bustle of life.
- It does not involve the financial (and psychological) burdens which can make Alpine skiing a problem. It can be learnt quickly and the sport can be practised as intensively as you wish.

It does not follow, however, that everyone who has become an enthusiastic cross-country rambler will also take to cross-country running on skis; he may well not have the necessary motivation. As distinct from simple walking, this variety of cross-country skiing calls for a fairly high level of performance and skill. This means that success in the sport is only possible if you are physically fit, have good endurance and the agility to maintain balance while performing fast dynamic movements. Compared to simple walking on skis, where the basic elements are few, it will be necessary to learn new forms of movement which have rhythm, elasticity, harmony and style.

But despite this, it does not mean that a recreational skier who started his cross-country skiing with simple walking cannot gradually come to *langlauf* if he systematically puts his mind to it.

For those seriously considering taking up the sport a medical examination similar to that recommended before starting a jogging course is advisable. Understandably, ambitious cross-country runners will find that having the correct equipment is much more important that it is for the gentler version of cross-country skiing. Poles that are too short or skis that are badly waxed can result in a whole range of unfortunate events; they may mean that too much strength has to be expended, they may lead to incorrect, uneconomical movements, and in the end they can be responsible for a discouraging experience or failure. It is absolutely essential to choose the right equipment and wax the skis well (see page 204), and, in practice, to have the expert advice and guidance of an instructor, coach or an experienced friend.

The basics of cross-country walking on skis can be learnt in two or three days, but the path to perfect cross-country running is much longer, and requires the will to practise hard and to train under professional advice. A skier who tries to teach himself is in danger of getting into bad habits without the example of an instructor who can check his movements and put mistakes right. Studying technique in a well illustrated book is certainly one way of learning – but it cannot replace the practical experience of instruction.

In cross-country running, the technique of top-class competitive skiers is, in principle, the right technique for everyone, and can safely be emulated. Everyone must, of necessity, do the basic movements, such as the diagonal stride or the two-pole technique. The difference between an ordinary and a top-class skier lies in the perfection of technique and the intensity with which they practise. Of course the constitution, strength and temperament of different athletes introduce a 'personal' note. Although the result, however, may be an individual style, it is built on a common technique.

Note: though the following pages represent the various techniques and combinations of movement in cross-country skiing, complex, dynamic movements carried out at the same time can only be described consecutively on the page. This can mean that the descriptions of some of the movements seem more complicated than they actually are. It is hoped that the combination of descriptions with illustrations will help you.

The diagonal stride

As mentioned in the section on simple walking on skis, a natural walking or running movement, extended by the gliding movement of skis, is the basis of the diagonal stride. This means the alternate movement of opposite arms and legs is typical of the sequence of movements in the diagonal stride.

The movement is divided into three phases:

thrust phase
gliding phase
swinging phase

Thrust phase

The thrust phase begins as the leg that is swinging forward passes the leg which is sliding. Bend the joints of the leg from which the thrust takes place; this bending of the hip, knee and ankle joints, together with a forward lean of the upper part of the body, places the centre of gravity further forward. The body therefore is in a good position to be pushed forward as the thrusting leg is stretched. The upper part of the body should be at an angle of about 45° during the thrust. If it is too upright, part of the force generated by the thrusting movement is directed upwards rather than forwards. As the thrusting leg is stretched the body is pushed forward, and the other ski glides along the trail.

The thrusting movement of the leg is reinforced by the final phase of the pole-plant, in which the body is pushed past the arm as it straightens. If it is the left leg that is stretching, the final push with the right pole is made during or just before the stretching of the leg, to reinforce the movement – and, alternately, stretching the right leg uses the left pole.

The gliding phase can be seen more clearly in the series of pictures showing Juha Mieto of Finland (below) than in the series showing Magne Myrmo of Norway (above).

Gliding phase
After the thrust with leg and arm, one ski glides. The weighted leg on which it is gliding is well bent, the shin forming an angle of less than 90° with the front of the ski.

During the glide the arm now swinging forward plants the pole at about the level of the gliding foot, or just ahead of it. The other arm swings out behind and almost straight during the gliding phase.

Swinging phase
After the thrust, the thrusting leg and the opposite arm swing out behind and then forward again. The foot of the swinging leg is brought into the track just behind the gliding leg – or level with it – without any interruption of the swinging movement. Then the start of the thrust phase of the next step is prepared.

A marked swinging phase is especially useful in competitive cross-country skiing and is often called 'resting the arm and leg'. The skier's muscles are briefly relaxed, and the movement becomes a steady alternation of tension and relaxation.

Note: in a perfectly performed diagonal stride these three phases merge smoothly into each other. The upper part of the body remains more or less still and does not jerk to-and-fro with every step.

Style and small details of technique vary from one top-class skier to another. Despite such small differences, however, it is interesting to note that the general movements are the same with all top skiers. Compare the pictures showing Magne Myrmo (above) and Juha Mieto (below). Both give a perfect textbook example of the separate phases of the diagonal stride.

The swinging step

In terrain with little variation in gradient, it is possible to straighten up by leaving out one or two pole-plants, and so give your arm and shoulder muscles a slight rest. Occasionally, obstacles in the terrain, unevenness of the ground or a trail running diagonally across a slope will also call for this technique.

In contrast to the 'ordinary' diagonal stride, the thrust of the leg is not linked to a thrust of arm and pole. The poles are planted only two or three times to four leg thrusts. Accordingly, we speak of a 'three-time' or 'four-time' step.

In the three-time step every third pole-plant on both sides is left out, or a pole is planted on one side but left out on the other side.

In the four-time step you leave out the pole-plants of two consecutive thrusts. During this phase the upper part of the body rises up and the poles are swung forward. The poles are used again to reinforce the next thrust.

Diagonal stride: climbing a slope

Good cross-country skiers can take slight inclines in their diagonal stride. They shorten the length of their steps and the gliding phase according to the gradient of the slope. The movement of arms and poles becomes very important. The ankle, knee and hip joints are bent further than during skiing on the flat. The upper part of the body remains bent forward the whole time, forming an angle of less than 45° with the ski.

As the inclination of a slope increases the gliding phase becomes shorter, and if the slope is steep there is no gliding phase at all. Racers (with properly waxed skis) have to make their own decisions as to whether gliding, and the use of the energy it entails, is an economical way of moving on an upward-sloping trail. On a steep slope the leg swinging forward is set down on the trail in front of the leg on which the skier is gliding. Care must be taken not to break contact with the snow during the backward thrust.

Note: the use of arms and poles is important for an effective technique. The 'swinging phase' of the arms is shorter – adjusting to the incline of the slope – but the poles are planted more vigorously. The rhythm of the pole-planting corresponds to the faster rhythm of the skier's leg movements. The pulling and pushing phase, however, calls for a lot of strength in the skier's arms and trunk.

The herringbone step

If a slope becomes steep even athletic cross-country skiers will change from the diagonal stride to the herringbone step (see pp. 70–1). An expert cross-

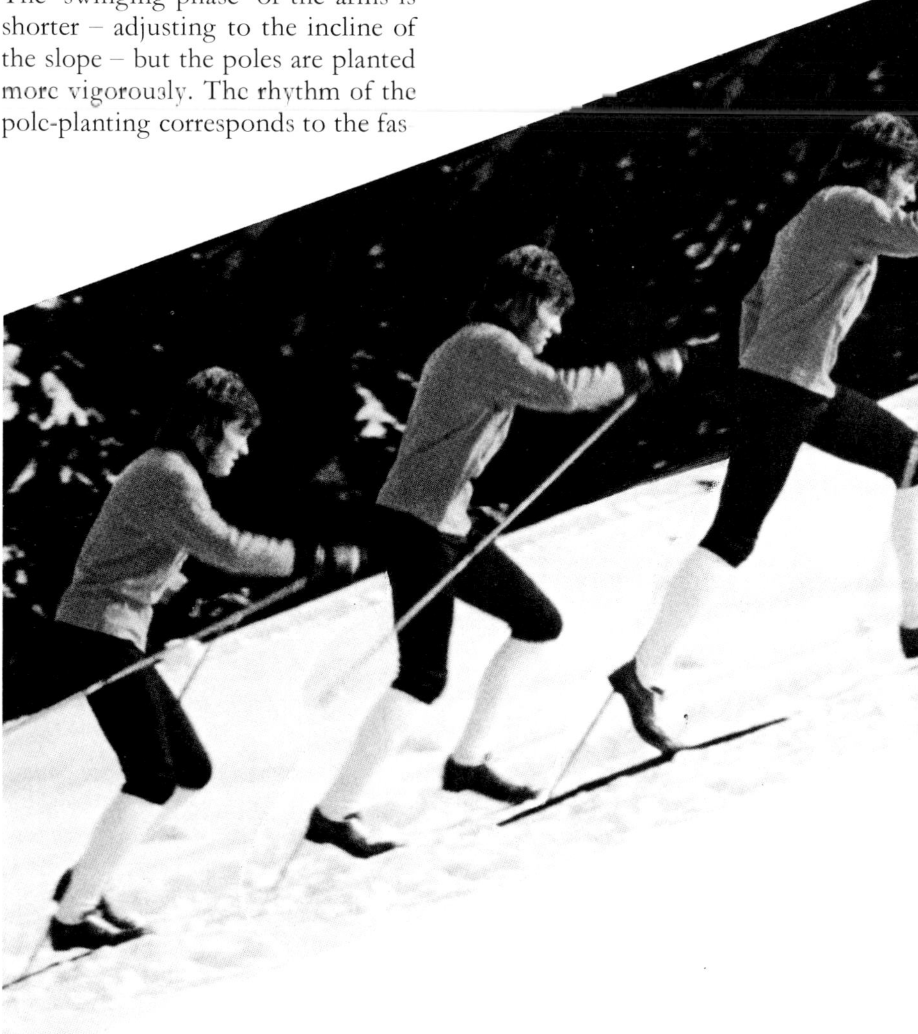

Diagonal stride going up a slope: abbreviated gliding phase, vigorous use of arms and poles, upper part of body leaning forward.

country skier will only angle out the skis as far as is absolutely necessary. He keeps to the rhythm of the diagonal stride. Here too he will have to plant his poles with considerable energy.

Herringbone step used climbing a slope.

Double-pole technique

Double-pole technique is used when the skis are gliding along so well and so fast that the diagonal stride is no longer an economical way of moving. Nowadays, this technique is used quite frequently, even on level trails, not just on downward slopes.

Recently cross-country skis have adopted the plastic surfaces which were once used only in the manufacture of Alpine skis; the technique of waxing has been improved and refined, and together these have improved the gliding qualities of the skis. This means that double-pole technique is more important now, especially in competitions.

As the name indicates, the technique entails simultaneous planting of both poles to help the skis glide along. If the pole-plant is preceded by an accelerating step, the combination is called a double pole-plant with intermediate step.

Note: the skier's trunk and back muscles are briefly relaxed by the bending of the upper part of the body and its subsequent straightening. This is useful as a help to good breathing (breathe in as you stand upright, breathe out as you push, i.e., when flexing down).

Double pole-plant without intermediate step

With the skis sliding along the trail side by side, the upper part of the body is raised, swinging the arms forward at the same time.

The poles are planted beside the trail in front of the feet, i.e., somewhere between the binding and the tips of the skis, according to the speed.

When the poles form an angle of less than 90° with the front of the skis, the pushing movement begins. The upper part of the body is flexed vigorously towards the thighs, the arms pulling the body forward to the poles.

As the movement proceeds the pulling motion becomes a pushing one – with the hands below the knees as they pass the legs. The vigorous push is finished by applying a final pressure as the arms are stretched back.

In the last phase of this double-pole technique, experts adopt a slight backward-leaning position. This unweights the tips of the skis, friction is less and the ability of the skis to slide is greater. (See the leaning-back position of racers in the egg or tuck in Alpine skiing, p. 74.)

After the final moment of pressure the arms are still stretched out behind in a relaxed manner. At this stage the hands are open and hanging through the loops of the poles.

The upper part of the body is not brought up again until this point. The relaxed arms are swung past the body and forward as both skis glide forward.

It is particularly important to breathe out hard during the flexing and to breathe in well as the trunk comes upright.

Double pole-plant with intermediate step

If the double pole-plant does not give enough acceleration, it can be linked with a preceding thrust from one leg.

In this combination of steps, both arms and poles are swung forward during the leg thrust.

The double pole-plant occurs at the end of the gliding phase, when the leg is left swinging forward after the thrust. The rest of the movement is as for double pole-plant without an intermediate step.

The pole push starts when the poles and the skis form an angle of less than 90°.

The leg swinging forward is set down on the trail beside or just behind the leg which is gliding (this often means the glide takes place in a slight stepping position). Again, the pushing movement of the poles is finished as late as possible, giving a final vigorous pressure as the arms stretch to propel the body forward.

During the glide on both skis the next thrust movement of one leg is prepared.

When skiing with this technique it is usual to alternate the legs used for the thrust. There are some skiers, however, who perform a 'one-sided' double pole-plant with intermediate step, preferring to thrust with the same leg each time.

There is another fairly common variation in which two or three intermediate steps are purposely inserted between the pole-plants.

Here the double pole-plant is preceded by two or three diagonal strides without pole plant.

ABOVE: double pole-plant without intermediate step.
BELOW: with intermediate step.

Changing from diagonal stride to double pole-plant and vice versa

Changing from diagonal stride to double pole-plant and vice versa should not mean a break in the rhythm.

From diagonal stride to double pole-plant
At that point of the diagonal stride where a skier would next plant his pole, he lets his arm and pole swing out in front, swinging the other arm forward too with the leg from which he has pushed off. After the next thrusting movement, the manoeuvre corresponds to double pole-plant *with* intermediate step (see top row of photographs).

From double pole-plant to diagonal stride
Changing from a double pole-plant to a diagonal stride is started by bringing both poles forward at the same time, as if for double pole-plant with intermediate step. Only one pole is planted diagonally to the leg which is gliding (little energy should be used for this pole plant), while the other stays out ahead ready to be planted during the following gliding phase (see photographs below).

Apart from the fact that techniques must be suited to the terrain, alternating techniques means that the same muscle areas are not always being used, which can bring relaxation and relief.

Changing direction

For the sake of completeness this technique should be mentioned (which is still described in all manuals), although hardly any top-class skiers use it in practice. It is only used when direction has to be changed sharply on short upward slopes. The outside ski is placed tail outwards, in the new direction, and weighted after removing pressure from the inside

Note: preparing to thrust, and the thrusting movement, should take place after passing the top of an undulation and, as a general rule, when going down into the dip.

Using the double pole-plant
When crossing dips and undulations using the double pole-plant technique the same principle applies as for the diagonal stride. The thrust and pole-plant should always occur when going down into a dip, after passing the crest of the undulation.

Note: when using the double pole-plant *without* an intermediate step, the pole-plant should begin after crossing the crest of the undulation, so that you push hard down into and through the dip.

When using the double pole-plant *with* an intermediate step, the one leg thrust, as for the diagonal stride, is done after passing the crest of the undulation, and the subsequent pole-plant drives the skis through the dip and up the next undulation.

ski. The inside ski is then brought up parallel and weighted again before the end of the outside ski is angled outwards again at the next step. The rhythm of arms and legs is as for the diagonal stride, but the gliding phase is sharply curtailed.

Undulations and dips

Using the diagonal stride
When crossing dips, bumps or undulations using the diagonal stride, it is essential to take off at the right moment. Delaying or curtailing your last steps means that you can time the thrust to take you down into the dip, i.e., the thrust starts from a ski sloping downhill, after passing the crest of the undulation, and thus giving the best possible propulsion forward. The gliding and swinging phases will then be sufficient to cross over the next undulation.

If the thrust, however, is made while coming out of the dip and upwards again, part of the force of the thrust will be dissipated upwards (see diagram right).

Crossing dips and undulations with double pole-plant.

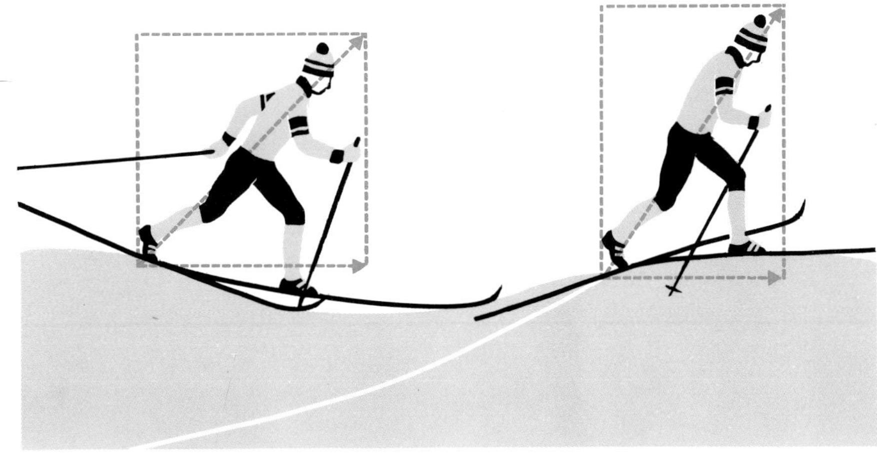

Crossing undulations and dips with diagonal stride.

Step turns

When gliding along on level or downward sloping terrain, direction can be changed with the help of the movement known as stepping a curve.

This is a repeated transfer of weight from one ski to the other, which is started by angling out the ski on the inside of the curve and placing it in the new direction. The ski on the outside of the curve is then pushed off from the inside edge and the outside ski is brought up parallel with the other. The outward angling of the inside ski is repeated. This technique achieves an acceleration if the thrust from the outside ski is reinforced by a double pole-plant (see photographs left).

Skating step

The skis, angled out alternately left and right, are accelerated by vigorous thrusting movements of the legs and arms. This technique is to be recommended mainly on flat and downhill slopes if the snow cover is hard and the trail gives no help.

It is started by weighting one ski, angling the other out sideways and pushing off vigorously from the inside edge of the weighted ski. There is then a gliding phase on the outward-angled ski, which now takes all the weight.

Meanwhile the raised unweighted ski is brought up and angled with its tip outwards. The thrust is again from the inside edge and the weight is transferred to the outward-angled ski.

Acceleration – as when stepping a curve – can be achieved by using a double pole-plant simultaneously with the thrusting movement of the legs.

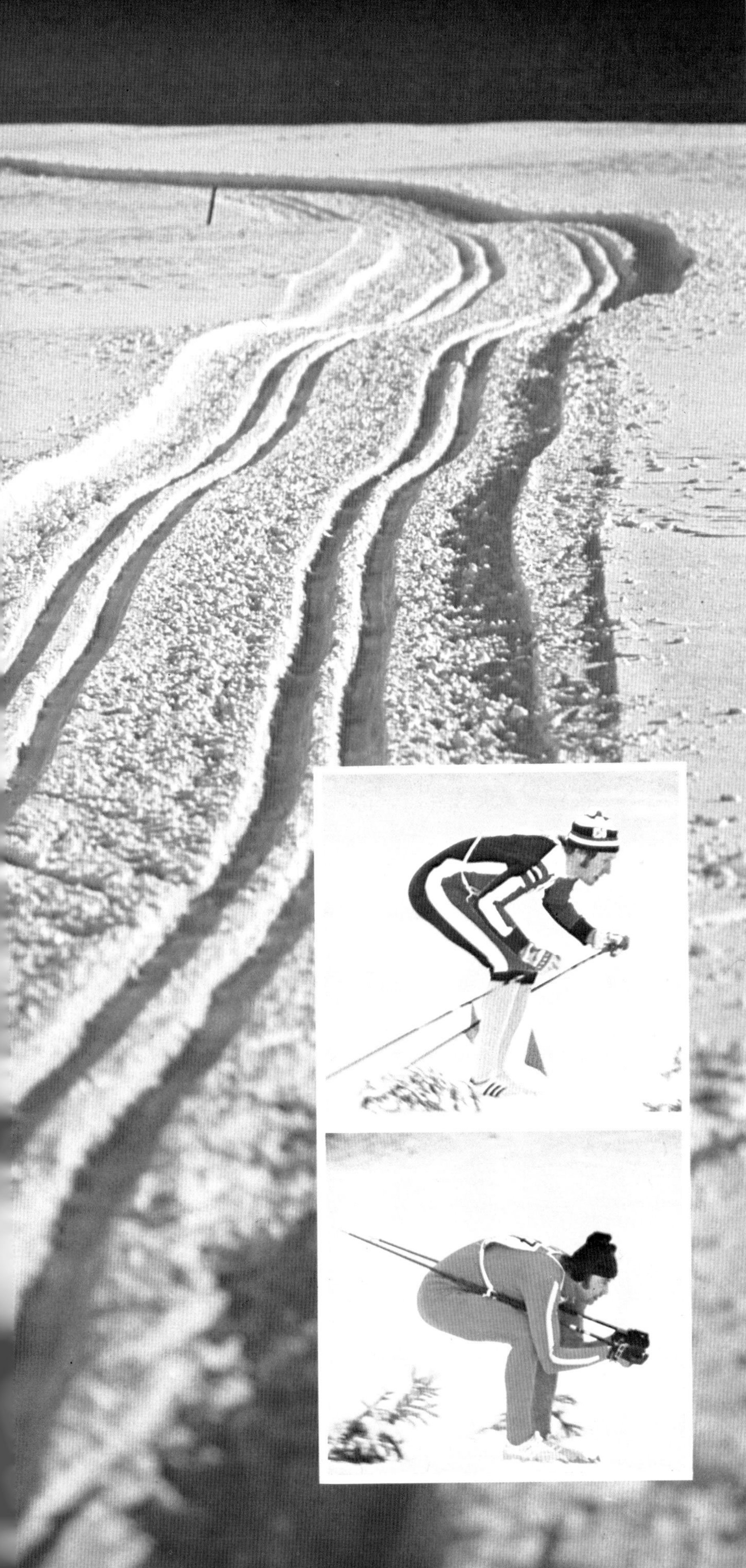

Cross-country downhill techniques

In the athletic variety of cross-country skiing it is possible to distinguish between three positions in which the body can be held while skiing downhill:

1. *Standing upright*, slight slopes can be skied quite restfully (providing speed and time are not involved). With the weight evenly distributed on the balls of both feet and with ankle, knee and hip joints only slightly flexed and the upper part of the body almost upright, the poles are carried with arms angled in to the side, the tips pointing backwards.
2. When skiing on steeper and more difficult slopes, and in competitive events, a *half-tuck* position is usually adopted by flexing ankle, knee and hip joints further and bending the upper part of the body well forward. Arms and poles are carried forwards, and laterally, to help balance. Most of the weight is on the heels, since any forward-leaning position entails the danger of a fall caused by the fact that the binding does not hold the heel.
3. If the downhill run is not technically difficult (and in a race fractions of a second matter), a *low tuck position*, familiar from Alpine racing, is used. The upper part of the body is rested on the thighs, poles clamped between the upper arms and body, and the lower arms extended far enough forward for the hands to meet. This is the aerodynamically favourable 'egg position', which reduces the body's resistance to the air and therefore increases its speed. The marked sitting-back position also means the skis slide faster.

The closed position of arms and

poles in this technique, however, means that it is harder to react rapidly in moments of insecurity.

Note: The position adopted will naturally vary according to the degree of skill. Good, experienced skiers, with some practice of Alpine skiing, can adopt the tuck even on difficult runs, while the less experienced skiers would do better to ski in the half-tuck, with arms stretched sideways and forwards.

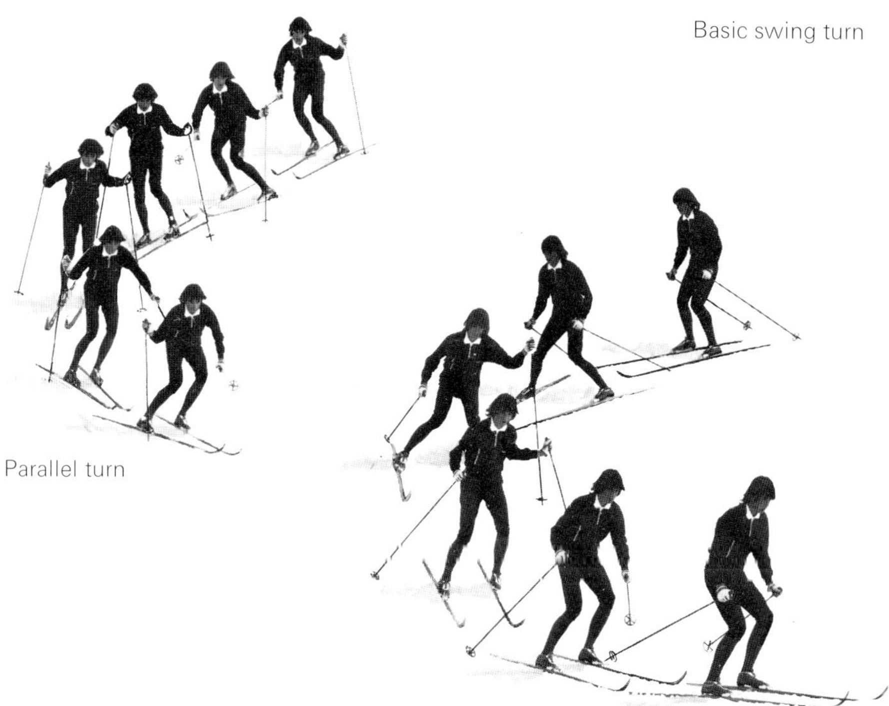

Parallel turn

Basic swing turn

Coming to terms with changes of terrain

The same principles apply as for simple walking on skis.

Dips and bumps are absorbed or 'swallowed' by the legs. If a full tuck is used on a downhill section this must be abandoned on the approach of an undulation, so that the legs can be flexed to absorb it.

Small dips can be stepped through, i.e., legs stretched down, pushing the skis well into the dip. If approaching in a relatively upright position, it will be necessary to bend ankle, knee and hip joints before entering the dip (see diagram, p. 187).

Curves and turns

The ability to come down a slope, to change direction and execute a turn, is certainly one of the peak achievements of a cross-country skier. It calls for considerably greater dexterity than the corresponding techniques in Alpine skiing, since the cross-country ski has several disadvantages compared with the Alpine ski:

- The fact that the skis are narrower makes it harder to guide them into the right position and to balance on them.
- Cross-country skis are easily deflected from their path by various unevennesses (trails, lumps of snow), because they are lightweight and flexible.
- It is harder to transfer turning movements from legs to skis, because of the relatively loose connection between boots and skis.
- The lack of sharp edges makes it considerably more difficult to judge how hard to set the edges.
- On hard snow, or when travelling fast, the cross-country ski tends to 'flutter' because of its light weight and relative instability when turning.

To compensate for these disadvantages, the following points should be taken into consideration when skiing downhill on cross-country skis:

- Always ski in a slight sitting-back position, so that the heel of the boot can be pressed into the teeth of the heel plate. This stops the heels sliding sideways off the skis when they are traversing and turning.
- Good use of the poles to support and help in a turn, and as 'first aid' when feeling unbalanced, is a great help.
- As a general rule, running and turning with skis well apart gives better balance. It is also easier to put things right from this position.

People who are not so expert at skiing downhill – especially cross-country skiers with no experience of Alpine skiing – should aim to master a good safe *basic swing turn* which is described in the Basic Technique section of the chapter on Alpine Skiing.

Basic swing turn

Sequence of movements:

- Approaching in a traverse or a controlled traverse slide-slip, the uphill ski is angled out into the snowplough position towards the fall line.
- Push off from the inside ski, pole-

plant and exert weight on the outside ski.

- Bring up the inside ski – and rotate both legs, carefully assessing the amount of movement needed to reach a new traverse.

Parallel turn

Skiers who have mastered the parallel turn on Alpine skis can apply the same technique to cross-country skis: Sequence of movements:

- Approach in a traverse or side-slip, and adopt a flexed stance with skis apart.
- Push off with pole-plant and upward unweighting.
- During the weighting phase, rotate the skis over the fall line into the new direction – flex gently, carefully assessing the amount of movement needed, and complete the turn on the new traverse.

The fact that the equipment is less steady than Alpine skis means you need great dexterity and a good sense of balance.

Racers should familiarize themselves with these techniques and train to achieve the sense of security which will keep them from falling on difficult downhill runs. It is easy to lose several seconds gained on long level stretches and upward-sloping sections of a run by falling just once.

Changes of technique

In the normal way cross-country skiing trails do not often call for quick changes of technique from one type of step to another. They usually demand the use of the diagonal stride and the double-pole techniques over long stretches of terrain, interspersed now and then with upward or downward slopes to be negotiated in the appropriate way.

For the purpose of training, a relatively short circular trail with plenty of variation in it is ideal, laid out in terrain that will enable all the techniques and combinations of steps to be used in quick succession (see diagram below).

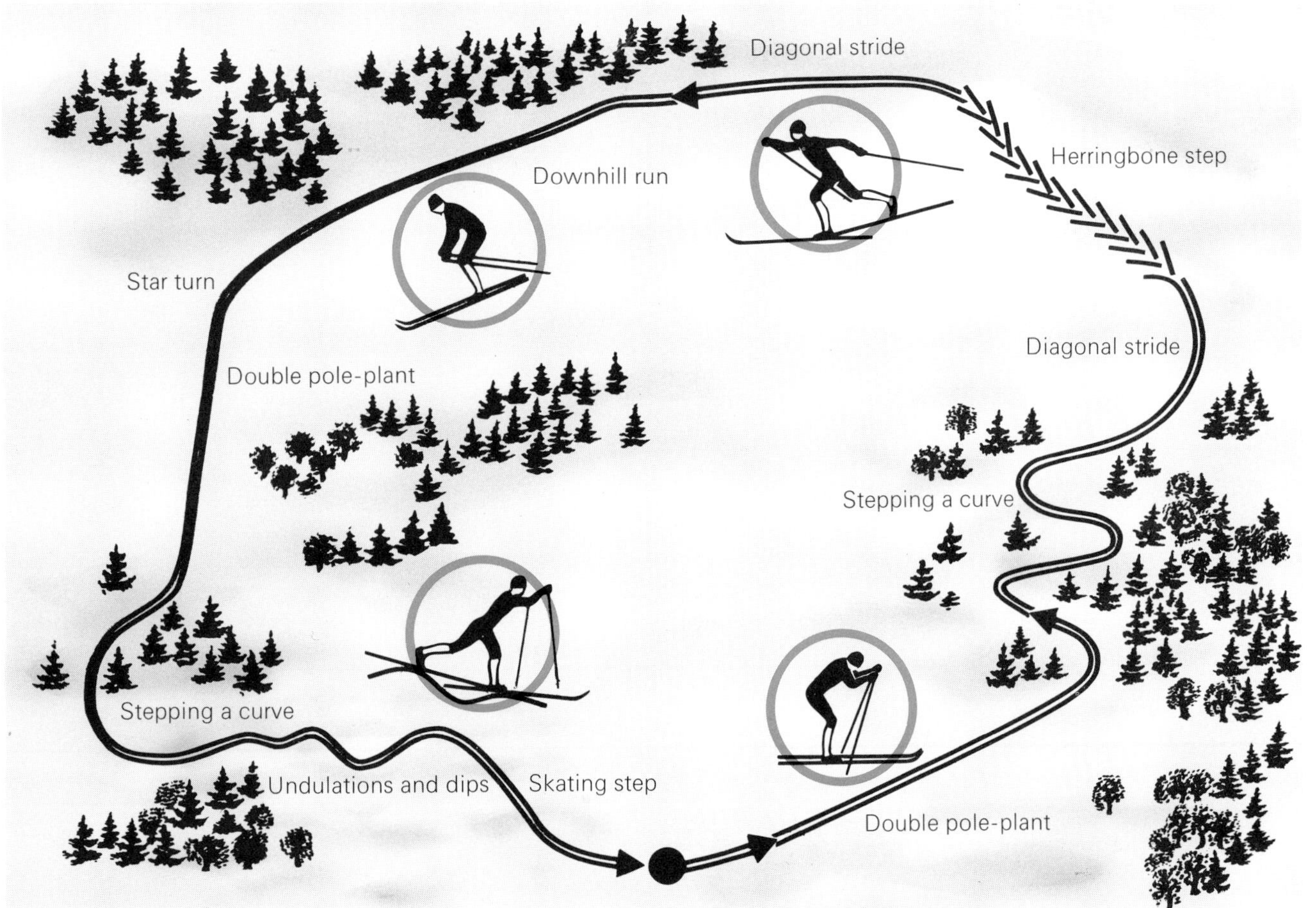

Cross-country skiing as a competitive sport

As with every sport practised competitively, which calls for endurance, cross-country skiing demands great physical effort and strength of will. Long-term systematic preparation and regular training are prerequisites for any athlete. As a rule people start competitive cross-country skiing by joining a club. After a carefully planned training course, the club coach will enter young people for their first modest competitive events. Later on the young skiers may continue in competition or take to the more relaxing life of a recreational sportsman, according to individual talent, inclination and success.

Anyone deciding to pursue the sport competitively should be quite clear about the demands that will be made.

- You must be physically capable of the considerable strains that training and competition will place on you. There should be a medical examination of fitness for the sport at the start, followed by regular check-ups.
- You should make up your mind just how far you want to go, and can go. You are unlikely to have time for a regular job or for study and also be in the top class as a national and international sportsman. It is one of the responsibilities of a good coach to discuss this problem with young people and their parents.
- As a competitive sportsman you should realize that you cannot separate your sport from your life-style. Anyone who wants to succeed in competitive cross-country skiing will need the courage and endurance necessary to lead what is, at times, an almost ascetic life.

Training

To be a successful competitor in cross-country skiing events – or at least take part in them without physical harm – year-round training is almost essential. Only a long-term training schedule drawn up by professionals will assure that an athlete is at his peak form at the right time, i.e., the time of the most important competitive events. It is no part of this book to lay down individual training schedules for anyone who might be interested; that is a job for club coaches. It is possible, however, to summarize the basic considerations to be born in mind when training schedules are drawn up – for competitive cross-country on a lower level as well as for the top-class sportsmen.

Training periods

The training year is divided into three stages:

In the northern hemisphere:

1. Preparation period (mid-May to mid-December)
2. Competition period (mid-December to end of March)
3. Transition period (April to mid-May)

In the southern hemisphere:

1. Preparation period (early November to mid-June)
2. Competition period (mid-June to end September)
3. Transition period (October to early November)

Snowfalls are fairly frequent in late May and the season officially begins in early June. Most skiers do not count on lasting snow until late June or early July. The season usually lasts about twelve weeks and finishes in late September though snow often falls in October. In parts of New Zealand some areas have a ski season from mid-May to December. In Australia, on the other hand, some winters have very poor snow cover.

An athlete's performance curve follows the course of the training programme (see diagram below).

Preparation period

In the *first phase* of the preparation period the emphasis is on general training for endurance, strength (strength and endurance combined), maintaining speed for long periods and mobility.

In the *second phase* training for general fitness is intensified and special training for strength and speed is combined with endurance; sequences of movements are added.

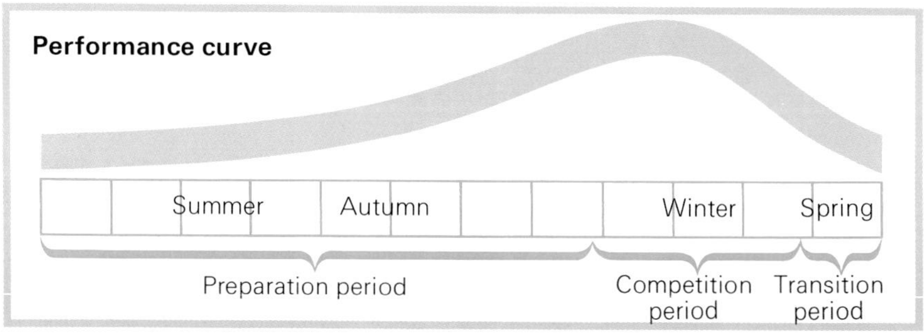

40
LANGLAUF

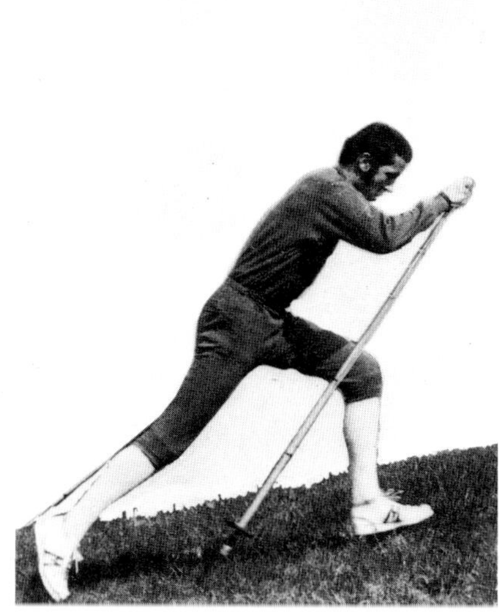

Training for fitness, with regard to cross-country skiing technique, is mainly in the form of jumps imitating the steps, and the use of roller-skis.

When *jumping* you imitate the sequence of movements in the diagonal stride by running up slightly sloping terrain taking large 'jumping' strides. Emphasis is laid on the powerful 'accelerating' thrust movement, followed by a brief retardation of the running rhythm to correspond to the gliding phase of the diagonal stride. If you use ski poles at the same time the muscles of your arms also receive the right training.

Roller-skis enable you to imitate the movements of cross-country skiing. There are several different models on the market, all of them corresponding in principle to cross-country skis on wheels. They can be used on roads and asphalt paths. (A device to prevent them running backwards enables the correct leg thrust to be done even when running and going uphill.) The best results in training are achieved on level or slightly rising terrain, by running, using the diagonal stride, and gliding with double pole-plants. This intensively trains your muscles for combined strength, speed and staying power.

The mobility needed for cross-country skiing is obtained by playing ball games throughout the preparation period, and most of all by doing exercises. There are suitable exercises in the chapter on Skiing Exercises (see pp. 48–55).

In the *third phase* of the preparation period emphasis is on the most effective possible changeover from 'dry' training to training in the snow.

Some useful hints:

- Take the time to wax your skis so that they grip well; skis that are too smooth lead to incorrect movement sequences from the start.
- Complete concentration on technique is only possible on a well-prepared trail. Often a perfect, small circular trail may be better than a longer but poorly prepared and much-trodden trail.
- Do not start by sprinting! The first few days' training in the snow should be over long distances at an easy, regular pace.
- After 'running yourself in' in this manner, interval training (or alternating stress and relaxation activity) should be incorporated; later, longer high-energy bursts can be added to the training. The idea is to improve speed and endurance.
- Mindless enthusiasm is a bad thing; training should perfect technique. Extreme fatigue or exhaustion often cause poor performance.
- If extreme exhaustion sets in, return to easy, regular skiing to recover. In principle every training session should end with a long gentle run.
- Intense private rivalries, or taking part too seriously in the first of the season's competitions, can do harm in the early phase of training in the snow. Keep strictly to a training plan.

Competition Period

The conduct and intensity of training during the competition season (mid-December to the end of March in the northern hemisphere) is an individual matter. Training must take into account the number and frequency of competitive events in which you may be taking part, as well as your own physical and mental condition. It is impossible to make general recommendations for this period. Coaches and skiers must judge for themselves whether hard training or relaxed, gentle skiing between competitions is best.

Transition Period

In the transition period (April to the end of May in the northern hemisphere), between the end of one season of competition and the start of training for the next, you should 'get your breath back'. The emphasis is on recuperation after the physical and mental strains of the competition season. Having a change from training especially geared to the needs of cross-country skiing gives you the chance to get to know other kinds of sport – and a pause of this kind whets the appetite for the coming preparation period. Make sure you do have a rest.

Competitive events

The following is a brief summary of the classic distances. More information about the rules of competition can be obtained from national and international skiing authorities.

Individual events
Women: 3 and 6 miles (5 and 10km); also 12½ miles (20km)
Men: 9, 18½ and 31 miles (15, 30 and 50km); also 9 miles (15km) cross-country combination.

Relays
Women: 2½ × 3 miles (4 × 5km)
Men: 2½ × 6 miles (4 × 10km)

In the individual events the competitors usually start one by one at intervals of thirty seconds; in the relays they start together from a starting line.

Both skis are marked before the start to prevent a change en route; in case of need, *one* ski (and one ski only) can be changed.

Sprinting
This means racing round a circular track with a group start. Two runners

form a team and take over from each other at the end of a round.

This is an attempt to make cross-country skiing an attractive spectator sport, which is impossible in individual events over long distances.

Biathlon
From the historical point of view, the biathlon evolved from the use of skis as a means of transport for winter hunting. Today this event is defined as 'cross-country skiing combined with shooting'.

Points are awarded according to the time taken skiing and the number of hits a competitor makes in shooting (standing or lying down). Depending on the particular competition, wide shots may be penalized by adding on time or a penalty distance of 490yd(150m).

International events comprise:

- 12½ miles(20km) individual competitions, four sets of shots being taken at ringed targets.
- 6 miles(10km) individual competitions, two sets of shots being fired at breakable discs.
- 2½ × 4½ miles (4 × 7.5km) relay competitions (each member of the team firing two sets of shots at breakable discs).

Popular marathons
These are mass events on the lines of

the traditional Swedish Vasaloppet Race, which covers 53 miles(85.8km) and has over 20,000 skiers taking part every year. In North America two of the best known events are the American Birkebeiner from Telemark Ski Centre to Hayward, Wisconsin and the 93 mile(150km), two-day Canadian Coureur des Bois in Québec. Among the most popular marathons in Europe are the Engadin Ski Marathon, 26 miles(42km), which was first run in 1969 with 900 competitors, both men and women, but which is now limited to a maximum of 10,000 each year; the Marcia Lunga from Cortina d'Ampezzo to Moena, Italy; the King Ludwig Run in Oberammergau, 56 or 28 miles(90 or 45km); the Koasa Run from Kitzbühel by way of Kossento St Johann in Austria, 45 or 26 miles(72 or 42km).

Ski marathons: competitive events for everyone

Parallel to the general boom in cross-country skiing over the last few years, interest in popular, competitive skiing events has also increased to a remarkable extent.

The idea of participating in a skiing marathon, especially with skiers who take up the sport later in life, often starts in quite a mild manner when you find how much you enjoy moving successfully along the trail. Then you realize that your condition and staying power are improving, and with the right technique you would be able to ski longer distances without any difficulty. Finally you start asking yourself how far you could go and what timing you would make.

Anyone can take part after paying the entrance fee, and set off over a distance of 15, 30, 50 or more miles(25, 50, 80 km), without experience, having to produce no proof of training, and usually without any medical check-up. No wonder skiing marathons of this nature sometimes make the headlines in an unfortunate manner; there have been individual cases of exhaustion, collapse and even death on cross-country skiing trails.

Such occurrences should not be dramatized but at the same time they should not be underestimated. It seems right to mention an unfortunate and dangerous tendency which is now threatening the skiing marathon movement in general: the original idea of participation in a kind of national migration on skis is becoming infected more and more by the 'competitive' virus. Many participants become over-ambitious and put all the strength they have into getting a good time or a placing. This is not to say that trying for your personal best time or a good placing is unhealthy in principle. In so far as it is a matter of enjoying yourself, improving your personal performance, and competing in a healthy way with others, there can be no objection to it.

But it has been observed that many skiers taking part in the marathons are putting pressure on themselves to reach a level of performance of which they are physically and mentally not capable. They often come back over-strained, even ill, from what should, in itself, have been a weekend's pleasant recreation. It would be a pity for this genuinely popular movement in skiing to lose the spirit in which it was conceived by developing along these lines. Organizers and participants alike should try to combat the tendency for skiers in marathons to place too much strain on themselves in their efforts to put up a good performance.

Training

Anyone who wishes to take part in a ski marathon should prepare themselves physically, over a long period of time. This applies to all skiers taking part in the competition, including those who 'only' want to complete the course. Those who do not train all the year round, and then try to test their powers of endurance in a skiing marathon, are asking for trouble.

It is not necessary, however, to ski for very long distances during dry training, or training in the snow.

This was how the popular cross-country skiing marathon began about fifteen years ago. At the start there were only a few idealists – the atmosphere was friendly, almost like that of a family.

TSV
O
VOLKSSKILAUF
START
Start
174
275
272

Many skiers take two 9 mile(15km) runs a week as the minimum. You should not take part in a skiing marathon if you have less than 250 miles(400km) training in the snow under your belt.

Medical examination

Before entering for a marathon everyone should have a medical examination. In particular, heart and circulation should be tested, and tested under stress. Organic disorders of any kind, high blood pressure, hyperthyroid conditions and similar symptoms of illness will not allow intensive training for endurance, and will naturally mean exclusion from marathons.

Acute infections
Probably the greatest danger threatening a basically healthy skier is for him to start a race when suffering from, or immediately after, an acute infection or inflammation. Apparently harmless cases of tonsillitis, toothache or a slight chill can affect the heart muscle if the body is overstrained, and serious injury may be the result.

However much you may begrudge the waste of a long preparation, the entrance fee you have paid, maybe even travelling to the starting point to no purpose – no one should start a race if they are not healthy *at that moment*.

Motivation

Before the start, you should be clear whether you are one of the ambitious, competitive athletes, or whether you belong to the large mass of cross-country skiers, assessing themselves on their performance and training as well as ambition. The laws and rules of competitive sport will apply to the competitive athletes; they are after victory, or a good place – and their motivation to take part will conform to their ambitions.

Other skiers taking part in marathons, on the other hand, should keep the fact that they are to have a pleasant weekend's sport in the forefront of their minds. In contrast to the top-class sportsmen, there is no need for them to put all their strength into trying for a place which is, in the last resort, an unimportant achievement for them.

Travelling to the start

Travel to the starting point of a skiing marathon either the day before – or a whole week before the start. Those who have time can benefit by eight days on the spot, becoming acclimatized, training daily and getting to know the trail. Especially at high altitudes like St Moritz in Switzerland, three or four days' acclimatization is not enough. Indeed, after that length of time people frequently find there is a slight deterioration in their general wellbeing. Arriving the day before circumvents this problem. Comfortable accommodation must be booked well in advance.

Medication

Those who cannot sleep well the night before the start, should on no account try self-medication. Even a sleepless night will make little difference to the form of a skier who has prepared over a long period. Sleeping pills and tranquillizers, however, can have disastrous results in the course of a long race – as disastrous as those of booster drugs!

Diet

During the week before the event, you should be on a diet rich in carbohydrates. Your daily requirement is about 6000 calories. Fat content should be kept as low as possible and fat in your daily diet should not amount to more than 25 per cent of the whole calorie intake.

Never start a race on an empty stomach! A meal about two hours before the start, consisting of easily digestible foods such as porridge or muesli, will give you a good foundation.

There is a popular misconception that you ought to consume a great deal of liquid with plenty of glucose before a race. There is no point in this; taking small quantities during the race is a better idea.

After each half-hour's or hour's exertion, you should take a glucose drink and later this should be changed to a salty liquid in the form of broth or soup. The right amounts of nourishment taken at the right time to replace the loss of salt and fluid from the body will help prevent muscle cramps and exhaustion. For the same reason there should also be salty fluids available at the end of the run. Nowadays all the best-known skiing marathons have refreshment stations along the course, providing properly chosen food and drink to nourish the participants.

Knowing the course

Knowledge of the marathon course through training, or from a previous event, enables you to adjust your capabilities to it a great deal better than if it were entirely new to you. You can also get a good idea of it by studying plans and sketches. A map showing the course, and a good sketch of it, will give information about each section, drawn to scale, with its level stretches, upward and downward slopes, as well as the refreshment stations and waxing stations (see diagram of the Vasa Race below).

It is a good idea for someone who is new to the course to join a partner whose skiing performance is the same as his and who knows the course.

Waxing

A skiing marathon is no time to try out experiments and refinements of waxing. As a rule you should follow the official advice given about waxing. The organizers and their waxing experts generally have the best information about snow and temperature

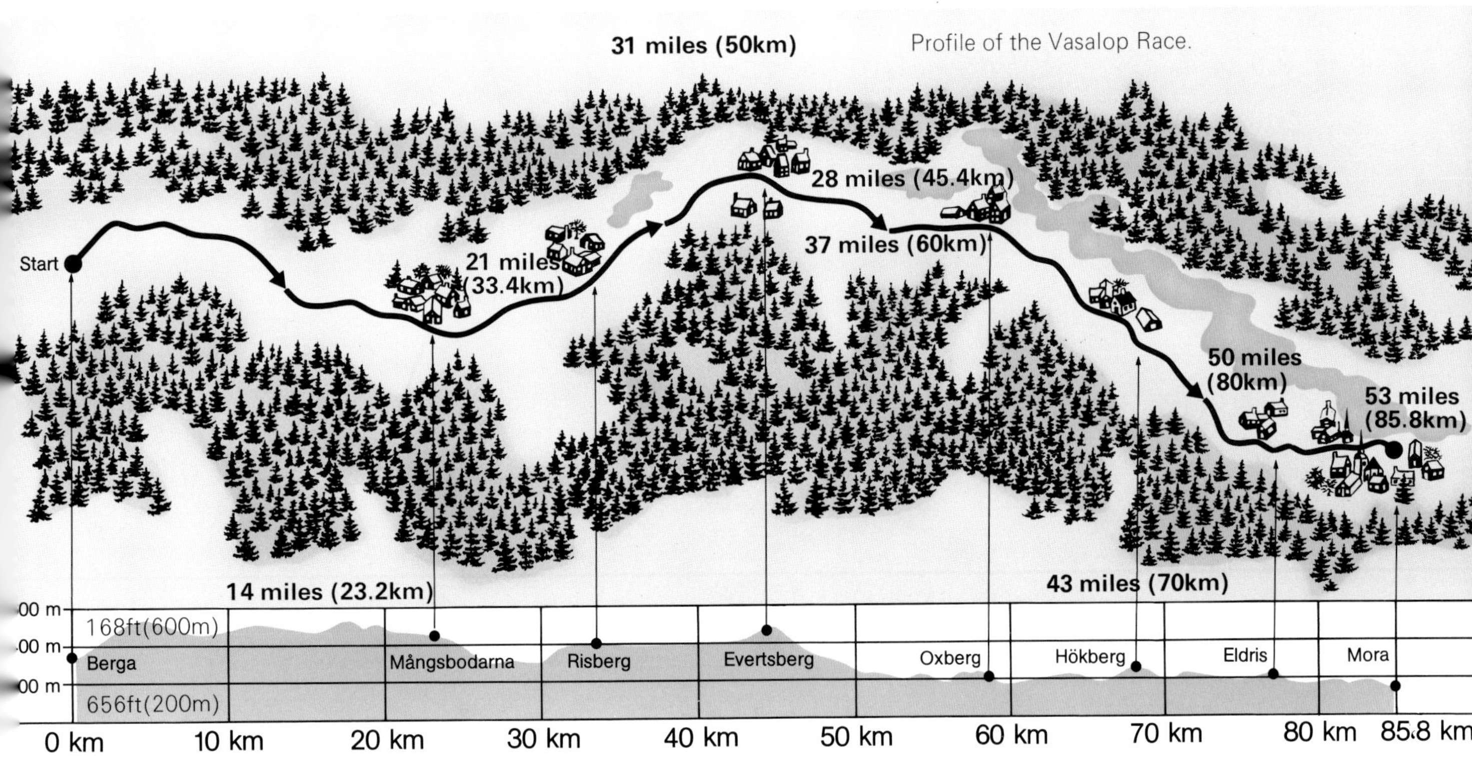

Profile of the Vasalop Race.

conditions along the course. When travelling over a long stretch of the course it is particularly important to use the right amount of wax. Even if the wax itself is the correct kind, making a mistake about the amount needed can mean that your skis are too blunt or too slippery. Skiers who find they have not waxed their skis properly while they are racing should stop and re-wax them; it will pay off. The time can easily be made up – if, that is, it is of any importance! In difficult, poor or variable snow conditions skis with no-wax surfaces have proved useful.

Warming-up

Purposeful warming-up at the start of a marathon is only important for those skiers who intend to be at the head of the field from the very beginning. Everyone else can take time warming-up for the first few miles. A race should be started gently – until heart, circulation, breathing and metabolism have become used to the effort. But saying that systematic running-in is not necessary, does not mean standing about for long, getting chilled, while your skis gather an accumulation of snow and ice, especially if soft wax is being used.

Speed

Every participant in the race will have to adjust his speed sensibly to his own powers of performance, from start to finish. He must keep something in reserve, and should never bring himself to the brink of exhaustion. From the start, it is important to have a good sense of the best speed you can make continuously. Experience has shown that a rough-and-ready guide-line for the average skier is 6 miles (10km) per hour. If this average speed can be maintained, it will put long laps of the course behind you in a very respectable time. If this speed does not feel comfortable it is essential to slow down at once.

More haste less speed

The cross-country skier, who does not worry about competition, can regard the way between start and finish as a long, athletic course to be completed within a generous time limit adjusted to his own capacity for performance. He will not let the clock or competition from other people put pressure on him. He will find time to admire the landscape, and will not feel hurried when stopping at the stations along the course; there is no reason why he should. A little cheerful chat with friends along the way does no harm. This kind of thing makes a skiing marathon a pleasant, friendly, as well as a sporting experience.

The wrong company

None of your good intentions will be any use if you find yourself in the wrong company during a skiing marathon. Naturally, taking part will be more fun if the pleasures and exertions of the expedition can be enjoyed with friends. But if a group intends to keep together the whole way, all the members must have the same capacity for performance, and they must share the same attitude to the race. Too often an over-competitive spirit arises in such groups, ending in pointless private rivalries. The fun of the thing – at least for the weaker skiers – is simply in skiing the course.

The popular marathons started out as a recreation but each has now become a true race. This does not mean that all participants have to be racers, nor do they need to compete in the true meaning of the word. It may be trite but very true to say that to take part is more important than to win. Any skier can derive great pleasure simply by testing himself against the standard of others. Just to have completed a Vasaloppet or Birkebeiner is an immense achievement and leaves a lasting feeling of pride and well-being. It is far, far better to finish rather than fail through trying too hard.

After the race

A feeling of elation at having completed the course, mingled with thirst and fatigue, often lead inexperienced marathon skiers to make silly mistakes after they reach the finish. A great deal of ice-cold beer and a heavy meal are not the right nourishment at the end of the race!

You should start by compensating for the fluids lost by taking salty drinks, soup and fruit juice. A small beer, as long as it is not too cold, will not hurt and it must be drunk slowly. After great exertions, the secretion of gastric juices is less than usual for some time, so for the first couple of hours after the race easily digested food, rich in carbohydrates, is advisable. (After prolonged exertion your muscles will be ready to absorb a good deal of carbohydrate, to replenish the stores of glycogen in the muscle cells expended during the race.) Experience has shown that the appetite is relatively small after considerable and prolonged effort, but it will come back in good measure later.

With these hints in mind a first skiing marathon can be approached with an easy mind. You will have plenty of fun and sporting enjoyment, and you will come home with a feeling of self-confidence and satifaction.

Equipment

With the boom in cross-country skiing all over the world, equipment for the sport has changed more over the last few years than for decades before. Industry and sports' manufacturers were, naturally enough, quick to see a gap in the market and plug it with attractive merchandise. The increased demand for skis and improvements in quality, however, have meant that cross-country skiing equipment, which used to be so cheap, has now risen in price.

To make a good buy when faced with such a variety of equipment you should get professional advice from an expert, and go to a really good sports' shop to make your purchases. These are the essential pieces of equipment:

Skis

The simple wooden ski, its running surface prepared with hot tar, has given way to a compound ski made of light, high-quality plastic materials with a polyethylene running surface.

The popular appeal of cross-country skiing – both the gentler and the more athletic varieties – was heightened by the development of the no-wax ski, i.e., skis whose running surfaces did not need to be waxed before use.

With these skis, structured surfaces of various kinds take over the function of the wax, making it easier to glide forwards but helping to prevent the skis sliding back as the skier thrusts off.

Nowadays there are models with strips of mohair scales running in either direction and stepped or herringbone ridges on their running surfaces.

The mohair strips have to be sprayed with a 'mohair spray', to increase their gliding ability and keep them from freezing up. You may also need to spray the scaly running surfaces; this spray can improve their sliding qualities and protect the surface itself.

- Beginners, and skiers who prefer ski rambling and have no great sporting ambitions, should choose a touring ski with a no-wax sole width $2-2\frac{1}{3}$in(53–60mm).
- For an athletic cross-country skier, or even someone keen to improve his performance and who has mastered the techniques well enough, a standard cross-country ski width $1\frac{3}{4}-2$in(46–53mm) is recommended.

  This group of skis contains models with defined sliding and thrust areas, partially equipped with suitable surface structuring.
- A technically expert skier, or a competitive athlete, will prefer a racing ski width $1\frac{3}{4}-3$in(45–77mm). This very light ski weighing 25oz(700gm) has an unstructured running surface and must, of course, be waxed. There is no doubt that a good professional racing ski, perfectly waxed, glides better and is just as good as, if not better than, a ski with a structured running surface for thrust. The exceptions to this rule are when the temperature is around 32°F(10°C) and the snow is variable. In these conditions you could use a racing ski with areas of carefully calculated structured surface (scales or a special roughened surface).

Rigidity

Whether you use waxed skis or skis with structured running surfaces, you will need to choose them with the right length and rigidity for your weight and skiing technique. A short and rigid central area of the ski, for instance, is suitable only for heavy skiers with a good technique. Athletic skiers will need to have the rigidity of their skis carefully distributed, so that there are distinct sliding and gripping areas. (The sliding areas are, roughly, in the front and back thirds of the running surface,

Rigidity of tip — Ridigity of end — Rigidity of centre

and the gripping areas in the centre.)

Beginners, and those who prefer ski rambling, should choose skis which are not too rigid in the centre, so that they can weight the entire running surface of the skis as evenly as possible.

Length

Cross-country skis should not be too short. They are very light and it will be more difficult to position them correctly if they are short as well. The following lengths are recommended for adults:

Women:
height up to 5ft(155cm)
ski length: height plus 14in(35cm)
height over 5ft(155cm)
ski length: height plus 12in(30cm)

Men:
height up to 5ft6in(170cm)
ski length: height plus 13–16in (34–40cm)
height over 5ft6in(170cm)
ski length: height plus 12–14in (30–35cm)

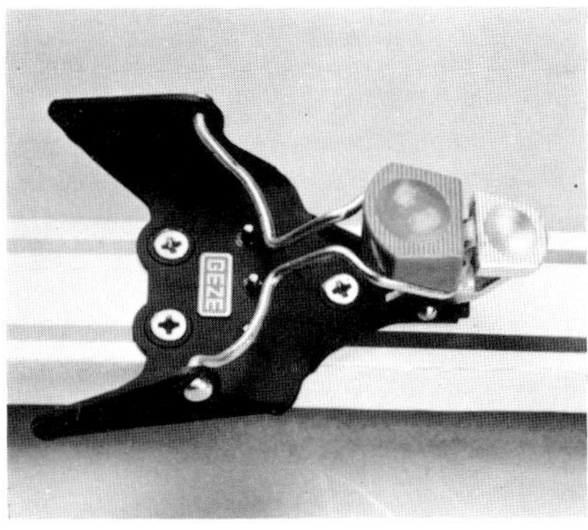

Binding on the Rottefella principle, easily opened with the tip of your ski pole.

Miniature binding for racers – combined with a special boot.

Bindings

The so-called 'Nordic' is now universal for cross-country ski bindings. Toe bindings with side pieces on the Rottefella principle are recommended for ski rambling; they will protect the boots and feet on crusted, icy trails. They are available in three standard widths: 71mm, 75mm, and 79mm. A wire clamp clipped into the binding side-pieces presses the welt of the boot soles down and into the short sole spikes that hold the boot in position.

Those who want to go in for more athletic cross-country skiing should look for one of the newer miniature bindings, which are lighter and offer less resistance to the snow. These bindings are often combined with a special shoe.

The binding is located by balancing the ski: it is laid over a knife-edge and moved until it is balanced. Before the binding is fitted, this balancing point is matched to the two outer spikes of the binding; it is placed roughly at the front of the foot.

When the binding is fitted the heel of the boot must lie flat on the ski. A 'grip plate' (or olive as it is known), must be fitted to the upper surface of the ski at this point; it stops the heel sliding sideways off the ski, especially when going downhill.

Ski boots

There are various models on the market, ranging from the very stable type, for touring or gentle trail skiing, which come up above the ankle bones, to the super-light racing type.

The higher type of boot, for touring, gives an inexperienced cross-country skier more support in the ankle-joint area and makes it easier for him to keep his balance. An elastic closure around the top of the boot is intended to keep out snow and water. The light racing shoe does not enclose the ankle.

Boots for cross-country skiing of any kind must have soles which make it possible for the foot to lift easily while skiing. The boots should fit any other comparable binding.

Cross-country ski boots can be made of leather, plastic, plastic-coated leather, or rubber. Recently racing boots made of proofed nylon have come on the market.

Ski poles

Nowadays cross-country ski poles are usually made of Tonkin (bamboo which does not splinter) or glass fibre. They must be stable and resistant to breaking, and at the same time they should be light and springy. (A springy pole gives extra impetus when planted.)

Hand grips are made of cork or roughened leather.

Loops are made of leather and must be adjustable.

Correct length: when stood on the groud, poles for cross-country skiing should reach to your armpit.

Ski wear
See pp. 16–23

Waxing

Waxing must perform two functions in cross-country skiing: it should help the skis to glide, and it should prevent them from slipping backwards as the skier pushes off.

Every time a skier thrusts his skis backwards the snow crystals will have to penetrate the layer of wax slightly if he is not to slip backwards. During the subsequent gliding phase the snow crystals must be wiped off the running surface of the skis. If the wax applied is too soft for the type of snow encountered, the crystals will dig themselves so far in that they are not removed during the forward gliding movement. The ski is then 'blunted', and the running surface becomes iced up or accumulates lumps of snow.

Too hard a wax in the prevalent snow conditions, and the crystals will not be able to penetrate the layer of wax at all during the thrust. The skis are too 'sharp', and will slip backwards.

Waxing apparatus: gas burner, cork, spatulas, wax remover, as well as several varieties of wax and a wax heater.

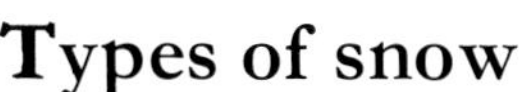

Types of snow

To learn the secret of waxing skis well, you will need to appreciate snow conditions. Roughly speaking, types of snow may be divided into three kinds:

New snow: the snow crystals are very sharp and pointed. Accordingly, they will penetrate the layer of wax easily. So in new snow conditions a thin and (according to the temperature) relatively hard layer of wax is required.

Settled and finely granulated snow: the snow crystals have either lost some of the sharp definition of their edges as they merge slightly into each other, or they have formed a more granulated structure. In snow of this kind a rather thicker layer of wax is needed, into which the granulated crystals can penetrate more easily.

A softer grade of wax (colour coding blue instead of green) may be required.

Old snow: in old snow, spring or crusted snow the crystals have thawed and then re-frozen. The layer of wax should be thick and fairly soft.

The principle of waxing

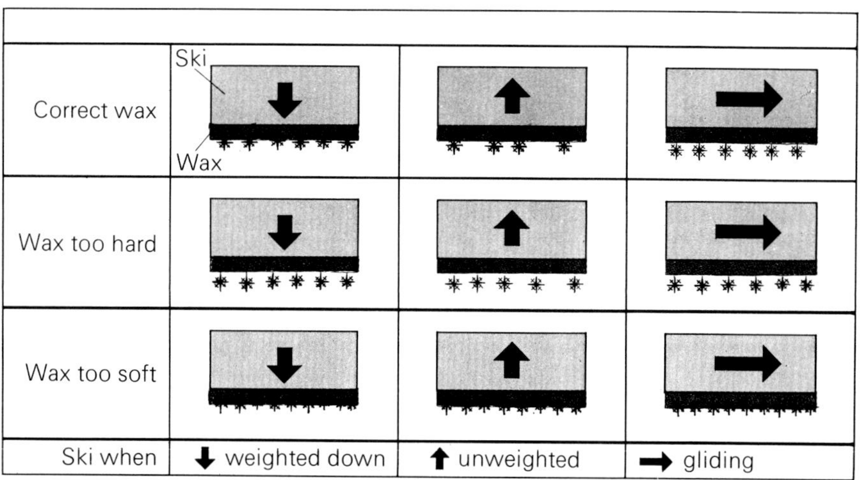

Temperature

The other factor to be taken into account in choosing the right wax is temperature. A thermometer should be part of a cross-country skier's basic equipment. Before reaching for the wax the temperature should be consulted: take the temperature of the snow when it is below freezing point (because early in the morning snow can often be colder than air), and take the air temperature when it is above freezing (because snow cannot be warmer than 32°F(0°C).

If you look at a crystal of new snow at a temperature of 28°F(−2°C), you will find it is as sharp and pointed as at 14°F(−10°C), but it will be noticeably harder at that temperature. Therefore a harder, thinner wax will be required if your skis are to glide well.

As a general principle, waxing is easier at temperatures below freezing, and slight errors are not so noticeable. The real problems arise when you have to choose the right wax for temperatures around 32°F(0°C).

Moisture of the snow

Around 32°F(0°C) the choice of wax depends to a great extent on the moisture of the snow. At this temperature snow may be either dry and almost powdery, or quite wet. This should be born in mind when choosing the wax to use.

Table of waxes

An international colour-coding table has been agreed to make it easier to choose the right waxes for cross-country skiing. Roughly speaking, a distinction is made between dry or hard waxes in cans, and soft waxes in tubes.

Waxing technique

Experts do not wax the running surfaces of their skis evenly from tip to tail; they divide the surfaces into *waxing zones* (some types of ski have these marked out).

The gliding areas (at the front and back of the ski) are waxed to be 'faster', the central area, which is pressed down on the snow as you thrust, is waxed to help the ski 'grip' well, and the waxing is adjusted to the consistency of the snow and the temperature.

- Hard wax is applied in an even layer and rubbed smooth with a cork. For a thick layer, three to four thin coats should be applied on top of one another.
- Soft wax is applied in dabs or short 'ribbons' and spread with a spatula to form an even layer. It can be finished off by rubbing it with the flat of the hand.
- The groove of the running surface is left free or treated with a running wax.
- The running surfaces must be dry and clean before you wax them. Old wax can be removed with a solution of wax remover.
- After waxing the skis should be left outside for five to ten minutes to 'temper' them. They must then be run in before use.
- Skis with ridges or fibre strips in the central area can have their sliding qualities at the front and back improved by waxing with a running wax.

Waxing for beginners

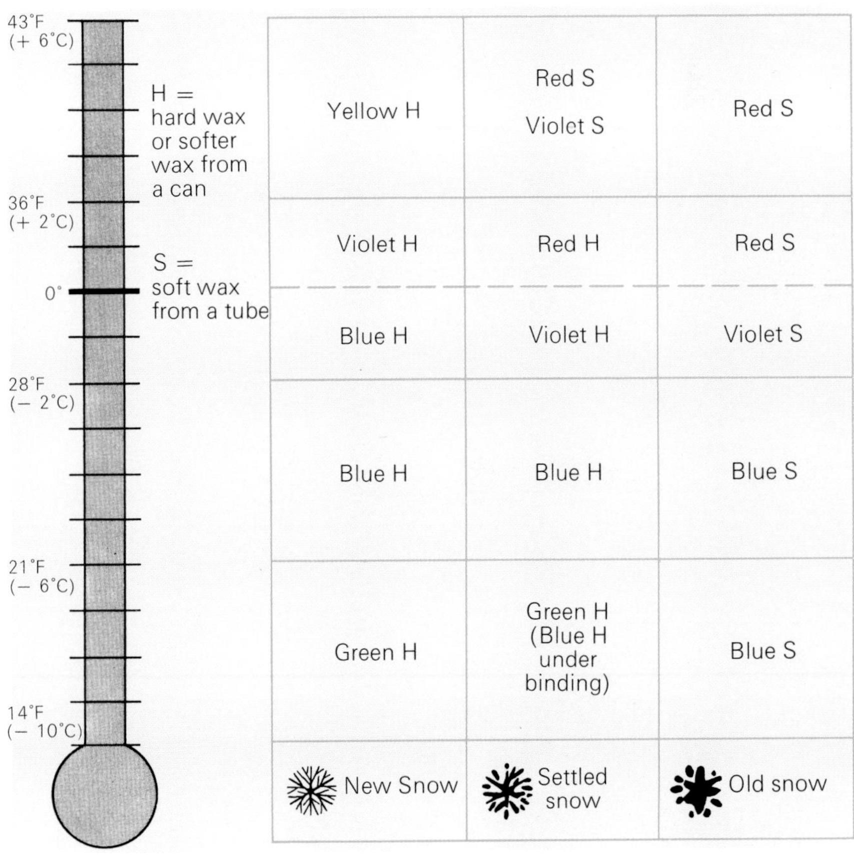

Skiing vacations

Millions of skiers go racing, turning, slipping and falling down the white slopes of ski resorts all over the world – every year in winter. A positive avalanche of skiers head towards the mountains in ones and twos, in families and in organized plane-loads. It is not all pleasure. A few come home injured, legs in plaster. Others catch every infection that is going the rounds of their resort. Many are disappointed by bad weather, poor snow conditions, uncomfortable hotels and over-crowded, ill-mannered lifts and trails. Most, if not all, of the negative experiences can be avoided by simple preparation and sensible precautions:

- Sound knowledge of technical factors (equipment).
- Consideration of local conditions (trails, transport and accommodation).
- Information on climatic conditions (sun, wind, mist, cold, snow, avalanches).
- Control of subjective factors (physical condition, trail discipline, skiing standards).

Many of the disappointments can be avoided if every holiday skier takes the trouble to make some preparation for his vacation and observes some commonsense rules during the vacation.

Insurance can be taken out against skiing accidents, illness, even lack of snow, but financial compensation is only partially successful in assuaging avoidable disappointment and disillusion.

Everyone's dream of a skiing holiday: blue sky, plenty of snow, well-prepared trails, hotels and lifts close together. More dream than reality ... Zürs, Arlberg, Austria.

Planning a holiday

Fitness

Spending the year sitting at a desk, taking no exercise, cannot be instantly remedied by going skiing for a week. Anyone going on a winter sports' holiday should be in reasonably good condition before he starts and should not expect that he will automatically become fit when he arrives. Skiing exercises started in good time help your heart, lungs and muscles to tick over properly.

Exercises are the way to avoid muscle stiffness (and, even worse, strained or pulled muscles) that may afflict skiers, who have not done any suitable exercises, in the first few days of their winter holidays.

To start a skiing holiday as fit as possible is a good rule but can be something of a problem for older people.

Feeling fit and being healthy are not necessarily the same thing. Someone in good health is not automatically fit, and similarly someone who feels fit is not necessarily in perfect health. Latent heart disorders, circulation or breathing problems may suddenly show up during a winter holiday – even if only on long walks or going up to high altitudes on a lift. Older people may be running more risks than others when they go skiing.

While coming down a long and difficult slope it is easy to think that the body is not actually working in the physical sense. The stress represented by such a downhill run, however, in what may be tricky snow conditions, raises the pulse rate to frequencies which would otherwise only occur in conditions of great physical exertion and produces muscle fatigue more commonly associated with long-distance running. Here the value of cross-country skiing cannot be over-emphasized; and more and more skiers are coming to recognize its attractions. This form of the sport gets your heart, circulation, breathing, muscles and joints all working together in an ideal way. It is a better form of holiday skiing for many older people and for housewives whose domestic duties leave them little time for recreational sport.

If possible all sporting arrangements should not be booked in advance. Some people feel compelled to finish a two-week course of ski instruction, come what may, even though they find it too much of a strain. You cannot expect to feel better for your holiday in such circumstances.

Choice of resort

It is a problem that bedevils all recreational skiers. Inevitably some compromises have to be made. In the case of a skiing family with children of school age, the question of when to go on holiday is already decided; it can only be in the school holidays or if there is a mid-winter school break. Beginners going on holiday at the height of the season should go only to small resorts, with easy slopes, away from the crush of the big skiing centres; they require somewhere which will be sure of having snow, with a well-run ski school, several nursery slopes, and small practice lifts. It is only sensible to save money and leave the more famous skiing resorts until you are more expert, and can really enjoy the more demanding slopes. If the peace and quiet of a small ski centre does not appeal, and a busier spot with cinemas, discos, night life and plenty of social activity as well as actual skiing is the choice of ambience, then the life in one of the big resorts may prove a better choice (though whether rest and refreshment has been part of the holiday is another question).

Most people have to rely on studying brochures. This is an art in itself. The following is what you will need to know:

- The character and height above sea level of the centre.
- Length and rise of the lifts.
- Type of lifts (ski-tows, chairlifts, gondolas, tramways).
- Length and difficulty of the downhill runs.
- Length and situation of the trails for cross-country skiing.
- The direction the skiing slopes face and the timberline.
- Location of hotel or other accommodation, distance from skiing and the lifts.
- Snowfall records; are the trail standards suitable, are they well groomed? Are the cross-country skiing trails groomed? Signposted? Are there prepared, measured racing trails? Or touring trails?
- For beginners: are the nursery slopes in sun or shade during the day? (Novices spend a lot of time standing around on the nursery slopes.) Do the nursery slopes have plenty of variety, and are they safe? Are there lifts near them? Do they lie well away from the busy trails used by the experts? Are there ski courses for children, and children's nurseries? Are there beginners' lifts on the nursery slopes?
- Finally, the accommodation, the road, plane or rail connections, relative costs of all-inclusive or partial board compared with self-catering – can all be assessed from sound brochures.

It is impossible to estimate the cost of a vacation in a ski centre; travel, unless undertaken as group travel or for special charter, will almost certainly exceed the cost of the accommodation unless low-cost, self-catering is acceptable. What can, however, be stated as a general guideline is that the cost of lifts, tuition, entertainment and extras will amount to approximately the same sum as the pre-paid cost of travel and accommodation. For example if the travel-agent price for a week on half-board (American Plan) comes to, all-in, $250(£125) per adult person, then the extras including lift passes will amount to a further $250(£125). If high-cost accommodation and first-class travel are chosen the proportion remains the same.

Ski schools for beginners

The best ski resort will be unsuitable for a beginner if it does not have a good ski school. The quality of a ski school depends on its organization and individual instructors.

A good ski school:

- runs courses for both Alpine and cross-country skiing
- divides the pupils into graded classes
- may divide the pupils into classes according to language spoken, age and physical condition
- never has more than twelve members to a class
- offers special courses for children
- guarantees the minimum of standing and walking about for its pupils, and plenty of practice and actual skiing
- teaches pupils how to behave safely and correctly on the trails, as well as actual ski techniques
- arranges 'races' and tests for its pupils
- keeps a watchful eye on the ski-and-boot rental organization
- keeps checking the instructor's teaching methods; makes sure they know the latest methods of instruction. A good ski school will also make sure that its pupils have access to terrain suitable for their degree of expertise. It will ensure

that the hours are as advertised (especially as advertised abroad), and that the relationship of time spent skiing to fees paid is reasonable.

In many centres better instruction can be obtained by private rather than group teaching. Many novices can overcome personal ski-blocks by well-timed private tuition.

During your holiday

The way to spend a skiing holiday is a personal matter of good sense and a little critical self-assessment.

An individual's powers of performance may vary a great deal according to the environment, especially at high altitudes. Everyone knows about the 'low' in performance encountered on the second or third day; self-assessment is important and a restday or some acclimatization with a little cross-country skiing can pay handsome dividends. Dragging a skiing weekend out as long as possible can have unfortunate results; people will have two or three 'last runs' on a Sunday afternoon, so as not to miss the remaining precious moments, and suffer for it as a result. Lack of concentration combined with physical weakness and overtired muscles are likely to lead to accidents.

Rest at the right time, and a suitable diet, are the best way to prevent emergencies caused by this kind of fatigue. Glucose and chocolate are quickly converted to replace the lost energy. At high altitudes the drier air requires a larger fluid intake. Avoid heavy, fatty meals. On the other hand, having nothing but a quick bowl of soup in a brief pause at midday, so as not to lose skiing time, is not going to provide the energy for a full day's skiing.

Long evenings spent at the bar, taking in large amounts of alcohol and nicotine, will do skiing performance no good at all. Trendy ski instructors who are back on the slopes next morning, apparently none the worse for wear after a convivial evening, are not an example for many skiers to follow.

In fact, long and merry evenings, if you go up to a high altitude by transport the next morning, can leave you feeling very ill.

Very painful muscles after a first day's skiing (more so than ordinary muscle stiffness) or joint pain after several falls may be cured by a timely rest day.

Sprains and pulled muscles which are not treated at the right time can lead to long-term damage.

Injuring yourself in this way is frequently due to the fact that muscles become cold and stiff while going up on a lift, especially a chairlift, and are not immediately capable of the sudden demands made by an immediate downhill run. A few loosening-up exercises can pay off handsomely (see pp. 88–89).

There are some special problems encountered at high altitudes.

Even if there is no great discomfort, performance is likely to suffer at high altitudes, especially where endurance is concerned. Heavy exertion will require a longer recovery period.

Any symptoms such as headache, dizziness, nausea and vomiting, as well as difficulty in breathing and a fast pulse, may indicate the onset of mountain sickness. These symptoms can appear as low as 6000ft(2000m) for anyone suffering from a heart, lung or circulation disturbance but generally do not become seriously noticeable below about 10000–11500ft(3000–3500m).

Skiers who go up to the sun and the snow in spring and summer are putting more strain on their systems than in winter, since they have to reach higher altitudes.

There are usually over 3000ft (1000m) between the spring flowers in the valleys and the last of the skiable snow on the mountains. Cable cars can whisk skiers up over these distances in a matter of minutes. The subsequent downhill run on a trail can lead to stress situations like those encountered in motor racing.

Most skiers may think the foregoing remarks are self-evident and hardly need to be mentioned. There are many first-timers, however, who are unaware of some of the problems associated with skiing in the high mountains. The problems that may arise are greater than those encountered on summer holidays in the mountains. Sensible training to become physically fit, combined with a critical self-assessment, are a good insurance for the pleasure and magnificent recreation the mountains in winter can offer.

Film and still photography

Snaps and film brought home from a skiing holiday are frequently disappointing. The pictures are boring, the colour flat or distorted, focus poor, the image blurred. Photographing snow and skiers has its own special problems, not least the simple choice of subject matter. This becomes especially evident from the yawns when an interminable slide show drags on and on or badly edited abroupt film sequences flicker past the eyes. There is much to be said for photo albums; at least they are little trouble to produce and even less trouble to look at.

Equipment, these days, is virtually fool-proof. Most cameras have automatic exposure setting and few skiers will be in a position to carry around heavy professional equipment or a

1 2 3 4

full case of interchangeable lenses. Home-movie cameras are now universally fitted with zoom lenses and even for the 35mm photo-buff a single 55–150mm zoom is a practical proposition. Ideally, three focus-lengths are required for all skiing eventualities: a wide-angle lens for impressive general scenes of mountains and skiing ground, a standard 50 or 55mm lens for general purposes and a long-focus lens – 150–250mm for action shots of skiers. Lens hoods and ultra-violet or polarizing filters are indispensable for all lenses even for the multi-coated variety which, theoretically, do not require these filters. The light on a mountain snow-scene is particularly rich in the blue to violet end of the spectrum, particularly at midday and on dull, lightly overcast days. Photographing without an ultra-violet filter can result in excessively blue colour or in a very flat and colourless result.

In general, photographing against the light or against the sun results in better colour and better definition of snow surfaces. Shadows thrown by an early or late sun emphasize snow structure and add drama to an otherwise dull skiing scene.

Most centre-weighted exposure systems will give a false light reading on account of the excess reflection from the snow added to the sky values. With an unfamiliar camera, a series of trial shots will save a great deal of disappointment. Rating the film value at one point over and one point under is the simplest method of bracketing the exposure value. As a general rule, photographing in bright sun on a snow surface, one stop faster than indicated (on the principle that an under-exposed colour shot is better than an over-exposed, bleached-out disappointment) is a simple answer if trial exposures are not feasible.

When photographing close-ups (i.e., faces) against a sunlit snow background, take an exposure value against the back of a hand held close enough to occupy most of the view-finder. Snow scenes can produce very strong shadows and when photo-

Photographing a skiing star, such as Rosi Mittermaier demonstrating a ski turn, is beyond the scope of most amateurs and requires a motor drive. For this kind of picture the focus should be fixed against an identifiable object which lies in the same plane as the skier. As a general rule, action shots of skiers should be taken from below and against the light. Exposure should be 1/500th or less and the depth of focus sufficient to cover the entire sequence.

Filming or photographing ski racers normally requires a tele-lens of 150 to 250mm. Exposure should be not less than 1/500th and for filming slow-motion is often very effective. The further away the photographer is, the less the camera movement required to follow the skier.

graphing people direct sunlight should be avoided. The best colour shots are made with the main light falling behind the shoulder of the person to be photographed.

Serious ski photographers who want to ski and photograph without too much delay and trouble will probably be best served by an old, small pocket camera, a Leica, Retina or one of the folding 35mm cameras that are supposed to have gone out of fashion.

Home-movie makers should remember the basic rules of filming. Ideally a script should be prepared and kept with sufficient film in hand

This photograph captures the joy of cross-country skiing together, taken in the Rockies.

for the unexpected and unplanned. Technical gimmickry should be avoided and the use of zooming kept to a minimum. Panning shots should be slow and if an automatic exposure camera is used, panning into the sun need not be avoided. Wherever possible a tripod or unipod should be used. It is extremely difficult to hold the camera still after some vigorous skiing, at high altitude and in a wind. Brochures, lift tickets, badges are good background material for subsequent stills and trail plans; lift notices and names make useful title material.

Additional lighting and flashguns are rarely required, even in dim après-ski dives if some fast film and wide-aperture lenses are available. Where artificial lighting is required, this should be kept to a minimum, if only to avoid irritating other customers. Most amateur flashes will only be effective up to a range of a few yards for photographing friends and neighbours.

Winter driving

Individual tyre clamps

These are still incorrectly regarded as a substitute for snow-chains. As they only surround the tyres partially, they give no sideways grip and are bumpy. They are usually easy to fit and are used only for getting out of a short stretch of difficult snow or a steep gradient. For along drive use snow-chains.

Snow-chains

When driving in high mountain areas in winter snow-chains are essential. In Switzerland they are compulsory on all mountain roads marked with the snow-chain sign. There are three types of snow-chain: ladder, zig-zag and cross-tracked.

All kinds of chain grip well, but only the cross-tracked chains grip well laterally. Chains can be fitted easily to radial and snow tyres. Wear of chains on snow is practically nil, but very high when driving on a dry road. On dry roads speed should not be faster than about 30 mph (50km/hour). On a snow-covered road, about 45 mph(75km/hour) is an acceptable maximum. Usually chains on the driving wheels only are adequate.

Brakes

When parking do not use the handbrake; it can freeze up. Put the car into gear to keep it from rolling away (first gear if pointing uphill, reverse if pointing downhill). On a steep slope turn the front wheels towards the kerb or a bank of snow.

Windshield (or windscreen)

Save yourself the trouble of having to scrape the windshield every morning by covering it with cardboard or foil fixed in place under the wipers. It is even better to use a de-icer spray.

Windshield wipers

The water bottle for the windshield wipers should be kept filled with water and antifreeze. You will have to judge for yourself at what temperature the contents will remain liquid. If necessary methylated spirits can be used; a mixture of one part of methylated spirits to three parts of water will give protection down to about 10°F(−12°C).

Rear window

If you do not have a heated rear window use clear-view film to prevent misting up.

Antifreeze

Without antifreeze the cooling system will freeze up in winter. Modern antifreeze can stay in the radiator all summer, but it should be changed at the latest after two winters. Sufficient antifreeze should be used for temperatures down to, at least, 4°F(−20°C).

Oil

Oil used in the summer months becomes viscous at temperatures near freezing point, making it harder to start the engine. Use a thin-bodied oil for the engine of your car in winter or a lower multigrade variety.

Battery

The capacity of all batteries decreases in low temperatures; more current is used in winter than under normal circumstances because lights, windscreen wipers, heater and heated rear window are in greater use. It is important to check that the battery is fully charged and the distilled water is at the right level before setting off into the mountains, where temperatures can be very low.

Jump leads

If you have forgotton to switch off your lights and your battery is flat, jump leads, 10ft(3m) long if possible, can be used to transfer current from a charged to a flat battery. Towing can often be difficult, and indeed impossible in the case of most cars with automatic transmission.

Door locks

Locks can freeze up if moisture gets inside them. There are various ways to thaw them out:

- Warm them with your hands.
- Warm up the key with a cigarette lighter, matches or a cigarette end, and place the key in the lock when hot.
- Before the winter begins coat the key with vaseline and work vaseline into the lock.
- Use a de-icer spray, which is the quickest way to do it.

This will only work, however, if you have your spray outside the car – it is no use leaving it in the glove compartment!

Lights

Even a slight film of dirt on the headlights will decrease the intensity of light let through; moreover, the light may be wrongly scattered. A slight grey film of dry dirt over the headlights will, in twilight conditions, decrease the amount of light by 40–50%. So for reasons of safety clean the lights repeatedly when driving by night in winter, or when driving in conditions of poor visibility.

Ski rack

Fit only good stable ski racks. The foot fixing the carrier to the top of the car should be at least 4in(10cm) wide.

Skis should be fastened to the ski rack with their tips pointing backwards. Many racks provide a locking mechanism as a protection against ski theft.

Tyres

Tyres with worn treads can be extremely dangerous on the road in winter and cause accidents. Bear the following hints in mind during winter:

- Cross-ply summer tyres are unsatisfactory in snow and ice.
- Cross-ply winter tyres are good in dry snow, but not on wet snow or a wet or slippery road.
- Radial-ply summer tyres are better in wintry conditions than cross-ply tyres, but should not be used on snowy mountain roads unless fitted with snow-chains. In any case the tread should be over $\frac{1}{5}$in (5mm).
- Radial-ply winter tyres have a good tread which will give a good grip in slush and snow.
- Winter tyres with only $\frac{1}{7}$in(4mm) tread will not have much traction on a snow-covered road, and should not be fitted.
- Never mix radial and cross-ply tyres, for reasons of safety.
- Winter tyres should be fitted to all four wheels.
- Pressure should be 0.2 higher on all wheels than in summer.
- Do not drive fast on winter tyres of any kind.

If in doubt, check with your local garage.

Winter accessories

Scraper, brush, de-icer sprays for windows and locks, de-misting cloth, folding spade in very snowy areas, sandbays to weight down the car when starting, and for scattering sand if necessary.

Winter driving in the mountains

If your car is not fitted with snow tyres or snow-chains it can get stuck going up a slope. To avoid this happening it is important to keep a steady speed up the hill.

If the care has manual gear-change, avoid changing gear unnecessarily since gear-changing causes a loss of speed. If your do get stuck try the following:

- Get the front wheels straight; they will start moving more easily than if they are on the slant.
- Start in second gear, using acceleration and a light foot on the clutch.
- If there is a sprinkling of new snow, or snow warmed by the sun on the road, rock the car backwards and forwards several times to give a harder surface and a long-enough run to start. If the car is thoroughly stuck your passengers will have to give a good push as you start.
- It can also help if a passenger gets on to the front fender or bumper of a car with front-wheel drive, or on the back fender or bumper of a car with the engine in front and back-wheel drive; or, better still, gets into the trunk (boot). It is a good idea to have a few bags of some heavy material as ballast in the trunk of cars with standard drive.

When coming down steep slopes, avoid braking sharply and making abrupt movements when steering.

Brake very gently on snow and ice. Locked wheels make the car uncontrollable. Sequence braking can prevent locked wheels.

Black ice can form at any time on the road if the temperature is around 34°F(2°C). The film of ice which forms at temperatures of 28°F(−2°C) to 36°F(4°C) is not as slippery as patches of ice at lower temperatures.

Skiing and the law

The days are long gone when a beginner simply got hold of a pair of turned-up wooden boards and made his first secret attempts at sliding in the snow on his own. Nowadays a skier finds himself confronted by a vast array of skiing equipment, the ski lifts are crowded, and the trails sometimes seem like a street in the rush hour.

This change in the situation has not just meant the coming of a technically sophisticated ronge of equipment and mechanical means of getting up the slopes, but it has brought with it a whole host of legal problems associated with the improvement of equipment and lifts, and the potential collisions between the skier and his surroundings.

Equipment

If you buy a car you will usually want to know how long it is under guarantee or when it last passed a test. In the same way a skier who sets store by having safe equipment will expect his skiing gear to correspond to the latest safety regulations. In Europe and North America the performance of the functional unit comprising ski, binding, boot and ski brake is under any guarantee only if each part of the unit corresponds to accepted national or international standards.

Ski boots

Ski boots have the most important part to play here, since they transfer the skier's movements to the skis, and must at the same time assist the safety binding to release. The soles of the ski boots must comply with established standards. Moreover, one must not only ski in a ski boot, but be able to walk and stand in it without being crippled. Investigations have shown that a skier spends most of his time in ski boots just standing, spends less time walking in them, and least time of all skiing.

Safety bindings

A safety binding must comply with accepted national and international standards to ensure that it does not release by mistake, causing unnecessary falls, but *does* release the boot in the course of a strong frontal or twisting strain before injury is caused.

Recent annual tests have shown that only about one third of the bindings used by skiers are properly adjusted. The retailer has the responsibility of fitting the bindings, adjusting them to the boots and the individual needs of the skier. This will be done if the top of the shin-bone is measured and the bindings adjusted accordingly – as shown in the IAS table (p. 35).

If you notice anything wrong with your equipment you should not try to repair it yourself; you would not try to fiddle about with the brakes of your car yourself if you did not have the technical knowledge to do so. And it is in the retailer's own interest to do his job properly, since he may be held responsible if it can be proved that an accident was caused by faulty equipment supplied by him.

One important point to remember is that the best kind of ski binding for adults is not suitable for children and young people. Children need a binding complying with different standards. The argument that children have more elastic bones and their injuries will heal faster is fallacious. Hospitals and clinics in ski areas can confirm that far more children and young people are admitted with injuries than should correspond statistically to the ratio of children to adults skiing. Quite often a broken leg may lead to a check in the child's growth and later to unequal growth of both legs. As children are able to ski expertly, the border area between the point where a binding should hold firm and the point at which force is exerted which will break a bone is a very small one. So children's bindings should function more accurately than bindings for adults.

Crash helmets

Head injuries incurred during skiing have often proved very dangerous. Wearing a crash helmet, especially for children while downhill skiing, is a sound precaution. Children will be ready to follow the example of top racers. Young people and adults, on the other hand, will only be persuaded to adopt this sensible form of protection when manufacturers succeed in producing a fashionable and comfortable crash helmet.

Retaining straps, ski brakes or stoppers

Ski equipment is not complete without a retaining device which complies with accepted standards. A retaining strap for a beginner skiing slowly or a skier in deep snow is recommended while a ski brake is preferable for a faster trail skier. The ski brake protects other skiers from a loose ski racing down the trail, and does not endanger the skier himself. The retaining strap has the disadvantage that the wearer of the ski may be injured by his own ski. New regulations laid down by many ski transport companies mean a skier may find himself barred from using them if he is not wearing one of these two devices on his skis.

Ski poles

Safety poles complying with accepted safety standards are an ideal but rare item of equipment.

Terrain

In most countries a skier has a legal right of way over public or common land but not over certain types of private land. This means that you cannot go skiing in your neighbour's front garden, but you are allowed to ski in fields, woods and meadows. The freedom allowed to individual skiers in this respect, however, does not apply to organized groups, competitions, or the laying out of downhill runs. Laying out runs and trails requires the authorization of the owner of the property. Fenced grazing or forestry land needs the permission of the owner or tenant unless there is a public right of way across such land.

Skiing rules

The boom in skiing means that you are seldom on your own on trails at the weekend. The rules of the sport should be known and obeyed if you want to avoid unpleasant surprises.

For example: a skier is standing at the edge of a trail, taking a breather and admiring the view, and then skis off. At that moment a more athletic skier comes shooting down fast from the slope above, and cannot avoid the first skier. There is a collision, resulting in injuries. Neither skier will take the blame for the accident. The second skier claims it was up to the first skier to look uphill before starting off again. The first skier objects that the second skier ran into him from behind, so it was *his* fault. Lawyers exchange letters and the case comes to court on a charge of bodily harm.

You might look long, and in vain, for a legal solution. The entire legal liability situation, insofar as it relates to a skier, his equipment and his surroundings is extremely complicated and legally obscure. In most countries the Common Law relating to product liability, misrepresentation, negligence and the like will cover the obvious cases. There is a vast grey area, however, which cannot be defined simply nor is it similar in different countries.

Various international and national organizations have established standards and norms for equipment; for example, the IAS has done so; this is, in theory, an international ski safety body. European industrial practice has established a series of standards which now have a quasi-international validity. In North America the association of sporting equipment manufacturers and suppliers operate a generally accepted list of standards. An annual conference discussing legal aspects of skiing has attempted to bring a degree of standardization to the claims and counter-claims for damages by, and to, third parties. A number of court cases, some still *sub-judice* years after the event, have indicated a disturbing degree of responsibility on the part of resorts and mountain transport management for the wellbeing of skiers whom they service. At present the cost of insurance is going to be passed on to the skier in the form of much higher lift-pass costs and even charges for the use of ski and cross-country trails.

The FIS has laid down ten international rules for skiers. You cannot claim that you need not observe these rules because you do not belong to a sporting association; the regulations have been in force since 1967 as the standard of behaviour to be observed by all skiers in the ski countries of the world. Below is the full, official FIS text.

Rule 0
Skiing is a sport and as in all other sports, it has a risk element and certain civil and penal responsibilities.

The FIS Rules must be considered the ideal expression of model conduct for a responsible, careful and keen skier.

The Rules enumerate the principle duties laid upon all who practise the ski sport.

A skier is expected to be familiar with, and to respect, the Rules for circulation on skis.

A skier who does not observe these rules is mistaken and lays himself open to liabilities in case of accident.

Rule 1: respect for others
A skier must behave in such a way that he does not endanger or prejudice others.

The FIS Rules apply to all skiers. Participants in competitions also come under existing national and international competition rules.

The integrity of the human being stands over and above all sports' results.

The FIS Rules apply to the pupils of ski schools. Ski teachers must respect the rules, teach them to their pupils and enforce them.

Rule 2: control of speed and skiing

A skier must adapt his speed and way of skiing to his personal ability and to prevailing conditions of terrain and weather.

A skier must adapt his speed and way of skiing to the nature of the course.

It is normal that a skier goes fast on a fast course (in general use by accomplished skiers).

It is normal that a skier goes slowly on an easy course (as a rule used by beginners).

To take care and show respect for the Rules is all the more imperative for an undisciplined skier who goes slowly on a fast course or fast on a slow course.

Experienced skiers and beginners must go slowly in narrow passages and especially at the foot of the course and at the departure of means of mechanical transportation.

A skier must be able to stop, make a turn or otherwise perform within his range of vision.

Rule 3: control of direction

A skier coming from above, whose dominant position allows him a choice of path, must take a direction which assures the safety of the skier below.

The priority of the skier below also covers normally anticipated activity of the skier who is in front of another skier.

Skiing is a sport of free activity where everybody may go as he pleases, provided he respects the rules of circulation and adapts his skiing to his own personal ability and prevailing conditions (such as the course, quantity of snow, visibility, obstacles, etc.).

FIS remains against the establishment of rigid rules of the road (such as right-left and below-above). Every skier must decide for himself how to handle an immediate situation. A normally careful and conscientious skier should be aware of what happens not only in front of him or below him but also on the sides, all within his normal range of vision, while continuing to descend.

Rule 4: overtaking

It is permitted to overtake another skier going up or down – to the right or to the left, but always leaving a wide-enough margin for the overtaken skier to make his turns.

The responsibility of a skier overtaking another skier extends to the moment when he has passed the overtaken skier. This is necessary in order not to cause any difficulties for the skier being overtaken.

The above responsibility is valid also when overtaking a skier who has stopped on the course.

Rule 5: duties of a skier crossing the course

A skier wishing to enter a course or passing a training ground must look up and down to make sure that he can do so without danger to himself or others. The same applies when starting again after a stop on the course.

All activity against the normal direction of a course may be dangerous and requires care especially when:

entering a course
crossing the training ground course
starting again after a stop
attempting 'fantasy turns', unforeseen movements, etc.

Rule 6: stopping on the course

If not absolutely necessary, a skier must avoid a stop on the course, especially in narrow passages or where visibility is restricted. In the case of a fall, a skier must leave the course free as soon as possible.

A stop creates a situation of disturbance on a downhill course. If a skier must stop, he should do so at the side of the course. It must be considered legally offensive to stop in dangerous places (narrow passages with bad visibility) where, in itself, a descending skier's activity is dangerous and liable to accidents.

Rule 7: climbing

A climbing skier must keep to the side of the course and, in bad visibility, keep off the course entirely. The same goes for a skier who descends on foot.

Climbing is a disturbing activity on a downhill course. It should therefore be kept to the side of the course. If not, anyone who climbs must, at all times, assure themselves that they are not endangering a descending skier.

Rule 8: respect for signals

A skier must respect the signals.

The signals for opening and closing the course and marking danger points must be respected.

The courses are marked in black, red, blue or green, indicating the difficulties the skier will meet when descending the different courses.

Every skier must choose his own course.

A slow skier, using a fast course, must redouble his attention so that he is sure to observe the Rules. The same is applicable for a skier going rapidly down a slow course.

Rule 9: conduct at accidents

At accidents everybody is duty-bound to assist.

As for penalties, the FIS hopes that the offence of 'desertion at accidents on skis' will be considered equivalent to desertion at road accidents, in all countries where the legislation has not already foreseen this.

Rule 10: identification
Witnesses at an accident, whether responsible parties or not, must establish their identity.

The reports of witnesses are of great importance for the establishment of the dossier of an accident. In this respect, everybody must be prepared to act as a witness. Reports of the competent authorities – the police and medical services – will be of considerable assistance when it comes to deciding possible liabilities.

It is of value to collect as many such reports as possible.

Third-party insurance

Damages arising from skiing accidents can be so high as to represent a real threat to the livelihood of the skier held responsible, if he has not insured against that eventuality. Third-party insurance must cover the skier adequately in all countries in which he expects to ski.

Conclusion

Skiing is a paradoxical sport. It evolved as a means of practical transport and developed into the largest participant sport and recreation in the world practised today by millions of people.

It is essentially a solitary occupation as every skier skis for himself, and by himself, however many other skiers may be in his immediate neighbourhood. The paradox lies in the inescapable fact that, in order to enjoy his skiing, every skier, whether Alpine or cross-country, is dependent upon the active co-operation of a great number of people, large and expensive machinery, the goodwill of a whole army of authorities, land owners and utility organizations (such as restaurants, lifts), all of which cost much money and which depend upon the willing or unwilling contributions, direct and indirect, of the skier.

This practical assistance can, in very general terms, be called the infrastructure of skiing. In order that the solitary skier can revel in his private solitude of snow and sun and mountains, the infrastructure has to provide him with his skis and clothes, transport him to his chosen place of exercise and transport him up the mountain where it will feed him, safeguard him and provide the best protection from outside dangers of weather and snow that is feasible under the circumstances.

In other words, the solitary skier is alone only in his imagination but surrounded not only by sophisticated modern artefacts but by a considerable number, often a very large number, of other skiers who are all equally concerned with their solitary skiing endeavours.

The paradox goes a lot further; modern skiing, notably Alpine skiing, gives a superficial impression of being a very controlled sport, even a protected sport where only the inherent risk element in any physical sport remains the unknown factor. This is a gross illusion. In practice, the cossetted urban citizen is transported, in considerable comfort and safety, from his accustomed, organized and regulated environment into the high mountains.

But immediately outside the double doors of the expensive mountaintop restaurant or down the concrete passage from the arrival station of the lift or cable car is a high-Alpine environment which, despite the most earnest endeavours of the infrastructure, remains as wild and untamable as it has been since the ice age retreated. The weather can change from blazing sun to Polar cold and blizzard in the blink of an eye; the well-marked trails, safely rolled and manicured, freed from potential avalanche danger and unseen potholes, can turn into a white desert where there are no distinguishing features. The wonderful sparkling powder of tomorrow morning is this afternoon's purgatory.

Many years ago, the Alpine skier – and the cross-country skier for that matter – were a minority, an eccentric band of mountain wanderers for whom few had understanding, none responsibility. Regrettably, for such is human nature, the moment the infrastructure provided amenities, there arose the threat of litigations and legal responsibilities and, to counter such threats, rules and regulations, do's and don'ts inevitably made their unwelcome appearance. These regulations were possibly doubly unwelcome, even though they were sincerely meant for the skier's own good, to save him, despite himself, from dangers of which he was only dimly aware and which were, truth be told, only a remote statistical possibility.

It was the popularity of the sport which brought about this first unwelcome change. Where, at one time, a mountain glade saw a skier once a week, there are now a thousand a day and unless total chaos is to prevail, rules and regulations are required and must, if need be, be enforced. It is a long journey from the solitary skier to the sport today.

Any skier who is out to enjoy his favourite run, a long-desired trail or just to exercise desk-tired muscles for an hour or two, will do well to remember that his personal pleasure is, to a large extent, dependent upon other people on the mountain with him following, in a very general sort of way, these rules and regulations. That rules should have touched the

last stronghold of the solitary sportsman, the lonely cross-country skier, is just another unfortunate paradox resulting from the universal attraction the sport has for a cross-section of western man.

You cannot teach yourself to ski with the aid of a book and some unruly tumbles. You cannot make yourself a pair of serviceable skis in your home workshop and expect to swoop like a swallow down the steepest trail. You can, indeed, climb your own mountain under your own foot-power, but if you should find yourself in mayday difficulties you will still expect help to come from some anonymous rescue service. You can carry your own food up to the top of your chosen mountain, but you cannot expect the local refuse company to collect your discarded orange peel and food wrappers and – be honest – you would be the first to object to finding an empty sardine tin littering your favourite resting spot under a sun-drenched rock.

Like it or not, as a skier you are dependent on our fellow skiers and an army of unseen collaborators to make our skiing as pleasant and safe as possible; the one great help to this end is knowledge: knowledge about the equipment we use, how to use it and how to care for it; how to behave towards our fellow skiers and how to safeguard ourselves against the dangers that the sport cannot avoid. That has been the purpose of this book and if it has, at times, seemed a trifle authoritarian, then it is only because thirty million skiers have made anything other than a minimum of rules and regulations, standards and norms a recipe for total chaos.

There is, however, a great deal that the skier himself can contribute with a minimum of effort and this is nothing more than the most fundamental of common courtesies. The unruly lift line, the inconsiderate trail cowboy, the ill-temper vented on others for our own minor faults – these are a contemporary evil of the ski trails, Alpine and cross-country. But they dwindle to nothing compared to the personal pleasure enjoyed by any skier, novice or expert, in a sport which has no equal.

Index

Guide to US ski areas

Ski Areas (*Telephone number for snow conditions in italics*)	Elevation (in feet): top (T), base (B)	Skiing terrain	Slope difficulty: B (beginner), I (intermediate), A (advanced)	Lifts	Lift capacity per hour	Length of season	Average annual snowfall (in ins)	Average temperature	Cross-country	Touring
Alyeska Resort Girdwood Alaska tel: (907) 783-6000	T:3000 B:200	Most skiing above timber-line in open glacial bowls; lower down tree-lined slopes; longest run: 2 miles	B:25% I:25% A:50%	6	3700	Nov 19-Apr 30		35°F. Sun 80% of season	At area	Nearby
Arizona Snow Bowl Flagstaff Arizona tel: (602) 774-0562 *(602) 779-4577*	T:11600 B:9500	Open beginner, high bowl powder, long consistant fall line for moguls; longest run: 1½ miles	B:29% I:27% A:44%	7	1600	Nov 20-Apr 5	150		At area	At area
Sunrise Ski Area McNary Arizona tel: (602) 334-2122	T:10740 B:9300	17 slopes and trails; longest run: 3 miles	B:30% I:45% A:25%	4	3500	mid Nov-mid Apr	250	20-30°F. Sun 75% of season	Nearby	Nearby
Alpine Meadows Ski Area Tahoe City California tel: (916) 583-4232 *916 583-6914*	T:8700 B:6970	2000 acres of skiable terrain on two mountains. longest run: 5420 ft	B:25% I:35% A:40%	13	8000	Thanks-giving to Mem-orial Day	180	29°F. Sun 80% of season	At area and nearby	At area and nearby
Badger Pass Yosemite California tel: (209) 372-4691 *(209) 372-4808*	T:8100 B:7200	10 runs, small area, tree-lined; longest run: 1 mile	B:30% I:50% A:20%	6		mid Nov-mid Apr	59		At area and nearby	At area and nearby
Boreal Ski Area Truckee California tel: (916) 426-3666 *(415) 982-1771*	T:7800 B:7200	24 slopes, some of which run into another forming one run; longest run: ⅞ mile	B:20% I:60% A:20%	7	4000	Thanks-giving to Easter (usu-ally)	96-144			
China Peak Lakeshore California tel: (209) 893-3316	T:8709 B:7030	200 acres of slopes and trails. All chairs over 1 mile; longest run: 2.9 miles	B:15% I:50% A:35%	7	4800	Nov 15-Apr 15	150 — 200		Nearby	Nearby
Dodge Ridge Pine Crest California tel: (209) 965-3474 *(415) 982-1771*	T:7600 B:6600	Bowl, open and tree-lined on 300 acres; longest run: 4200 ft	B:20% I:60% A:20%	12	10800	Thanks-giving to Easter	450		Nearby	Nearby
Goldmine Ski Area Big Bear Lake California tel: (714) 585-2517/8	T:8600 B:7100	Many runs and trails; longest run: 2½ miles	B:20% I:35% A:45%	6	3600	Thanks-giving to April			Nearby	Nearby
Heavenly Valley South Lake Tahoe California tel: (916) 541-1330 *(800) 822-5977*	T:10167 B:6100	Bi-state ski complex over 20 miles of varying terrain; tree bowl and packed surface skiing; longest run: 7 miles	B:25% I:50% A:25%	25	19100	mid Nov-mid May	300 — 500	29°F. Sun 84% of season	Nearby	Nearby
Kirkwood Ski Resort Kirkwood California tel: (209) 258-6000	T:9800 B:7800	Open bowl 2000 acres, 50 major runs, excellent beginner terrain; longest run: 2½ miles	B:20% I:60% A:20%	9	10500	Nov 17-Apr 29	450	29°F. Sun 60-70% season	At area & nearby	At area
Mammoth Mountain Ski Area Mammoth California tel: (714) 934-2571 *(714) 934-6166*	T:11053 B:7953	Over 60 open slopes, bowls, and trails; longest run: 2 miles	B:30% I:40% A:30%	22	25000	Oct-June (approx)	130	35°F. Sun 80% of season	Nearby	Nearby
Mountain High Ski Area Wrightwood California tel: (714) 249-3226	T:8100 B:6900	Open slopes & trails; longest run: 1100 ft	B:34% I:35% A:31%	2	2400	Thanks-giving to Apr 30			10 miles	
Mt Baldy Mt Baldy California tel: (714) 982-4208	T:8600 B:6500	Snow conditions change frequently. Mostly int-ermediate with some interesting advanced runs	B:20% I:50% A:30%	4	3100	Jan to late March				
Mt Reba at Bear Valley Bear Valley California tel: (209) 753-2301 *(415) 982-1771*	T:8506 B:6400	21 miles of well-groomed well-balanced terrain; longest run: 3 miles	B:25% I:50% A:25%	8	8900	Nov-end Apr	450	15-20° F. Sun 65% of season	Nearby	Nearby
Mt Waterman La Canada California tel: (213) 790-2002	T:8000 B:7200	15 trails tree-lined; longest run: 4000 ft		3	2400	Nov-Apr			Unmarked	
Northstar-at-Tahoe Truckee California tel: (916) 562-1111 *(916) 562-1330*	T:8600 B:6400	39 marked trails and runs, north-facing ski bowl sheltered by two wooded ridges on 1200 acres; longest run: 2½ miles	B:33% I:50% A:17%	8	8600	mid Nov-mid Apr	300	29°F. Sun 75% of season	At area	At area
Papoose Ski Area Olympic Valley California tel: (916) 583-4826	T:6500 B:6200	Longest run: 500 ft		6	2000	Thanks-giving to May 1			Centre for Squaw Valley	Centre for Squaw Valley
Plumas-Eureka Ski Bowl Quincy California tel: (916) 836-2317	T:6200 B:5550	Open bowl skiing, tree-lined trails; longest run: 1 mile		4	1000	Dec 15-Mar 31				
Powder Bowl Ski Area Tahoe City California tel: (916) 583-4373	T:6300 B:5450	Beginner-intermediate: 3 miles of trail		3	1300	Nov-Apr			At area	At area

Shirley Meadows Ski Area Wofford Heights California tel: (805) 376-6780	T:6000	Longest run: 1400 ft	B:40% I:30% A:30%	3		Dec-Mar				
Signal Hill Norden California tel: (916) 426-3632	T:7800 B:7500	Mostly intermediate/beginner skiing. One open slope, two wooded bowls		1	450	Thanksgiving to Easter			At area	At area
Sierra Ski Ranch Twin Bridges California tel: (916) 659-7475	T:8852 B:7282	Open slopes with 21 tree-lined runs; longest run: 2½ miles	B:25% I:40% A:35%	6	6700	Jan 3-Apr 10	450 — 500		Nearby	Nearby
Ski Sundown Kirkwood California tel: (209) 258-8543 *(209) 258-8300*	T:7650 B:6450	14 runs, 12 miles of trails	B:20% I:60% A:20%	3		mid Nov-Apr	93			
Snow Valley Running Springs California tel: (714) 867-3677/7182 *(714) 867-2434*	T:7800 B:6800	19 open runs; longest run: 1¼ miles	B:45% I:30% A:25%	10	8500	Thanksgiving to Apr 1	120			
Squaw Valley Olympic Valley California tel: (916) 583-6985	T:8900 B:6200	Mostly open slopes, few trails; longest run: 3 miles	B:30% I:40% A:30%	23	26300	Nov 15-May 15	450	25°F. Sun 60% of season	At area	At area
Soda Springs Ski Area Soda Springs California tel: (916) 426-3626	B:6800	Family skiing	B:45% I:35% A:20%	3		Thanksgiving to April			At area	
Stover Mountain Chester California		5 runs; longest run: ½ mile	B:25% I:45% A:30%	2	1000	Thanksgiving to Easter				
Sugar Bowl Norden California tel: (916) 426-3651	T:8383 B:6881	7 miles of trails, 33 slopes mostly tree-lined; longest run: 2 miles	B:25% I:25% A:50%	9	7000	Nov-May 15	500	20°F. Sun 50% of season	Nearby	At area
Tahoe Donner Truckee California tel: (916) 587-6046	T:7350 B:6750	2 miles of trail, 75% open bowl; longest run: 1mile	B:50% I:50%	3	1500	Thanksgiving to Easter			At area	At area
Tahoe Ski Bowl Homewood California tel: (916) 525-7479	T:7880 B:6250	Expanded challenging runs; ski in any direction from top of mountain; longest run: 1½ miles	B:40% I:40% A:20%	5	3240	Thanksgiving to Easter	120		Nearby	
Wolverton Ski Bowl Sequoia Nat. Park California tel: (209) 565-3381	T:7400 B:7200	Beginners to advanced, 3 slopes, open and tree-lined; longest run: 1000 ft		3	1000	Nov 24-Easter Sunday			Nearby	
Arapahoe East Golden Colorado tel: (303) 277-0833	T:7400 B:6900	Well-groomed slopes and trails; longest run: ½ mile	B:60% I:40%	3	2200	Nov 25-Mar 10				
Aspen Highlands Aspen Colorado tel: (303) 925-5300	T:11800 B:8000	77 miles of slopes, bowls, open trail, glades; longest run: 2 miles	B:25% I:50% A:25%	12	10000	Nov 23-Apr 15	220	24°F. Sun 80% of season	Nearby	At area
Aspen Mountain Aspen Colorado tel: (303) 925-1220	T:11212 B:7930	Over 500 acres of runs and trails; longest run: 2+ miles	I:25% A:75%	7	6575	Nov 23-Apr 15	300	24°F. Sun 80% of season	Nearby	Nearby
Berthoud Pass Idaho Springs Colorado tel: (303) 572-8014	T:12000 B:11022	Varied terrain	B:40% I:40% A:20%	3	1100	Oct-Apr				
Breckenridge Breckenridge Colorado tel: (303) 453-2368 *(303) 893-2201*	T:11843 B:9630	Front and back bowls on peak 8. 780 acres of skiable terrain; longest run 2.6 miles	B:30% I:45% A:25%	14	14383	Nov 23-Apr 15	295		At area	At area
Buttermilk Mountain Aspen Colorado tel: (303) 925-1220	T:9840 B:7868	420 acres of groomed trails for beginners and intermediate. Tiehack side offers expert skiing; longest run: 2 miles	B:38% I:44% A:18%	7	6647	Nov 23-Apr 1	200		At area	At area
Copper Mountain Copper Mountain Colorado tel: (303) 668-2882	T:12050 B:9600	45 trails approx. 50 miles; all below tree line, some back bowl skiing; longest run: 2½ miles	B:20% I:60% A:20%	10	10500	Nov 18-Apr 30	250	24°F. Sun 75% of season	At area	At area
Eldora Ski Area Nederland Colorado tel: (303) 447-8012 *(303) 447-8011*	T:10650 B:9250	[illegible] acres of trails and 36 slopes; longest run 2 miles	B:10% I:40% A:50%	5	5550	Oct 28-early Apr	150		At area	At area
Geneva Basin Grant Colorado tel: (303) 789-1426	T:11750 B:10500	21 trails; longest run 1 mile	B:25% I:45% A:30%	4		mid Nov-Apr			At area	At area
Hidden Valley Estes Park Colorado tel: (303) 586-4887	T:11400 B:9400	Longest run: 1¼ miles	B:30% I:40% A:30%	4	3200	Dec 1-mid Apr			Nearby	
Keystone/ Arapahoe Basin Keystone Colorado tel: (303) 468-2316	T:12440 B:10800	22 trails covering 185 skiable acres; powder skiing in bowls	B:10% I:50% A:40%	5	5400	Nov 17-June	450		At area	At area
Keystone Mountain Keystone Colorado tel: (303) 468-2316 *(303) 468-5050*	T:11640 B:9300	37 miles of trail, open bowl glade and trail skiing; longest run: 3 miles	B:20% I:65% A:15%	9	9400	Nov 17-Apr 15	200	27°F. Sun 75% of season	At area	At area
Loveland Ski Areas Georgetown Colorado tel: (303) 569-2288	T:12430 B:11000	540 acres of above timber-line bowls & tree-lined lower slopes; longest run: 1½ miles	B:25% I:55% A:20%	8	8200	mid Oct-1st Sun in May	275		At area	At area
Monarch Winter Sports Garfield Colorado tel: (303) 539-4060	T:12000 B:11000	19 slopes, extensive open, wooded powder skiing, well groomed for all levels; longest run: 1¼ miles	B:25% I:65% A:10%	3	2840	Nov 15-May 1	354		Nearby	Nearby
Pikes Peak Colorado Springs Colorado tel: (303) 684-9868	T:11500 B:10500	Longest run: 1 mile	B:75% I:20% A: 5%	3	1000	Nov 7-Apr 1				
Purgatory Durango Colorado tel: (303) 247-9000	T:10500 B:8950	43 trails on 450 acres, plenty of tree and open-bowl skiing, groomed trails; longest run: 2 miles	B:25% I:55% A:20%	6	4200	Pre-Thanksgiving to Apr 15	300		At area	At area
Ski Broadmoor Colorado Springs Colorado tel: (303) 634-7711	T:6800 B:6200	Open slopes; longest run: ¾ mile	B:60% I:20% A:20%	2	600	Thanksgiving to Apr 1				

Snowmass Mountain Aspen Colorado tel: (303) 925-1220	T:11808 B:8250	13,000 acres of tree-lined trails. Expansive 'Big Burn' slope dotted with sparse trees; longest 4 miles	B:10% I:65% A:25%	12	13575	Nov 23-Apr 15	300	25°F. Sun 85% of season	Nearby	Nearby
Steamboat Steamboat Springs Colorado tel: (303) 879-2220 *(800) 525-2501*	T:10600 B:6900	614 acres or 33 miles of skiable terrain, 53 trails plus gladed tree areas and open meadows; longest run: 2½ miles	B:23% I:49% A:28%	15	14700	Dec 2-Apr 15	325	28°F. Sun 65% of season	At area	At area
Sunlight Glenwood Springs Colorado tel: (303) 945-7491/7270	T:10200 B:8500	27 miles of trails; longest run: 4 miles	B:40% I:40% A:20%	3	1500	Thanks-giving to Apr	145		At area	At area
Telluride Ski Area Telluride Colorado tel: (303) 728-3856	T:11930 B:8730	40 miles of terrain, 27 slopes all tree-lined; longest run: 4 miles	B:25% I:45% A:30%	6	3300	Nov 23-Apr 1	400		At area	At area
Vail Vail Colorado tel: (303) 476-5601	T:11250 B:8200	Largest single mountain skiing complex in North America. 10 sq. miles of skiing terrain, about 89 trails. 700 acres of natural bowl area; longest run: 4½ miles	B:30% I:40% A:30%	18	20830	Nov 22-Apr 15	317	24°F. Sun 70% + of season	At area	At area
Winter Park Winter Park Colorado tel: (303) 726-5514 *(303) 892-1453*	T:11125 B:9000	800 acres, 52 trails, glade skiing; longest run: 2 miles	B:24% I:39% A:37%	13	15800	Nov 15-Apr 22	250	25°F. Sun 90% of season	Nearby	Nearby
Bogus Basin Boise, Idaho tel: (208) 336-4500 *(208) 336-2300*	T:7600 B:5800	37 runs plus open slopes and powder glades; longest run: 8000 ft	B:25% I:52% A:23%	11	7340 + ropes	Thanks-giving to Apr	100		At area	
Brundage Mountain Ski Area McCall Idaho tel: (208) 634-2244	T:7600 B:6000	Variety of runs for all skiers, powder to packed runs	B:40% I:40% A:20%	3	1920	Nov 15-Apr 15				
Kelly Canyon Ski Area Idaho Falls Idaho tel: (208) 538-6261	T:6600 B:5600	7 runs and 3 trails over 300 acres; longest run: 6800 ft		5	2100	Dec-Apr				
Lookout Pass Ski Area Wallace Idaho tel: (208) 744-1301	T:5400 B:4720	3 miles of trail, 3 main faces, 1 ridge run; longest run: ¾ mile		4	825	Dec 15-Apr 1			Nearby	
Pomerelle Ski Resort Albion Idaho tel: (208) 638-5555	T:9000 B:8000	16 open slopes and trails groomed daily	B:25% I:50% A:25%	3	2000	Nov-Apr	60-80		At area	At area
Schweitzer Ski Area Sandpoint Idaho tel: (208) 263-5147 *(509) 838-4052*	T:6389 B:4400	Open bowls and glades, groomed runs for all skiing levels. 3500 acres served by lifts; longest run: 2¼ miles	B:20% I:50% A:30%	8	7600	late Nov-Apr 10	180	20°F. Sun 45% of season	Nearby	Nearby
Silverhorn Ski Area Kellogg Idaho tel: (208) 786-6141 *(208) 786-7661*	T:6020 B:4120	14 runs, beginner to advanced; longest run: 2 miles		3	1500	Nov 1-Apr 15				
Soldier Mountain Ski Area Fairfield Idaho tel: (208) 764-2260 *(208) 764-2519*	T:7200 B:5800	36 runs — 30% tree-lined; longest run: 2 miles	B:20% I:50% A:30%	5	2200	Thanks-giving to Apr 15			At area	
Sun Valley Sun Valley Idaho tel: (800) 635-8261 *(208) 622-8261*	T:9150 B:5750	1175 skiable acres, 66 runs, mogul glade, groomed runs, isolated beginning mountain; longest run: 3 miles	B:25% I:50% A:25%	18	22804	Dec 9-Apr 15	119	Sun 80% of season	At area	At area
Tamarack Ski Resort Troy Idaho tel: (208) 835-4714	T:4100 B:3500	3 slopes, 3 trails; longest run: 4000 ft		2	600	Jan 1-early Apr			At area	
Taylor Mountain Idaho Falls Idaho tel: (208) 524-0202		Open slopes, novice to expert; longest run: 2850 ft		2		Dec 15-Apr 1				
Beef Trail Butte Montana tel: (406) 792-2242	T:5280 B:2680	5 slopes, 12 miles of trail; longest run: 3650 ft		2	500	Dec 15-Easter			At area	At area
The Big Mountain Whitefish Montana tel: (406) 862-3511	T:7000 B:4750	25 miles of slopes, 25 different runs, open and tree-lined; longest run: 2½ miles	B:20% I:60% A:20%	6	3000	Nov 23-Apr 22	300		At area	At area
Big Sky of Montana Big Sky, tel: (406) 995-4211/4708	T:9800 B:7500	32 miles, 19 slopes, bowl, tree-lined and meadow trees; longest run 2½ miles	B:25% I:25% A:50%	5	5200	Thanks-giving to end Apr	400 +	20°F. Sun 70% of season	At area	At area
Bridger Bowl Ski Area Bozeman, Montana tel: (406) 586-2787/2111 *(406) 586-2389*	T:8100 B:6100	Open bowls, packed slopes, powder runs, gullies, chutes and glade skiing; longest run: 1½-2 miles	B:25% I:45% A:30%	8		mid-Dec-Apr 8	400 +		Nearby	Nearby
Discovery Basin Anaconda, Montana tel: (406) 563-2184	T:8100 B:6800	30 acres of slopes, novice and expert trails; longest run: 1¾ miles	B:15% I:70% A:15%	2	1200	Dec 26-Apr 9	81		Nearby	
Marshall Mountain Ski Area Missoula, Montana tel: (406) 258-6619	T:5500 B:4000	7 open slopes & trails through trees; longest run: 7000 ft		6	7300	Dec 15-Apr 1			At area	
Montana Snow Bowl Missoula, Montana tel: (406) 549-9777	T:7600 B:5000	Natural bowl skiing with challenging trails; longest run: 3½ miles		4	1800	Thanks-giving to Apr 11				
Lee Canyon Ski Area Las Vegas, Nevada tel: (702) 870-4778	T:9540 B:8510	6 slopes, groomed daily; longest run: 5000 ft		4	3000	Thanks-giving to Easter	210			
Mt Rose/Slide Mountain Reno, Nevada tel: (702) 849-0704 *(702) 849-0706*	T:9700 B:8200	High in Sierras, 30 runs, open and bowl-type skiing; longest run: 3 miles	B:30% I:40% A:30%	8	5100	mid Nov-late Apr	200	25°F. Sun 85% of season		
Tannenbaum Reno, Nevada tel: (702) 849-9925	T:7000 B:6600	5 trails & 2 open slopes; longest run: 1800 ft		3		Christ-mas to Easter				

Angel Fire Angel Fire, New Mexico tel: (505) 377-2301 *(1-800) 243-5250*	T:10680 B:8500	19 miles of ski runs; longest run: 3½ miles	B:40% I:45% A:15%	3	2300	Thanksgiving to Easter	120		At area	At area
Powder Puff Mountain Red River, New Mexico tel: (505) 754-2382	T:8700 B:8600 500 ft	Open slopes, well groomed; longest run:	B:50% I:40% A:10%	5	5000	Nov 1-Apr 2	155		Nearby	Nearby
Raton Ski Basin Raton New Mexico tel: (505) 445-3015	T:9000 B:8000	Beginner meadows, intermediate and advanced trails; longest run: 2 miles	B:25% I:50% A:25%	1	1200	Dec-Apr	130			
Red River Ski Area Red River, New Mexico tel: (505) 754-2223	T:10274 B:8750	Beginner to expert on 100 acres; longest run: 2½ miles	B:35% I:40% A:25%	6	5350	Thanksgiving to Easter	155	44°F.	Nearby	
Sandia Peak Ski Area Albuquerque New Mexico tel: (505) 296-9585	T:10378 B:8600	Total of 24 runs, tree-lined from beginner to expert; longest run: 2½ miles	B:15% I:75% A:10%	6	2600	Dec-Apr	150		At area	
Santa Fe Santa Fe, New Mexico tel: (505) 982-4429 *(505) 983-9155*	T:12000 B:10350	Excellent mix of good trails for all skiers. Wide open timber on Upper mountain; longest run: 3 miles	B:20% I:40% A:40%	5	4400	Nov 25-Apr 10	160			
Taos Ski Valley Taos Ski Valley, New Mexico tel: (505) 776-2291	T:11819 B:9207	Over 1000 acres, vast variety of bowls, chutes, slopes; longest run: 5¼ miles	B:24% I:13% A:63%	8	5500	Nov 18-Apr 15	317	38°F. Sun 88% of season	At area	At area
Anthony Lakes North Powder, Oregon tel: (503) 898-2261	T:8000 B:7125	7 major runs for all types of skiers, open timber slopes, lots of powder	B:25% I:50% A:25%	2	1920	mid-Nov-early May	120		Nearby	
Hoodoo Ski Bowl Sisters, Oregon tel: (503) Hoodoo Toll Station No. 1 or 2 *(503) 345-7416*	T:5703 B:4668	Mostly open, 16 runs over 85 acres from top; longest run: 5280 ft	B:29% I:39% A:32%	5	4800	Thanksgiving to mid-Apr	240		At area	At area
Mt Ashland Ski Area Ashland, Oregon tel: (503) 482-6406	T:7600 B:6500	11 tree-lined slopes plus bowl skiing; longest run: 1 mile	B:20% I:30% A:50%	4	2600	Dec-Apr	100		At area	At area
Mt Bachelor Bend, Oregon tel: (503) 382-8334 *(503) 382-7888*	T:7700 B:6000	6-mile area, variety of open bowls, over 30 slopes, natural tree terrain; longest run: 1 mile	B:30% I:30% A:40%	8	8460	Nov 1-June 25	192	16°F. Sun 30% of season	At area	At area
Mt Hood Meadows Mt Hood, Oregon tel: (503) 337-2222 *(503) 227-SNOW*	T:7300 B:4523	Groomed slopes gentle to challenging; longest run: 2 miles	B:25% I:40% A:35%	9		Nov 15-June	275		Nearby	
Multorpor-Ski Bowl Government Camp, Oregon tel: (503) 272-3330 *(503) 224-9221*	T:5200 B:3700	Variety of terrain, open slopes, hills groomed, trails cleared	B:20% I:50% A:30%	12	4800	Nov 15-mid Apr	300		At area	At area
Spout Springs Ski Area Weston, Oregon tel: (503) 566-2015	T:5500 B:4950	4 open-slopes, 5 trails; longest run: 4000 ft	B:30% I:60% A:10%	5	4800	mid Nov-mid Apr	120		At area	At area
Timberline Government Camp, Oregon tel: (503) 272-3311 *(800) 574-1406*	T:8500 B:5000	23 trails & slopes; longest run: 2 miles	B:30% I:50% A:20%	6	2580	Year round	252		At area	At area
Warner Canyon Ski Area Lakeview Oregon tel: (503) 947-2932	T:6450 B:5750	2 major trails, 2 main slopes; longest run: ½ mile		1		Jan 1-Apr 10			At area	
Willamette Pass Ski Bowl Sisters Oregon tel:	T:6700 B:5200			5		Nov-May				
Alta Alta Utah tel: (801) 742-3333	T:10550 B:8550	Open and bowl skiing; longest run: 3 miles	B:25% I:50% A:25%	9	5430	Nov 18-Apr 29	500	15-25°F.	At area	At area
Beaver Mountain Ski Area Logan, Utah tel: (801) 753-0921 *(801) 753-4822*	T:8775 B:7235	16 groomed runs, acres of scattered aspen & pine; longest run: 2¼ miles	B:25% I:35% A:40%	4	3300	Dec-Apr	350		Nearby	Nearby
Brighton Brighton, Utah tel: (801) 359-3283	T:9870 B:8730	31 designated runs, 12 miles open slopes and bowl skiing; longest run: ¼ miles	B:25% I:50% A:25%	4	4000	Nov-until snow melts			At area	
Brianhead Ski Resort Cedar City, Utah tel: (801) 586-4636	T:11000 B:9800	12 major trails for all levels; longest run: 1½ miles	B:20% I:60% A:20%	4	2800	Nov-May 1	300		At area	At area
Park City Ski Area Park City, Utah tel: (801) 649-8111 *(801) 649-9571*	T:10000 B:6900	2200 acres; over 65 trails 650 acres of open bowl; longest run: 3½ miles	B:17% I:46% A:37%	11	12700	Nov 17-May 6	300	27°F. Sun 80% of season	At area	At area
Mt Holly Beaver Utah tel: (801) 477-8003 49-8111 *(801) 649-9571*		12 runs beginner to advanced		3		Nov 24-Apr 16				
Nordic Valley Eden Utah tel: (801) 745-3511		beginner to advanced		2						
Park West Ski Resort Park City, Utah tel: (801) 649-9663	T:9000 B:7000	34 miles of groomed runs; longest run: 2½ miles	B:20% I:40% A:40%	7	5600	Nov 19-Apr 15	275		At area	At area
Snow Basin Ogden, Utah tel: (801) 392-9196	T:8800 B:6600	Open terrain, 48 runs; longest run: 2½ miles	B:15% I:70% A:15%	5	5000	Nov-Apr			Nearby	Nearby
Snowbird Snowbird, Utah tel: (801) 742-2222 *(801) 521-6040*	T:11000 B:7900	Gad Valley open meadows, 2 bowls; longest run: 2½ miles	B:20% I:40% A:40%	6	6500	Nov 18-May 1	450	28°F. Sun 65% of season	At Alta	At Alta
Solitude Ski Resort Salt Lake City, tel: (801) 534-1400	T:9800 B:8100	Wide open slopes & trails, bowl skiing; longest run: 2½ miles	B:25% I:30% A:45%	4	4000	mid Nov-May	400		At area	At area

Sundance Provo, Utah tel: (801) 225-4100	T:7800 B:6100	25 major runs open & tree-lined; longest run: 2½ miles	B:10% I:50% A:40%	3	4350	Dec 1-Apr 15	60		Nearby	Nearby
Alpental Snoqualmie Pass Washington tel: (206) 434-6112 *(206) 623-3418*	T:5400 B:3200	11 slopes, 4 trails	B:20% I:40% A:40%	9	4294	Nov-May	160		Nearby	Nearby
Badger Mountain Waterville Washington tel: (509) 745-4201	T:4500 B:3000	Beginner Advanced & Intermediate runs		5	1800	Dec-Mar				
Crystal Mountain Crystal Mountain Washington tel: (206) 663-2265 *(206) 634-3771*	T:6830 B:4400	4500 acres, 6 major trails, extensive open slopes; longest run: 3½ miles	B:10% I:20% A:70%	17	7700	mid Nov-mid May	204	28-30°F. Sun 25% of season	At area	At area
49° North Ski Resort Chewelah, Washington tel: (509) 935-6649 *(509) 924-5252 or (509) 838-4966*	T:5773 B:3850	700 acres & 80 acres reserved for powder skiing 12 major runs; longest run: 3.2 miles	B:30% I:30% A:40%	4	4200	Dec 1-Apr 15	120		At area	At area
Mission Ridge Wenatchee Washington tel: (509) 663-6543 *(509) 663-7631*	T:6740 B:4600	30 runs; longest run: 5 miles	B:30% I:50% A:20%	7	3710	Dec 3-Apr 23	60		At area	
Mt Baker Bellingham Washington tel: (206) 734-6771 *(604) 688-1595*	T:5500 B:3500	Variety of slopes, open, tree-lined and bowl skiing; longest run: 6500 ft	B:15% I:60% A:25%	11	6000	Nov 1-June 1				
Mt Hyak Ski Resort Snoqualmie Pass Washington tel: (206) 623-0330	T:4060 B:2800	Open slopes and trails	B:25% I:50% A:25%	5	5000	Dec 6-mid Apr			At area	
Mt Spokane Spokane Washington tel: (509) 484-3908 *(509) 238-6223*	T:5881 B:4367	23 runs and open slopes; longest run: 1½ miles	B:20% I:50% A:30%	9	5000	Dec 15-Apr 15				
Snoqualmie Summit Area Snoqualmie Pass Washington tel: (206) 434-6161 *(206) 634-0200*	T:3990 B:3000	Open slopes and high bowls	B:20% I:45% A:35%	18	11200	mid Nov-Apr	170			
Stevens Pass Leavenworth Washington tel: (206) 973-2500 *(206) 634-0200*	T:6000 B;4500	Longest run: 6047 ft	B:14% I:39% A:47%	13	8210	Nov-May 1				
White Pass Village White Pass, Washington *(206) 634-0200 or (503) 222-9128*	T:6000 B:4500	Open slopes, several miles of trail; longest run: 2 miles	B:20% I:60% A:20%	5	3300	Thanks-giving to Mem-orial Day	100 — 150		At area	At area
Jackson Hole Teton Village, Wyoming tel: (307) 733-2291	T:10450 B:6311	100 miles of slopes, 3200 acres, bowls, tree-lined and open trails; longest run: 7½ miles	B:10% I:35% A:55%	7	6700	Late Nov-mid Apr	456	21°F.	At area	At area

Meadowlark Ski Area Worland Wyoming tel: (307) 366-2409	T:9100 B:8500	5 slopes, 5 miles of combined terrain; longest run: 600 ft		2	450	Thanks-giving to mid Apr			At area	
Sleeping Giant Ski Resort Cody, Wyoming tel: (307) 587-4044	T:7200 B:6700	6 miles of trail; longest run: ¾ mile		2	1200	mid Dec-mid Apr			At area	At area
Snow King Mountain Jackson, Wyoming tel: (307) 733-2851	T:7808 B:6237	Open slopes and trails; longest run: 1 mile	B:20% I:30% A:50%	4	1750	Dec 15-Apr 15			At area	At area
Targhee Resort Alta, Wyoming tel: (307) 353-2304	T:10200 B:8000	Open slopes, excellent bowls; longest run: 2½ miles	B:10% I:70% A:20%	4	3600	Nov 17-Apr 22	500		At area	
Chestnut Mountain Lodge Galena Illinois tel: (815) 777-1320		13 runs, open slopes	B:30% I:50% A:20%	10		Dec 15-Mar 5	30	20°F. Sun 30% of season		
Four Lakes Ski Area Lisle Illinois tel: (319) 964-2550/51		Longest run: 1100 ft	B:20% I:80%	6		mid Dec-Mar 1				
James Park Winter Sports Evanston Illinois tel: (312) 869-9449		1 open slope longest run: 300 ft		1		Dec 1-Apr 1				
Marriott's Lincolnshire Resort Lincolnshire Illinois tel: (312) 634-0100 *(312) 695-SNOW*		1 slope	B:100%			Dec 10-Feb 28				
Villa Olivia Ski Area Bartlett, Illinois tel: (312) 742-5200		12 runs, open slopes; longest run: ¼ mile		13		Dec 3-Mar 20			At area	
Bendix Woods County Park New Carlisle, Indiana tel: (219) 654-3155	T:998 B:898	4 open slopes; longest run: 960ft		4	600	Dec 15-Feb 15			At area	At area
Pines Ski Area Valparaiso, Indiana tel: (219) 462-4179		7 slopes, 1 trail; longest run: ¼ mile		10	9000	Dec 1-Mar 1			At area	At area
Crescent Hills Crescent Iowa tel: (712) 328-9547	T:1300 B:1100	Open slopes longest run: 1400 ft		3	2500	Dec 7-Mar 7				
Duck Creek Davenport Iowa		1 slope longest run: 700 ft	B:100%	1		Dec 1-Feb 8				
Holiday Mountain Estherville Iowa tel: (712) 362-2264		5 slopes, tree-lined; longest run: 1200 ft		4		Dec-Mar			At area	

Ski Valley Boone Iowa tel: (515) 432-2423		10 runs longest run: 1800 ft		3		mid Dec-mid Mar				
Sundown Dubuque Iowa tel: (319) 556-6676/6730	T:1075 B:625	Glade skiing, through red cedar trees; longest run: ½ mile	B:20% I:70% A:10%	5	4000	Dec 10-Mar 15	42		Nearby	Nearby
Mont Bleu Ski Area Lawrence Kansas tel: (913) 843-2363		longest run: 1400 ft	B:100%	1	600	Nov 15-Mar 15				
Marriott's Tan-Tar-A Resort Osage Beach Missouri tel: (314) 348 3131 x266		Longest run: 1200 ft		2		Dec 15-Mar 1				
Alpine Valley Milford Michigan tel: (313) 887-2180 *(313) 887-4183*	T:1160 B:910	17 slopes; longest run: 1800 ft	B:20% I:50% A:30%	23	8400	Dec-mid Mar	50 +			
Big Powder-horn Mountain Bessemer, Michigan tel: (906) 932-4838	T:1840 B:1218	17 slopes and trails; longest run: 1 mile	B:15% I:65% A:20%	7	7000	Thanks-giving to Easter	200		At area	
Bintz Apple Mountain Freeland Michigan tel: (517) 781-0170		Open slopes with few scattered trees; longest run: 800 ft		10	6000	Dec 1-Mar 15			At area	
Blackjack Bessemer Michigan tel: (906) 229-5115		2 runs, groomed; longest run: 1 mile	B:50% I:40% A:10%	5	3600	late Nov-Mar				
Boyne High-lands Harbor Springs Michigan tel: (616) 526-2171	T:1310 B:805	Well groomed, wide slopes, a few trails; longest run: 5200 ft	B:30% I:35% A:35%	8	15000	Thanks-giving to Easter	150		At area	At area
Boyne Mountain Boyne Falls Michigan tel: (616) 549-2441		13 ski runs, wide open slopes; longest run: ¾ mile	B:20% I:40% A:40%	11	14400	Thanks-giving to Easter	145	30°F. Sun 35% of season	At area	At area
Caberfae Ski Area Cadillac, Michigan tel: (616) 862-3400 *(616) 862-3300*		580 acres, 36 groomed trails; longest run: 1 mile	B:30% I:50% A:20%	22		Thanks-giving to Easter			At area	At area
Cannonsburg Ski Area Cannonsburg, Michigan tel: (616) 874-6711 *(800) 253-8748*		60 acres, open slopes; longest run: 1800 ft	B:25% I:60% A:15%	20	15000	Thanks-giving to mid Mar	68		At area	At area
Crystal Mountain Thompsonville Michigan tel: (616) 378-2911	T:1132 B:757	18 slopes, 12 illuminated trails & slopes; longest run: ½ mile	B:25% I:40% A:35%	5	5200	Thanks-giving to Apr 1	120		At area	
Grand Haven Ski Bowl Grand Haven Michigan tel: (616) 842-3210		2 slopes		2						
Hilton Shanty Creek Lodge Bellaire, Michigan tel: (616) 533-8621	T:975 B:675	15 slopes, trails and open; longest run: 2000 ft	B:20% I:60% A:20%	4		Dec 5-Mar 15			At area	
Indianhead Mt Wakefield Michigan tel: (906) 229-5181 *(800) 338-1240*	T:1935 B:1297	240 acres of trails, 15 runs; longest run: 1 mile	B:25% I:50% A:25%	7	8400	Thanks-giving to Easter	200		Nearby	Nearby
Kandahar Ski Club Fenton Michigan tel: (313) 629-9109	T:1200 B:940	10 slopes, trails; longest run: ½ mile				Dec 10-Mar 15			At area	At area
Maplehurst Ski Area Kewadin Michigan tel: (616) 264-9675		6 slopes 4 trails longest run: 2500 ft		4		mid Dec-mid Mar			At area	
Mio Mountain Ferndale Michigan tel: (517) 826-5569		13 runs on 60 acres; longest run: 1500 ft		4		mid Dec-Apr 1			Nearby	
Mont Ripley Houghton Michigan tel: (906) 487-2340	T:1120 B:700	Open slopes and bowls; longest run: 2200 ft		2	2400	Dec 2-Mar 25			Nearby	Nearby
Mt Grampian Ski Area Oxford, Michigan tel: (313) 628-2450		12 slopes, open skiing; longest run: 1800 ft		8		Dec 1-mid Mar			At area	At area
Mt Holly Ski Area Holly, Michigan tel: (313) 634-8269/8260	T:327	10 slopes, 1 trail; longest run: 1800 ft	B:25% I:35% A:40%	16	8400	Dec 1-Mar 15	50		Nearby	
Mt Maria Ski Lodge Spruce Michigan tel: (517) 736-8377		5 open slopes, trails tree-lined; longest run: 1500 ft		4	4800	Dec-Apr			Nearby	
Nub's Nob Habor Springs, Michigan tel: (616) 526-2131	T:1340 B:915	150 acres of skiing; longest run: ¾ mile	B:25% I:35% A:40%	7	6200	Thanks-giving to Apr 1	120		Nearby	Nearby
Petoskey Winter Sports Park Petosky Michigan tel: (616) 347-5550		Small ski run.	B:30% I:70%	1		Dec 15-Mar 1				
Pine Knob Ski Resort Clarkston, Michigan tel: (313) 394-0000	T:1300 B:1000	8 slopes; longest run: ¼ mile	B:30% I:40% A:30%	12		Nov 25-Mar 15	32		At area	
Pine Mountain Pine Mountain Michigan tel: (906) 774-2747	T:1800 B:1400	50 acres, 9 slopes & trails; longest run: ¾ mile	B:20% I:60% A:20%	4	3700	Thanks-giving to Mar 30	80		At area	At area
Porcupine Mts State Park Ontonagon Michigan tel: (906) 885-5798		3 slopes, 1 open slope; longest run: 1 mile		6	4100	Dec 20-Apr 1	180 - 210		At area	

Royal Valley Ski Resort Buchanan, Michigan tel: (616) 695-3847 *(616) 695-5862*	T:810 B:600	Tree-lined trails; longest run: 1800 ft	B:20% I:45% A:35%	11	8400	Nov 25-Mar 15	60	Nearby	
Schuss Mountain Mancelona Michigan tel: (616) 587-9162 *(800) 632-7170*	T:1142 B:742	50% open slope, 50% trails; longest run: 4800 ft	B:25% I:40% A:35%	5	5000	Nov 24-Apr	200	At area	At area
Ski Brule Mountain Iron River, Michigan tel: (906) 265-4957 *(800) 338-7174*	T:1861 B:1440	7 slopes; longest run: 1 mile	B:30% I:40% A:30%	5	2700	Thanks-giving to Apr 3	130	At area	At area
Swiss Valley Jones Michigan tel: (616) 244-5635		10 slopes 2 trails; longest run: 1800 ft		13	1800	Dec 15-Mar 15		Nearby	Nearby
Sugar Loaf Mountain Resort Cedar Michigan tel: (616) 228-5461		23 runs; longest run: over 1 mile	B:30% I:30% A:40%	6	6000	Thanks-giving to Apr 8	180 ins	At area	At area
Sylvan Knob Ski Area Gaylor Michigan tel: (517) 732-4733	T:1400 B:1175	17 runs; longest run: ½ mile		8	4500	Dec 15-Apr 1			
Timber Ridge Ski Area Kalamazoo Michigan tel: (616) 694-9449		Tree-lined, 14 slopes; longest run: 2000 ft	B:40% I:40% A:20%	10	3000	Nov 25-Mar 1		Nearby	
Timberlee Ski Area Traverse City Michigan tel: (616) 946-2600		16 slopes beginner-intermediate	B:25% I:50% A:25%	5	4000	Early Dec-mid Mar		At area	
Traverse City Holiday Traverse City Michigan tel: (616) 946-5035		12 slopes		7		Dec 15-Mar 15		Nearby	
Vulcan USA PO Box 491, Vulcan, Michigan tel: (906) 563-9222	T:1320 B:900	9 runs; longest run: 3000 ft		3	2400	Thanks-giving to Apr		Nearby	
Afton Alps Hastings, Minnesota tel: (612) 436-5245		31 slopes & trails; longest run: 3000 ft	B:20% I:60% A:20%	19	18000	Late Nov-late Mar			
Buck Hill Ski Area Burnsville, Minnesota tel: (612) 435-7187	T;1205 B:900	12 slopes; longest run: 2000 ft	B:40% I:45% A:15%	9		mid Nov-to early Apr	35	Nearby	Nearby
Buena Vista Bemidji Minnesota tel: (218) 243-2231		12 runs; longest run: 1800 ft	B:50% I:40% A:10%	8	4720	Thanks-giving to Easter		At area	
Coffee Mill Ski Area Wabasha Minnesota tel: (612) 565-9994	T:1230 B:730	Tree lined; longest run: 4000 ft		3	2500	Dec 20-Mar 15		Nearby	Nearby
Glenhaven Ski Area Glenwood Minnesota tel: (612) 634-9912		7 runs; longest run: 950 ft		2					
Golden Gate to Fun Camp-ground Sleepy Eye, Minnesota tel: (507) 794-6586	T:1300	5 runs; longest run: 1350 ft	B:50% I:50%	5				At area	
Hyland Hills Ski Area Bloomington, Minnesota tel: (612) 835-4604		17 slopes; longest run: 2000 ft	B:60% I:30% A:10%	7	3800	Thanks-giving to Mar 15	50	At area	At area
Lutsen Ski Area Lutsen, Minnesota tel: (218) 663-7966/7212 *(218) 436-5218*		18 runs all tree lined; longest run: 1½ miles	B:15% I:52% A:33%	6	6300	Thanks-giving to Easter	160	Nearby	Nearby
Mt Frontenac Red Wing, Minnesota tel: (612) 388-5826	T:1120 B:700	9 slopes; longest run: 1 mile		9	1200	Dec 1-Mar		At area	
Old Smokey Fergus Falls Minnesota tel: (218) 736-2251		Small ski hill in city limits, 4 runs; longest run: 600 ft		2		Dec 15-Mar 15			
Powder Ridge Ski Area Kimball, Minnesota tel: (612) 398-7200		9 runs, several trails; longest run: 2650 ft		7	12000	Thanks-giving to Apr 1		At area	
Sugar Hills Grand Rapids Minnesota tel: (218) 326-3473	T:1752 B:1350	23 slopes over 3 ridges; longest run: 5000 ft	B:20% I:50% A:30%	9	10000	Thanks-giving to Easter	85	At area	At area
Val Chatel Park Rapids, Minnesota tel: (218) 266-3306		Trails, slopes & bowls; longest run: 1452 ft		6		Dec 10-Apr 8		At area	At area
Welch Village Welch, Minnesota tel: (612) 222-7079/258-4567	T:1050 B:700	21 trails through trees; longest run: 4500 ft	B:30% I:30% A:40%	8	8400	Nov 25-Apr 1	50		
Wild Mountain Ski Area Taylors Falls Minnesota tel: (612) 465-6365. *291 7980*	T:1113 B:813	12 slopes, lots of trees; longest run: 4500 ft	B:30% I:40% A:30%	5	9600	mid Nov-late Mar	50	At area	
Frostfire Ski Area Walhalla North Dakota tel: (701) 549-3600		7 slopes & trails open and tree lined		3	1500	Thanks giving to mid Mar		At	area
Skyline Skiway Devils Lake North Dakota tel: (701) 766-4479 *(701) 662-5618*	T:1740 B:1430	4 slopes 1 trail; longest run: ½ mile		2	1000	mid Dec-early Mar			
Trestle Valley Minot North Dakota tel: (701) 839-5321	T:1510 B:1315	10 trails; longest run: 1400 ft		3	2500	Dec-Mar		Nearby	Nearby

Deer Mountain Ski Area Deadwood, South Dakota tel: (605) 584-3230	T:6600 B:6000	20 trails & open slopes, bowls and tree-lined; longest run: 5000 ft		5	2500	Thanksgiving			At area	At area
Great Bear Ski Valley Sioux Falls, South Dakota tel: (605) 338-1351		3 large open slopes, 9 runs; longest run: 1500 ft		4	1200	Dec 1-Mar 15			At area	
Terry Peak Ski Area Deadwood South Dakota tel: (605) 584-2165, *1-800 843-1930*	T:7076 B:5000	17 trails including 3 new; longest run: 1¼ miles		6	5500	Dec 1-Apr 1	150		At area	At area
Boston Mills Ski Area Peninsula, Ohio tel: (216) 657-2334		7 slopes & trails; longest run: 1700 ft	B:50% I:40% A:10%	10	6500	Dec 1-Mar 15				
Brandywine Ski Centre Northfield, Ohio tel: (216) 467-8197	T:911 B:670	4 bowls, 1 trail, 40 acres; longest run: 1710 ft	B:50% I:40% A:10%	16		Dec 1-Mar 15				
Clear Fork Ski Area Butler, Ohio tel: (419) 883-2000 *(419) 522-2464*		7 slopes; longest run: 1 mile	B:30% I:40% A:30%	9		Dec 1-Mar 15	50-60			
Snow Trails Ski Area Mansfield, Ohio tel: (419) 522-7393	T:1290 B:990	Open slopes & trails; longest run: 2000 ft	B:20% I:70% A:10%	10	5980	Nov 25-Mar 15	39		Nearby	
Sugar Creek Ski Hills Bellbrook Ohio tel: (513) 848-6211		5 slopes; longest run: 1600 ft	B:20% I:60% A:20%	4	5000	mid Nov-mid Mar				
Alpine Valley Resort East Troy Wisconsin tel: (414) 642-7374		8 tree-lined slopes, 2 beginners areas	B:20% I:60% A:20%	17		Dec 1-Mar 15		24°F, Sun 60% of season		
Birch Park Ski Area Houlton, Wisconsin tel: (612) 439-3723	T:930 B:700	18 groomed slopes & trails; longest run: 1800 ft	B:30% I:50% A:20%	11	16800	Nov 19-Mar 31	45			
Bruce Mound Winter Sports Area Neillsville Wisconsin tel: (715) 743-2490		7 slopes; longest run: 2400 ft		4		Dec 20-Mar			Nearby	
Camp 10 Rhinelander Wisconsin tel: (715) 362-6754		7 runs; longest run: 2000 ft		5	1000	mid Dec-mid Mar			Nearby	
Chanticleer Inn Eagle River Wisconsin tel: (715) 479-4486		Beginner ski hill intermediate run; longest run: 150 ft		2		Dec 15-Mar 15			At area	
Devil's Head Lodge Merrimac Wisconsin tel: (608) 493-2251 *(312) 236-0891*		7 slopes, tree lined, 2 beginner areas; longest run: 4500 ft	B:20% I:60% A:20%	9	7000	Dec 1-Apr 15	20		At area	
Gateway Lodge Land O'Lakes Wisconsin tel: (715) 547-3321		11 runs; longest run: 2000 ft		3					At area	
Hardscrabble Ski Area Rice Lake, Wisconsin tel: (715) 234-3412		10 runs; longest run: 4000 ft		7	3000	Nov-MAr			At area	
Hilly Haven Ski Area De Pere, Wisconsin tel: (414) 336-6204		Tree-lined scenic slope; longest run: 500 ft		5	2000	Dec 15-Mar 15			Nearby	Nearby
Mont du Lac Ski Area Superior, Wisconsin tel: (715) 636-9991	T:917 B:617	3 miles of trail, 7 slopes open and tree-lined; longest run 2400 ft		5	2500	Dec 1-Mar 31				
Mt La Crosse La Crosse, Wisconsin tel: (608) 7888-0044	T:1136 B:620	13 slopes & trails; longest run: 5300 ft	B:20% I:50% A:30%	5	3500	Thanksgiving to mid Mar	50		At area	At area
Navarino Hills Shiocton Wisconsin tel: (715) 758-2211		1 bowl 10 trails; longest run: 1200 ft		6	1200	Dec 15-Mar 15			Nearby	
Nest of Eagles Spooner Wisconsin tel: (715) 635-8447	T:1360	3 runs tree lined; longest run: 1500ft		1	240	Nov 26-Apr 1			At area	
Nordic Mountain Wild Rose, Wisconsin tel: (414) 787-3324 *(715) 249-5703*	T:1137 B:887	2½ miles of trails all tree-lined; longest run: 3500 ft	B:15% I:50% A:35%	7	4000	Dec 1-Mar 15	100		At area	
Olympia Ski Area Oconomowoc, Wisconsin tel: (414) 567-0311		10 slopes open, west tree-lined; longest run: 2800 ft	B:10% I:70% A:20%	4		End Nov mid Mar			At area	
Playboy Ski Area Lake Geneva Wisconsin tel: (414) 248-8811	T:1296 B:1085	18 acres varied terrain longest run: ¼ mile	B:20% I:60% A:20%	5	4200	Dec 1-Mar 15	46		At area	
Port Mountain Ski Area Bayfield, Wisconsin tel: (715) 779-3227	T:1280 B:963	13 slopes & trails; longest run: 3200 ft		5	5500	Dec 1-Apr 1			At area	
Rib Mountain Ski Area Wausau Wisconsin tel: (715) 845-2846	T:1942 B:1242	4 slopes, tree-lined; longest run: 3800 ft	B:25% I:50% A:25%	7	6000	Dec 8-Mar 12	60		At area	At area
Ski Majestic Lake Geneva Wisconsin tel: (414) 248-6128		5 slopes; longest run: 1400 ft	B:50% I:33% A:17%	8	4380	Dec 1-Mar 15				
Snowcrest Ski Area Somerset Wisconsin tel: (612) 439-2427 *(715) 247-3852*		18 runs on 80 acres, tree-lined; longest 3800 ft	B:25% I:50% A:25%	10		Nov 19-Mar 30	60		Neary	Nearby

Standing Rocks Stevens Point Wisconsin tel: (715) 824-3949		3 runs; longest run: 1000 ft		2					At area	
Telemark Ski Area Cable, Wisconsin tel: (715) 798-3811	T:1770 B:1400	100 acres of open slopes; longest run: ½ mile	B:40% I:40% A:20%	7	13000	Thanks-giving to Easter	70		At area	
page 52										
Trollhaugen Dresser, Wisconsin tel: (715) 755-2955 *(612) 433-5141*		13 slopes groomed daily; longest run: 2500 ft	B:20% I:65% A:15%	11	10800	Nov 15-Mar 15	45	20°F.	At area	
Whitecap Mountains Montreal Wisconsin tel: (715) 561-2227		15 miles of trail, 1 open slope, 1 bunny bowl; longest run: 5000 ft	B:25% I:50% A:25%	9	9400	Nov 25-Apr 1	200	20°F. Sun 50% of season	At area	At area
Wilmot Mountain Wilmot Wisconsin tel: (414) 862-2301 *(312) 736-0787*		30 open slopes & runs; longest run: 2500 ft	B:30% I:30% A:40%	17	20000	Dec 1-Mar 31				
Woodside Ranch Resort Mauston Wisconsin tel: (608) 847-4275		100% beginner slope tree lined & open; longest run: 1200 ft		1		Dec 20-end Mar			At area	At area
Cloudmont Resort Mentone Alabama tel: (205) 634-3841	T:1800	1000 foot slope & 1 artificial slope		2	800	Dec 1-Mar 15				
Vining's Ridge Ski Area Atlanta Georgie tel: (404) 432-9563		1 open slope; longest run: 500 ft		1	800	All year				
Ober Gatlinburg Gatlinburg Tennessee tel: (615) 436 5423	T:3500 B:2700	4 slopes, tree-lined; longest run: 4800 ft		9	2000	Dec 1-Mar 15				
Wisp Oakland Maryland tel: (301) 387-5503 *(301) 387-4000*	T:3080 B:2470	12 miles of slopes & trails, 3 open and 6 tree-lined; longest run: 2 miles	B:25% I:55% A:20%	5	4000	Dec 16-Mar 11	90		Nearby	Nearby
Bryce Mountain Resort Basye Virginia tel: (703) 856-2121 *(703) 856-2151*	T:1750 B:1250	3 slopes; longest run: 3500 ft	B:34% I:33% A:33%	5	800	Dec 15-Mar 15	30			
The Homestead Ski Area Hot Springs, Virginia tel: (703) 839-5079	T:3050 B:2500	4 slopes & 3 trails; longest run: 4000 ft		4	1000	Dec 15-Mar 15				
Massanutten Harrisonburg, Virginia tel: (703) 289-2711 *(703) 289-2181*	T:2525 B:1730	9 slopes; longest run: 5600 ft	B:25% I:50% A:25%	5	5200	Dec 1-Mar 15	34			

Wintergreen Wintergreen Virginia tel: (804) 361-2200 *(804) 361-2100*	T:3450 B:2925	6 slopes, over 55 acres; longest run: 2800 ft	B:22% I:70% A: 8%	3	4600	Dec 1-Mar 10	46			
Appalachian Ski Mountain Blowing Rock, North Carolina tel: (704) 295-7828	T:4000 B:3635	6 runs; longest run: 2700 ft		5	2200	Thanks-giving to Mar 30				
Wolf Laurel Mars Hill, North Carolina tel: (704) 689-4111	T:4700 B:4000	6 slopes; longest run: 3500 ft		3	1000	Dec-mid Mar				
Beech Mountain Ski Area Banner Elk, North Carolina tel: (704) 387-4231	T:5484 B:4675	18 slopes & trails; longest run: 1½ miles	B:50% I:30% A:20%	10	10000	mid Nov-Mar	90			
Sugar Mount-ain Resort Banner Elk North Carolina tel: (704) 898-4521 *(704) 898-5256*	T:5300 B:4100	12 slopes; longest run: 1½ miles	B:35% I:30% A:30%	5	5200	mid Dec to mid Mar	52			
Canaan Valley Ski Area Davis West Virginia tel: (304) 866-4121 *(800) 624-8632*	T:4280 B:3430	5 slopes, 14 trails; longest run: 1 mile	B:28% I:44% A:28%	4	1200	mid Dec to mid Mar	170 — 200		Nearby	
Coonskin Park Charleston West Virginia tel: (304) 345-8000	T:850 B:725	1 gently rolling slope; longest run: 600 ft		1	200	Dec-Mar 1				
Snowshoe Ski Resort Slatyfork West Virginia tel: (304) 799-6600 *(800) 624-8636; (800) 642-9058*	T:4848 B:4000	120 acres of slopes & trails; longest run: 8200 ft	B:10% I:50% A:40%	4	1200	Thanks-giving to Easter	180		At area	At area
Brooklyn Brooklyn Connecticut tel: (203) 774-5937		1 trail 1 slope; longest run: 1800 ft	B:100%	1						
Lakeridge Ski Area Torrington Connecticut tel: (203) 482-3591		2 downhill trails longest run: ½ mile		1	460	Dec 18-Apr 1			At area	At area
Mohawk Mountain Ski Area Cornwall Connecticut tel: (203) 672-6100		12 trails, 5 slopes; longest run: 1½ miles		7	6200	Dec 1-Mar 31			Nearby	Nearby
Mt Southing-ton Ski Area Southington Connecticut tel: (203) 628-0954	T:560 B:110	6 trails, 5 slopes; longest run: 1 mile		8	3800	Thanks-giving to Mar 15				
Powder Ridge Ski Area Middlefield Connecticut tel: (203) 349-3454 *(800) 243-3760; (1-800) 622-3321*	T:990 B:450	12 slopes & trails; 7 open, 5 tree-lined; longest run: 1¼ miles	B:30% I:50% A:20%	7	9000	Nov 15-Apr 10			At area	At area

Woodbury Ski & Racquet Woodbury Connecticut tel: (203) 263-2203	T:850 B:550	4 open slopes, 2 wide trails, 2 tree-lined; longest run: ¾ mile		3	2544	Dec 1-Mar 15			Nearby	
Pine Top Ski Area Escoheag, Rhode Island tel: (401) 397-5656	T:580 B:300	4 slopes, 2 trails	B:100%	4	4000	Dec-mid Mar				
Ski Valley Cumberland Rhode Island tel: (401) 333-6406	T:475 B:200	5 trails, 5 open slopes; longest run: 3000 ft		3	2000	Dec 1-Mar 15			At area	At area
Camden Outing Club — Snow Bowl Camden Maine tel: (207) 236-3438 *(207) 236-4418*	T:1000 B:100	7 miles of trail, 1 open slope; longest run: 1¼ miles	B:10% I:80% A:10%	3	2400	mid Dec-mid Mar	90		At area	At area
Chisholm Winter Park Ski Area Rumford Maine tel: (207) 364-8977	T:2500 B:1000	2 open slopes, 4 tree-lined trails; longest run: ½ mile		1	720	mid Dec-late Mar			At area	At area
Lonesome Pine Trails (Fort Kent) Fort Kent Maine tel: (207) 834-5202		Beginners slope & intermediate run; longest run: 2000 ft		2	360	Dec-Apr			Nearby	
Evergreen Valley Resort E. Stoneham Maine tel: (207) 928-3300	T:1636 B:1050	12 trails; longest run: 1¾ miles	B:20% I:40% A:40%	3	3000	Nov 23-Apr 1	100		At area	At area
Lost Valley Ski Area Auburn Maine tel: (207) 784-1561		8 trails 4 open slopes; longest run: ¾ mile	B:40% I:30% A:30%	4	1200	early Dec-Mar 15	50 ins		At area	At area
Pleasant Mountain Bridgton Maine tel: (207) 647-2022	T:1905 B:650	20 trails, 2 open slopes; longest run: 1½ miles	B:40% I:40% A:20%	6	4000	Dec-Apr	90-100		At area	
Saddleback Mountain Ski Area Rangeley Maine tel: (207) 864-3380	T:3500 B:2300	17 trails & 1 open slope on 10 acres; longest run: 2½ miles	B:50% I:25% A:25%	4	3139	Thanksgiving to Easter	200		Nearby	Nearby
Squaw Mountain at Moosehead Greenville Maine tel: (207) 695-2272	T:3250 B:1350	14 trails, 30 miles of terrain; longest run: 2½ miles	B:25% I:40% A:35%	3	2500	Nov 27-Easter	200		At area	At area
Sugarloaf/USA Carrabassett Maine tel: (207) 237-2000	T:4237 B:1637	36 miles of trails, 1 gladed slope; longest run: 3 miles	B:30% I:40% A:30%	11	9300	Nov 17-Apr 17	170	26°F. Sun 50% of season	At area	At area
Amesbury Ski Tows Amesbury Massachusetts tel: (617) 388-9205		3 large open slopes		4		mid Dec-mid Mar				

Berkshire Snow Basin West Cummington Massachusetts tel: (413) 634-8808	T:1725 B:1175	8 trails 3 slopes; longest run: 1 mile		4		Christmas-Apr 1				
Boston Hills Ski Area North Andover Massachusetts tel: (617) 683-2733	T:440 B:100	7 slopes, tree-lined; longest run: 2100 ft		4	4700	mid Dec-to mid Mar			At area	At area
Bousquet Ski Area Pittsfield, Massachusetts tel: (413) 442-2436	T:1875 B:1125	200 acres of terrain, 5½ miles of trails & slopes; longest run: 1½ miles		9	9500	Dec 1-Apr 1				
Brodie Mountain New Ashford Massachusettes tel: (413) 443-4752	T:12700 B:11450	17 miles of slopes & trails; longest run: 1½ miles	B:30% I:50% A:20%	7	6000	Nov-Apr	60		At area	At area
Butternut Basin Great Barrington, Massachusetts tel: (413) 528-2000	T:1800 B:800	14 miles of trail and 2 open slopes; longest run: longest run: 1½ miles	B:15% I:60% A:25%	6	6800	Dec 4-Mar 28	70		At area	At area
Chickley Alp Ski Centre Charlemont Massachusetts tel: (413) 339-4802		4 slopes 10 trails; longest run: 1 mile		4	1000	Dec 15-Mar 15				
Jericho Hill Marlboro Massachusetts tel: (617) 485-9730		Beginner & Intermediate		2		Dec-Mar				
Jiminy Peak Hancock Massachusetts tel: (413) 738-5431	T:2500 B:1300	9 slopes & trails; longest run: 2 miles	B:30% I:30% A:40%	5	4000	Thanksgiving to Apr	90		Nearby	
Mt Tom Ski Area Holyoke Massachusetts tel: (413) 536-0416	T:1380 B:700	12 open slopes & trails; longest run: 3600 ft	B:30% I:60% A:10%	8	3800	Dec 15-end Mar			At area	
Nashoba Valley Ski Area Westford Massachusetts tel: (617) 692-3033	T:440 B:200	7 slopes, 1 trail; longest run: 1400 ft		10	13400	Dec 15-Mar 15				
Otis Ridge Ski Area Otis Massachusetts tel: (413) 269-4444		14 slopes & trails, some open; longest run: 4500 ft		8	3500	Dec 5-Apr 5			At area	At area
Prospect Hill Ski Area Waltham Massachusetts tel: (617) 893-4837		2 advanced trails, beginners slope		2		mid Dec-to mid Mar				
Ward Hill Shrewsbury Massachusetts tel: (617) 842-6346		5 open slopes, 2 trails; longest run: 2000 ft		7	1000	Thanksgiving - Mar 10				
Attitash Bartlett New Hampshire tel: (603) 374-2369 *(800) 258-0316*	T:2300 B:743	30 trails, tree-lined; longest run: 2 miles	B:25% I:50% A:25%	4	5000	Dec 15-snow melt	111		Nearby	Nearby

page 60

Black Mountain Jackson New Hampshire tel: (603) 383-4490	T:2300 B:1200	14 trails, 2 slopes; longest run: 1 mile		4	2900	mid Dec-late Mar			At area	At area
Bobcat Ski Area Bennington New Hampshire tel: (603) 588-6330/1	T:2003 B:1362	15 trails; longest run: 1 mile	B:25% I:35% A:40%	4	3000	Thanksgiving to Apr	120		Nearby	Nearby
Bretton Woods Ski Area Bretton Woods New Hampshire tel: (603) 278-5000 *(603) 278-5051*	T:3100 B:2000	10 trails; longest run: 1.2 miles	B:33% I:45% A:22%	3	1200	Dec 16-mid Apr	180		At area	At area
Cannon Mountain Franconia New Hampshire tel: (603) 823-5563 *(617) 338-6911; (603) 823-7771*	T:4176 B:2000	21 miles of trails & wide open slopes; longest run: 2⅓ miles	B:30% I:45% A:25%	8	5500	Nov 25-Apr 16	156	20°F. Sun 50% of season	At area	At area
Brickyard Mountain Inn Laconia New Hampshire tel: (800) 258-0343	T:1000 B:580	6 tree lined trails & 1 slope; longest run: 3000 ft		2	1200	Nov 25-Mar 30			At area	At area
Campton Mountain Campton New Hampshire tel: (603) 725-3082	T:2000 B:1600	3 slopes beginner to advanced; longest run: 3000 ft		1	1200	Dec 26-late Mar				
Crotched Mountain Francestown New Hampshire tel: (603) 588-2836	T:1900 B:1200	3 slopes, 7/8 miles of runs; longest run: 1⅛ miles		4	3000	late Nov-early Apr				
Dartmouth Skiway Lyme Center New Hampshire tel: (603) 795-2143	T:1900 B:1000	10 trails, 1 open slope; longest run: 6000 ft		3	2500	Dec 15-mid Mar			Nearby	At area
Gunstock Area Laconia New Hampshire tel: (603) 293-4341	T:2400 B:900	5 open slopes, 19 trails, 20 miles of trail; longest run: 2½ miles	B:25% I:50% A:25%	7	5200	mid Dec-Apr 1	100		At area	
King Pine Ski Area East Madison New Hampshire tel: (603) 367-4648	T:850 B:500	2 slopes open, 12 trails; longest run: ¾ mile		4	2600	Dec 23-Mar 30			Nearby	Nearby
Loon Mountain Lincoln New Hampshire tel: (603) 745-8111 *(603) 745-8100*	T:2750 B:950	13 miles of trails & slopes; longest run: 2½ miles	B:20% I:45% A:35%	5	4400	Dec-Apr 9	160	25°F. Sun 70% of season	At area	At area
McIntyre Ski Area Manchester New Hampshire tel: (603) 669-7931		2 open slopes 1 trail; longest run: 1000 ft		3	1000	Christmas-mid Mar			At area	
Mittersill Franconia New Hampshire tel: (603) 823-5511 *(603) 823-7772*		3 slopes, 6 miles of trail; longest run: 1½ miles		3	2200	Dec 20-Apr 1				
Mr Cranmore Skimobile North Conway New Hampshire tel: (603) 356-5544	T:2000 B:500	12 trails, 4 open slopes, 300 acres; longest run: 2 miles	B:20% I:60% A:20%	6	5000	Dec-Apr 2	100		At area	Nearby
Mt Whittier W. Ossipee New Hampshire tel: (603) 539-2268	T:2100 B:400	50 acres of slopes, 8 miles of trail; longest run: 1 mile		4	6000	Dec-Mar/Apr	150		Nearby	Nearby
Pat's Peak Ski Area Henniker New Hampshire tel: (603) 428-3245 *(617) 262-5454*	T:1400 B:690	13 trails & open slopes; longest run: ¾ mile	B:37% I:39% A:24%	6	6000	late Nov-early Apr	85-120		Nearby	Nearby
Temple Mountain Ski Area Peterborough New Hampshire tel: (603) 924-6949	T:2084 B:1486	24 acres, 3 slopes, 9 trails; longest run: 2200 ft		5	6700	Dec-Apr			At area	At area
Waterville Valley Snow's Mt Waterville Valley New Hampshire tel: (603) 236-8391	T:2095 B:1520	3 open trails; longest run: 4000 ft		1	1200	Dec 25-Mar 20			At area	
Waterville Valley Mt Tecumseh Waterville Valley New Hampshire tel: (603) 236-8311 *(800) 258-8983; (800) 552-0388*	T:3870 B:1850	32 wide, fall-line slopes; longest run: 3 miles	B:30% I:40% A:30%	7	8760	Nov 17-Apr 15	158		At area	At area
Woodbound Inn Ski Area Jaffrey New Hampshire tel: (603) 532-8341	T:1330 B:	2 slopes		2		Dec 26-Mar 15	105		At area	At area
Wilderness Ski Area Dixville Notch New Hampshire tel: (603) 255-3400 *(617) 227-8288; (603) 255-3951*	T:2700 B:1700	7 slopes, 12 trails; longest run: 2 miles	B:20% I:65% A:15%	3	2800	Early Dec-Apr	200+		At area	At area
Wildcat Mountain Jackson New Hampshire tel: (603) 466-3326 *(800) 258-8902; (800) 552-8952*	T:4050 B:1950	14 miles of trails; 3 open slopes; longest run: 2¾ miles	B:20% I:45% A:35%	4	2100	Nov 19-late Apr	174		At area	At area
Campgaw Mountain Ski Area Mahway New Jersey tel: (201) 327-7800	T:720 B:450	Open slopes & trail; longest run: 1800 ft		3	1800	Dec-Mar				
Craigmeur Ski Area Newfoundland New Jersey tel: (201) 697-4501	T:1300 B:1050	4 slopes & 2 trails; longest run: 1700 ft		4	3000	Nov 15-Mar 31			At area	
Hidden Valley Vernon New Jersey tel: (201) 764-6161	T:1400 B:780	4 trails & 1 beginner slope; longest run: 3600 ft	B:25% I:50% A:25%	2	2800	Dec 6-Mar 15	60			
Vernon Valley/Great Gorge McAffee New Jersey tel: (201) 827-2000 *(201) 827-3900*	T:1480 B:440	13½ miles of trail on 10 slopes; longest run: 7920 ft	B:25% I:45% A:30%	17	6000	Thanksgiving	89	28°F. Sun 60% of season	At area	At area

Belleayre Mountain Pine Hill, New York tel: (914) 254-5601 *(914) 254-5600*	T:3365 B:2100	7 slopes, 15 miles of trail all tree-lined; longest run: 7500 ft	B:27% I:40% A:33%	7	6300	Dec 1-Apr 1	169		At area	At area
Big Birch Ski Area Patterson New York tel: (914) 878-3181 *(914) 878-6292*	T:1270 B:820	3 slopes, 11 trails; longest run: 2400 ft	B:40% I:30% A:40%	5	1000	Dec 15-Mar 15				
Big Tupper Ski Area Tupper Lake New York tel: (518) 359-3651	T:3050 B:2000	3 slopes, 22 trails; longest run: 1 mile	B:60% I:30% A:10%	5	5240	Dec 15-Easter	128		At area	
Big Vanilla At Davos Woodridge New York tel: (914) 434-5321		19 slopes & trails; longest run: 3900 ft		9					At area	
Bobcat at Catskill Ski Center Andes, New York tel: (914) 676-3143	T:3365 B:2315	Wide open slopes, narrow trails; longest run: 1¾ miles		2	1800	Dec 15-Mar 31			At area	At area
Bova Ski Slopes Salamanca New York tel: (716) 354-2535	T:1700 B:1500	4 open slopes; longest run: 1000 ft		2	600	Dec 15-Mar 15			At area	At area
Bristol Mountain Canandaigua New York tel: (716) 374-6422 *(716) 271-5000*	T:2050 B:1000	8 trails & 4 slopes; longest run: 8700 ft	B:30% I:40% A:30%	5	4800	Early Dec-late Mar	90		Nearby	
Catamount Ski Area Hillsdale New York tel: (518) 325-3200 *(800) 628-5030*	T:2000 B:1000	17 trails & 3 open slopes, all others tree-lined; longest run: 2 miles	B:40% I:40% A:20%	6	5400	Dec 1-Apr	55		At area	
Cockaigne Cherry Creek New York tel: (716) 287-3223 *(216) 221-5070; (716) 287-3545*	T:2022 B:1592	4 slopes, 7 trails; longest run: 3100 ft	B:20% I:50% A:30%	3	1500	Nov 12-Apr 11	220		At area	At area
Cortina Valley Ski Area Haines Falls New York tel: (518) 589-6500 *(800) 243-6600*	T:2650 B:1925	8 slopes, 35 acres; longest run: 5200 ft	B:20% I:60% A:20%	3	3400	Thanksgiving-Apr	60-80			
Frost Ridge Le Roy New York tel: (716) 768-9730	T:790 B:640	4 open slopes, 7 trails; longest run: 850 ft		4	3000	Dec 15-Apr 1			Nearby	Nearby
Gore Mountain Ski Center North Creek New York tel: (518) 251-2411 *(518) 251-2523*	T:3600 B:1500	24 trails, 2 slopes & 2 cross-country trails; longest run: 3½ miles	B:20% I:50% A:30%	8	6500	Dec 1-Mar 31	80	24°F. Sun 50% of season	At area	At area
Dynamite Hill Chestertown New York tel: (518) 494-2711		Small slope	B:100%	1						
Fahnestock Ski Area Carmel, New York tel: (914) 225-3223	T:1000 B:750	4 trails, 3 open slopes; longest run: 1500 ft		4	2500	mid Dec-early Apr				
Frost Ridge Le Roy New York tel: (716) 768-9730	T:790 B:640	4 open slopes, 7 trails longest run: 850 ft		4	3000	Dec 15-Apr 1			Nearby	Nearby
Fun Haven Lebanon New York tel: (315) 837-4812		1 slope	B:100%	1					Nearby	Nearby
Greek Peak Cortland New York tel: (607) 835-6111	T:2100 B:1320	4 slopes, 21 trails; longest run: 1½ miles	B:48% I:42% A:10%	8	6400	Nov-Apr	110		At area	At area
Hickory Ski Center Warrenburg New York tel: (518) 623-9866	T:1900 B:700	3 slopes, 12 trails; longest run: 1¼ miles		4	2250	Christmas-Mar 15			At area	At area
Holiday Mountain Ski Area Monticello New York tel: (914) 796-3161	T:1300 B:900	10 open slopes; longest run: 4500 ft	B:30% I:40% A:30%	10		Dec 1-Mar	50		Neary	Nearby
Holiday Valley Ellicottville New York tel: (716) 699-2345 *(216) 621-1800; (716) 699-2644*	T:2250 B:1500	31 slopes & trails, tree-lined; longest run: 4300 ft	B:25% I:50% A:25%	8	7900	Nov/Dec Apr	168			
Hunter Mountain Ski Bowl Hunter New York tel: (518) 263-4223 *(212) 683-4933*	T:3200 B:1600	32 miles, 35 open slopes & tree-lined trails; longest run: 2 miles	B:20% I:40% A:40%	15	1400	Thanksgiving to Easter	125	25°F. Sun 50% of season		
Juniper Hills Harrisville New York tel: (315) 543-2737		6 slopes 2 trails		2						
Kutsher's Country Club Monticello New York tel: (914) 794-6000		2 slopes		2					At area	At area
Kissing Bridge Glenwood New York tel: (716) 592-4963 *(716) 592-4961*	T:1750 B:1250	23 slopes & trails on 700 acres;	B:30% I:50% A:20%	11	10000	Dec 11-Mar 18	185		Nearby	Nearby
Labrador Ski Area Truxton New York tel: (607) 842-6221 *(315) 458-3553*		3 open slopes, 13 trails longest run: 4500 ft	B:40% I:30% A:30%	5	1200	Dec 1-Apr 1			Nearby	
Mt Cathalia Ellenville New York tel: (914) 647-7171	T:1725 B:1200	15 trails tree-lined; longest run: 3000 ft		2	1000	Nov-Apr				
Mt Peter Ski Area Glenwood Lake New York tel: (914) 986-4992	T:1000 B:600	5 wide slopes, 5 wooded trails, longest run: ½ mile	B:50% I:35% A:15%	2	2500	Dec 15-Mar 15	35	30°F.		

Mt Whitney Ski Center Lake Placid Club Resort New York tel: (518) 523-3361	T:2408 B:200	5 slopes open and tree-lined; longest run: ¾ mile		2	800	mid Dec-mid Mar			Nearby	Nearby
Peek'n Peak Ski Center Clymer New York tel: (716) 355-4141	T:1800 B:1400	16 slopes & trails; longest run: 3000 ft	B:20% I:60% A:20%	7	7000	mid Nov-Apr 1	200 +		At area	
Pines Ski Area South Fallsburg New York tel: (914) 434-6000	T:1800 B:1600	3 slopes & 3 trails; longest run: 2000 ft		3	600	Nov 22-Apr 10				
Silver Mine Ski Center Bear Mountain New York tel: (914) 786-3791	T:2100 B:1750	3 wide, long slopes; longest run: 1400 ft		5		mid Dec-early Apr			Nearby	Nearby
Scotch Valley Stamford New York tel: (607) 652-7332	T:2950 B:2200	11 slopes & trails; longest run: 1 mile	B:20% I:50% A:20%	5	3700	Thanks-giving to Easter			At area	At area
Ski Minnewaska New Paltz New York tel: (914) 255-6000 *(914) 255-5500*	T:1260 B:875	3 slopes, 7 tree-lined trails, 200 acres; longest run: 3500 ft	B:20% I:70% A:10%	4	3600	Dec 15-Mar 15	49		At area	At area
Sterling Forest Ski Center Tuxedo New York tel: (914) 351-2163 *(914) 351-4788*	T:1400 B:815	6 slopes, 1 racing slope; longest run: 3000 ft	B:20% I:70% A:10%	4	3800	Dec 11-Mar 11	36			
Swain Ski Center Swain New York tel: (607) 545-6511	T:2007 B:1400	10 miles, 24 slopes & trails; longest run: 5300 ft	B:40% I:45% A:15%	5	6000	Thanks-giving - Apr 15	150		At area	
Toggenburg Ski Center Fabius New York tel: (315) 683-5842 *(315) 446-6666*	T:2000 B:1400	12 slopes & trails; longest run: 6000 ft	B:20% I:60% A:20%	5	4800	Dec 1-Apr 1	150	25°F. Sun 30% of season	Nearby	Nearby
West Mountain Ski Area Glens Falls New York tel: (518) 793-6606	T:1401 B:450	5 slopes, 11 trails; tree-lined and open; longest run: 7800 ft	B:15% I:75% A:10%	6	4300	Dec-Apr	60		Nearby	Nearby
Whiteface Mt Ski Center Wilmington New York tel: (518) 946-2223 *(518) 946-7171*	T:4436 B:1220	13 miles of trails; 25 slopes; longest run: 2½ miles	B:35% I:45% A:20%	9	7200	Dec-Mar 31	130	Sun 60% of season	Nearby	Nearby
Willard Mountain Greenwich New York tel: (518) 692-7337		2 slopes 4 miles of trail; longest run: 3000 ft		4	3000	Dec 15-Apr 1				
Williams Lake Rosendale New York tel: (914) 658-3101		1 slope	B:100%	1					At area	
Windham Mountain Club Windham New York tel: (518) 734-4300	T:3050 B:1400	11 slopes & trails, tree-lined, 1 open slope; longest run: 2¼ miles	B:20% I:40% A:40%	4	4500	Nov 24-Apr 16	110		Nearby	Nearby

Big Boulder Ski Area Lake Harmony Pennsylvania tel: (717) 722-0101	T:2200 B:1725	7 slopes & 4 trails; longest run: 2900 ft	B:40% I:40% A:20%	6	6000	Dec 1-Mar 30	60			
Blue Knob Claysburg Pennsylvania tel: (814) 239-5111	T:3150 B:2100	7 miles of trails, 14 slopes tree-lined, 80 acres; longest run: 9200 ft	B:15% I:70% A:15%	4	3100	Nov 19-mid Mar	100			
Camelback Ski Area Tannersville Pennsylvania tel: (717) 629-1661 *(800) 233-8100*	T:2000 B:1200	17 slopes & trails, over 6 miles of trail; longest run: 6500 ft	B:40% I:40% A:20%	7	7260	Early Dec-late Mar	50	35°F. Sun 70% of season		
Elk Mountain Ski Center Union Dale Pennsylvania tel: (717) 679-2611	T:2693 B:1693	16 slopes & trails tree-lined & open	B:30% I:30% A:40%	5	5400	Early Dec-mid Apr				
Chadds Peak Chadds Ford Pennsylvania tel: (215) 388-6476		Longest run: 1000 ft		4	5000	mid Dec-late Mar			Nearby	
Fernwood Resort Bushkill Pennsylvania tel: (717) 588-6661 *(800) 233-8103*		1 slope for beginners & other runs		1		Dec 1-Apr 1				
Hickory Ridge Ski Area Honesdale Pennsylvania tel: (717) 253-2000	T:2500	2 open slopes, 3 trails; longest run: 1 mile		2	1400	Dec 25-mid Mar			Nearby	
Hidden Valley Resort Somerset Pennsylvania tel: (814) 445-6014/8575	T:2950 B:2550	7 slopes, 3 trails, 2½ miles of trail; longest run: 3600 ft	B:25% I:50% A:25%	7	5000	Dec 15-Mar 15	150		At area	At area
Jack Frost Mountain White Haven Pennsylvania tel: (717) 443-8425	T:2000 B:1500	11 slopes; longest 3200 ft	B:25% I:50% A:25%	6	6400	Nov 19-Mar 27	95			
Masthope Ski Area Lackawaxen Pennsylvania tel: (717) 685-7101	T:1350 B:700	3 slopes longest run: 5400 ft		2	2000	Thanks-giving - Mar 30				
Mount Tone Lake Como Pennsylvania tel: (717) 798-2707		9 slopes & trails on 2 mountains		3						
Pocono Manor Pocono Manor Pennsylvania tel: (717) 839-7111		4 slopes & trails		2					At area	
Saw Creek Bushkill Pennsylvania tel: (717) 588-6611		7 slopes & trails		1	1200	Dec 15-end Feb				
Seven Springs Mountain Resort Champion Pennsylvania tel: (814) 352-7777	T:2940 B:2075	Variety of runs over 1 mile across mountain; longest run: 4320 ft	B:15% I:65% A:20%	12	10200	Dec 1-Apr 1	130	24°F	At area	

Ski Liberty Fairfield Pennsylvania tel: (717) 642-8282 *(800) 233-7521; (717) 642-8297*	T:1150 B:580	8 trails tree-lined, 3 miles of trails; longest run: 4800	B:30% I:50% A:20%	4	3600	Thanks-giving-Mar 15	24			
Ski Roundtop Lewisberry Pennsylvania tel: (717) 432-9631 *(800) 424-9415; (717) 432-9755*	T:1200 B:650	6 trails, 4 slopes; longest run: 4100 ft	B:40% I:30% A:30%	6	6500	Nov 15-Mar 15	20			
Sugarbush Mountain Latrobe Pennsylvania tel: (412) 238-9655	T:200 B:1900	1 tree lined slope, 2 trails; longest run: 1000 ft		1		Dec 1-Apr 1			At area	At area
Timber Hill Canadensis Pennsylvania tel: (717) 595-7571	T:1100 B:700	2 slopes, 7 trails; longest run: 5000 ft		3		mid Dec-mid Mar				
Bromley Mountain Manchester Center Vermont tel: (802) 824-5522	T:3275 B:1990	20 trails & 2 open slopes; longest run: 2½ miles	B:20% I:60% A:20%	6	6000	Thanks-giving to Easter	150	18°F. Sun 40% of season	Nearby	Nearby
Bolton Valley Ski Resort Bolton Vermont tel: (802) 434-2131 *(800) 451-3220*	T:3200 B:2150	40 acres, 23 trails, 15 miles of trails; longest run: 9000 ft	B:20% I:60% A:20%	4	3800	Thanks-giving to mid Apr	275		At area	At area
Burke Mount-ain Recreation E. Burke Vermont tel: (802) 626-3305	T:3200 B:1200	28 trails, 3 open slopes; longest run: 3½ miles	B:38% I:38% A:24%	5	3480	Thanks-giving to Easter	170		At area	At area
Glen Ellen Waitsfield Vermont tel: (802) 496-3301	T:4083 B:1450	36 slopes & trails; longest run: 2½ miles	B:25% I:50% A:25%	5	4500	Thanks-giving to late Apr	200		Nearby	Nearby
Carinthia West Dover Vermont tel: (802) 464-5461	T:2800 B:2000	8 slopes; longest run: 4000 ft		2	1200	Dec 1-Apr 15			Nearby	Nearby
Cochran Ski Area Richmond Vermont tel: (802) 434-2479	T:850 B:350	3 open slopes; longest run: 3000 ft		3	2000	Dec 15-Mar 30	110		Nearby	Nearby
Haystack Wilmington Vermont tel: (802) 464-5321 *(802) 229-0531*	T:3200 B:1800	90 acres, 23 trails and slopes; longest run: 2+ miles	B:25% I:50% A:25%	6	4300	Early Dec-end Mar	100		Nearby	Nearby
Jay Peak Ski Area Jay, Vermont tel: (802) 988-2611	T:3968 B:1815	24 trails, over 50 miles tree-lined; longest run: 2½ miles	B:45% I:30% A:25%	12	6000	Nov 20-May 1	275	12°F.	At area	At area
Killington Ski Resort Killington Vermont tel: (802) 422-3333 *(800) 451-4301; (802) 422-3261*	T:4220 B:1060	60 trails & slopes, 450 acres on 4 mountains; comprised of 7 skiing areas; longest run: 5 miles	B:41% I:25% A:34%	12	16400	late Oct-late May	300	28°F. Sun 65% of season	Nearby	
Hogback Mountain Marlboro Vermont tel: (802) 464-3942	T:2350	19 slopes & trails		4		Dec-Apr			Nearby	
Mad River Glen Waitsfield Vermont tel: (802) 496-3551	T:3600 B:1600	25 trails; longest run: 3½ miles	B:20% I:40% A:40%	4	3000	Dec 9-end Mar	120		Nearby	Nearby
Mount Snow Mount Snow Vermont tel: (802) 464-3333 *(802) 464-2151*	T:3556 B:1956	51 trails on 3 complete mountain faces; longest run: 3 miles	B:23% I:65% A:12%	14	13000	mid Nov-late Apr	150	Sun 20% of season	Nearby	Nearby
Magic Mountain Londonderry Vermont tel: (902) 824-5566 *(802) 824-5566*	T:3000 B:1400	22 trails & 5 slopes; longest run: 2½ miles	B:30% I:50% A:20%	5	3650	Thanks-giving-early Apr	120		Nearby	At area
Pico Rutland Vermont tel: (802) 775-4345	T:3967 B:2000	2½ miles of glade skiing; longest run: 2½ miles	B:20% I:60% A:20%	9	8400	Thanks-giving-May 1	200		Nearby	Nearby
Pinnacle Mountain Keene New Hampshire tel: (603) 352-9882 *(603) 352-5477*		4 slopes 2 trails	B:40% I:50% A:10%	2	1500	Dec-Mar/Apr				
Round Top Ski Area Plymouth Vermont tel: (802) 672-3363 *(802) 672-5152*	T:2600 B:1300	4 slopes, 15 miles of trails longest run: 1½ miles	B:30% I:35% A:35%	4	3000	Thanks-giving-Apr	130		Nearby	Nearby
Smugglers' Notch Jeffersonville Vermont tel: (802) 644-8851 *(800) 451-3222*	T:3610 B:1100	32 slopes, 55 miles of trail on 3 mountains; longest run: 3½ miles	B:25% I:41% A:34%	4	3100	Thanks-giving to Apr/May	260	15°F. Sun 40% of season	At area	At area
Stowe Stowe Vermont tel: (802) 253-7311 *(802) 253-8521*	T:4393 B:1300	32 slopes & trails; longest run: 4½ miles	B:10% I:70% A:20%	8	8000	mid Dec-mid Apr	120		At area	Nearby
Stratton Mountain Stratton Mountain Vermont tel: (802) 297-2200 *(802) 297-2211/2*	T:3875 B:2120	59 miles of trails & slopes, 6 slopes, 53 trails; longest run: 4+ miles	B:45% I:30% A:25%	8	10500	mid Nov-mid Apr	230		At area	At area
Sugarbush Valley Warren Vermont tel: (802) 583-2381	T:4013 B:1625	45 miles of trails, all tree-lined; longest run: 2½ miles	B:20% I:30% A:50%	8	7900	Thanks-giving to mid Apr	267		Nearby	Nearby
Suicide Six Woodstock Vermont tel: (802) 457-1666	T:1200 B:550	17 trails & slopes; longest run: 5700 ft	B:35% I:40% A:25%	5	4200	mid Dec-Mar	80			Nearby

Guide to Canadian ski areas

Ski Areas (Telephone number for snow conditions in italics)	Elevation (in feet): top (T), base (B)	Skiing terrain	Slope difficulty: B (beginner), I (intermediate), A (advanced)	Lifts	Lift capacity per hour	Length of season	Average annual snowfall (in ins)	Average temperature	Cross-country	Touring
Hemlock Valley Harrison Mills British Columbia tel: (604) 792-3966 *(604) 522-7220/ 859-6211/ 792-8485*	T:4500 B:3300	20 trails, 16 miles of open skiing; longest run: 5450 ft	B:30% I:35% A:35%	6	4200	Dec-Mar	600		At area	
Kimberley Ski Resort Kimberly British Columbia tel: (604) 427-4841	T:6500 B:4200	30 trails, N bowl skiing; longest run: 4 miles	B:25% I:50% A:25%	5	4200	Early Dec-end Mar	96	23°F.	Nearby	At area
Panorama Mountain Invermere British Columbia tel: (604) 342-3223	T:6900 B:3800	15 runs; longest run: 13000 ft	B:22% I:63% A:15%	5	4200	Early Dec-end Mar	105		At area	
Red Mountain Ski Area Rossland British Columbia tel: (604) 362-7384 *(604) 362-5500*	T:6600 B:3800	2 mountains — Red Mt has 1420 vertical, Granite Mt has 2700 vertical; 25 runs from trails to alpine slopes; longest run 4½ miles	B:20% I:40% A:40%	5	4000	Mid Nov-Early Apr	120		At area	At area
Silver Star Vernon Vernon British Columbia tel: (604) 542-6229/3618 *(800) 663-3444*	T:6280 B:4680	32 major runs & 20 miles of open skiing, groomed slopes and deep powder skiing; longest run: 10000 ft	B:25% I:45% A:30%	8	7500	mid Nov-mid Apr			Nearby	Nearby
Whistler Mountain Whistler British Columbia tel: (604) 932-5528 *(604) 687-6761*	T:6400 B:2120	2 large alpine bowls, 23 tree-lined runs; longest run: 5 miles	B:10% I:65% A:25%	11	9339	mid Nov-end May	450	24°F. Sun 20% of season	At area	At area
Fortress Mountain Calgary Alberta tel: (403) 264-4626 *(403) 288-1411*	T:7800 B:6700	27 tree-lined and open slopes, limited bowl skiing longest run: 11/5 mile	B:30% I:40% A:30%	4	5000	late Nov-end Apr	200		Nearby	
Lake Louise Lake Louise Alberta tel: (403) 522-3555 *Calgary: 244-6665 Banff: 762-2097*	T:8700 B:5500	34 designated runs, thousands of acres of bowl and gladed timber-line skiing; longest run: 5 miles	B:24% I:32% A:44%	8	7600	early Dec-end Apr	185	14°F. Sun 106 hrs month	At area	At area
Marmot Basin Jasper Alberta tel: (403) 852-3816	T:7980 B:5680	25 runs, tree-lined and open bowl skiing; longest run: 3½ miles	B:35% I:35% A:30%	5	4600	early Dec-end Mar	200 – 250		Nearby	
Sunshine Village Banff Alberta tel: (403) 762-3383 *(403) 261-8075*	T:8950 B:7200	Packed & powder runs, sheltered slopes amidst trees & open treeline; longest run: 2¼ miles		7	6500	mid Nov-end May	400		At area	
Table Mountain North Battlefield Saskatchewan		Longest run: 3380 ft		4	2720					
Holiday Mountain La Riviere Manitoba tel: (204) 242-2172	T:1550 B:1250	9 open slopes; longest run: 200 ft		5	4000	mid Nov mid Mar			At area	
Beaver Valley Markdale Ontario tel: (519) 986-2520 *(416) 231-2931*	T:1345 B:840	17 runs, dual slalom course; longest run: ⅞ mile	B:20% I:50% A:30%	6	4300	Dec-early Apr	130		At area	
Blue Mountain Collingwood Ontario tel: (705) 445-0231 *(416) 967-7152; (313) 964-2320*	T:1425 B:725	27 slcpes & trails on 800 acres. tree-lined; longest run: ¾ mile	B:25% I:50% A:25%	17	14884	early Dec-mid Apr	110	20°F. Sun ⅓ of season	At area	At area
Calabogie Peaks Calaboogie Ontario tel: (613) 752-2720	T:1265 B:505	9 miles of downhill trails, 70 acres of groomed slopes; longest run: 9000 ft	B:25% I:35% A:40%	5	5300	early Dec-mid Apr	80		At area	
Georgian Peaks Ski Club Thornbury Ontario tel: (519) 599-3737/2620 *(519) 599-2621*	T:1426 B:605	18 interconnecting runs, 6 slopes, 8 trails	B:25% I:50% A:25%	7	5000	early Dec-early Apr	95		At area	
Hidden Valley Highlands Ski Club Huntsville Ontario tel: (705) 789-5942 *Toronto: 364-2011*	T:1275 B:945	7 open slopes & 4 trails, all tree-lined; longest run: 2500 ft	B:30% I:50% A:20%	4	3960	mid Dec-early Apr	200		At area	
Horseshoe Valley Resort Horseshoe Valley Ontario tel: (705) 835-2014; Toronto (416) 364-9509		17 tree-lined slopes & trails; longest run: ½ mile	B:30% I:50% A:20%	6	7700	Nov 26-Apr 10	130	23°F. Sun ⅔ of season	At area	At area

Area	Elevation (ft)	Trails	Difficulty	Lifts	Capacity	Season	Acres		
Loch Lomond Thunder Bay Ontario tel: (807) 577-8926	T:1500 B:700	12 slopes & winding trails; longest run: 1¼ miles	B:25% I:40% A:35%	4	4500	late Nov-mid Apr	200	Nearby	
Mansfield Skiways Mansfield Ontario tel: (705) 435-5302	T:1375 B:975	12 open slopes with 20 possible run combinations; longest run: 2640 ft	B:30% I:60% A:10%	6	5400	mid Dec-early Apr	70	Nearby	
Medonte Mountain Barrie Ontario tel: (705) 835-2001		19 slopes & trails; longest run: 4000 ft		6	5600	Dec-Apr		At area	
Moonstone Ski Resort Coldwater Ontario tel: (705) 835-2018 *(416) 368-6900*		11 slopes & 1 trail, tree-lined; longest run: 5000 ft	B:20% I:60% A:20%	7	6500	Dec 10-end Mar	60	At area	
Oshawa-Kirby Ski Club Oshawa Ontario tel: (416) 983-5983	T:1175 B:875	3 open slopes, 10 tree-lined and one bowl		8	6000	mid Dec-mid Apr			
Talisman Resort Kimberley Ontario tel: (519) 599-2520		7 slopes, open & tree-lined; longest run: 4000 ft	B:25% I:50% A:25%	5	4200	Dec-Apr	50-75	At area	
Bromont Ski Center Bromont Quebec tel: (514) 534-2200	T:1850 B:550	15 miles of groomed trails and slopes on two mountains	B:5 r I:8 r A:2 r	5	4950	early Dec-end Apr		At area	At area
Camp Fortune Old Chelsea Quebec tel: (819) 827-1717 *(819) 827-2323*	T:1200 B:600	15 slopes		6	8400	early Dec-mid Apr		At area	
Edelweiss Valley Wakefield Quebec tel: (819) 459-2859	T:1200 B:570	15 slopes & trails covering 150 acres; longest run: 5000 ft	B:30% I:40% A:30%	7	7000	mid Nov-mid Apr	225	At area	
Gray Rocks St-Jovite-Mt, Tremblant Quebec tel: (819) 425-2771	T:1340 B:730	18 slopes; longest run: 1 mile +	B:33% I:29% A:38%	5	5300	mid Nov-mid Apr	120	At area	At area
Le Chantecler Ste Adele Quebec tel: (514) 229-3555		13 slopes; longest run: 3000 ft		9	8640	mid Nov-mid Apr		At area	
Mont-Gabriel Mont Gabriel Quebec tel: (514) 229-3547	T:1360 B:570	18 slopes	B:10% I:50% A:40%	11	5000	mid Nov-mid Apr		At area	
Mont Orford Ski Area Magog Quebec tel: (819) 843-6548 *(514) 878-4467*	T:2850 B:1200	20 miles of trail; longest run: 2½ miles	B:40% I:33% A:27%	7	5700	late Nov-Apr	150 — 250	At area	At area
Mont St-Castin Des Neiges Lac-Beauport Quebec tel: (418) 849-4461		6 slopes, groomed and open; longest run: 2740 ft		7	6640	mid Nov-mid Mar			
Mont Sainte-Anne (Parc du) Beaupré Quebec tel: (418) 827-4561 *(514) 861-6670; (418) 827-4579; (416) 482-1796*	T:2625 B:575	Full range of ski runs on 2 m sides; longest run 15850 ft	B:6 r I:11 r A:10 r	14	9300		150	At area	
Mont Saint-Saveur Saint-Saveur Quebec tel: (514) 866-7190		16 slopes; longest run: 4600 ft		8	8110	late Nov-Mar			
Mont-Sutton Sutton Quebec tel: (514) 866-5156 *(514) 866-7718/7639*	T:2950 B:1400	25 slopes & trails. 18 miles of tree-lined & gladed run; longest run: 2¼ miles	B:30% I:40% A:30%	6	5400	late Nov-early May	216	At area	At area
Mont Tremblant Mont Tremblant Quebec tel: (819) 425-2711 *(514) 861-1925*	T:3001 B:870	25 tree-lined trails on 2 sides of the mt; longest run: 3½ miles	B:16% I:56% A:28%	11	10000		165	At area	At area
Owl's Head Mansonville Quebec tel: (514) 292-5592	T:2450 B:680	11½ miles of groomed slopes; longest run: 1200 ft	B:20% I:60% A:20%	6	6000		180	At area	At area
Saint-Gérard St Mathieu Lac Bellemare Quebec tel: (819) 539-5451		15 slopes & trails; longest run: 3900 ft	B:50% I:30% A:20%	1	7200	Nov-Apr			
Ski Montcalm Rawdon Quebec tel: (514) 834-3139		12 slopes; longest run: [illegible]000 ft		6	5760	late Nov-Mar			
Sun Valley Ste Adele Quebec tel: (514) 229-3511; (514) 861-4801	T:1300 B:1800	8-10 slopes; longest run: mile	B:33% I:33% A:33%	6	5760	mid Nov-Mar		At area	At area
Sugarloaf Provincial Park Cambellton New Brunswick tel: (506) 753-6258	T:657 B:150	7 trails, all tree-lined and groomed		3	3200	mid Dec-early Apr	175		
Martock II Ski Area Windsor Nova Scotia tel: (902) 798-4728 *(902) 798-5421*	T:695 B:95	5 slopes; longest run: 4800 ft		2	2400	mid Dec-early Apr	120		

The information contained in this guide was selected from *The White Book* published by Inter-Ski Services, Inc. PO Box 3635, Georgetown Station, Washington DC 20007 and can be obtained from them at $7.95 + $1.25 for postage and handling.

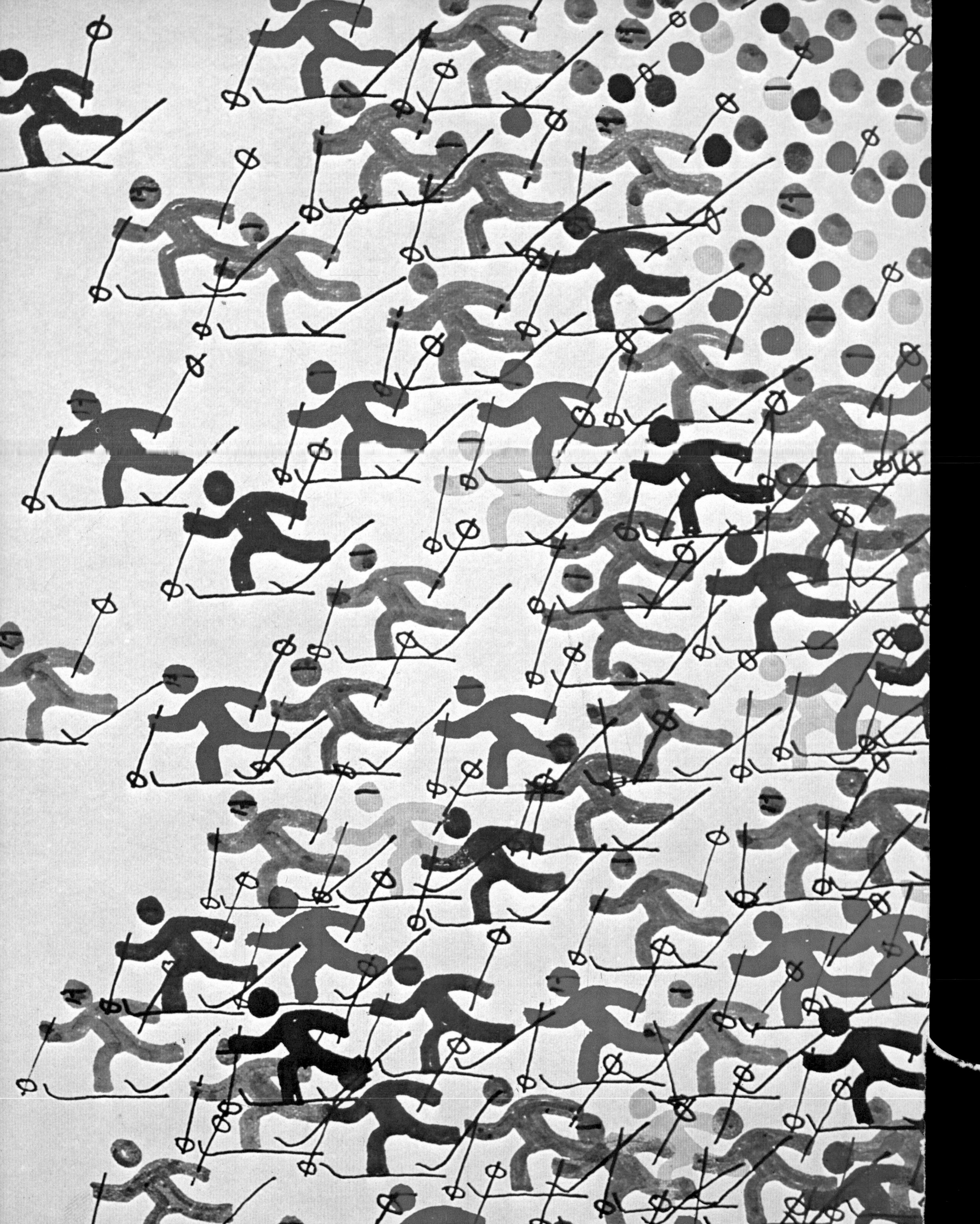